Get More on Nolo.com

Go to this book's companion page at:

 www.nolo.com/back-of-book/DIMO.html

Checking the companion page is a good way
to stay informed on topics related to this book.

More Resources
from Nolo.com

 Legal Forms, Books, & Software
Hundreds of do-it-yourself products—all written in plain English,
approved, and updated by our in-house legal editors.

 Legal Articles
Get informed with thousands of free articles on everyday legal
topics. Our articles are accurate, up to date, and reader friendly.

 Find a Lawyer
Want to talk to a lawyer? Use Nolo to find a lawyer who can
help you with your case.

NOLO
LAW for ALL

14th Edition

Divorce & Money

Make the Best Financial Decisions During Divorce

Attorney Lina Guillen

FOURTEENTH EDITION	OCTOBER 2023
Editor	AMY LOFTSGORDON
Book & Cover Design	SUSAN PUTNEY
Proofreading	MARTHA C. BENCO
Index	RICHARD GENOVA
Printing	SHERIDAN

ISSN: 2473-4497 (print)
ISSN: 2473-4500 (online)
ISBN: 978-1-4133-3107-3 (pbk)
ISBN: 978-1-4133-3108-0 (ebook)

This book covers only United States law, unless it specifically states otherwise.

Please note

Accurate, plain-English legal information can help you solve many of your own legal problems. But this text is not a substitute for personalized advice from a knowledgeable lawyer. If you want the help of a trained professional—and this book will always point out situations in which that's a good idea—consult an attorney licensed to practice in your state.

MH Sub I, LLC dba Nolo, 909 N. Pacific Coast Hwy, 11th Fl., El Segundo, CA 90245.

Dedications

This book is dedicated to …

Those grappling with the enormity of divorce and, thus, most in need of guidance.

My family and friends, who kept me sane through the writing process.

A special dedication to my little ones, M and L, who inspire me daily and help me keep things in perspective.

Thank You

Victoria F. Collins and M.C. Blakeman, who contributed so much to the earlier editions on which this work is based and who deserve recognition for their hard work, creativity, and cooperation.

Amy Loftsgordon, Editor at Nolo, for keeping me on track and on time with this latest edition and for her hard work and eye for detail throughout the editorial process.

Special Acknowledgments

To the late Dale Fetherling, who will always be remembered for his gifts of balance, tolerance, organizational skills, and for his boundless respect for our readers.

About the Author

Lina Guillen is a seasoned trial attorney with over 22 years of experience in a wide range of legal matters, including family law and civil litigation. She focuses her practice on high-asset dissolution in the San Francisco Bay Area as an associate at one of the largest family law firms in Northern California. As Nolo's Family Law Legal Editor, she has edited a variety of Nolo books, written numerous legal articles on divorce and family law issues, and managed the development of legal content on several Nolo websites. In addition to being the coauthor of *Neighbor Law* and author of *Divorce & Money: Make the Best Financial Decisions During Divorce*, Lina has been quoted in several publications, including the *New York Times, U.S. News & World Report, Real Simple* magazine, and *How Stuff Works*. Lina is an active member of the California State Bar and received her law degree from the University of California College of the Law, San Francisco. Before law school, she was an editorial assistant for *The Press Democrat* newspaper in Sonoma County.

Table of Contents

Introduction:
Your Financial Companion During Divorce

The week when you take the first steps to end your marriage has been the worst week of your life. Suddenly, the person you're divorcing calls and demands copies of your tax returns for the past five years.

You brown-bag your lunch and take the bus to work so you can make ends meet while your divorce is pending. But then, you receive an unexpected bill for a joint credit card you never canceled. Your soon-to-be ex-spouse charged an expensive vacation on your joint credit card, and now you must pay for it.

Money is often the last thing you want to deal with when your marriage is ending, but there might never be a more crucial time to take control of your assets.

In fact, making financial decisions is possibly the most important job you have in your divorce.

How can you make the right decisions? How do you deal with tedious financial details when you're going through such a stressful event? Unfortunately, it's hard to find answers to those questions.

Legal advice is plentiful, and therapists or support groups can help you through emotional upheavals. But who can show you how to make sense of your financial life?

That's where this book comes in. It explains what you must know to avoid the potential financial disasters of divorce. Specifically, this book will help you understand:

- what you own and owe
- how divorce affects your taxes
- how to divide your property, investments, and other assets
- what can happen to your retirement savings or your business when you divorce
- what to do about alimony and child support
- how to prepare to negotiate a final settlement, and
- how to gain financial stability in your new life as a single person or single parent.

Each divorce is different, of course, so this book can't provide complex financial advice for every possible situation. But it can let you know where you can turn to find answers.

Divorce is a crash course in managing personal finances—a course you need to complete whether you signed up for it or not. However daunting this course may seem, the first lesson can be stated plainly: There is a big difference between legal reality and financial reality.

The financial truth about divorce is this: Just because you "get it in writing" doesn't mean you will get it for real. In other words, even though your settlement might be perfectly legal and fair, it can still be costly in financial terms. For example:

- How will you pay for debts that mounted during the marriage if your spouse refuses to come up with any part of the money— even if you weren't supposed to pay those bills under your settlement agreement?
- If you leave the division of your property up to the courts, the tax consequences of your transactions will most likely be ignored. But the IRS may still collect those taxes.
- What will you do if your spouse agreed to pay child support but is consistently late or fails to pay?

As you divorce, you must be on the alert for the limitations of the law. Throughout this book, we'll show you how to write a strong financial settlement without ignoring the blind spots of the legal system.

Keep in mind that divorce doesn't have to be messy and expensive. Even if you have a great deal of property, you don't need to spend a fortune. One couple, for example, had $5 million in assets, yet spent only $5,000 in legal fees. This couple evaluated their property, analyzed tax consequences, and negotiated fairly.

By contrast, another couple, whose property totaled only $100,000, ended up spending $20,000 on attorneys' fees alone—all because they couldn't be realistic about their personal finances and instead let their emotions interfere with reason.

Whether you and your spouse have a little money or a lot, it is important that you look at your divorce from the perspective of financial reality. This means protecting your financial well-being, whether or not your spouse cooperates. Without this perspective, you might one day find yourself painted into a financial corner, saddled with debts, or burdened with assets you can't afford or sell.

The choice is yours. Divorce is painful enough; don't let money problems make it worse.

If You Are Feeling Overwhelmed ...

Congratulations. You're normal. Feeling overwhelmed is a very common experience during divorce. Even extremely capable people might suddenly find it difficult to balance a checkbook or perform other simple tasks.

If that happens to you, slow down. You can't expect to consider every financial aspect of divorce at once.

Although every divorce is different, the process seems to have one universal effect—temporary paralysis. Whether you're a hard-driving executive or a stay-at-home spouse, a traumatic separation can cause otherwise competent people to become immobilized by the emotion of the situation and the gravity of the financial questions they face. Should we sell the house? How much alimony will I get or pay? What will happen with our taxes? Who will support the children?

Feeling overwhelmed, confused, angry, or depressed—these are normal responses to the stress of divorce. As with any major undertaking, the best tactic is to break it down into small, manageable pieces. And because the hectic pace of life today puts so many demands on your time, this book presents this plan in step-by-step segments. When you complete several small goals each day, you are less likely to become overwhelmed and immobilized. That feeling of accomplishment helps you stay out of crisis mode and works to your benefit both emotionally and financially.

Managing Your Divorce in Troubled Financial Times

Money problems cause terrible stress in the best of times. When divorce is added to those problems, the mix is often personally and emotionally devastating. As you read this book, you often will be encouraged to get past the emotional import of your situation before you make a financial or legal decision. It always makes sense to consider the financial implications of splitting up and, if possible, measure them against the emotional costs of staying together. Before you even embark on that difficult calculus, you should look hard at your marriage, especially if you have children. Have you done everything you would reasonably expect your friends to do if their marriages were in crisis? Are there emotional wounds that might be healed through counseling? Extended work with a marriage therapist is not cheap, but the cost of divorce is almost always greater. And even if you can't save your marriage through therapy, you might learn better ways to communicate with your spouse that will serve you well if you end up divorcing.

Of course, in some cases, particularly those where domestic violence, addiction, alcoholism, or child abuse is a factor, divorce is often the only way out. You shouldn't stay in a marriage where you feel unsafe.

Only you know when there's no turning back. But be aware that divorce doesn't repair feelings of hurt, sadness, disappointment, or failed expectations. It's a good idea to attempt to address your problems through other means before you consider a divorce.

Alternatives to Traditional Litigation

If you decide that divorce is your best and only option, be aware that the traditional, bare-knuckles "see you in court" approach is the most expensive route you can take, especially if your case ends up in court. Moreover, with budgetary cutbacks and ongoing post-COVID-19 virtual protocols and case delays still happening in many states, judicial calendars remain overcrowded, which can make divorce litigation a painfully long process.

If the decision to divorce is mutual, and you have good reason to believe that your spouse will be honest and forthcoming with information concerning joint and separate assets, debts, income, and expenses, you might want to consider the following options. (There's more about them in Chapter 7.)

Mediation. For divorcing spouses who are realistic and cooperative, working with an experienced mediator is a great option. In this scenario, a couple reaches a marital settlement agreement with the help of a trained mediator, who serves as a neutral facilitator—the divorcing couple makes the decisions, not the mediator. Mediation saves you money on costly attorneys' fees and allows you to avoid spending wasteful hours, days, or weeks in our clogged court system.

Arbitration. Divorcing spouses can resolve some of their divorce issues through binding arbitration in several states. (Check with an attorney to find out what your state allows.) Arbitrators, unlike mediators, hear arguments and evidence from each side to decide disputes and issue formal orders. While the laws vary a bit from state to state, in most cases, custody and child support issues can't be determined through arbitration, or if they are, a public court judicial officer must review the decisions to make sure they're in the best interest of the child.

Private judging. In most states, spouses can avoid the public courthouse by using private judging, where all divorce proceedings take place in a conference room—either at the private judge's office or in one of the attorneys' offices. Using a private judge is not the same as mediation or collaborative law: It's traditional litigation, which can include formal divorce discovery, depositions, and custody hearings, and may even go all the way to a full divorce trial. The main difference is that every status conference, hearing, and trial will take place outside of the public purview before a single judge, who's being paid to hear the case. The couple can avoid delays generated by busy court calendars and overly burdened family court systems. Generally, private family law judges are retired judges or family law attorneys with many years of divorce law experience. To use private judging, you must:

- file for divorce at your local courthouse
- reach an agreement with your spouse about which private judge to use—ask your attorney for referrals, and
- ask the family law judge assigned to your case to approve the appointment and transfer jurisdiction (authority) over your case to the private judge.

Depending on the laws in your state, a private judge can resolve all or most of the same divorce-related disputes that the public court can decide. However, private judges charge high hourly rates or daily flat fees, so they are typically used only in high-asset divorce cases. For example, in California, depending on where you live, a private judge might charge $800 an hour or $5,000 per day.

Limited-scope representation. You might be able to minimize legal fees by hiring a lawyer to perform a limited amount or type of work, such as one court appearance to help you argue about support or a custody schedule. With this type of representation, the attorney isn't responsible for your case, just a specific issue(s). Limited scope can be appealing to couples that, because of income constraints or prior training, are able to undertake a do-it-yourself approach to divorce.

Collaborative divorce. Here, each spouse has a lawyer who's committed to resolving the issues without litigating. All meetings include both spouses and both attorneys, and all parties commit to full disclosure of financial documents. The goal is to reach a written agreement to take to a judge and use as a final divorce decree.

Flexibility on Key Financial Issues

If you or your spouse is experiencing unemployment or other financial problems, being creative and flexible on certain divisive issues can help minimize additional financial losses.

Rethinking living arrangements. The most common ways divorcing couples deal with the family home is a sale to a third party or a "buyout," where one spouse pays the other and keeps the house. For more on house options, see Chapter 13.

Hold off cashing out assets. Divorcing spouses are often eager to get a fresh start, putting bad memories and poor decisions quickly behind them—and many often think this means assets must be cashed out. But if the values of homes, businesses, and retirement accounts have fallen, spouses may consider dividing holdings in kind and waiting for them to regain some value. For more on these choices, look at Chapters 7, 13, and 14.

Be flexible with spousal and child support. If one or both spouses are unemployed, it might be wise to defer a decision on alimony and child support for a few months in hopes the situation will improve. You will save money if you include a provision in the divorce agreement that allows you to revisit child or spousal support later without having to file additional paperwork. See Chapter 18 for more about support.

Stay nimble as to who claims the kids as a tax deduction. In some cases it might make sense for the noncustodial parent to claim the children if, for example, the custodial spouse is unemployed and has no income. Chapter 18 details the tax consequences of child support.

How to Use This Book

The advice in these pages is gender neutral. With more and more women taking on breadwinner roles and more men running households or earning less than their wives, the power dynamics in relationships continue to shift. Meanwhile, the traditional divorce between a working husband and homemaker wife, while still common, is outdated as a template. Women who earn more than their husbands and men who have spent years caring for children must be careful not to identify with the wrong parent when shaping a divorce strategy. This also applies to same-sex marriages and domestic partnerships where the duties of earning income and child rearing are not evenly divided.

Before you jump ahead and try to figure out what your house is worth or what you will need to do about alimony or child support, read Chapters 1 and 2, which give the framework for the legal and financial reality that you *must* understand as your divorce progresses.

For tips on dealing with emotional upheavals, read Chapter 3.

Chapters 4 through 7 cover "the first 30 days" and are especially important if you are in the initial stages of divorce. Chapters 8 and 9 help you start gathering financial data and thinking about the future.

In Chapters 10 through 12, you begin to seriously evaluate your assets, debts, income, and expenses. Whether you are a "do-it-yourselfer" or working with an attorney, you must figure out what you own and owe, and what it costs you and your family to live. We've provided several worksheets in Chapter 12 to help you.

Chapters 13 through 16 cover specific assets—the family home, retirement benefits, investments, and employee benefits. Chapter 17 deals with debts. And in Chapter 18, you'll evaluate the likelihood of paying or receiving alimony and child support—and in what amounts.

Your analyses and calculations from Chapters 12 through 18 are brought together in Chapter 19 to help you structure your final settlement. Finally, Chapter 20 provides guidelines for establishing a healthy financial life once the marriage has officially ended.

A Note on Same-Sex Marriage and This Book

In June 2015, the U.S. Supreme Court decided the historic *Obergefell v. Hodges* case and legalized same-sex marriage across the country. Today, all states must issue marriage licenses to all couples, regardless of sexual orientation. As a result, legally married same-sex couples are now entitled to the same state and federal marital benefits that opposite-sex couples enjoy. And same-sex married couples that want to end their marriages must follow the same legal divorce procedures as well.

All of the divorce-related financial information contained in this book applies to same-sex married couples. It doesn't, however, cover the unique dissolution procedures and tax consequences that apply to couples registered in domestic partnerships or civil unions in states where those are still offered. (Ask an attorney if you want to find out if domestic partnership registrations or civil unions remain available in your state.) If you're currently registered—or you registered before getting married—and you've decided to end your relationship, you should speak to a local attorney for advice that's tailored to your situation. ●

Legal vs. Financial Realities of Divorce

S ooner or later during your divorce, you will discover one insight that is central to this book *and* to the successful outcome of your settlement:

Legal reality and financial reality are fundamentally different.

A seemingly simple idea—but you'd be surprised how long it takes to sink in. To help you understand why this concept is so important, take a few moments to consider the following real-life divorce stories. In each, read the Legal Reality first. Then, see the true outcome on the Financial Reality side.

Legal Reality	Financial Reality
Jonathan and Penny were married for five years before they divorced. During that time, Penny frequently ran their credit cards to the limit buying clothing and had trouble balancing their checkbook.	After the divorce, Penny didn't pay off the credit cards, and creditors began hounding Jonathan for the money. Jonathan ended up footing the bills, because a divorce settlement assigning debts—even one included in a divorce judgment—can't change a couple's original joint obligation to their creditors.
When they reached the final settlement hearing, Jonathan was greatly relieved when the court made Penny solely responsible for paying the $10,000 in credit card debts she had accumulated during their marriage. The settlement was included in the final divorce judgment, which made Jonathan feel safe.	Had Jonathan raised the issue before their settlement was finalized, he could have demanded more property in exchange for paying Penny's debts or insisted that they sell some jointly held property to pay off their creditors.

Moral of the story:
Getting something "in writing" from the court
doesn't always mean you'll get it for real.

Legal Reality	Financial Reality
During their 15-year marriage, Sharon and Bill were committed to building up a good portfolio of stocks and mutual funds for their retirement.	Sharon paid attention to basic financial facts that Bill ignored: costs and taxes that decrease the value of an asset.
Because Sharon avidly followed the market, she wanted to keep a batch of stocks she had recently purchased and asked Bill to take stocks of equal value, which they had purchased early in their marriage. After negotiating over a few other assets, Bill and Sharon reached an agreement in which each of them would receive the exact same dollar amount in cash or assets at the end of the divorce. The court accepted the terms of their settlement, and the books on their marriage were quickly closed.	Sharon wisely picked the stocks most recently purchased. Because these stocks had not increased substantially in value, the taxable capital gains were low. Bill, however, blithely accepted the older stocks, which had gone up a lot in value since the time of purchase. Even at a capital gains rate of 20%, he owed substantial taxes when he sold the stocks. Had he taken the time to calculate his potential tax burden before agreeing to the settlement, he could have suggested splitting the stocks so that each spouse took half of the older stocks and half of the newer stocks.

Moral of the story: A 50-50 settlement isn't always equal.

Lessons in Legal Reality

The legal and financial perspectives on divorce are two distinct views of the same event. Ending your marriage with no assets or huge debts is the hard way to learn about the difference between these two realities. But if you are proactive from the get-go, your lessons don't have to be so costly.

If you intended to master Chinese cooking, you wouldn't begin by picking up Julia Child's *Mastering the Art of French Cooking*, even though it covers the same *general* topic of cooking. Similarly, you must take the time to consider the crucial differences between the legal and financial perspectives on divorce.

These four basic guidelines help define the legal perspective of divorce:
- Most divorces are settled out of court.
- Generally, divorce law is local.
- Don't expect the legal system (or a lawyer) to take care of you.
- It's easier to write laws than to enforce them.

Most Divorces Are Settled Out of Court

You might imagine that your divorce will be capped by a courtroom trial where you'll explain to a wise, kindly judge exactly how your spouse wronged you or where your lawyer wins the day.

Don't count on it. Legal TV scripts don't reflect reality.

An estimated 90% of divorce cases are settled without a court trial, most of which is done through meetings between spouses or their lawyers, and often on the courthouse steps. As the trial date nears, you'll quite likely be rushed into conferences in the courtroom hall or a coffee shop. In these frantic last-minute meetings, your spouse and/or the attorneys may confront you, demanding instant decisions on issues that will affect the rest of your life.

Most divorce courts today are primarily concerned with money, not morals. The legal system's main job is to resolve property disputes and to ensure the welfare of children. Spousal misconduct, of course, could affect custody, and economic mischief (such as hiding assets) can change the outcome of a final settlement. But judges don't have time to let you (and every other wronged spouse) vent in open court about your mate, when numerous other cases, with more urgent problems, also need to be heard that day. Emotional pain is not part of the legal or financial reality of divorce.

The impersonal atmosphere of court might baffle or intimidate you, but this reaction isn't necessarily a bad thing. A divorce that ends up in court is a protracted, expensive affair that many couples are wise to avoid. Often, it is to your advantage to stay out of the courtroom.

As long as you and your spouse work toward a settlement without involving the court, you can trade property, negotiate terms, and still maintain some measure of control over your destiny. *If you can't reach a settlement and must have a trial, however, you put your fate into the hands*

of a judge—a stranger who knows nothing about your children or property.
Yet, you'll have to live with whatever that judge decides.

Even in cases that are resolved before trial, there are often numerous
pretrial court hearings, such as those for temporary support, temporary
custody, and attorneys' fees, to name a few. These hearings alone can be
incredibly expensive, yet many could be settled beforehand, with a little
more effort at compromise.

Divorce Law Is Local

Not only do divorce laws differ from state to state, but interpretations of
divorce law can vary from judge to judge. Whether you ultimately hire
an attorney and whether or not you have a court trial, you should ask
a local lawyer to assess the most likely outcome of a your divorce case.
Find out how the local courts and individual judges view mediation.
Also ask about judges' attitudes and the prevailing mood regarding, for
example, joint custody, moving away with the children, or alimony.

Divorce courts are unlike other courts. They are called "courts of
equity," which means that the judges have wide discretion (leeway) in
making decisions. While a lawyer can educate you on the law, a lawyer
can't ethically or realistically promise what the judge will do in your case.

You might not like what you hear when you see a lawyer, who might
tell you that the things you want in your divorce are impossible to get.
Another attorney might promise you everything, but ultimately deliver
nothing. Interviewing several attorneys for a cross section of opinions
can give you a more accurate picture of your situation. (See Chapter 7
for information on hiring an attorney.)

If you know how individual judges normally rule in your locale,
your expectations will be more realistic. Even if you don't have a trial
(remember, 90% of cases settle), divorce lawyers tend to give advice
that is consistent with local court rulings. Granted, it's hard to ignore
sensational newspaper stories about high-dollar-amount divorces in other
parts of the country. But those cases are irrelevant. You must concentrate
on what happens in your backyard, because that's where your divorce
and your financial future will be decided.

Affording Attorneys

This book tells you to "check with an attorney" on various questions. That's because the individual circumstances of your divorce might require legal information beyond the scope of this book.

But who's going to pay for this costly legal advice?

Attending a brief consultation with a lawyer shouldn't bankrupt you. Organize your thoughts and questions before you seek legal advice so you can save time when the attorney's meter is running. At an initial visit, spend an hour—not a day. Then go home and think about how much more you may have to spend on an attorney.

In some cases, if your spouse makes substantially more income than you do, your spouse might be required to pay all or some of your attorneys' fees. The lawyer should be able to advise you about this at the initial consultation.

If you feel you truly need legal advice, but you have very little money and your spouse isn't obligated to pay your attorneys' fees, consider borrowing money or using a credit card to help pay for legal fees. Check with local law schools or bar associations, which may run divorce clinics where students assist low-income clients. Some law firms provide pro bono (free) legal services to clients who fall below certain income levels. Check with your local court, and visit its website, which may provide help in filling out paperwork. Many will also provide valuable explanations of different aspects of the divorce process.

No matter what other decisions you make, here's an important rule: Do not let your spouse's attorney or anyone else chosen by your spouse represent you. If your spouse has an attorney, you should too. One attorney can't represent both parties in a divorce action. For more information on finding—and working with—lawyers, see Chapter 7.

Don't Expect the Legal System to Take Care of You

Always remember that the professionals you hire to represent you in a divorce are simply working for you: They are not living your life, and they expect you to be an active advocate for your own interests. Even if you have the money to hire expert negotiators, don't fall into a passive attitude. You should be thinking like an entrepreneur during a divorce, not like a victim.

If you were starting a business, you would first sit down with accountants and financial professionals to crunch the numbers and determine whether your new venture has a good chance of turning a profit. Only then, after the financial aspects have been examined, would you consult an attorney about potential legal problems. Likewise, when you know you're heading toward divorce, you should determine (as best as you can) the value of all separate and joint assets and try to reconstruct a paper trail of financial information *before* you consult a divorce attorney.

Don't Be Afraid to Ask Questions

Don't be intimidated or afraid to ask questions if something is unclear. One divorcing woman admitted that some of her troubles resulted from her own unwillingness to appear ignorant. In an interview with sociologist Terry Arendell in the book *Mothers and Divorce*, the woman recalled her divorce and commented, "Part of the problem was my own fault. I gave the appearance of being knowledgeable. I knew more about buying property and bank accounts than my lawyer did, but I didn't understand all the tax things. And so I was reluctant to ask some of the things I should have asked."

However, becoming your own financial expert might be a very tall order—especially for spouses who aren't accustomed to managing finances and are starting out from a position of no control. If your spouse has held the financial reins tightly, don't despair. You can get up to speed with some expert assistance. If you're a financial neophyte, you should immediately seek legal help to understand your rights and begin preparing for the negotiations to come.

Definition: Settlement Agreement

This book refers to "marital settlement agreements," "property settlement agreements," "settlement agreements," or simply "agreements." They all mean the same thing. A settlement agreement is a written contract between you and your spouse outlining how you will divide your property and debts, the amount of alimony and child support owed and who will pay it, who will have custody of or visitation with the children, and all other major issues. If you and your spouse are unable to reach an agreement on any of these issues (on your own or with the help of a mediator), you will have to go to court to have a judge resolve them. Once these issues are finalized—either through an agreement or by a judge—they are incorporated into the final divorce decree.

Use the checklists and forms in this book to learn the basics of documenting your separate and joint assets. As you assemble documents, find a safe place (*not* in your home) to store them. Never underestimate the value of financial statements in a divorce.

You must also realize that the legal system is not designed to help you with your finances once the divorce is granted. For example, you may legally and fairly split the benefits of a pension plan in a divorce settlement, but when the time comes to retire, you might have less income than you need to live on. The court can't anticipate or resolve that problem for you.

Further, the implications of future taxes on property are not taken into account in settlement agreements in most states. Generally, only existing—or impending—taxes can be factored into a division of assets. Anything beyond these taxes is considered speculation—and speculation isn't normally welcome in the courtroom.

For example, if, as part of the divorce settlement, you and your spouse will sell $40,000 of stock at a profit, you could agree that the taxes owed on the profit will be factored into the settlement and split between the two of you. But, if you decide instead to keep all of the stocks and your spouse gets another asset of the same value in exchange for your spouse's portion of the stocks, the court will not (on its own) award you more at the time of trial to cover whatever amount of taxes you might owe in the future.

You will need to call the shots today to keep a grip on your future. You can't leave complex, speculative questions about your financial future to the one-dimensional perspective of divorce law.

Don't expect the legal system to make the best financial decisions for you. Only you can do this.

Covenant Marriages

Three states (Arizona, Arkansas, and Louisiana) provide marrying couples with the option of entering into "covenant" marriages. A covenant marriage makes it more difficult to get a divorce and is an alternative to a traditional marriage permitting divorce without restrictions. In addition to undergoing premarital counseling prior to their wedding, a couple wanting to end a covenant marriage must wait a full two years before proceeding, and may divorce only for reasons such as adultery or alcoholism. Parties in states offering covenant marriage are free to enter into a traditional marriage if they prefer. Opponents claim covenant marriages will force some women to stay in an abusive relationship.

Most estimates indicate that only a very small number of couples—between 0.25% and 3%—have opted for covenant marriages in the states where they're legal.

It's Easier to Write Laws Than to Enforce Them

Laws concerning child support payments are among the most stringent on the books. Yet every year, countless parents fail to pay court-ordered child support. Nonenforcement of court orders is one aspect of legal reality for which you must prepare yourself. As you go through each step of your negotiations, ask, "How will I handle this if my ex refuses to abide by the agreement or the judge's orders? What options do I have to enforce this agreement?" And most important, "How much will enforcement cost me?"

When you recognize these risks ahead of time, you can take steps to minimize them.

To enforce your divorce agreement, you will probably have to go to court. The process is expensive, time-consuming, and emotionally draining. If at all possible, keep animosity to a minimum after the divorce so that both parents' custodial or visitation time with the children goes smoothly. In turn, that may make it more likely that your ex will make alimony and child support payments on time.

Your Best Strategy: Think Financially—Act Legally

Make your financial concerns the centerpiece of your divorce, and work within the framework of the law. That is the most powerful position you can take. If you think financially and act legally, you will be able to anticipate risks and assess your needs, before a financial disaster hits.

No one wants to negotiate for an asset in a divorce and then be unable to sell it because they'd owe too much in taxes. Why should you go through the nightmare of settlement negotiations only to end up losing everything you fought for after the divorce is over?

Remember: The legal process of divorce is something you will live *through*—but the financial reality is what you will have to live *with* for the rest of your life.

In a divorce, it's not what you get that counts—it's what you keep.

Legal vs. Financial Stages of Divorce

Use the following table to help you understand the relationship between the legal and financial stages of divorce. These stages will be explored in more detail throughout the book. Keep in mind that few divorces will follow the steps in this exact order.

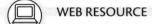 WEB RESOURCE

Nolo's websites, www.nolo.com and www.divorcenet.com, contain legal information and resources that will help you through your divorce. These sites include legal information on topics such as alimony, custody, child support, mediation, property and debt division, grandparent issues, and divorce in the military. They can also help you find local lawyers to assist you in your divorce. Divorce information online has exploded in recent years, and many other sites also specialize in divorce information, resources, and referrals to specialists, including therapists, mediators, and financial advisers.

You will need to be discriminating when you search. Information available on the sites of private firms, for example, might be technically accurate, but this content is often more of a marketing tool than a reliable legal source. Government or nonprofit sites (which typically end in .gov or .org) such as those belonging to states, local courts, state bar associations, and law schools tend to be more reliable. These sites often offer online self-help centers, links to law libraries, clinics, and general information about the law in your county or district:

- www.aaml.org
- www.divorceasfriends.com
- www.divorcecare.org
- www.divorceinfo.com
- www.divorcesource.com, and
- www.divorcewithoutwar.com.

Legal Stages	Financial Stages
Consult an attorney or do some research at a law library to learn about your legal rights and responsibilities. In particular, investigate how your state's laws regarding separation affect custody, alimony, child support, debts incurred after separation, and changes in the value of marital assets after separation.	Gather together your financial papers. Investigate the financial impact of separation and complete a cost–benefit analysis of your options. Make copies of all documents relating to assets, liabilities, income, and expenses whether or not you believe they're important. Use the Financial Facts Checklist (Chapter 8) as a tool (but not a limitation) to what you copy. Close or freeze access to joint accounts. (See Chapter 6.) Open accounts in your own name before filing for divorce. Visit the Federal Trade Commission's website to begin the process of obtaining free copies of your credit reports (https://consumer.ftc.gov/articles/free-credit-reports).
Physically separate. For some couples, this means moving apart. For others, it's living in different parts of the house and no longer sleeping together. Additionally, your state law may use its own criteria to define the date of marital separation. Consult with an attorney to determine the rules in your state.	Keep track of debts incurred before and after separation, joint bills paid, and improvements made to property during separation. Keep receipts for moving and other expenses. Update insurance as necessary. Think about whether you will file taxes jointly or separately.
One spouse files a complaint or petition requesting a divorce. This step begins the formal divorce proceedings. The other spouse must file an answer or response.	

Legal Stages	Financial Stages
One spouse files a request for temporary orders regarding custody, visitation, alimony, or child support. The request may also ask that the other spouse pay both partners' attorneys' fees.	Document all temporary alimony payments made, and write down your agreements about alimony.
Conduct legal discovery (the procedures used to obtain information during a lawsuit) or win spouse's cooperation to share documents. Determine the amount of alimony, child support, and attorneys' fees you will pay or receive, if applicable.	Conduct financial fact-finding. Complete the net worth and cash flow statements in Chapter 12. Hire a forensic accountant if necessary to search for hidden assets. Analyze your assets and debts—use appraisers, accountants, tax advisers, actuaries, and others to help you assess values, tax consequences, and other risks of keeping or giving up property.
Begin settlement negotiations, using one of these possible scenarios: • Use mediation to negotiate the settlement. • Negotiate between yourselves. • Negotiate through your attorneys. • If you are unable to settle certain issues, bring those issues to a judge.	Before settlement negotiations, make a list of all items you want the agreement to cover. Be sure to carefully analyze the tax ramifications and other financial pitfalls of each offer and counteroffer. Reduce attorneys' fees by doing much of the legwork on your own, settling without an attorney, keeping anger out of your negotiations, and avoiding a trial. Remember that a trial can be very expensive. You'll have to pay lawyers' fees as well as the fees of the experts (accountants, actuaries, and the like) whom you bring in to testify.
Draft your marital settlement agreement to incorporate terms of the settlement or the court order. The agreement is incorporated into the final judgment of divorce.	If you settle by agreement, carefully check it against your wish list.

Financial Realities No One Talks About

The true cost of divorce is rarely discussed openly.

Y ou're probably better prepared to negotiate a car purchase than to negotiate a divorce. Most of us accept that the advertised "sticker" price of the car isn't the final price. A new car often has a "dealer markup," taxes, and other fees that will be tacked on before you drive the car off the lot. If the car is preowned, you might have the opportunity to negotiate a lower price. You'll also need to factor in the cost of insurance, registration fees, repairs, and maintenance.

Many people enter divorce looking for a "sticker price," which will be final and all-inclusive. But there's just no way to predict the cost of divorce. Divorce has too many unforeseeable variables, even for spouses who know their net worth. Costs and fees, such as those related to refinancing and transferring property, conducting research, and hiring experts, can turn what you thought was a great deal into one with devastating financial consequences.

You will need to keep a sharp eye out for additional amounts you may be charged, but were unaware of when you agreed to a settlement. Divorce clients who focus primarily on the legal or emotional implications of their situation often fail to consider important financial angles of their settlements.

Take the family home as one example. You must consider much more than the price you paid for it and the eventual sale price. In addition, you must:

- Make sure property taxes are paid and current.
- Search for any liens on the property.
- Keep the mortgage payments current and free of late charges.
- Confirm no judgments are recorded against the property in the land records, which must be paid before title can be cleared for transfer.

If you were going to sell your house under conditions other than a divorce, you would have to consider and negotiate the cost of necessary repairs or inspections and a real estate agent's commission (unless you sold the house yourself). You would also consider the implications of a capital gains tax. Under current tax law, if you have lived in your home for two of the past five years, you pay taxes on any profit beyond the first $250,000, or $500,000 if you are married and file jointly with your spouse.

In our experience, these important considerations are rarely discussed during a divorce. Many courts must, by law, consider only the home's equity value. The costs of sale, federal and state taxes, and other subsidiary expenses are beyond their scope. Spouses often pay their exes for a full share of a home's equity, while totally ignoring the other normal costs and benefits of the house sale.

Only after the sale is final does one spouse recognize the benefits or risks of carrying those costs alone. And most divorcing couples *do* sell their family homes—either at the time of judgment or within five years after the divorce.

At divorce, you and your spouse are essentially "selling" everything you own—by way of transfer either to the other or to an outsider.

It is critical that you approach divorce the way you would any other business transaction. Look at your situation from a realistic perspective that takes all predictable financial events into account, especially those with tax-related consequences.

Financial reality begins where legal reality ends. To help you close the gap between the two, this book provides you with worksheets and instructions on specific issues. It also suggests that you keep in mind five general observations on financial reality. These are the basic "truths" about money and divorce you should refer to whenever you face your toughest financial decisions:

- In divorce, everything takes longer and costs more.
- When you're connected to another person financially, you're at risk.
- The IRS is watching your divorce—even when you're not.
- Cash is king.
- You're playing for keeps; don't sell off tomorrow for today.

In Divorce, Everything Takes Longer and Costs More

One of the universal misconceptions about divorce is that it will end quickly so that all parties move on with their lives, free of the animosity that brought their marriage to an end. This is rarely the case, especially when a court gets involved.

In fact, your divorce can cost more money and take a longer time to settle than you ever imagined. For many couples, the process takes one to two years—even for simple divorces the spouses thought would take only six months. The cost can range from several hundred dollars to many hundreds of thousands. (Many clients start off intending to settle, get stuck on one issue, and then end up spending millions in litigation, only to settle just before trial.)

To understand the costly nature of divorce, you must recognize the high price of splitting one economic unit in half. On the surface, an equitable property division would seem to mean each person walks away with half of what was shared by two and is, therefore, left with enough to support one.

But in the mathematics of divorce, that's not how the equation works out. Most spouses have unequal salaries and earning potential. Even during times of economic hardship, many people live beyond their means. When it comes time to divide one household into two, there is rarely enough money to go around. That holds true as much for young married couples with little property as it does for older, wealthy couples with assets accumulated over many years. In a divorce, dismantling these arrangements is not like performing a surgical procedure; it's more like experiencing a natural disaster. When couples separate, their fragile economic bases are torn apart, much as an earthquake loosens a house from its foundation, leaving everything in disarray. Spouses, children and extended families are left fearful of the unknown.

Recognizing that everything takes longer and costs more can help you through those moments when you are suddenly faced with an unexpected debt or an unwanted delay in your divorce.

Accept the Fact That Money Is Tight

Maybe you already understand that your divorce will cost you dearly. What do you do with that knowledge?

Be willing to accept a change in your lifestyle. Face it, you might have to borrow money, move, get a second job, or buy a used car instead of a new one. Be prepared for an economic pinch—at least for a while.

You will have to resist the very understandable temptation to splurge when your marriage is ending. The fact that you have to prepare for lean times also means that you must pay special attention to each financial decision you will make in divorce. In the end, the expense of the divorce itself means you must begin conserving your financial resources now.

You're at Risk When You're Financially Connected to Another Person

This truth seems obvious, yet it's often ignored. Divorcing partners tend to resist or "forget" that they must cut the financial ties that bind them, or pay for those ties long after the marriage ends.

You're at risk any time you hold a joint interest with your spouse, are jointly responsible for obligations related to that interest, or are financially dependent on your spouse or ex-spouse. You have no control over their health, disability, death, employment, ability to earn income, or any third parties they may bring into their lives (and yours). If your ex-spouse defaults on payments, commits fraud, goes bankrupt, dies, or becomes disabled, your future could be jeopardized unless you've completely severed your financial relationship.

These risks often are overlooked—even through a divorce—because of the common human aversion to change. If you've maintained a joint checking account for 20 years, it might feel strange to close it. Reorganizing your financial position often forces people to accept that their marriages are really over. It's a difficult, but critical adjustment.

A spouse might feel overly responsible for the other partner's welfare—and continue paying for something like a car long after it's no longer appropriate. Resentments over an affair or some other perceived wrongdoing, such as lying, gambling, or abusing alcohol, can also cause one partner to remain financially entangled with the other.

People often leave themselves at risk with their former partners because they simply don't think about it. As you work through this book and your divorce, you'll learn some of the most common financial risks divorcing couples face and get tools for protecting yourself. Because your divorce is unique, however, you must stay alert to the risks in your particular case. Identify the areas where you and your spouse could remain connected financially, then work to break those connections wherever possible.

You'll need courage and support from people you trust, but you should also get professional help from qualified attorneys, certified public accountants (CPAs), and/or financial planners. Base your decisions on their advice, rather than divorce horror stories you might hear from friends.

Start thinking like a problem solver. Avoidance isn't the problem solver's method. Avoidance only creates more risk, uncertainty, and fear.

The IRS Is Watching Your Divorce

You must consider the tax implications of each major financial move you make during your divorce. To you, selling your property might seem like a simple business transaction—but to the Internal Revenue Service, your actions could create something called a "taxable event." Be sure you're managing those events to your best advantage. Factor in tax costs anytime you make a financial decision in your divorce, because someday, the IRS will want to collect.

As a general rule, a transfer of property between spouses related to a divorce is a nontaxable event. However, you might face major tax consequences in the future when that asset is sold postdivorce. Generally, with anything you keep as part of your settlement, you become solely responsible for the taxes due on all gain (profit) on that asset from the time the two of you originally purchased it.

It is in your best interest to consult with tax accountants or other financial professionals who can help you calculate the impact of taxes on your property division.

You will also need to decide how you will file tax returns once a divorce is underway. If you expect refunds on joint returns, decide how you will split the money. Be sure you know how the tax bill will be paid if money is due.

The point is not to become paralyzed with worry about the IRS, but to recognize that your changing marital status definitely affects your tax status. Throughout the rest of the book, you'll get guidance and formulas regarding some tax matters. For more complicated issues, you should contact an experienced CPA or tax expert.

 WEB RESOURCE
The IRS continues to improve its resources so they are more user-friendly. The IRS website (www.irs.gov) offers plain-English answers to many difficult tax questions, and keyword searches will produce many articles and bullet point lists explaining how a divorce can affect both spouses' taxes.

Cash Is King

Quick—which would you rather have:
- A retirement plan that promises to pay $125,000 in ten years, or $100,000 today?
- A Mercedes currently valued at $35,000, or a mutual fund with a current market value of $35,000?
- A secured note from your spouse promising to pay you $500 a month for the next five years, or a lump sum payment of $30,000 today?

The simple answer is: Take the money and run.

Like the proverbial "bird in the hand is worth two in the bush," a dollar you get today is worth more than a promise of one tomorrow. In the examples above, the retirement plan may be riskier than you think, the Mercedes will depreciate and could be expensive to repair, and your spouse might never make good on the promised payments. (While the $35,000 mutual fund is not exactly in cash, a mutual fund is a liquid asset and can be converted to cash much more quickly than a car that is depreciating in value.) "Cash is king" holds true whether you are speaking of actual cash or cash-equivalent liquid assets.

Three basic financial concepts explain why cash is king: inflation, the time value of money, and the risk-free nature of cash.

Inflation. "Inflation" is the rise in the prices of goods and services. In brief, your dollar might not be capable of buying as much tomorrow as it will today. Suppose you currently have $1,000. With a typical inflation rate averaging as low as 3.5% per year (with the exception of the inflation rate at the time of writing, which is higher than the long-term average and expected to drop in the coming year), your $1,000 would only have the power to buy $503 in goods in 20 years.

What if you and your spouse agree that you will be paid $10,000 as part of your settlement? If you're paid at the time of the divorce, you'd get $10,000 in today's dollars. If you have to wait three years for your money, that $10,000 will be worth less. Consequently, if you are offered a divorce settlement payment to be collected in the future, you must account for inflation.

Time value of money. Quite simply, if your money is working for you today—by growing in a quality mutual fund, producing profits in your business, or even earning interest in a bank account—you are getting more value than if you have to wait until tomorrow to put that money to work. Why should you have to wait, and give your spouse the use of your money for months or years to come? Better to get your payments in cash at the time of the divorce than to miss the opportunity of using your money to best advantage.

Risk-free nature of cash. The value of a lump sum payment doesn't fluctuate and isn't taxed upon receipt when it's paid as part of a divorce settlement. That might make it attractive enough for you to accept cash in exchange for getting less than the full amount to which you might otherwise be entitled.

You're Playing for Keeps

In the rush to reach a settlement, some divorcing couples seek the quickest way out—regardless of the future cost. When the dust settles, mistakes might surface that end up costing you greatly in money and time.

To manage money effectively, you need alternatives to help solve unexpected problems and to meet your goals. When you trade away long-term options for short-term needs, you're forcing yourself into a corner. You literally take future choices away from yourself. Accepting property without considering maintenance costs and your future lifestyle can strap you with debt for years to come. Agreeing to pay your spouse's bills just to hasten the divorce process may take care of some emotional needs, but it probably does not make sense financially. Nor should you calculate your finances based on a situation or arrangement that hasn't yet come to fruition or that may prove only temporary.

> **EXAMPLE:** Marla was divorcing and calculating her cost of living. During the divorce, Marla's mother provided free child care, and Marla assumed that would continue indefinitely. She did not stop to think of what would happen should her mother become unable to babysit. After Marla's divorce was final, her mother found a new part-time job and could no longer care for her grandson. Marla spent a great deal of time and money renegotiating her support payments to reflect her true cost of living and child care.

When you are in the middle of a divorce, you might overlook obvious problems unless you apply long-term thinking to your divorce decisions. Anytime you feel rushed or pressured, either by your spouse or by the legal calendar of your divorce proceedings, take a moment to step back and look at your divorce from a future-oriented perspective. That view should help you withstand the pressures and make more informed decisions.

Money Is Not Math

Anxieties and phobias about math might hamper your ability to make financial decisions when a marriage ends. Don't feel embarrassed if you're intimidated by columns of numbers and fine-print paperwork. The formulas in this book are purposely simplified so that everyone can understand the financial information needed at divorce.

Don't worry about mastering math. You only have to gather current and accurate information about your financial situation. Getting the right numbers to plug into the formulas is much more important than learning how to make complicated tax or other calculations.

Years ago, computer scientists coined the term "GIGO," which stood for "garbage in/garbage out." If they fed the computer the wrong data (garbage in), they would get the wrong answers (garbage out). Likewise, if you try to calculate your cost of living or the value of your property using outdated information or guesswork, you will end up with "garbage" in your final settlement. So gather the correct data. If you don't want to plug the numbers into the formulas yourself, you can hire a bookkeeper, an accountant, or a financial planner to work with you.

Emotional Divorce:
Managing the "Money Crazies"

To make the best financial decisions during divorce, you must be alert to the emotional states that can sabotage your settlement negotiations.

Be on guard if you find yourself attempting to:
- get even
- get it over with, or
- get back together.

These three "gets" show the influence of strong emotions, which will hamper your ability to see both the upside and downside of your decisions. Anger, resentment, and running away are reactions. But in a divorce, you must not simply react; you need to think clearly, carefully, and coolly.

Start by checking your attitude. Do any of the following sound like you?

"I'm going to get even no matter what it takes. You're going to pay for what you did to me. Just you wait. I'll see you in court."

You might feel that this attitude conveys strength, but the "get even" approach rarely leaves people satisfied, even when their divorce settlements or the court's orders are totally equal according to the numbers on paper. Bitter feelings linger long after the settlement, especially if you use poor financial judgment motivated by revenge. The hostility between warring parents can have terrible consequences for their children, which might linger for years.

What's more, vengeful spouses' attorneys' fees are often the highest. If you insist on going to court to get even, a trial will likely cost you at least three times as much as an out-of-court settlement. Besides that, you're unlikely to get what you want from a judge; even if you do, there is no guarantee that your ex will follow the court's orders.

While you should certainly pursue your legal rights, the judicial system is no place to satisfy your emotional demands.

"Holding on to anger is like grasping a hot coal with the intent of throwing it at someone else. You are the one who gets burned." (Variously attributed)

"I don't care what happens. I just want to get it over with."

Stop right there. In a divorce, running away or becoming defenseless is the equivalent of playing the victim, and being victimized is perhaps the worst strategy you can take when it comes to your finances. The decisions you make during your divorce will affect you (and your children) for the rest of your life. It's no time to choose the path of least resistance. Your financial survival depends on participating in each step of your divorce settlement. And if you take too many shortcuts, you could create unexpected money problems that won't take effect until later. In a year or two, your emotional life will be different, but the financial agreements you make during divorce, will affect you permanently.

"Maybe if I don't cause problems financially, we can work it out. I won't make waves. I'll just give in so we can get back together."

Certainly this attitude is understandable when you're hoping to reconcile or if both of you are committed to a fair and equitable settlement. But it's futile—and dangerous—to think you can save the relationship by surrendering your financial leverage. Avoiding conflict is often another expression of victimhood or passive aggression, neither of which will set things right. Why should someone come back into a faltering relationship if you're agreeing to everything anyway? Meanwhile, if you and your partner do get back together, your relationship will be much healthier if you're on equal footing— financially and emotionally.

All this advice might make sense, but in reality, how do you deal with money when you are emotionally involved with your spouse?

That question is perhaps the most important one to ask when you embark on a divorce, and it is central to the purpose of this book.

The primary concept can be stated simply: The better you manage your emotions, the better equipped you'll be to manage financial decisions during divorce. But applying this rather simple concept can be a very difficult task. The emotional toll of divorce is so high that some therapists and counselors use the label "crazy time" to describe it.

Ironically, you'll need to make calm, rational financial decisions that affect your future while you're under intense emotional pressure. Your two tasks—the logical and linear management of money and the release of emotional tension—pull you in opposite directions. Balancing between these poles is an insane proposition. No wonder you feel as if you have the "money crazies."

You will need to be cool and focused while you manage your finances during divorce, which means you need to limit the hours you spend wrestling with your emotions. When you take steps to understand the divorce process in emotional terms, you might avoid some of the common pitfalls that lead to victimization and unchecked anger. Forewarned is forearmed.

Depression During Divorce

Depression often begins quietly, but it can linger long after your divorce is over. The CDC estimates that one in every ten adults experiences depression in a given year. Figures aren't available for people undergoing divorce, but experience suggests the percentages climb much higher for this group.

If left untreated, depression can be devastating to your physical as well as mental health. Depression has many possible symptoms, with common ones being:

- anxiety
- fatigue
- no longer enjoying things that made you happy
- difficulty making decisions (an especially severe symptom in divorce)
- feelings of hopelessness or unworthiness, and
- suicidal thoughts.

Depression is a very common and treatable condition. Please seek medical advice and/or therapy if you're feeling overwhelmed by the the emotional and financial toll of divorce. Being responsible and efficient when you're at your worst might not seem fair, but remember that this difficult period of time is temporary and you will get beyond the pain of splitting up.

Reduce Stress Whenever You Can

No matter how eager you might be to get on with a divorce, it's probably going to be a struggle for you to achieve the financial-emotional balance necessary to see it through. That struggle means stress, perhaps more than you've ever experienced. Research indicates that only the death of a spouse creates more stress than divorce. Some counselors contend that when other factors are considered—separation anxiety, moving from a long-term residence, and loss of status, to name just a few—divorce is *the* most stressful life event you can ever face.

Money is a difficult topic—taboo—for most people. Even happily married couples can experience stress when discussing it. If you're now handling money on your own, especially if your spouse took exclusive charge of the family finances during the marriage, the unknowns can seem overwhelming. Worries about financial survival, the divorce settlement, finding a job after staying home for years, or paying attorneys can be crushing, especially when you can no longer "talk things through" with your spouse.

Stress can manifest in dozens of ways. Sleeplessness, fatigue, loss of appetite, disruption of work patterns, lack of focus, and emotional explosions over frustrations, large or small, are all common symptoms. It's critical that you do whatever is necessary to take care of yourself. If you have children, good self-care is even more important. Your frustrations are less likely to spill over onto the children if you're attending to your own needs.

If you have disposable income, schedule a massage, go out to dinner or a movie, or even arrange a weekend away. These quick fixes can take the edge off during a rough patch. But even if money is tight, you have no excuse for ignoring your stress. No-cost forms of self-care, like taking a walk, practicing meditation, reading, listening to music, simply sitting under a tree, or watching a sunset, are available to all of us. These types of quiet intervals can help reduce stress and ease the strain on your bruised emotions.

Even if you don't feel like it, try to keep your sleeping and eating patterns close to normal. Rest and good nutrition are essential to good health.

Regular exercise is one of the smartest and most efficient antidotes to divorce stress. It will combat fatigue and provide an essential outlet for physical and emotional tension.

These stress reduction techniques sound simple and can be applied to many life events, but make no mistake: They are crucial in your fight against the money crazies. The stress of divorce can last months and even years—you have to learn to manage it.

Safeguard Your Sanity

During a divorce, it's important to safeguard your emotional well-being. Spend more time with people who can give you positive reinforcement and less with those who criticize you or your divorce. Join a divorce support group. Since the COVID-19 pandemic, many support groups have gone virtual and now meet online. As a result, more people who simply couldn't find time in their schedules to make these types of meetings before COVID are able to join, especially single parents or divorcing spouses with busy work or travel schedules.

If you find that you're unable to shake feelings of sadness or you start to feel like you're slipping into depression, it's time to consider therapy with a licensed professional. In the long run, the money you spend on your mental health will be less than what you'd lose if, for example, you got fired from your job or engaged in self-destructive behaviors.

Rely more on voicemail, email, and text. Not only can you screen nuisance calls or messages if your spouse is hostile, but you can set up your notifications to let others know that you are unreachable or busy when you need to be alone.

Some days you'll feel like talking and other days it will be the last thing you want to do. You might have just calmed down, and then, when you run into a friend and retell your story, emotions rise again—the catch in the throat, the anger, the frustration. That could be a healthy experience, but if you're feeling that it's too much, limit your personal conversations just as you would your calls and messages.

Take control of your home environment. Clean a closet, paint a room, or move the furniture. There's an almost universal tendency during divorce to think about the past—obsessively and excessively. Most people find it is simply easier to put away the family pictures, the mementos, and the visual cues that can trigger feelings of loss and depression.

You are affected not only by what you see, but also by what you hear. Instead of sitting back and allowing a favorite old song or heart-tugging commercial or movie to make you sad, listen to or watch something new. You'll be amazed at how good it can feel to exert control over something when so much of your life seems to be out of control.

"No, We Can't Afford It Now"

Few parents enjoy denying their children toys, gifts, or other pleasures. During divorce, you might find yourself repeating the phrase, "No! We can't afford it now!" more times than you care to count. Disappointing your children can only add to your frustration. But while you might want to protect them from harsh realities, you must also be honest and help your family adjust to the new circumstances.

Make sure discussions about money are age appropriate, and make sure your children are mature enough to understand the difference between making hard choices (such as choosing to fund one after-school activity instead of two) and a real crisis (losing the family home to foreclosure). If your children are too young to understand the concept of money, you'll need an extra supply of patience to handle their confusion and mood swings.

Take heart in the fact that millions of children have survived divorce, and that many benefit from learning about how to live well under a tight budget and watching their parents manage a divorce courageously. And don't forget: The better you handle your divorce today, the more likely your children's future will be grounded in a positive and healthy lifestyle, instead of negative thinking.

We Need to Talk: Money & Kids After Divorce (Volume 1) by Linda Leitz, CFPA (Bright Leitz Publishing, LLC), contains useful advice for broaching these tough subjects with your children.

Watch Out for Sore Spots

You probably already know which financial issues are likely to get you upset. All couples have sore spots—resentments about an unpaid bill, spending sprees, bounced checks, interfering in-laws, loans to relatives, or gifts to a lover.

If you know that you will be dealing with an issue that's been a particular long-term irritation, prepare yourself for it instead of merely reacting to the inevitable pressure. Get a good night's sleep before tackling such a problem, or postpone a confrontation until you feel strong enough to be at your best. Taking these basic steps can go a long way toward reducing the tension in your life. Remember, reducing stress means increasing your ability to make sound financial decisions.

Be Prepared for the Worst

Some emotional problems of divorce offer no easy solutions—when people are under stress, they tend to revert to their base, survival behaviors. This can lead to excessive drinking, shouting matches, and other bad scenes. If someone tends to be absent-minded, selfish, or controlling, those tendencies will be exaggerated when a marriage is ending.

During divorce, couples are facing the psychological task of separating, and consciously or unconsciously look for ways to break their connections to each other. During courtship, partners do everything possible to build the relationship, while in divorce, energy goes into destroying it. Amplified by stress, these destructive impulses create many of the horror stories you might hear about divorce—sweet irrational gestures of romance are reversed by equally ridiculous acts of "vengeance."

Even if you believe that you and your spouse are capable of proceeding with a "civilized" divorce, it helps to prepare for the worst-case scenarios. Remember, survival instincts can also stimulate awareness, which is something you'll need when it comes time to think about money.

Don't Let Threats Throw You

In the process of divorce, your soon-to-be ex-spouse might try to threaten you in some of the following ways.

"Unless you play this my way, you'll never get a dime."

Keep calm. Of course the person making this threat wants to scare and intimidate you and continue the power plays that have worked in the past. When you hear such statements, tell yourself that coercion won't work. The property will be divided fairly, and support will be awarded in accordance with guidelines.

"I'll go to jail before I'll pay you a dime of support."

Don't panic. Know that support can be enforced through a wage assignment, which means that your check will come directly from your ex-spouse's employer. If your ex-spouse doesn't work for someone else and falls behind in support payments, a number of enforcement methods are available. Ultimately, failing to pay support can mean a jail term, but most people pay voluntarily before going to jail.

"I'll quit my job before I'll pay you that kind of money."

A lot of divorcing spouses have tried this approach, many judges have seen this tactic, and it doesn't typically work. It's more than a little suspicious when one spouse suddenly and voluntarily quits a long-held job just before they're supposed to start paying spousal and/or child support in a divorce. This move is not smart. If you can show a judge that your ex-spouse quit a job to avoid support, the court will probably continue support at the same level, and your ex will have to find a way to pay.

"I will reconcile with you only if you put everything in my name."

Nice try. If you're going to reconcile, why do you need an agreement that is lopsidedly in favor of the person making such a demand? Be extremely suspicious of such statements, and don't sign anything without consulting your attorney.

If you're on the receiving end of a threat, don't be intimidated or give in. Ignore threats as best you can and continue to work toward a reasonable resolution.

If you believe your spouse might cut off any connection to you—by wiping out the checking account, running off to another state, or ruining the family's credit—you might be able to short-circuit potential damage. Even if the worst-case scenarios never come to pass, you will have done yourself a favor by simply drawing up a plan of action.

Whatever happens, you must do your best not to take bizarre or vengeful behavior personally. This approach will help you to remain detached from the short-term drama of divorce, and therefore better able to concentrate on the long-term money questions that demand your attention.

Develop a Financially Focused Mental Attitude

To combat a devious spouse during divorce, you must develop a strong mental attitude and a solid legal strategy. You're certainly entitled to feelings of outrage and betrayal. You can utter the cry "How can you do this to me?!?" as much as you want to. In fact, that phrase is a common chorus in divorce cases. Yes, many things that happen in divorce *are* unfair.

But the fact remains that you will have to keep going and keep fighting for your financial life regardless of the injustices your spouse (or your spouse's attorney) perpetrates. You can stand up for yourself. If you stay focused on the future and the financial realities of your life, you'll be in a much stronger position as your divorce progresses.

Avoid the "All at Once" Syndrome

Most likely, you will experience a wide range of feelings and moods: anger, hatred, elation, excitement, sadness, loss, depression, bitterness, rejection, loneliness, guilt, and hostility. Sometimes it will feel as though you're experiencing those feelings all at once. This phenomenon seems to be a hallmark of the divorce money crazies.

You might also feel that everything is coming apart all at once. Just as soon as you get the car fixed, the washer or the stove breaks.

One explanation is that you simply notice problems more because of your heightened and chronic stress levels. Moreover, by the time most people separate, a great deal of their energy has been focused on the relationship—not on the normal chores that can keep a household running. You might not be in the mood to defrost the refrigerator or check the oil in the car as usual. That lack of maintenance can catch up with you as the machinery in your life begins breaking down.

The all at once syndrome in divorce can manifest itself in other ways as well. Some people decide that while they are changing a mate, they should change everything else in their lives as well. They try to lose weight, quit smoking, get a new job, and redecorate the house, all at once. This approach is never helpful. Give yourself time. Go slowly. You'll have your hands full just getting through the divorce.

Manage the Ebb and Flow of Emotions

Keep in mind that emotions tend to be experienced in waves. One day you feel fine; the next day, life is awful. Such fluctuations are common in divorce, and eventually the wave action subsides. Don't attempt to handle important money tasks on the bad days—wait until the storm passes.

Because the level of tension in a divorce is often compared to the stress that accompanies the death of a loved one, some psychologists claim the grief processes are also similar. Elisabeth Kübler-Ross's groundbreaking work on death and dying pinpointed five stages of grief: denial, anger, bargaining, depression, and acceptance. These stages do not necessarily occur in this order. How you go through these stages is unique to you, but it is important that you experience them.

Marriage counselors note that people who avoid grieving by jumping into a new relationship too quickly are only prolonging the process. Those who do allow themselves to grieve for the marriages they had (or the marriages they wished they had) actually get through their divorces more quickly—and carry less psychological baggage when the marriage is over. As a consequence, they are often able to manage their financial lives better, too.

While the grief processes are similar in death and divorce, some important differences do exist. Social attitudes have changed greatly, but widows and widowers still get more sympathy than those who have divorced. With divorce, too, the door to your relationship doesn't close with the same finality. You might still have contact with your former spouse for years and go through the grieving process many times as you continue to make contact and separate.

Ambivalence—the love-hate relationship with your former spouse—is common when marriages end. Actually, the push and pull in and out of the relationship characterizes the separation process that began before the actual divorce. Commonly, one person in the relationship becomes discontented before the other, and this "initiator" is usually the one to ask for the divorce.

If your partner was the initiator, don't be surprised if that person seems to have already moved on. In fact, the initiator has a head start on the psychological work needed to separate. Just don't let yourself lag behind financially, or get pushed into doing something you're not ready for.

The initiator might already be out the door and pressuring you to "get on with it"—to sign over the condo, to sell the house, to separate the silverware. Meanwhile, you might still be at the "starting gate," emotionally shocked and dazed, unable to finalize a process you have only begun.

If you initiated the divorce, realize that it is probably in your best financial and family interests to be sensitive to your partner's pace of accepting the separation. Your negotiations are likely to be more successful if you present your financial proposals to someone who has had a chance to assimilate what is happening in the relationship on a personal level.

Psychologists have found that the hardest part of the divorce process tends to be the time just before the actual physical separation. Tensions often mount dramatically until the real break occurs. Some couples separate and reconnect several times in an attempt to save the marriage. Whatever is happening to you emotionally, continue taking steps to put your financial life in order. Should you and your partner ultimately reunite, your relationship will be stronger if you have not used money as a weapon against each other.

Mixed Emotions—Working With Attorneys

Controlling your emotions is important—particularly when it comes to working with an attorney on your divorce settlement. Remember, your attorney is not your therapist or confidante. As you proceed through this book and through your divorce settlement, be honest with yourself about whether you are being a model client (and one who will save attorneys' fees) or a client whom your attorney would like to avoid. The following questions will help you make that determination:

- Have I given my attorney accurate and complete information on time?
- Have I thought through the objectives of my divorce agreement?
- Do I waffle in making decisions or compromises?
- If I'm not clear on a legal issue, do I ask for clarification?
- If I have a disagreement with my attorney, am I willing to talk it through to resolution?
- Do I neglect to cover issues and later blame my attorney for forgetting certain items?
- On a continuum between being a pest and being unavailable, where am I?
- Am I paying my bills on time?

Don't Let Financial Tasks Overwhelm You

As you move through your divorce, it will be easy to become overwhelmed with the financial details. You might suffer from math anxiety or money phobias. Or perhaps you and your partner shared a complicated financial life, one that will take effort to untangle.

Whatever your feelings, you can get some relief by breaking down your tasks into small steps. Reward yourself for completing an item. Hire a math whiz to help you when necessary. If you're upset, see a counselor or join a therapy group. That strategy makes much more sense, and is less costly, than using your attorney as a therapist or asking your friends to help you understand a situation that calls for expert analysis.

Anything you can do to build your self-esteem is important now. Divorce tends to make you feel worse about yourself, and it's easy to confuse money issues with your sense of self-worth. Besides the stress-management techniques already described, you may also find it helpful to keep a journal. Having a notebook handy to jot down feelings throughout the day helps dissipate tense moments. This record can serve as an "invisible calculator" to tally the emotional costs of financial decisions. Tracking feelings and reactions in this way can make it easier to reach those bottom-line decisions.

While it might seem as though the inner turmoil from your divorce will never end, it is a finite process that only takes time. For some people, the process lasts one or two years, while for others, recovery from a divorce could take longer. You are very likely to become a different person in that time, with different needs and attitudes. Keep that in mind as you manage the money crazies of your divorce—and make sure the financial choices you make today will work for you tomorrow.

Divorce—on a Spiritual Level

For some people, divorce stress is more than emotional. It becomes a religious or spiritual crisis. This book can't attempt to address such a crisis. You can, however, contact local churches, synagogues, or clergy members for referrals to divorce ministries.

One note of caution: No matter how you feel about your divorce from the spiritual point of view, you can't ignore its legal and financial consequences.

For example, one client insisted on working exclusively with attorneys and other professionals who shared her faith. While there is nothing inherently wrong with this, it didn't work in her case. She didn't judge the professionals she hired on their competence or abilities. In the end, she had to go through the costly process of finding a new attorney and accountant to help her complete the divorce.

For more information on selecting professionals, see Chapter 7.

The Hardest Part: Is My Marriage Really Over?

Legally, a final decree from the court marks the end of your married life.

Emotionally, it might be years before you feel complete peace of mind about the end of your marriage. But from a strictly financial standpoint, the marriage ends when you or your spouse begins to take unilateral actions without considering the effect on the other person.

It's that moment when one spouse stops acting like a trusted friend or partner and starts putting the other spouse in economic jeopardy. One spouse might empty a bank account, leaving the other with nothing to pay the bills. Or a soon-to-be ex might run up joint debts unbeknownst to the other.

A great deal of financial damage can take place in the early stages of divorce. You must protect your interests whether or not you feel sure the marriage is over.

Couples often go through several phases of splitting up and getting back together before the final and permanent break in the marriage. While you're going through this push and pull, you might find yourself walking a tightrope between conflicting demands and emotions— watching out for your personal property without antagonizing your spouse, or taking care of your individual needs while not letting your spouse off the hook for joint responsibilities.

Eventually, you'll know when the marriage has reached a point of no return. Even then, you might hold out hope for a reconciliation. Nothing is wrong with having hope—as long as you protect yourself and continue taking care of business. That means knowing precisely where your financial interests and risks lie and what to do about them. The following stories illuminate the dilemma you're in at this early stage of divorce—and the danger of ignoring its consequences.

A Happy Ending	An Unhappy Ending
When you're in the midst of a crumbling relationship, it might be hard to believe that resolving money problems can sometimes help clear up other troubling issues in a marriage. Alice came in for a financial consultation and said she was considering a divorce. Although she had always worked outside the home, her husband managed the finances and kept her in the dark. Unwilling to tolerate the situation any longer, Alice began educating herself and learning about the couple's cash flow, taxes, and investments. She also consulted an attorney to assess her legal rights. Secure with her knowledge, she confronted her husband and demanded a greater financial role in the marriage. They argued bitterly and almost divorced at several points along the way. Through patience and counseling, however, they resolved their differences and kept the marriage intact.	The infamous Palm Beach divorce of Roxanne and Peter Pulitzer in the 1980s demonstrates what can happen if both parties are not equally committed to a reconciliation. Roxanne claimed that in trying to save her marriage, she lost her financial power and leverage as a mother. Upon receiving divorce papers concerning hearings and proceedings, she said she followed her husband's instructions to throw them in the garbage because he did not intend to end the marriage. Doing just that placed Roxanne at a great disadvantage when her husband did, in fact, continue the divorce proceedings. "I lost the case before it even started," she said once it was over. Instead of focusing on the reality of her situation, she put her energy into reconciliation—and lost.

No one can really predict which marriages will come apart or stay together, because every couple, and the dynamic between them, is unique. If you're still questioning whether you have a viable marriage or not, you might want to consider the following options.

Counseling. Now is the time to find out whether your marriage is worth saving. Some people can't—and perhaps shouldn't—let go until they have explored every avenue of reconciliation. But if your spouse refuses to cooperate, you might have little choice but to accept the inevitable and move on with the divorce.

Temporary separation. For some couples, a period of time apart is healing. At the same time, it's important to keep your financial house in order. Make a list of your joint obligations and expenses. Through mediation or counseling, you and your spouse might be able to reach agreements about dealing with the practical demands of life while you work on your emotional relationship.

After you give yourself some time to consider this information and your options, you must confront the main decision presented in this chapter: Is your marriage really over? This question is not meant to rush you toward divorce, but rather to help you clarify your position. You can afford to leave some questions open in life—but this isn't one of them. Once you've made this decision, it will be significantly easier for you to tackle the hard tasks ahead. But if you're unclear on this, all decisions that follow become much harder to make.

Okay—take a deep breath. Write out your answer below, or speak it out loud to someone you trust. Either way, the time has come to make the decision that only you can.

Is my marriage really over?

Whatever Stage You're in, Don't Ignore Legal or Financial Realities

Whether you attempt counseling, a trial separation, or something else, don't ignore your financial responsibilities and potential liabilities. Just as you would consider legal notices or documents important at any other time in your life, so, too, must you recognize the serious implications of any legal actions in the early stages of divorce—even if your spouse tries to convince you otherwise. Don't ignore court orders or papers. And, if you have any reason to suspect your spouse is moving assets or taking funds from your joint accounts, you should immediately read Chapter 6 for information on how to protect your interests.

The Separation: What Happens When One Spouse Moves Out?

"I told him I wanted him out by the end of the month."

"I can't stand it another minute—I'm getting out of here."

"It's over and it would be easier on all of us if you would just go."

Don't be surprised if you find yourself saying—or hearing— any of these statements before you separate. At the outset of a divorce, feelings might run high, and emotions seem to dictate the schedule of events in your life. Old arguments and long-held resentments commonly surface in this difficult period, just before or during the actual physical separation. Power plays could become more troublesome as one of you might try to force the other out of the family home.

No matter how you feel about your spouse, neither of you necessarily has to be the one to move—unless you or your children would be in physical danger if you stayed together. If your spouse has been abusive, you can request a restraining order from the court, which would prohibit your spouse from remaining in the family home. In many states, you might be able to find resources on the local court's website or the court's family law help center so you can file this paperwork yourself, without a lawyer's assistance. In other states, however, court clerks must assist you in completing papers to apply for a restraining order. Many legal aid clinics and women's legal clinics also provide pro bono (free) legal help—including assistance in applying for restraining orders—for victims of domestic violence. (See the appendix.)

Even when violence is not an issue in your marriage, practical reasons might dictate that one spouse move out rather than the other. For example, many divorcing couples who live under the same roof find making agreements difficult. If one of the spouses moves out, the divorce often proceeds more smoothly and with less pain.

In the midst of ending a marriage, you might not want to look at your situation in the cold, harsh light of financial reality. But that denial could ultimately cost you thousands of dollars. Before you insist on leaving or having your spouse move out, take a little time to consider the financial consequences of the separation date.

Whether you view this time period as a trial separation (where you continue to work on your marriage) or a final and permanent separation (as in the beginning of divorce), the following information is important to you.

Protect Your Child Custody Rights If You Plan to Move Out

If you have children, the primary caretaker might want to stay in the family home while the other spouse rents a place, housesits for someone else, or moves in with a friend. However, by moving out of the family home without your children, you could jeopardize your chances of getting physical custody of them. Few judges like to change the status quo when it comes to kids. So before you move out, be sure to make arrangements with your spouse as to the conditions under which you will each see the children. Define each parent's schedule with the children, including who will drive them to and from school, tutoring, extracurricular activities, friends' homes, and social events, such as birthday parties.

If you have any question about your rights as a parent or feel that you're being pushed away from your children by moving out of the house, or if you're considering moving out of state, be sure to consult an attorney who can help you establish custody arrangements before you move.

If either parent moves out of state with the children for six months or longer before filing for divorce, your divorce case could end up being split between two states, with the monetary aspects determined in one state and the custody aspects determined in another. Be sure to consult an attorney and think carefully before making such a move or agreeing to a move by your spouse.

The Separation Date

Determining who will move out of the family home might be the first really difficult question you'll have to tackle. The next question—when—is also extremely important. Depending on your state's laws, the date you and your spouse formally separate can affect your credit, health insurance, pension benefits, and other assets.

Before the date of separation, you and your spouse are still married and subject to the same laws you've been living under since you got married. After your separation, however, you enter a gray area of financial and legal reality that won't be fully clarified until the divorce is final. You'll have no control over the actions of your spouse during this time, yet you are still connected in some ways—and any connection might result in your being held responsible for your spouse's bills, even bills that were racked up after your legal separation.

In addition, the value of a retirement plan, dividends, and other assets can be thousands of dollars more or less at settlement time, depending on whether your state defines marital property from the date of separation or the date of divorce.

Generally speaking, the definition of the separation date is the date on which there was a final and permanent break in the marriage and no hope of a reconciliation. The circumstances courts believe tend to show the date of separation vary between states but, generally speaking, include the following:

- one spouse formally announces that they intend to file for divorce
- the couple begins to conduct life differently (such as when one spouse starts sleeping in a guest bedroom or occupies another section of the house)
- the date on which divorce papers are filed, or
- the date on which one spouse physically relocates from a shared dwelling.

Note that in all but the last case, couples may continue living together after the separation date. While this can be to your advantage if neither can afford to move right away, the advantage can be tempered by the loss of privacy, the increasing hostilities as the divorce battle heats up, and the effect any parental conflicts might have on the children.

The date that's determined to be the date of separation could have financial advantages for one spouse or the other. If you are going to be responsible for the credit card charges your spouse incurred during the marriage, for instance, you'd want the date of separation to precede your spouse's shopping spree.

A competent divorce attorney can help to explain the laws of your state and their implications for your finances. The expense of speaking with a lawyer can be far outweighed by the benefits of being prepared for possible credit scares as you disentangle your finances from those of your spouse.

In six months to a year, you will have the advantage of hindsight and a different perspective, but with some planning and research now, you can anticipate the most critical effects separation will have on your financial outlook.

Separation Agreements in Writing

Even if you are clear about your state's definition of the separation date, you might need a formal, written separation agreement to ensure that you and your spouse are legally in accord concerning your divorce procedure, how the bills will be paid, who moves out, and how temporary child custody or spousal support will be structured. Relying only on oral agreements is never a good idea. Unwilling spouses sometimes claim that verbal separation agreements never happened or were not legally binding. If your spouse relocates, your spouse could still list your shared home as a primary address or attempt to claim that the separation was an experiment, or a "time-out," to think things through.

If you don't trust your spouse to act in good faith, make certain that you understand the details of your written separation agreement and that it supports your version of events. Both parties must enter the agreement voluntarily (never under duress) and understand the consequences of signing it. This is another reason why it often makes sense to get legal advice before either of you files for divorce. Remember: It's you, not the court, who should be the steward of your financial well-being.

If You Must Move

Although you might not like the idea, it's possible that you'll have to move from your home. Feelings of separation and abandonment can be exacerbated by stress and anxiety about where you'll live next.

To cope with your emotional reactions, look at your situation in practical terms and separate real concerns from unfounded fears. Here are a few things to remember:

- Movers often charge a premium for their hectic summer season, while offering lower prices between late September and April. The first and last days of the month are also busy times for movers, so you might be able to save money by moving midmonth or midweek. The American Movers Conference suggests that you question a mover carefully about rates, liability, pickup, delivery, and claims protection. If you have time, get estimates from at least three movers so you can determine if their prices and terms are fair. To move locally, you'll probably be charged an hourly rate or a flat fee. Long-distance movers usually charge by weight and mileage.

- In addition to moving costs, you'll need money for utilities, phone and internet services, and other "new house" expenses like kitchen staples and cleaning products.

- If you move your children out of state without your spouse's consent, a judge may order you to return the children to the state immediately and could ultimately deny you custody. Judges don't look favorably on parents who move their children away from the other parent, school, friends, and community ties. Consult an attorney before making such a move.

- If you move out of the house during the divorce, it can still be considered your principal residence for tax purposes, which affects capital gains taxes. This happens when ownership of the house is transferred to one spouse in a divorce and that spouse moves out. In other words, if you have to move out of the house during the divorce, you can still claim it as your principal residence for tax purposes, as long as you and your spouse have a written agreement about your intention that the house will remain your primary residence.

D-Days
During your divorce, you may see or hear these abbreviations used to refer to certain milestones: DOM: Date of marriage DOS: Date of separation DOD: Date of divorce

Debts and Credit

Bill collectors don't suddenly stop sending their statements just because you're going through a divorce. When you enter the limbo of separation, pay particular attention to its impact on your debts and credit standing.

Debts

In general, both spouses are responsible for paying debts generated during the marriage. Once the divorce is final, neither is responsible for the debts the other created. Debts incurred during separation, however, can be tricky. The general rule is that debts incurred after the separation date but before the divorce is final are the responsibility of the spouse who incurred them and must be paid by that person.

One exception is for "family necessities." For example, if, during the period of separation, one spouse incurs a debt for food, clothing, shelter, or medical care, the other spouse may be obligated to pay a portion of that bill. Children's expenses, too, usually fall into this category. The law views a spousal support or child support obligation as more important than one to a creditor.

The general rule—that the person who generated debts during separation must pay them—doesn't always protect you, however. If your partner defaults or simply refuses to pay, the creditors no doubt will come after you for payment. Because you were still married when the debts were created, the creditor will assert a right to collect from you. Your only remedy might be to try to get reimbursed by your ex-spouse.

EXAMPLE: Janet's husband, Jim, had dental work done after he moved out of their apartment, but he never paid the bill. Janet did not know anything about his dental work, and Jim left town as soon as the divorce was final. The dentist turned the bill over to a collection agency, which then went after Janet for the money. Eventually she settled the bill, spending lots of her time, energy, and money to resolve the problem.

Debt Collection After Divorce

It's important to remember that while divorce means the end of your legal relationship with your spouse, creditors may continue to see you and your ex as joint debtors. In community property states, both spouses may be liable for a credit debt, even when only one of them signed the credit agreement. The rules vary from state to state, but it's best to be cautious, and assume that any expense incurred for a joint purpose may result in a collection attempt against you.

If you carry debt into your separation, you should be aggressive in monitoring your credit status. Freeze all joint credit card accounts and home equity lines of credit (HELOCs) with carried balances to make sure the bleeding stops. You should both call your creditors to deactivate accounts and write letters confirming the dates and times you called, who you spoke with, and the details of what each of you said. For more on handling credit card debt, see Chapter 6.

Credit

Remember the warning given in Chapter 2: When you're financially connected to someone else, you're at risk. You are responsible for any use of a credit or charge card by either cardholder on a joint account.

Most of the time it is best to close joint credit accounts, because you can't control your spouse's use of them. But before angrily closing all joint credit accounts, check first to see how your individual credit will be affected by such an action. If you don't have credit in your own name, be sure to establish it before you separate.

In certain circumstances, you might need joint credit. For instance, if you'll both be buying maintenance items for your house, rental property, or children, it might be convenient to have a joint checking account to which both you and your spouse contribute. You can make a formal written agreement as to how the account will be used and even require that all checks written on the account must have both spouses' signatures. Keep in mind, however, that even though you might need to retain joint accounts, you shouldn't consider starting any new joint financial ventures.

RESOURCE

Extensive information on debts, creditors, establishing credit in your own name, and other similar issues can be found in *Solve Your Money Troubles* **and** *Credit Repair*, **both by Amy Loftsgordon and Cara O'Neill (Nolo).** You can also find a variety of informative articles on this subject on Nolo's website at www.nolo.com.

Request Your Credit Reports Now

During a separation, getting copies of your credit reports is a good idea. You're entitled to one free credit report per year from each of the three major credit-reporting agencies: Equifax, Experian, and TransUnion. (At the time of writing, Equifax, Experian, and TransUnion continue to offer free weekly online credit reports, a service they started in response to the COVID-19 pandemic. However, this service could end suddenly. Also, under a legal settlement, you can get six free credit reports from Equifax each year through 2026 at AnnualCreditReport.com.) You can begin by visiting the Federal Trade Commission's article on credit reports (https://consumer. ftc.gov/articles/free-credit-reports). From there, you can link to the Annual Credit Report Service, a site maintained by the three nationwide credit agencies, and submit an order for your reports. You can order copies of your reports online or by phone or mail.

Central Source LLC
P.O. Box 105281
Atlanta, GA 30348-5281
877-322-8228
www.annualcreditreport.com/index.action

Request Your Credit Reports Now (continued)

To get your reports by mail, you need to download and fill out a request form at www.annualcreditreport.com/gettingReports.action and mail it to the address above.

You must provide your name, address, Social Security number, and date of birth when you order. You also might be required to provide information that only you would know, such as the amount of your monthly mortgage payment.

If you want additional copies of your credit reports within a year, or you need to correct information in your credit reports, you'll probably need to contact the credit bureaus directly. Contact the following:

Equifax
P.O. Box 740241
Atlanta, GA 30374
888-378-4329
www.equifax.com

Experian National Consumer Assistance Center
P.O. Box 2002
Allen, TX 75013
888-397-3742
www.experian.com

TransUnion
2 Baldwin Place
P. O. Box 1000
Chester, PA 19016
800-888-4213
www.transunion.com

If you want to get a combined report that shows what information each of the reporting companies has on you, you can go to any of their websites or to www.myfico.com. You can get combined reports and credit reports for a fee.

Your credit reports will provide you with valuable information about your outstanding debts. In addition, you'll have the chance to make corrections should there be any errors in your reports. The credit bureau will enclose information with your reports on how to dispute incorrect information in your credit files, or you can find that information on the website.

Building Better Credit Reports and Credit Scores

Good credit reports and high credit scores can go a long way toward making your financial life easier after divorce. A credit *report* is a file that shows potential creditors what credit accounts you have open, your bill-paying habits, and other information affecting your credit-worthiness, such as whether you've declared bankruptcy or have been sued or arrested. Credit-reporting companies collect this information and sell it to creditors, insurers, employers, landlords, and others who may wish to do business with you.

A credit *score* is a number that encapsulates information about you and your credit experiences. Using statistical formulas, creditors compare your information with the credit performance of customers with similar profiles. One commonly used scoring system, known as FICO, scores using a range from 300 to 850. The median FICO score is 714, and a score below 600 suggests a particularly risky borrower.

Having good credit reports and high credit scores means it will be easier for you to get credit as well as to benefit from, for instance, loans with lower interest rates and smaller monthly payments.

You're entitled to a free copy of your credit report from each of the three main credit-reporting bureaus (Equifax, Experian, and TransUnion) once every 12 months. (See "Request Your Credit Reports Now," above.) You can get your credit scores from the three nationwide credit-reporting agencies, but you will need to pay a fee. Other companies offer credit scores for sale alone or as part of a package of products.

Although consumers often believe—and the media suggests—there's just one score per consumer, actually many different credit scores may exist for any individual. For instance, a car dealer may use a score designed for auto lending, while others exist for mortgage lending and insurance purposes as well as for specific types of lenders, such as credit unions or traditional banks.

If you need to improve your credit scores, paying your bills on time is the most obvious way. But also important are the amount of your debt and your credit utilization rate—that is, how much of your credit limit you're using up by making charges on your credit cards.

If you get copies of your credit reports—and you should—you need to check them carefully. If you find *inaccurate negative* information in any of the reports, be sure to tell the credit-reporting company that produced the report (in writing) what you believe is false, and submit documents that support your position. If you prevail, the credit agency must correct your report and send copies of the revised report to you and to anyone who's requested the report during the past six months.

If you find *accurate negative* information, such as a bankruptcy or a foreclosure, understand that only the passage of time can ensure its removal. A credit agency can report accurate negative information for several years and bankruptcy information for up to ten years for a Chapter 7 bankruptcy and seven years for a Chapter 13 bankruptcy.

Retirement Plans and Pension Benefits

In most situations, the marital portion of your retirement plan is defined by the date of your divorce. So, you'll probably be entitled to any growth in the account that occurred during the entire marriage, even if you separated months earlier.

Many companies provide an accounting of retirement benefits only on an annual basis. The amount in a pension fund, a profit-sharing plan, or another type of benefit program could differ significantly from one part of a year to the next. By the time your divorce becomes final, a year or two could have passed since your separation, and the retirement fund may have grown by thousands of dollars.

To safeguard your interest, get a copy of the benefit brochure issued by your own or your spouse's employer if possible. It's also helpful to have copies of the actual retirement plan itself or a summary of it. (Chapter 14 covers retirement plans in detail. It includes a letter you can send to request information and give notice of your interest in your spouse's retirement benefit plans.) Because so many factors affect your retirement benefits, it is best to consult an attorney, a financial adviser, a pension plan expert, or an actuary who can analyze your particular situation. (See Chapter 7 for more information on seeking advice from a professional.)

Income and Income Taxes

Under the laws of many states, the income that you earn after the date of separation is yours and yours alone. Therefore, you are solely responsible for the taxes due on this income. Also, the date of your separation may influence your decision to file your income taxes jointly or separately. (See Chapter 11.)

Investments and Business Assets

Many states value assets at the date the divorce is final, not the date of separation. This means that if one spouse moves out of the house and the assets appreciate between that date and the date the divorce becomes final, the spouses will share in the appreciation. The valuation of investments and business assets should be double-checked, however, as the rules do vary from state to state.

> EXAMPLE: Having assets valued from the date of divorce instead of the date of separation cost Harry a bundle. On the date of separation, his extensive portfolio was valued at $5 million. By the date of the divorce, his holdings had almost doubled because of the stock market boom during the period between separation and divorce. So instead of having to split $5 million with his soon-to-be ex-wife, Celeste, he had to share the full $10 million.

Alimony

Be aware that your separation date can have a significant effect on alimony you pay or receive. In many states, a nonworking, dependent, or lower-wage-earning spouse is presumed to be in need of alimony for a longer period of time after the end of a long-term marriage (usually one lasting at least ten years from the date of marriage to the date of separation). If you're a few months shy of the ten-year presumptive period for alimony (or the time length mandated by your state), you might want to stay around to avoid jeopardizing the length of those future payments. Read more about alimony in Chapter 18.

Social Security Benefits After Divorce

If you were married for at least ten years and are at least 62 years old, you are entitled to Social Security benefits based on your ex-spouse's contributions. These benefits become available after you have been divorced for at least two years. You are entitled to these benefits regardless of whether your ex-spouse claims benefits. Your receipt of benefits will not reduce the benefits payable to your former spouse (or any other former spouse of your former spouse).

A few additional facts:

- Benefits are based on your ex-spouse's total contributions, not just those made during your marriage.
- If you were married (and divorced) twice and both marriages lasted more than ten years, you can claim benefits through the ex-spouse with the larger Social Security account.
- If you remarry before you reach the age of 60 and stay married to your second spouse, you cannot claim benefits based on your first spouse's account—but you can get benefits on the record of your new spouse.
- If you receive disabled, divorced, widow's, or widower's benefits, your benefits will continue if you remarry when you are age 50 or older.

 CAUTION
Divorce can alter your Social Security benefits and options.
For instance, a surviving divorced spouse who plans to remarry before age 60 might consider delaying the wedding until turning 60, to avoid the remarriage penalty. Also, delaying a divorce until the marriage has lasted ten years can mean the difference between getting Social Security benefits and missing out. Check out the Social Security website or contact the Social Security office to learn more.

Because each worker's Social Security file is confidential, you might not be able to find out the status of your spouse's benefits. You can try to get this information by asking your spouse or by contacting the local or national office of the Social Security Administration (SSA). Call 800-772-1213 to get a *Request for Earnings and Benefits Estimate Statement* (Form SSA-7004). You can also visit the SSA website at www.ssa.gov. The site includes downloadable copies of many publications and forms, including Form SSA-7004. Once you have the form, complete it and send it back to the SSA.

If these methods fail, you will probably need a lawyer's help to get information about your spouse's benefits. (See Chapters 7 and 12 for information on working with lawyers. For more on different types of retirement benefits, see Chapter 14.)

Before You Move

Before you move out of the family home, you should make copies of all documents that may have any relevance to your financial settlement. When in doubt, copy the document first, and evaluate it later. Refer to the Financial Facts Checklist in Chapter 8 for the most important documentation. Even if you don't have your spouse's cooperation in this project, it is important that you get the copies. If you must resort to the legal process of discovery (see Chapter 12), your legal bill might run sky high—with no guarantee that you'll get all the information you might ultimately need.

You should also do an inventory of all shared or individual property. Use photos or video to document the condition of property at stake in your divorce. (For more information on dealing with property, see Chapter 6.)

Questions to Ask an Attorney

As you can see, you'll need to assess your legal and financial positions carefully before separating. Because the legal definition of the separation date varies from state to state, this book can't explain the nuances of your state's law. But below, you'll find a list of important questions for you to ask an attorney or research at your local law library.

1. Who should move out of the house? Can I be forced to move?
2. In our state, what defines the date of separation? Is it when one of us:
   - moves out?
   - files for divorce?
   - declares the marriage is over?
3. What other legal or financial ramifications of the date of separation should I know about?
4. Which debts—incurred after the date of separation but before the divorce becomes final—is each spouse responsible for?
5. What date is used—separation date, date of final negotiations, or date closest to the final divorce—to calculate the value of assets?
6. Can the court award alimony to a spouse for an indefinite period? If not, what end date is the court likely to apply to spousal support? Does the court consider the length of the marriage in awarding spousal support?
7. What is the average length of an alimony award in our state?
8. Who should make payments on joint debts during the divorce?
9. Do I have the right to reimbursement for payments I make on joint obligations during the divorce?
10. Can I get divorced before our property is fully divided?

Closing the Books:
What Do We Do With Joint Property?

Your spouse might not want to ruin you—but their actions can leave you at risk.

When you and your spouse are splitting up, you come face to face with a hard fact. You're at risk when you're financially connected to another person.

Does that mean you need to rush out in a panic and close all your joint accounts? Not necessarily—it's never wise to act in panic, and very few spouses deliberately destroy each other financially. But even if your spouse doesn't purposely ruin your financial life, your spouse's actions can leave you vulnerable.

One way to gauge how much financial damage your spouse could inflict is to measure the level of hostility between you. For example, if you're no longer on speaking terms, you should probably separate your financial lives quickly.

Even if your divorce is "friendly," don't count on that goodwill to determine what you should do about joint accounts. Look at your situation objectively and apply common sense. You should be moving toward eliminating shared financial obligations. Because income is often reduced—and expenses increased—by a divorce, it might not be possible to cut all connections, but nevertheless, you can still reduce your risks.

Joint Account Checklist

The material that follows should alert you to common trouble spots.

Credit Cards

Before closing joint credit card accounts, be sure you have established credit in your own name, based on your own income. A department store, for instance, may open an individual account for you when you close a joint one. You might be tempted to include your ex-spouse's income when applying for separate credit. Don't do it. Because you won't be able to use your ex's income to repay your bills, it would border on fraud.

If you don't qualify for credit based on your own income, you can apply for a secured credit card. Many banks will give you a credit card if you secure it by opening a savings account. Your credit limit equals a percentage of the amount you deposit into your account. Depending on the bank, you'll be required to deposit as little as a few hundred dollars or as much as a few thousand. Many secured credit cards have a conversion option. This option lets you convert the secured card into a regular credit card (one not tied to a savings account) after a certain time period and if you use the card responsibly.

Search online to find banks that issue secured credit cards. Check www.bankrate.com for specific information about credit cards.

Once you've established your own credit, write simple emails (or letters if required) to close any jointly held credit cards or revolving loan accounts. Even if a credit card account hasn't been used for years, close it to prevent your ex-spouse from using it in the future without your authorization. Closing these accounts might not fully protect you from obligations for your spouse's later-incurred debts, but it puts the burden on the creditors to take action.

Your credit reports should give you all the information you need to close credit card accounts. (See Chapter 5 for information on how to get copies of your credit reports.) If you have questions, call the creditor (a toll-free number is usually on your statement).

After 30 days, check your credit reports to ensure they reflect the account was "closed by consumer request."

Most of the time, you will have little trouble terminating joint accounts. On occasion, however, a creditor may demand that you pay off the balance first. If you can afford to pay the bill, do so. That's better than leaving the account open and allowing your spouse to run up more debts.

If you can't pay off the entire balance, you can still ask that the account be made inactive while you make payments. This strategy prohibits further charges from being made on the account. Once the balance is paid, the creditor should have no problem closing the account completely. Most customer service representatives will take care of your request. If you can't make satisfactory arrangements through a customer service representative, however, ask to speak to a supervisor, and continue up the chain of command. Explain that you are going through a divorce and that you are closing out your joint accounts. Remember to put all communications with credit card companies in writing, keep copies, and document your payments.

During your separation, if your spouse uses a joint credit card account (before you get a chance to close it) to charge basic items such as food or clothes, you might be responsible for the payments. (See Chapter 5.)

Sample Letter for Closing Joint Accounts

[*Date*]

To:

Re: Account number _____

      Card member _____ [*your name*]

      Social Security number _____

Dear_____:

This letter is to inform your company that the above-referenced account is to be closed, effective immediately. At this time, my spouse, [*name of spouse*], and I are seeking a divorce.

I am requesting a "hard close" of the account so that neither party may incur new charges. If [*spouse's name*] is the primary signer on the account, that person does not have my permission to reestablish the card at any time using my name and/or credit.

If you are unable to close this account with only my authorization, you are instructed to terminate my relationship with this credit card account immediately, and any charges made to the account after the date of this letter will be the responsibility of [*spouse*].

If the account has an outstanding balance, you may keep the account open for billing purposes only, but I request that you keep it inactive so that neither party can incur new charges. Please advise me immediately of any outstanding charges on the account.

Please notify the three major credit bureaus that this account has been "closed by consumer" and kindly send me written confirmation that you have done so.

Thank you for your assistance.

Sincerely,

[*Your name*]

Equity Credit Lines

A frequently overlooked area of joint financial liability involves equity lines of credit also called "home equity lines of credit" or "HELOCs." A HELOC is an open-ended loan made by a lending institution—usually a bank, savings and loan, or credit union—against the equity in your home. The lender gets a secured interest in your home, and if you don't repay the loan, the lending institution can force the sale of your house (foreclose).

Some equity credit lines supply a checkbook and/or credit card that can be used just as they would with a joint checking account. Whichever spouse has the checkbook and card has access to the money.

If you and your spouse have a HELOC, pay a visit to your lender. Take a letter with you requesting that the account be closed or frozen because of your divorce. If you have a checkbook and/or HELOC credit card, be sure to destroy them, and request that no additional checks or cards be issued. By leaving a HELOC open during the divorce, you risk losing your home.

Similar to an equity line of credit is a margin account, which stock brokerage firms offer. You might not want to close a margin account right away, because opportunities to profit from trading may arise during the course of the divorce. Instead, you and your spouse should make agreements about what kind of activity is allowed, including an agreement that neither spouse may take any funds out of the account without either the written consent of the other spouse or a court order. If one spouse normally does the trading, you can authorize that spouse to continue trading under specified circumstances. Whatever you agree, put it in writing! You should convey your agreement in a letter to the brokerage firm. When you're closer to finalizing your divorce, you can divide the asset and close the account completely.

!

CAUTION

Beware of fraudulent loans. If your spouse claims to have borrowed money during your marriage from friends or relatives, proceed with caution. It might be a scheme to snatch joint assets. Here's how it works: One spouse falsely claims to have borrowed money during the marriage, unbeknownst to the other spouse, from a close friend or relative. The false loan is then paid back from joint assets. The friend or relative who receives the money then returns it surreptitiously once the divorce is final, and voilà! What was once a joint asset now belongs only to one spouse. The way to prevent this is to ask your spouse to produce records that prove when, how, and why the loan was made and in what amount. What was the money used for? Marital expenses? Demand to review records showing the flow of money in and out, and check income tax returns to determine whether interest was paid on purported loans to relatives. If your spouse can't provide this information, or if you never agreed to this loan, you should argue that you're not responsible for paying it back and that it's 100% your spouse's responsibility. This way, your spouse can't dip into your assets to pay back this fake loan.

Joint Checking, Savings, and Other Deposit Accounts

As with joint credit cards, you might not want to close joint checking or saving accounts unless you have an account in your own name or will open one immediately. If you don't close a joint account, however, you run the risk that your spouse could come in and empty it without your knowledge.

You have a few options:

- Ask the bank to freeze the account and not allow either you or your spouse to move money in or out without both of your signatures.
- Take out half the money in the account and place it into your individual account.
- Close the account and place all the money into a dual-signature account. You'll need an agreement with your spouse to use this option.

CAUTION

If your spouse takes all the money from your joint accounts, your settlement—or a court—will probably provide for your reimbursement. That repayment, however, could be months or years away. Until then, you have to deal with losing your share of a joint account. If you don't have a personal savings or checking account, you may have to borrow money to cover the shortfall.

If You Are Broke

If you're out of money, you're probably safe in withdrawing half of the cash in joint accounts to pay for necessities. But, generally, you'll be required to disclose the withdrawal and document what you used it for, and you might have to pay it back. (If you have any doubts, ask an attorney.) Of course, the old standby methods of calling Mom and Dad or using credit cards are also available. You could also ask for temporary alimony. (See Chapter 9.)

Joint Title to Property

How you hold title to property can be important. The two most common ways for married people to hold title are joint tenancy and tenancy in common.

Joint Tenancy

Many couples hold property, especially real property, in joint tenancy. Joint tenancy's major advantage is that when one joint owner dies, the remaining owner or owners automatically inherit the deceased's portion of the property without having to go through the long, expensive probate process. If you don't want your spouse to automatically inherit your share, then change your joint tenancy ownership to tenancy in common.

Tenancy in Common

With tenancy in common, married couples may own equal shares, but upon the death of one spouse, that spouse's share goes to whomever is named in a will or another estate planning document. If you die without a will or another estate plan, your property passes under the laws of your state. Usually the property is divided between the spouse and/or children, if any; if there is no spouse and no children, it goes to the parents or siblings.

The best way to convert property from joint tenancy to tenancy in common is to secure your spouse's agreement and then change the title together. For example, a couple could transfer their house "from Herbert and Donna Walker as joint tenants to Herbert and Donna Walker as tenants in common." You can obtain a blank deed from a title insurance office, a real estate office, or online.

If you can't find a blank deed, you could simply draft a statement saying, "Herbert and Donna Walker hereby transfer their real property located at 4555 Ellison Boulevard, Fargo, North Dakota, from Herbert and Donna Walker as joint tenants to Herbert and Donna Walker as tenants in common." Be sure you both sign the statement before a notary public. Then record the deed or statement in the office where your original house deed is recorded.

> **CAUTION**
> **Whether the change in property ownership is unilateral or jointly agreed upon, make sure you update your estate plan after any changes.** In addition, be sure your title change follows all of your state's laws regarding notice to your spouse. And if you're in the midst of a divorce, make certain you're not violating any order restraining you from transferring title.

> **CAUTION**
> **By closing accounts or serving your spouse with a restraining order, recognize that you may be upping the ante by increasing the degree of conflict in your divorce.** You (and any professional advisers you use) must assess the risks and the consequences, because sooner or later, you will meet your spouse at the negotiating table.

If your spouse will not consent to the change, you can complete the deed or statement yourself. Write, "Donna Walker hereby transfers her interest in the real property located at 4555 Ellison Boulevard, Fargo, North Dakota, from Donna Walker joint tenant to Donna Walker tenant in common." Any one person can unilaterally terminate their interest in a joint tenancy. Again, sign it before a notary and record it in the office where your original house deed is recorded.

Joint Investments and Other Holdings

Make a list of any investments or other joint assets you can think of. Immediately call your broker, your discount brokerage house, and any other financial institutions where you have holdings. Tell them that you and your spouse are divorcing so no assets or money should be moved or transferred without the knowledge and approval of both spouses. Be sure to tell the broker to make a note in your file. That way, when your spouse speaks to anyone else at the firm, that person will see the account has been frozen. Also, if the account has check writing or credit card privileges, specify whether the freeze applies to those transactions. Follow up the call with a letter or email identifying the person with whom you spoke, noting the date and time of the call, and giving a summary of the conversation.

When it comes to joint investments, you have to move quickly because most stock transactions are completed online.. If your spouse is the one who normally handles these transactions, all of your joint holdings could be sold and the money transferred out of the account in a matter of seconds. If you call first to freeze the accounts, you stand a good chance of protecting your interests.

Sample Letter to Broker

November 27, 20xx

Rodney Washington
Bull and Bear Investment Company
3400 Financial Square, Suite 1740
Boston, MA 02000

Dear Mr. Washington:

This letter is to inform you that my spouse and I are in the process of divorce. Please freeze our account, #12345-67890, so that no transactions occur until further notice. Please make a note to this effect on the firm's "online" file on the computer. This freeze is to be effective immediately, and this letter confirms my instructions to you by telephone on November 24, 20xx.

These instructions apply to the assets in our account as well as the check writing and/or the credit card privileges we currently have with this account.

Yours truly,

Lenore Kwong

Safe-Deposit Boxes

Just as one spouse can remove all money from a joint checking account, so too can a spouse take all of the items out of a joint safe-deposit box. Unfortunately, safe-deposit boxes are one of those items in which "get there first" is the operative rule. Try to take possession of both keys to the safe-deposit box if at all possible. If your spouse empties the box before you do, you might have little chance of reclaiming the contents.

The best way to legally protect yourself is to get a restraining order from the court and give a copy to the bank. The order would prevent either spouse from having access to the box until you reach a settlement or the court removes the restraining order.

You might possibly protect yourself if you can get to the box, write an inventory of the contents, and take photos of the items. Then have the bank officer sign the list documenting your inventory. If your spouse removes anything later, you'll have some proof of what was taken.

Shared Property and Special Collections

While your furniture, appliances, and knickknacks around the house might not be as valuable as other assets and investments, this property can cause more irritation and antagonism than almost anything else. Emotions flare up when you reach for a favorite tool only to find it missing or look for your mother's antique brooch and discover it is gone.

To avoid future problems, do an inventory of your home and possessions similar to the kind you would conduct for insurance purposes. Obviously, it will be simpler to do such an inventory while you're still living in the family home and have access to your property—so do it before you move out.

List the contents of each room and take pictures and a video of each room and all the contents for documentation. Your ultimate goal is to divide these items as fairly as possible. Few couples split the small items exactly 50-50, but you should try to value bigger property items so your division is not horribly one-sided. For used items like household furniture and electronics, you can get simple estimates by running a Google search for your item to see what it's currently selling for. You might find your item for sale on websites like Craigslist, Facebook Marketplace, and Nextdoor, which will give you a good idea of its current fair market value (FMV). If you can't find your item anywhere, one rule of thumb for FMV that applies to most used furniture and clothes is to take the original purchase price and discount it by 50% to 75%, which gives you an estimated FMV.

A reputable appraiser should appraise any coins, gold, jewelry, art, or other valuable collectible.

In the meantime, jointly owned household property should not be disposed of unless both spouses agree, as neither one owns an item outright until the settlement. You only own your personal, separate property. Your children's property, such as furniture or toys, should be given to the children and not valued or divided in the divorce settlement.

Financial First Aid for Divorce Emergencies

If a stranger stole your wallet with all the credit cards inside, you'd probably have more protection than if your spouse wipes out your joint accounts. Almost nothing can stop one spouse from closing a joint account without the knowledge of the other. During a divorce, it can come down to who gets there first—to the bank account, the computer files, the brokerage office, or the safe-deposit box.

However, it's important to know that many states, such as California, include automatic restraining orders (ATROs) in their initial divorce petitions, which means that once the paperwork is served, *both* spouses are prohibited from transferring property without the other's permission. If your state does not do this, and if you are concerned that your spouse might empty out a joint account or otherwise take assets to which you are entitled, you may need to obtain a temporary restraining order prohibiting the removal, sale, transfer, or other use of the property. Not only can restraining orders be placed against your spouse, but they can also be served on third parties, such as bank managers and others with control over your assets.

Restraining orders are also used to bar a violent or abusive spouse or parent from having contact with the other spouse or children. Domestic violence organizations can help you obtain that kind of restraining order. See the appendix for more help.

Questions to Ask an Attorney

Closing accounts isn't always a straightforward procedure and can vary from state to state. Below is a list of important questions for you to ask an attorney or research at your local law library:

1. Does the divorce petition in my state include an automatic temporary restraining order? If so, can I send a copy of that to third parties, such as banks, to freeze our joint accounts?

2. Do any state laws prohibit me from withdrawing half of the cash in our joint accounts or borrowing money on joint accounts?

3. Can I unilaterally change property from joint tenancy to tenancy in common, or do I need my spouse's consent?

4. Would it be advisable to close my joint accounts and move the funds to an account solely in my name or into a joint account requiring both signatures on the checks?

5. Do any state laws prohibit me from canceling or changing beneficiaries on my life or medical insurance policies during divorce?

6. What would I need to do to prevent my spouse from taking money out of our home equity line of credit? ●

Getting Help: Whom Can I Turn To?

During divorce, you're going through a time of transition unlike any other in your life. Everything is changing. No matter how capable you are, you'll need help to get through this transition.

Even if you have little money and few resources, it's important to get support. Check with local legal aid organizations, libraries, churches, community organizations, law schools, colleges, or government agencies for low-cost services. In some areas, divorce specialists and centers can advise you for a small fee.

The kind of help you seek will depend on what you need. For some, a personal counselor or therapist is crucial; others want only a temporary adviser to handle financial details. As your divorce progresses, you might also need to call on a variety of specialists ranging from attorneys to real estate agents, credit counselors to appraisers. Because your future is at stake, don't cheat yourself; get the best you can afford. Comparison shop and check references before signing contracts for outside services.

Questions to Consider When Seeking Outside Help

The following four questions are useful ones to ask yourself when choosing professionals.

Is the Person Competent and Suited to Handle My Specific Case?

Obviously, you want to work with someone who does a good job and can be trusted. Beyond those basic qualities, it's essential to determine that the person's training and services match your needs. In other words, you don't hire a bookkeeper if your situation calls for an accountant to make complex calculations or compute taxes. By the same token, an experienced divorce attorney is better than a lawyer who specializes in business transactions. Interview potential consultants on the phone, or use introductory sessions to outline your case and find out exactly what to expect, before you hire anyone.

> (!) **CAUTION**
> **Accepting a free session with a lawyer or another professional might mean that you end up being pressured into hiring that person.** You might be sold a service that you don't want or need. To avoid such problems, clearly state that you are only gathering information in the initial session and don't intend to make a hiring decision until after you have had a chance to sort through the information you receive. Remember, too, the adage that if something sounds too good to be true, it probably is. Be wary of any lawyer who seems to promise you the world, making guarantees that you can get anything you want in your divorce. There are no guarantees.

How Is This Professional Paid?

How a professional is paid—by the hour, on a retainer, or through commissions—inevitably affects you. This is a statement of fact, not a matter of philosophy or morals. If you will be paying by the hour, you must understand how that time will be billed. Does the professional bill in six-minute, ten-minute, or longer intervals? Are you going to be charged for time on the phone? Does the clock begin to run the minute you walk in the door? Find out.

In contrast, when people work on commission, their livelihood depends on selling you something. Again, nothing is wrong with that— you just need to recognize that reality and act accordingly. For instance, when you call for information about insurance coverage, the agent might try to sell you a new policy or different kind of coverage. Only you can decide whether it's appropriate to make such a purchase. Because of the emotional strain of divorce, take extra time to make decisions, or insist on getting a second opinion before you buy anything.

What's the Best Use of This Professional's Services?

Like many people going through a divorce, you might sometimes feel that you don't know where to turn. As personal and financial pressures mount, you could go to the wrong people for the wrong services. Trying to use your lawyer as a therapist or your banker as a tax consultant is an exercise in frustration. Think about your needs first and be sure you are using each professional's expertise appropriately.

Recognize the limits of each adviser you contact. Your local real estate agent, for example, might not be able to appraise the value of commercial property or of a vacation house located in a different city. If necessary, ask for referrals to specialists, and keep asking questions until you find the right person to answer them. You can save time and money by gathering much of the data the professional will need, especially financial information. Chapter 8 details the kind of information you'll need.

Am I Evaluating This Professional Objectively?

It's fine to ask friends and associates for referrals, but don't give up your own objectivity and accept a referral blindly, even if it comes from someone you trust. When you first meet with the professional, ask questions to determine if the person is knowledgeable, capable, and a good match for you and the unique facts of your case. If you feel uncertain, take your concerns seriously.

Similarly, don't feel compelled to use your sister just because she is an attorney or your uncle just because he is an accountant. Objectivity—on their part and yours—is very important. Your relatives may have your best interests in mind and be very trustworthy, but they might not have the expertise and/or experience you need. You might not want to disclose personal but important facts to relatives, or they might miss creative solutions and the big picture because they are too close to your situation. Empathy may feel soothing, but a professional's clear eye for detail and probing for the facts is what matters most.

Selecting Professionals to Assist You

Besides providing quality service, a good professional should explain potential risks in your situation and offer realistic appraisals of results and consequences. Keep that in mind as you review these descriptions of professionals who can help you during divorce. (For handy reference, you can enter names, addresses, and phone numbers of your professional advisers at the end of the appendix.)

Lawyers

Generally speaking, divorce attorneys charge hourly rates. These fees vary widely across the country and locally, too, mostly based on the lawyer's experience level. Be sure to find one that fits your budget. Be aware, too, that most lawyers require that you pay an up-front retainer before they do any work, sometimes amounting to thousands of dollars. As the lawyer spends time working for you, the bill is paid out of your retainer.

When the retainer is used up, your lawyer will either bill you directly or ask for another lump sum from which to draw. If you hire a lawyer who requests a retainer, be sure that you get monthly statements showing the precise work done, the amount billed, the amount deducted from your retainer, and the amount left. If there's a balance remaining at the end of the case (or if you change lawyers), you're entitled to get back any unused funds.

Financial negotiations and lines of authority remain clearest when each party is represented by an independent attorney. In most states, courts can order the wealthier spouse to pay a lower-earning spouse's attorneys' fees in a divorce. So if you really can't afford an attorney, check into whether that's a possibility in your case. You can also look into limited-scope representation, described below.

Limited-Scope Representation or "Unbundling"

Hiring a lawyer to represent you in a divorce can be enormously expensive, way beyond the reach of many people. In California, for instance, about 70% of divorce petitions involve self-represented parties. But many of the folks representing themselves in family court could benefit greatly from even a little bit of legal advice.

Many states now authorize attorneys to provide limited legal services to their clients—a practice that was frowned upon in the past. This is called "limited-scope representation" or "unbundled" legal services. While aspects of limited-scope representation are still controversial, the American Bar Association now encourages its members to offer unbundled services, and many advocates believe that in divorce cases, it can be particularly useful.

With limited-scope representation, instead of an attorney representing you in all aspects of your case, you and the attorney can agree that you will perform some of the work in your case yourself and the lawyer will help with tasks you can't or don't want to do. Examples of how you can use unbundled legal services are:

- consulting a lawyer for legal information and advice about your case when you come upon something you don't understand, or for help with the more complicated parts of your case (such as discovery and legal research) while you do the simpler tasks yourself
- hiring a lawyer to represent you on certain issues in your case (such as child custody, child or spousal support, or dividing property) while you do the rest yourself
- hiring a lawyer to prepare forms and court documents, which you then file yourself and follow up by appearing in court
- hiring a lawyer to make a court appearance for you, or
- hiring a lawyer to review documents you've prepared, coach you on how to represent yourself at court hearings, or instruct you on how best to present evidence in court.

The cost of limited-scope representation varies. Attorneys generally charge their regular hourly rate for the hours they work. Whether you pay a retainer depends on the scope of services requested.

CAUTION

States have not developed uniform rules about the nature and extent of limited-scope services attorneys are allowed to offer—and some states don't allow it at all. The American Bar Association website (americanbar.org) includes a resource center that can help you find information about unbundled services in your state: www.americanbar.org/groups/delivery_legal_services/ resources.

If you hire a lawyer to provide unbundled services, it is critical that you discuss in detail which tasks each of you will undertake, and sign a written agreement spelling that out. Be sure to ask questions about issues that are not clear to you. Your success depends on working together as a team.

Not all lawyers are comfortable offering limited-scope representation, so you may have to look around to find someone who will work cooperatively with you.

Tips on Working With Your Lawyer

You should expect your lawyer to:
- provide you with a clear understanding of how you will be billed and what costs to expect, including retainer, court costs, expert witness fees, and other expenses
- provide you with copies of all documents related to your case
- maintain detailed time records and send you accurate and understandable bills
- return your phone calls promptly
- explain your rights and how the lawyer will go about securing them for you
- keep you up to date on settlement negotiations, and
- put significant effort into trying to settle your case out of court and, if that is not possible, prepare your case—and you—for trial.

Remember, communication is a two-way street. Just as your attorney should provide you information, you must provide complete and honest information to your attorney. This includes filling out requested forms and gathering requested documents. (This topic is covered in detail in Chapter 8.) If your attorney has incomplete or inaccurate information, the advice you receive may be inappropriate for your particular circumstances.

Don't be concerned if your attorney is friendly with your spouse's attorney ("opposing counsel"). In fact, this often works to your advantage. Even if the attorneys are friends, they will each work for their client's interest. Attorneys who cooperate with each other are better able to negotiate and settle out of court, which will result in lower legal fees. In addition, if the attorneys are enemies and drawn into an emotional fight, the end result will be higher fees and a lower quality of representation for you.

Expect your lawyer to be pleasant but not to act as your de facto therapist. The lawyer's job is to guide you through the legal maze, not to listen to how your marriage might have turned out better if only you or your spouse had done this or that. If, as is often the case, you're suffering emotionally because of the breakup, you *should* see a therapist (see below). Therapists usually don't charge as much as lawyers, and they're much better equipped to deal with emotions.

Mediators

A private mediator is a neutral third person, trained in conflict resolution and family law, who works with both parties together to help them reach agreement on some or all of the issues involved in the divorce, including property division, child custody, and child and spousal support.

In some counties, mediators associated with the family courts work with divorcing couples on child-related issues only—they don't deal with support or property issues. This type of court-connected mediation is often mandatory, even if you are also seeing a private mediator.

In mediation, you and your spouse are in control of the decisions about how to divide property and deal with alimony and child custody and support. The mediator won't give legal advice or advocate for either party's position as a lawyer does. Instead, the mediator—along with your lawyers, if you have them—can help you explore different options and find a resolution that works for both of you. (For more about when mediation is appropriate, see "When to Use Private Mediation," below.)

Mediators are often lawyers themselves; sometimes they are therapists, social workers, or clergypeople. You pay for mediation by the hour, and the rates will be what a lawyer, therapist, or social worker normally charges. If the mediator is an attorney with lots of experience in family law, you can expect to pay the same rate that you are paying your own lawyer. In fact, you could pay more—but keep in mind that mediation tends to be an efficient, cost-effective way to settle cases. Generally, the parties share the cost of mediation equally, unless they agree otherwise.

What to Look for in a Lawyer

Choosing the right attorney is one of the most important decisions you will make. The right lawyer can help you achieve financial security as well as ease the strain of the divorce process. But the wrong lawyer can add to your woes.

When selecting an attorney, make sure your schedules are compatible. If they're not, you will have difficulties together. Because your lawyer is working on more than one case at a time, don't expect to always be able to connect on the first phone call—but the lawyer should return your calls promptly. You must also promptly return phone calls from your attorney or the attorney's office staff and respond to any correspondence to keep your case moving along.

Take the time and make the effort to choose a lawyer who is strong and experienced, yet sensitive to your needs. You need to resist the urge to quickly choose a lawyer just because a friend or relative says "so-and-so is good." Instead, interview at least three lawyers and compare them using the following criteria:

- **Knowledge and experience in family law.** An attorney who's practiced five years or more and whose practice is completely or primarily devoted to family and divorce law would be ideal. In addition, ask how much courtroom experience the attorney has, how many contested custody cases the attorney has handled, and whether the attorney has given lectures or written articles on divorce (often a sign of in-depth knowledge). Does the attorney belong to the American Academy of Matrimonial Lawyers, a professional group that certifies experts? In some states, such as California, consider hiring a certified family law specialist. These attorneys must pass an examination that tests their specific knowledge of divorce law. Most keep current on developments in divorce law by attending continuing legal education programs. They might know more about divorce law—including support, custody, and property division questions—than nonspecialists, and they might charge more as well.
- **Interest in your case.** Does the lawyer seem interested and excited, or bored and preoccupied? A divorce case tests any lawyer's zest for facts and details. You want someone who seems energized and up to the challenge.

What to Look for in a Lawyer (continued)

- **Availability of a team.** Does the attorney have the assistance of other lawyers and paralegals? Particularly in a complex case, the lawyer might need backup. You might ask how many others in the firm handle divorce cases and ask to meet with them as well. Similarly, because divorce cases often involve other fields of law—such as real estate, taxes, trusts, and the like—you should ask whether the firm has other attorney resources available for consultation if needed.

- **Coherent strategy.** All legal cases involve a plan of action that's based on goals on which the lawyer and client concur. After you explain your situation, ask the prospective attorney: What results can I reasonably expect? How will we achieve those results? How will we decide whether to try the case or settle? If we do try the case, how much will that cost?

- **Rapport.** Ask yourself: What's my gut feeling about this person? Charm is no substitute for competence. But you are going to be spending lots of time with your attorney, so you'll need a certain comfort level. Look for a lawyer who is pleasant but also confident and assertive.

In short, you want a lawyer who is going to solve problems, not create them. To get such an able advocate means you need to choose well, not necessarily quickly or cheaply. Take your time and be thorough.

For further help finding a lawyer, see the appendix.

RESOURCE

To find a private mediator, ask friends and professional colleagues for referrals. The court clerk at your local family or domestic relations court may be able to give you some referrals. You can also contact the national Association for Conflict Resolution (ACR) for a list of mediators in your area. ACR's website, www.acrnet.org, lists mediators all over the country.

Used properly, mediation can be much less costly than a prolonged legal battle—even when you have a lawyer as well. Often, couples who are mediating their divorces use consulting attorneys to help them consider their options and make proposals for settlement, and to draft or review the agreement that comes out of mediation. If you don't use a lawyer during your mediation, you might still need one to help you at the end. In some cases, the mediator will draw up a "memorandum of understanding" that outlines your agreement—then you can ask a lawyer to spend a relatively short time looking over the agreement and putting it into the proper form to be submitted to the court and made into a final judgment.

When to Use Private Mediation

As mediation becomes more and more common, most people going through a divorce will consider using the process. If you're not sure whether mediation is for you, consider some of the following questions:

- Do you and your spouse both want to resolve your divorce with the least conflict possible? If so, then mediation should be your first stop.

- Are both of you able to stand up for yourselves? If so, mediation can work. But if you're easily intimidated by your spouse and end up agreeing to things just to avoid an angry confrontation, you might be better off with an attorney.

- Was the decision to divorce mutual, and are you both clear that reconciliation isn't an option? The less conflict there is about who left whom and whether the marriage is over, the more likely you'll be able to cooperate in mediation. If either of you is still dealing with intense feelings of anger or you're having difficulty just being in the room together, it will be much more difficult. But even if the answer to this question isn't an unqualified yes, mediation can still work.

- Do you respect and support your spouse's relationship with your kids? If you have children, it's enormously important that you and your spouse be able to communicate effectively and make decisions together. Mediation is a great way to practice this with the help of a skilled professional.

When to Use Private Mediation (continued)

- Is there a history of violence or emotional abuse by one spouse, or does either spouse abuse drugs or alcohol? In these circumstances, it's best for both parties to have attorneys advocating for them.

- Are you willing to share all financial information, and do you trust your spouse to do the same? To be successful, mediation requires full disclosure of financial information by both parties.

There may be other factors that seem important to you. The following is by Gary Friedman, author of *A Guide to Divorce Mediation: How to Reach a Fair, Legal Settlement at a Fraction of the Cost* (Workman Publishing):

Central to determining mediation's appropriateness is whether or not the parties can deal fairly with one another.

Differences in the parties' openness to the process, the tendency of one party to dominate the other and inequalities in ability (or willingness) to deal with the subject matter must all be examined. Before jumping into mediation, ask yourself several questions:

- Are we both open to reaching a result that is fair to the other?
- Are we able to communicate clearly with each other? Can we each express ourselves and hear the other?
- Can we each identify what is important to us as a realistic and solid base for making choices? Can we each express that?
- Is either of us unwilling to seek outside support or unable to use it effectively when it is needed?

The decision whether or not to mediate should be an informed one, and one that can be reconsidered. Either party's hesitation should be taken seriously; both must be willing for the process to be meaningful. A decision not to mediate or to stop the mediation does not mean that adversary litigation is the sole choice. You can bring in a co-mediator, use a type of mediation more protective of the parties or work with lawyers committed to collaborating with their clients."

Collaborative Divorce

If it doesn't seem like mediation is for you because you want the support of having a lawyer of your own, but you are committed to the peaceful resolution of your divorce, consider using a process called collaborative law.

In a collaborative process, each spouse is represented by an attorney who is committed to a fair resolution of all the issues in the divorce. To begin the process, both spouses and their attorneys sign an agreement that calls for the following:

- Each spouse agrees to fully disclose and exchange all financial documents that will allow for fully informed financial decisions.
- Both spouses and their attorneys agree to maintain absolute confidentiality during the process, creating a safe environment for spouses to freely express needs and concerns.
- The spouses agree to reach a written agreement on all issues and not to seek a judge's intervention, and agree that the attorneys may use the written agreement to obtain a final court decree.
- Both spouses and both attorneys agree that if either party ends the collaborative process before they've reached an agreement, both attorneys must withdraw from the case and can't represent their respective clients in a court fight. To go to court, the spouses must hire new lawyers.

Central to the collaborative law process is the commitment by everyone involved to resolving instead of litigating. While the attorneys advocate for their respective clients, they also support the collaborative process, participate in full disclosure of all assets and liabilities, and encourage agreements for both spouses and their children. The "no court" agreement is critical, as it provides a major incentive to settle and avoid incurring the cost of starting over again with a new attorney.

During the process, the parties and their attorneys meet in a neutral setting to begin negotiations. All meetings include both spouses and both attorneys. All participants must contribute to positive discussions. At some point the spouses may agree to jointly retain experts, such as forensic accountants, to prepare accounting analyses, value assets, and assist with other technical issues. Other professionals may provide financial and tax advice, and in some cases, the spouses may hire a child specialist and even a mental health professional to provide ways to cope with the emotional stresses of divorce. What assistance is needed will vary from case to case.

Pros and Cons of Collaborative Divorce

Some important benefits to the collaborative process include the following:

- You receive support from your attorney's advocacy, expertise, and problem-solving and negotiating skills, while still retaining control over creating a negotiated agreement.
- You stay focused on finding positive solutions instead of getting derailed by threats of going to court.
- You negotiate a comprehensive settlement, instead of receiving an order made by a judge with too little time to understand the issues important to you or the nuances of your case.
- You increase the likelihood of compliance with the terms of a negotiated agreement when each spouse had a stake in the settlement. Working together cooperatively creates a positive environment for coparenting and can improve your relationship.

On the other hand, collaborative divorce has its downsides. It can be expensive and also cumbersome if too many professionals become involved with too many issues. And it can be unfair to the less powerful spouse, who might not have the resources to start over with another lawyer in a court battle if the collaboration is aborted.

RESOURCE
For more detail about divorce mediation and collaborative practice, take a look at _Divorce Without Court: A Guide to Mediation & Collaborative Divorce_, by Katherine E. Stoner (Nolo).

Arbitrators and Private Judges

Arbitrators differ from attorneys, who represent the interests of one spouse, and from mediators, who represent the interests of neither but act as neutral facilitators with no decision-making power. Instead, arbitrators and private judges (often retired from the bench) hear a case and make decisions regarding disputed issues. These decisions are then incorporated into a court judgment.

Arbitrators and private judges charge hourly or daily rates. Typically, these fees are somewhat more than what a top-paid attorney receives. However, arbitration is usually far less expensive than going to trial with an attorney, because fewer attorney hours are required.

Arbitration can be a better option than going to court. It can be most useful in resolving specific issues on which you can't agree, such as what a business is worth. Each side presents its case, and the arbitrator decides. Arbitration is not about negotiation and, in fact, may come up as an option after all negotiating efforts have stalled. You might want to consider this relatively quick and effective way to reach a decision.

RESOURCE
The best way to find an arbitrator is to ask your professional adviser—attorney, CPA, financial adviser, or insurance agent—for a referral. You can also contact the American Arbitration Association (AAA) for lists of arbitrators, at www.adr.org.

Financial Planners

A financial planner can help you prepare for your financial future as a single person. A planner might be able to help you identify potential risks in your settlement agreement and evaluate the potential tax consequences of decisions you're contemplating. Planners can review your net worth and cash flow statements as well as your retirement benefits, investment portfolio, and business holdings.

A financial planner can help you prepare for your financial future as a single person. A planner may be able to help you identify potential risks in your settlement agreement and evaluate the potential tax consequences of decisions you are contemplating. Planners can review your net worth and cash flow statements as well as your retirement benefits, investment portfolio, and business holdings.

There are three types of financial planners. Fee-only planners charge as much as several thousand dollars to develop a full financial plan addressing every aspect of your finances or offer consultations to answer your specific questions for a fee based on an hourly rate.

Commission-only planners derive all of their income from 3%–5% sales commissions on the investments they sell you. While they might give good advice, if they earn the majority of their income selling products, they might have a conflict of interest that can bias their recommendations.

Lastly, some financial planners are compensated by a combination of fee and commission, and might also have a conflict of interest when they advise you to buy certain products.

To find a financial planner, ask for a referral from an accountant, a banker, or an attorney you trust. You can contact the Financial Planning Association at 800-322-4237 or info@OneFPA.org, or visit its website at www.fpanet.org.

To be certain you're dealing with a reputable professional, check references and credentials. Planners who have undergone a rigorous program offered through the College for Financial Planning in Denver earn the title of Certified Financial Planner (CFP). Chartered Financial Consultant (ChFC) is another credential to look for. It's given to financial planners who pass a series of courses at The American College, located in Bryn Mawr, Pennsylvania.

In hiring a financial planner, look for someone who can analyze the financial impact of divorce on you—not someone whose primary focus is on selling investments. You also want someone who can communicate with your attorney, because your planner should help you identify and assess risks so you can protect yourself. Few of us manage our finances as well as we could, but you will find it to your benefit if you choose a planner who is willing to tell you what you would rather not hear.

How Financial Planners Can Help With Your Divorce

As you go through your divorce, a financial planner can help you:

- set long-term and short-term goals
- develop an action plan to reach those goals
- identify cash flow needs, sources of income, and expenses
- put yourself on a budget
- evaluate current investments in terms of risks and objectives
- determine which assets are most appropriate for you to keep
- develop an investment portfolio for your needs and goals
- learn the costs and tax consequences of keeping or not keeping your family home
- determine whether the proceeds from a retirement plan should be rolled over to an IRA or a Roth IRA
- determine whether to take an immediate or a deferred distribution from a retirement plan
- evaluate whether your current insurance coverage is appropriate and cost-effective
- decide how to invest for education funding, and
- make estate planning decisions.

Divorce Financial Analysts

The growing popularity of assets that can be tricky to value, such as hedge funds, stock options, private-equity ventures, and other sophisticated financial investments, has led to a new brand of adviser known as the "certified divorce financial analyst." Previously known as "certified divorce planners," these specialists help couples wade through the fiscal intricacies of splitting up. In fact, many have a financial title, such as certified public accountant (CPA) or CFP, in addition to their divorce financial analyst designation.

In recent years, some 2,500 of these divorce specialists have been trained, according to the Institute for Divorce Financial Analysts, and some big financial houses, like Merrill Lynch and Morgan Stanley, have divorce financial analysts on staff. For fees of $250 to $500 an hour, such advisers help couples and individuals navigate the economic aspects of divorce while leaving the legal issues, like custody, to divorce lawyers.

Divorce financial analysts are most effective working with clients on specific, complex financial issues, like avoiding tax snafus, dividing a stock portfolio, obtaining health insurance after a split, and deciding which assets to fight for and which to concede. While they're open to all clients, it's usually higher-asset couples (with estates of at least $3,000,000) who have been married more than ten years—so that alimony is a major issue—who can make the best use of their services.

To find a divorce financial analyst, contact the Institute for Divorce Financial Analysts, the body that certifies these professionals, at 800-875-1760 or on the Web at www.institutedfa.com.

Stockbrokers and Money Managers

Stockbrokers tend to focus on individual stock, bond, mutual fund, and insurance transactions. Money managers look at the overall performance of investment portfolios and evaluate how they meet short-term and long-term needs for growth, income, and safety.

In gathering information on your financial condition, you may have to contact your stockbroker for copies of brokerage accounts or other items. Again, as with other professionals who work on commission, recognize that your stockbroker may try to sell you products when you call for financial information.

Stockbrokers receive commissions on sales charges, which are paid by the client—usually 1% to 5% of the amount of money invested in stocks, bonds, mutual funds, or annuities. Money managers, on the other hand, receive a fee for the service they provide, which is designing and managing investment portfolios. They charge a percentage of the value of the money they manage.

Accountants

Accountants can provide a variety of services ranging from auditing a business to assessing employee benefits packages. Accountants charge by the hour or by the project. A certified public accountant (CPA) can work as a tax consultant—but don't assume that all CPAs can provide personal tax services. If you have income tax concerns, you might want to start by consulting an enrolled agent (EA), a tax specialist qualified to practice before the IRS. If you think your spouse is hiding assets or covering up financial facts, you might want to hire a forensic accountant. These specialists can trace marital property, evaluate financial reports, and value businesses.

To find out about EA, and to find one in your area, you can contact the National Association of Enrolled Agents at 202-822-6232 or www.naea.org.

Bankers

Your bank and banker can prove quite useful in helping you with various financial issues of divorce, such as canceling or opening lines of credit, establishing new accounts, or getting loans. Do not expect a banker, however, to advise you on investments or other complex issues. Also, while bankers work on salaries, they often function as salespeople for their own institutions, promote their own products, or sell mutual funds with a commission. Your banker may advise you to park your money in a certificate of deposit even though your long-term goals might be better served by investing in stocks or mutual funds. Get information from several different sources or consult with your financial planner before making any long-term decisions.

Insurance Agents

Insurance is one way to protect yourself from risks, and during divorce it's important to review your coverage. Contact your insurance agent to double-check your policies for life, health, disability, property, and business. Also check the cash and surrender values of the policy—they might be different from the amount stated in your contract because the actual rate of interest paid could differ from the rate of interest assumed when the policy was originally bought. You might also be charged a fee if the policy is cashed in.

Divorce is a good time to check the cash value of any life insurance policies because this value represents marital property to be divided. In addition, the policy can provide emergency cash if necessary. But be aware that the surrender value might be lower than the cash value. When you divide the family cars, be sure to check your auto insurance to make sure you are paying only to insure yourself (and perhaps your driving-age children) on the car(s) you keep.

Insurance agents are paid commissions. The insurance company pays the commissions, but the company prices its policies to include the commission—so ultimately, the customer pays the commission.

If you don't have an insurance agent, shop around and talk to several to find one with whom you feel comfortable. Be aware that insurance agents hold sales positions and might ask you to buy a new policy or expand an old one when you call for information. Resist their pressures and be sure you absolutely need any new insurance you purchase.

Real Estate Agents

When a real estate agent is involved in the sale of a home, that agent usually receives a commission from the seller, even if the agent has been working with the buyer. An agent who appraises a house usually will do so for free, in hopes of getting your business later when you sell.

Because your house might be the most valuable asset in your divorce settlement, it's important to get an accurate assessment of its current market value. Try to get estimates from several real estate agents or from a certified appraiser so you can negotiate with your spouse or a third-party buyer from a knowledgeable position. The best agents to ask are those familiar with the neighborhood. If you used an agent when you bought the house, that person is often well suited to appraise the property now.

Certified appraisers are covered in Chapter 13. You can get referrals from real estate agents, escrow companies, and lending institutions.

Therapists

In the stress of divorce, a therapist or counselor can be a valuable resource for helping resolve personal issues. To find someone, ask friends for referrals, or contact a local mental health association, church, or family service agency.

Therapists charge by the hour, with 50 minutes counting as an hour. Especially if money is tight, find out whether your medical insurance might reimburse you for all or part of your therapy sessions.

As with any professional, it's important to check credentials, but also make sure the therapist's approach feels appropriate to you. Don't hire a Freudian who does long-term psychoanalysis if you want short-term counseling to help you get through the divorce. If you can't afford one-on-one therapy, you might be able to find help and encouragement through a support group, a community service agency, or a program sponsored by a religious group.

Credit Counselors

Credit advisers can help you negotiate with your creditors and set up systems to manage your finances. These agencies generally receive most of their funding from major creditors, such as department stores, credit card companies, and banks.

Use the services of credit counselors who are affiliated with nonprofit organizations, such as the United Way, a local "Y," or a church- or synagogue-run association. A few other nonprofit credit counselors operate nationwide. The best is the National Foundation for Credit Counseling. This nonprofit organization generally charges nothing or a nominal fee for setting up a payment plan to get your commercial credit accounts paid off.

To use a nonprofit credit adviser to help you pay your debts, you must either have some disposable income or be willing to sell some of your property. A credit adviser contacts your creditors to let them know that you've sought assistance and need more time to pay. Based on your income and debts, the adviser, with your creditors, decides on how much you pay. You then make one or two direct payments each month to the agency, which in turn pays your creditors. A credit adviser can often get wage garnishments revoked and interest and late charges dropped. These agencies also help people make monthly budgets.

Actuaries

If a pension or retirement plan is at stake in your divorce, you may need the services of an actuary, a specialized financial professional. For details, including fees charged, see Chapter 14.

Business Appraisers

To determine the financial value of any business—including a sole proprietorship or professional practice—a business appraiser conducts a detailed analysis.

Call the IRS and request a copy of Internal Revenue Rulings 59-60 and 83-120 if you or your spouse operates a business or is a professional— doctor, lawyer, accountant, psychotherapist, and the like—with a private practice in the form of a closely held corporation. You will want to know the value of the business or practice. IRR 59-60 deals with methods of valuing closely held corporations; 83-120 concerns valuation of stock.

Private Investigators

Private investigators, or private detectives, can sometimes be helpful in a divorce by locating missing or misused funds, or exposing fraud or an affair in fault states where courts may consider that type of misconduct. Contrary to the "gumshoe" image spawned by countless movies and TV shows, a private detective is much more likely to wield a database than a pistol. Computers allow access to massive amounts of information from probate records, motor vehicle registrations, credit reports, association membership lists, and other sources.

Most states require that private investigators be licensed, and a growing number of states specify training requirements. California, for example, requires 6,000 hours of investigative experience, a background check, and a qualifying score on a written exam; 4,000 hours and a college or law degree; or 5,000 hours and an AA degree in police science, criminal law, or justice. In addition to formal licensing requirements in some states, many private detectives have experience in the military, law enforcement, insurance, collections, or the security industry.

A good investigator is curious, aggressive, persistent, assertive, and a good communicator. Skilled private detectives are able to think on their feet and have strong interviewing or interrogation skills. Most bill on an hourly basis and ask for reimbursement of expenses.

Online Do-It-Yourself Divorce Services

State and county court systems and bar associations have done a great deal to provide the public access to the legal system, especially in family law matters. Their websites are generally user-friendly and more reliable than most internet sources that cover the legal process of divorce. Many have self-help centers where you can begin the divorce proceedings yourself (if money is tight).

A growing number of websites provide legal forms for divorce and offer varying degrees of help in completing them. For fees ranging anywhere from $500 to $1,000 (a fraction of what most lawyers charge even for an uncontested divorce), these sites offer to help you prepare the paperwork and represent yourself in your divorce.

Much as over-the-counter remedies might help clear up minor health problems but can't replace a doctor when it comes to serious health concerns, these sites might be useful for the simplest of divorce procedures. But if the spouses disagree on any important issue and/or if they have children or complex finances, there's a substantial risk to relying on these sites alone, without consulting a lawyer.

CAUTION
When researching on the internet, stick to governmental sites in your state. Because divorce law is local, you need to stay focused on your regional courts, one of which ultimately will process and perhaps render a judgment in your case.

RESOURCE
More about online resources. There's an entire chapter on how to find divorce information yourself in *Nolo's Essential Guide to Divorce*, by Emily Doskow (Nolo). Also check with Nolo.com and Divorce.net for legal articles and state-specific information on divorce laws and procedures. ●

Financial Fact-Finding: What Must I Know and When Must I Know It?

Frequently, one spouse handles all the financial paperwork and decision making during the marriage. This approach can be practical when you're together, but a potential disaster during divorce.

The answers to the questions posed in this chapter's title are straightforward: You must know everything possible about your finances, and you need to know it as soon as you can, preferably before filing for divorce.

No one can make proper financial decisions without adequate information. How can you tell whether to keep the family home if you don't know what it costs to maintain it? On what will you base requests for alimony or child support if you're in the dark about living expenses? Both you and your spouse will need to document your financial life as you go through the divorce. Now, in the early stages, is the best time to start.

If you left the bookkeeping to your partner, you may feel as though you are starting from scratch. It's important not to panic. Take control by finding out as much as you can about your finances.

Linda, a 35-year-old mother of two, recalled that when she first separated from her husband, she was terrified at the thought of confronting her financial life. As she kept at it, however, the job became easier. "Now I can look at all of these complicated papers and forms and not feel scared," she reported.

SKIP AHEAD
If you were the family bookkeeper, you will be in much better shape than your spouse who did not participate in managing the finances. You can move on to "Don't Forget the 'Easy-to-Forget' Assets," below, and begin verifying the financial information you will need during your divorce. Otherwise, continue reading.

Whatever role you played previously, by the time the divorce is over, you will probably know more about the details of your financial life than you ever cared to. You gain this knowledge by going through these three steps:

1. **Information gathering.** Find and sort all financial information, such as files, receipts, bills, bank statements, mortgage statements, and other similar documents.
2. **Information analysis.** After sorting your papers, review your files, appraisals, and valuations. It's also important to calculate taxes and other costs—either by yourself or with an accountant or financial adviser.
3. **Decision making.** Once you analyze what you own and owe and what it costs to live, you can begin to decide what to do with your property in the divorce.

Start investigating your financial position now. Don't wait until you're at the bargaining table to figure out how much your house or your spouse's 401(k) is worth. By the time you enter settlement negotiations, you want to have as much up-to-date information as you can.

In this beginning stage of the divorce process, focus on information gathering only. Even if you don't understand all of it, do not get sidetracked from your fact-finding mission. Later on, you can concentrate on decision making. For now, your time is best spent on documenting your economic situation. Staying focused may seem hard, but it gets easier as you go along. Besides, it will help you:

- save time and money, especially once you hire an attorney
- distinguish your separate property from the marital assets
- negotiate a settlement from a position of strength, and
- begin building a foundation for a secure financial future.

Advice to the Terminally Disorganized

Ideally, your accounts and files are up to date and in order. More likely, however, you'll have to hunt for records. You're not alone. Few people are as on top of their personal finances as they would like to be.

Fortunately, you have a number of options in finding what you need. Tax returns, for instance, are gold mines of information in a divorce. The "Financial Facts Checklist" at the end of this chapter will give you other clues for finding financial data. But before you get there, here are some ideas to get you started.

Tax returns. You will need the information found in your tax returns from as far back as you can go, with the past three years as the bare minimum. This is one time when you will be grateful that the IRS keeps records (often electronically) of everything you send them.

You can get complete copies of your returns by using IRS Form 4506. However, retrieving these copies requires considerable time and money.

The IRS will provide you with the "transcript" of any tax return you filed within the last three years, free of charge. A transcript will display most of the line items in the return and is often sufficient for divorce purposes. It can be helpful to start with these free transcripts and then decide whether you need to pay for copies of your actual returns. Transcripts can be useful when time is a factor, as they are generally delivered within five to ten days. You can order transcripts of your returns online, using Form 4506-T or 4506-T-EZ.

You may also order a transcript of your tax account, which will show any adjustments that have been made (by you or the IRS) to your returns. Both these transcripts can be ordered free of charge on the IRS website or by calling 800-908-9946.

If you require an exact duplicate of a complete tax return for any given year (or if no transcript is available), it can be ordered for a fee. Copies of tax returns may take up to 60 days to be processed.

The IRS generally sends your tax information to the address shown on your previous return. If you've moved or are concerned about arousing your spouse's anger or suspicion, ask that the forms be sent to your office, your attorney, a friend, or a post office box. Once you have copies of the tax returns, you can review them with a trusted accountant or financial planner who can show you how to find basic financial information on the forms.

Loan applications and account statements. Check recent copies of credit or loan applications, canceled checks, and bank, brokerage, and credit union statements for information on assets or debts.

Insurance policies. Look for the names of the beneficiaries on any insurance policies. Determine whether the insurance is term or whole life. If it is whole life, find out the cash value.

Estate plans. You may find a wealth of information about property you and your spouse own by reviewing wills, trusts, and other estate planning documents.

Retirement plans. Keep track of work-related pension or savings plans, both your own and your spouse's.

Financial professionals. Make a list of accountants, lawyers, and other financial advisers you and your spouse have been using.

Credit reports. You can get a copy of your credit report periodically from one of the major credit bureaus. (See Chapter 5.)

Title reports. Visit your county land records office and conduct a title search, or have an escrow company do one for you, if you suspect there might be liens against your home or other real estate. (See Chapter 13 for details on liens.)

If you know you'll have trouble staying organized once you begin collecting your paperwork, you can hire a bookkeeping service, a virtual assistant, or a professional organizer. Before hiring one of these professionals, make sure the person has references, listens to you, and asks what you want—instead of telling you what you need.

No matter what approach you take in organizing your documents, keep it simple. You can buy an inexpensive three-ring binder to hold your papers. As your stack of information grows, create categories of documents by using the divider tabs that come with the binder. The "Net Worth" and "Cash Flow" statements in Chapter 12 will give you an idea of the kinds of divisions you can make.

When you begin to feel overwhelmed, remember that you're not just shuffling papers to get through your divorce. You're completing the groundwork for your financial decision making and security for many years to come—and that is worth the effort it takes to become informed and get organized.

Taxes and Power of Attorney

You may have a tax return transcript sent to a third party by completing the instructions on Form 4506-T. This can be useful when you're working with an accountant, an actuary, a financial manager, or an attorney in your divorce.

However, in some circumstances you might need greater involvement from a third party, such as your attorney. IRS Form 2848 provides authorization for a third party to communicate with the agency about your tax filings. In some cases, when a client is impaired or simply overwhelmed, an attorney in good standing with the state bar may be authorized to practice with the IRS and receive documents on the client's behalf.

This type of authorization would be helpful, for example, where a client's husband prepared all tax returns for his spouse over several decades, but never provided her with copies of the forms. If the client becomes subject to collection, she may want to sign a limited power of attorney that allows her lawyer to receive documents from the IRS and resolve the collection attempt.

Make sure your attorney is a professional in good standing with the state bar before you grant them even limited power to uncover previously unknown documents and negotiate on your behalf.

If You Think Your Spouse Might Be Hiding Assets

Unfortunately, divorce can be the occasion for a game of financial cat and mouse in which one spouse hides assets or makes other unethical moves. In some cases, the gaps in the financial information you get from your spouse occur because of honest mistakes. Many people are not detail oriented when it comes to personal finances and, in the stress of divorce, may forget some specifics.

On the other hand, some spouses purposely conceal the value of a business or switch funds into secret accounts. If the judge finds out, the spouse who hides assets may be deemed guilty of "economic misconduct." This misconduct is likely to affect the final settlement—the misbehaving spouse will probably get less than the innocent spouse.

Winning Big?

One California woman learned the hard way how seriously judges take the duty to disclose assets to the other party. In 1996, Denise Rossi won a $1.3-million lottery jackpot and 11 days later filed for divorce from her husband of 25 years. She kept her lottery winnings secret from her husband during the divorce proceedings. Two years later, he inadvertently learned of her windfall when he received a misdirected piece of mail. In 1999, a Superior Court judge ordered that the entire jackpot be given to the husband after determining that the wife violated state disclosure laws and acted out of malice or fraud. News reports indicate that the wife filed for bankruptcy in early 2000.

If you have any reason to believe your spouse is being less than candid with you about income or other assets, you will have to do a little detective work on your own.

If your own review of records like old income tax returns doesn't yield results, consider hiring a special type of certified public accountant called a forensic accountant. These specialists will comb through your records and can usually create an accurate picture of your spouse's financial position. Their services, however, can be expensive. You must weigh the cost of hiring a forensic accountant against the dollar amount at stake in your divorce.

The legal process of "discovery" can be used to force a reluctant spouse to turn over records and statements. Discovery is a formal information-gathering process used in lawsuits. Spouses (usually through lawyers) send papers to each other asking that questions be answered or documents turned over. Another procedure used in discovery is taking depositions—that is, orally asking questions of a witness who is under oath.

Discovery is usually time-consuming and costly, and may ultimately turn up nothing of importance. Therefore, gather information informally if at all possible.

No matter how you feel about your soon-to-be ex-spouse, you have an obligation to be financially responsible as long as you are legally married. In other words, each spouse must handle the family finances in a prudent manner. Financial misconduct is a breach of a spouse's fiduciary duty, and a court may find that a spouse engaged in "waste-dissipation" if the person squanders or destroys marital resources—including misusing cash or credit. Each spouse is also responsible for making all financial information available to the other.

In some states (for example, California, Maine, Colorado, and Arizona), as soon as divorce papers are served, automatic temporary restraining orders (ATROs) take effect, which state that neither party may transfer, encumber, conceal, sell, or dispose of property (whether marital or separate), unless there's a written agreement or court order. However, most other states require a formal request before a court will restrict either spouse's right to control property and are reluctant to prohibit the use or transfer of marital assets unless there's a history of past dissipation or recent threats to dissipate assets or incur debt.

Every divorce court will consider a party's financial misconduct when dividing property. A spouse who engages in financial conduct that is detrimental to the other spouse may find the judge dividing property in favor of the "innocent" spouse.

Don't Forget the "Easy-to-Forget" Assets

Many assets divided during the divorce aren't difficult to account for: the house, cars, retirement plans, and stocks. For other assets, you might have to search a little if your spouse is trying to hide them, as discussed above. Still other assets are in plain view, but you might overlook them

Searching for Hidden Assets

This checklist was adapted from one created by Ginita Wall, a CPA and certified financial planner in San Diego, California. It includes common ways in which a spouse might undervalue or disguise marital assets. You might have difficulty finding some items or getting the proof you need to show they exist. As mentioned, a forensic accountant, formal discovery procedures, or both might help. Hidden assets may involve:

- Collusion with an employer to delay bonuses, stock options, raises until after the divorce, or salary paid to a nonexistent employee with checks that will be voided after the divorce. You might find this information by taking the deposition of your spouse's boss or payroll supervisor, but more likely you'll need a forensic accountant
- Money paid from the business to someone close—such as a father, mother, girlfriend, or boyfriend—for services that were in fact never rendered. The money will no doubt be given back to your spouse after the divorce is final
- A custodial account set up in the name of a child, using the child's Social Security number
- Delay in signing long-term business contracts until after the divorce (although this might seem like smart planning, if the intent is to lower the value of the business, it is considered hiding assets)
- Skimming cash from a business
- Antiques, artwork, hobby equipment, gun collections, and tools that are overlooked or undervalued (look for lush furnishings, paintings, or collector-level carpets at the office, reflecting income that is unreported on tax returns and financial statements; document any of the cash expenses you know your spouse has incurred)
- Debt repayment to a friend or family member for a fake debt
- Expenses paid for a girlfriend or boyfriend, such as gifts, travel, rent, or tuition for college or special classes, and
- Cash kept in the form of traveler's checks and money orders. You might be able to find these by tracing bank account deposits and withdrawals.

nevertheless. While these "easy-to-forget" assets might not be worth a great deal of money, they can turn out to be valuable when you and your spouse are negotiating over who gets what in your divorce settlement. They could include such things as country club memberships, points for hotel, airline, or credit card programs, or equity in an auto lease.

Here are some other commonly overlooked assets and some suggestions for how to handle them.

Stock options. The right to purchase the employer's stock at a bargain price some time in the future may have significant value. Usually, the spouse who owns the stock options keeps them in exchange for an asset the other spouse wants to keep. Alternatively, you can agree to exercise the option jointly in the future if the company's buy-sell agreement permits this. (See Chapter 16 for more on stock options.)

Cryptocurrency. Cryptocurrency (crypto) is a type of virtual currency that's treated just like any other form of property for tax purposes. Crypto is becoming increasingly popular, and not just for tech industry insiders or the uber-wealthy.

Crypto is monitored and organized by a peer-to-peer network called a "blockchain," a secure ledger of transactions for buying, selling, and transferring crypto. Unlike physical money, crypto is decentralized, which means the government or a financial institution, doesn't issue it. People can use crypto to buy, sell, or trade securely without needing a third party, such as a government or financial institution to validate a transaction. For example, Bitcoin was created as a form of payment that isn't controlled or distributed by a central government, and the stablecoin Tether is pegged to the U.S. dollar. However, certain virtual currency transactions must still be reported on your tax return. So, check your tax return if you're wondering whether your spouse has sold any crypto during your marriage. For more information about virtual assets and taxes, check the IRS website at www.irs.gov/businesses/small-businesses-self-employed/digital-assets.

Although cryptocurrency isn't as easy to locate as a savings account, it isn't completely impossible to trace. One of the most common ways for consumers to store their crypto is through the use of a virtual custodial wallet. This is where you use a third-party website or app to hold your crypto for you. When you buy coins from cryptocurrency exchanges, apps, or stockbrokers, they put them in a custodial wallet they control. If you want to store the crypto yourself, you can transfer it from their custodial wallet to your own hot (online) or cold (offline) wallet. However, some stockbrokers and apps only let you buy and sell crypto but not transfer it anywhere. In that case, the only option is to use their custodial wallet.

Who Gets the Miles?

Many millions of Americans belong to frequent flyer programs. With the average active member logging 12,000 miles yearly, the number of banked miles is growing by 400 billion per year. In addition to the usual credits from airline flights, car rentals, and hotel stays, miles are offered for use with certain credit cards and other purchases.

Often one spouse accumulates most of the couple's frequent flyer miles through business travel, though they may be used for the couple's joint vacations. Thus, the miles might become an issue in divorce, with one spouse asserting that the other's accumulated miles should be split upon dissolution of the marriage.

Some divorce and estate lawyers place a value on air miles—two cents apiece—that approximates what the airlines charge when they sell miles to their corporate partners. So, 500,000 miles could be worth $10,000.

But valuation can be more complicated than that. For example, one spouse might be a present or former airline employee who as a retiree will be entitled to fly free. How can that privilege be valued and divided? That would depend on the number of years until retirement, the average present cost of total flights, and the presumed inflation rate between now and retirement.

Further complicating the issue of frequent flyer miles is that some airlines do not permit division of this asset. If a significant number of frequent flyer points (more than 25,000) are at issue in your divorce, you or your attorney should review the airline's latest frequent flyer program statement. Be sure to specify in any agreement or court order the points being transferred and a deadline for the transfer before the expiration date of the points. Similar steps should be taken for other bonus plans, such as those sponsored by hotels, credit card issuers, banks, rental car companies, and department stores.

If you think your spouse might have purchased crypto during your marriage or you discovered virtual asset information on your joint tax return, start by asking your spouse about it. If your spouse isn't forthcoming, you should speak to a local attorney about how to discover this information.

Tax refunds. If you file a joint tax return, the tax refund check will be in both names. Your divorce agreement should clearly state how the refund will be split. (See Chapter 11.)

Property taxes. If property taxes are paid partly for the past and partly for the future, the spouse paying those taxes for a period in which both spouses used the house may be entitled to a reimbursement of half of the taxes paid during that period of joint use.

Prepaid insurance. Because all insurance is paid for in advance, including life, disability, and casualty insurance, consider these prepayments when you are valuing and dividing property.

Vacation pay. The value of accumulated vacation hours should be based on the spouse's pay rate. If the employed spouse will be compensated now or later for unused sick pay, it may also be valued.

Frequent flyer points. To split these points, you can divide the miles themselves, have free tickets issued in the other spouse's name, or determine the monetary value of the travel benefits and compensate the other spouse accordingly (see "Who Gets the Miles?" above).

Season tickets. For some couples, season tickets for a hot sports team or important cultural events can be practically priceless. Whether you have tickets for the 50-yard line or a box at the opera, be sure you know their financial value and whether they can be replaced or replicated. Otherwise, you could find yourself losing an asset you cherish—or fighting for something that's not worth the effort.

Timeshares. A resort timeshare is often worth less than the amount still owed on it. You must decide whether one of you will accept it at a lesser value or whether you will continue to own it jointly, sell it, or let it go into foreclosure.

Professional dues and magazine subscriptions. Discounts are frequently offered for two- and three-year memberships in professional associations or for subscriptions to academic journals or other magazines. A spouse preparing for divorce might make substantial prepayments using money from marital funds in order to avoid using separate funds in the future. The amounts spent might not be much, but every bit matters when you're dividing it all up.

The W-2 and the Tax Return

Your financial fact-finding process should include an examination of your own and your spouse's W-2 forms, as well as your marital tax return or the returns you and your spouse file separately. There are several good reasons for doing this. First, it is never too soon to educate yourself on your finances, and the W-2 and the tax return are two primary tools. In addition, these documents provide information about how much income is available for alimony and child support payments (see Chapter 18). Finally, if you think it's possible your spouse might be concealing assets, the information contained there may point you toward sources you were not aware of.

Early every year, employers are required by law to issue a W-2 to each employee for the tax (calendar) year that has just ended. The employee attaches copies of the W-2 when filing federal and state tax returns.

 WEB RESOURCE
The W-2 form and the information included may change from year to year. For comprehensive information and instructions on the W-2 form, go to the IRS website www.irs.gov and, under "Forms and Publications," type in "W-2."

Of the numbered boxes on the W-2, the most important for this discussion are:

- **Box 1: Wages, tips, other compensation.** This is where the total of straight wages earned during the year appears. Also included are some employee business expense reimbursements, moving expense reimbursements, and employer contributions to certain fringe benefits, such as stock option compensation (for more on stock options, see Chapter 16). However, Box 1 does not include wages that the employee has deferred under certain employer-sponsored retirement plans, such as contributions to a 401(k) plan or a SIMPLE IRA (see Chapter 14).

- **Box 5: Medicare wages and tips.** This is usually a larger number than Social Security wages. Medicare wages are gross wages and are not reduced by contributions to salary deferral and other tax-deferred employee benefit plans. Generally, all income reported in Box 5 is considered gross wages, and is the amount used in calculating child and spousal support.

- **Box 11: Nonqualified plans.** Money that the taxpayer has received from certain retirement plans and certain deferred-compensation plans appears here.

22222	a Employee's social security number			
		OMB No. 1545-0008		
b Employer identification number (EIN)			1 Wages, tips, other compensation	2 Federal income tax withheld
c Employer's name, address, and ZIP code			3 Social security wages	4 Social security tax withheld
			5 Medicare wages and tips	6 Medicare tax withheld
			7 Social security tips	8 Allocated tips
d Control number			9	10 Dependent care benefits
e Employee's first name and initial Last name Suff.			11 Nonqualified plans	12a
			13 Statutory employee Retirement plan Third-party sick pay	12b
			14 Other	12c
				12d
f Employee's address and ZIP code				
15 State Employer's state ID number	16 State wages, tips, etc.	17 State income tax	18 Local wages, tips, etc.	19 Local income tax	20 Locality name

Form **W-2** Wage and Tax Statement   **2023**   Department of the Treasury—Internal Revenue Service
Copy 1—For State, City, or Local Tax Department

As for income tax returns, the format of the forms varies. Sources of funds may be marital income or separate income, and a joint return may reflect marital property, separate property, or both.

Several items on a tax return and its supplementary schedules are especially important:

- **Schedule A: Itemized Deductions.** This schedule may include several types of deductions that can figure into the earning-power equation for support. When you read the schedules filed by you and your spouse, look for entries that reveal items such as:

- **Medical and dental expenses.** Most taxpayers may claim a deduction only for expenses that exceed 10% of adjusted gross income. If this number is large, it might indicate that medical expenses will be an important part of a supported spouse's needs or that a supporting spouse might be unable to pay.

- **Real estate taxes.** An entry here indicates homeownership or investment property. Holdings you didn't know about might be reflected here.

- **Home mortgage interest.** An entry here suggests a family residence or possibly a vacation home. If home mortgage interest is being paid, request a copy of the note. Whether the note is for fixed or variable interest could affect support calculations. Also check whether the property has been refinanced.

- **Schedule B: Interest and Ordinary Dividends.** The entries on this schedule reflect interest from banks, money market accounts, brokerage accounts, and the like, as well as dividends paid by corporations to stockholders. These amounts are generally considered income, and thus they are available for child and spousal support. On this schedule, you'll see entries for:

  - **Interest earned.** This indicates the size of the current balance of invested funds. Thus, this may be helpful in assessing disclosure statements in other aspects of the divorce process. Whether the interest is taxable or tax free will affect the support calculation.

  - **Dividends.** These are funds paid by securities. An entry here indicates that one or both spouses hold corporate stock or other securities. But many securities do not pay dividends, and those that don't may not be reflected on the tax return.

- **Schedule C: Profit or Loss From Business.** Unless the two of you can come to an agreement, the job of placing a dollar value on a business owned by spouses at divorce is best done by a forensic accountant or a business appraiser. But the annual tax return can reveal clues about the earning power of a sole proprietorship or a sole practice.

You won't necessarily get easy, clear information from a business tax return. As scandals involving Fortune 500 companies have shown, business accounting can be an inexact science, with much room for fudging. A businessperson can manipulate figures by delaying the deposit of checks; overstating travel and meals ostensibly related to business, putting nonworking friends or relatives on the payroll to inflate "expenses," buying personal items with business money, or writing off automobile expenses. If you suspect such practices, you might want to hire a forensic accountant to do a detailed cash flow analysis and to value the business.

If you decide to wade into the world of business accounting, you need to know a few things. Different businesses use different accounting methods. Some operate on a *cash basis:* They report to the IRS only cash income received, not money that their customers owe them, and they deduct expenses actually paid during the year. Others work on an *accrual basis*: They report income when it is earned, not necessarily received, and they deduct expenses when incurred, not necessarily when paid. Understanding the type of accounting method used is essential for determining a business's profit or loss and, thus, its cash flow for purposes of support.

- **Schedule D: Capital Gains and Losses.** On this schedule, the taxpayer notes the sale or exchange of a capital asset, which is an asset owned and used personally or kept as an investment. Almost everything you own, including your house, household furnishings, car, jewelry, and personal collections, is a capital asset. If an item is a capital asset, its sale generates a capital gain. If you exercise a stock option, that's also capital gains income. (For more on capital gains and losses, see Chapter 11 and Chapter 13. For stock options, see Chapter 16.)

Many capital gains don't count as income for support purposes. The determining factor may be whether the gain is considered a one-time gain or a recurring gain. For example, if the periodic sale of chunks of land from a large parcel has been funding the lifestyle of the parties and there's a reasonable expectation that this pattern will continue, the sale proceeds may be considered income. In such a case, the tax effect of the capital gains portion of income may have a significant impact on the after-tax amounts available to both the supporting and the supported spouse.

Most state courts have said that income realized from the exercise of stock options is income available for child support. One Ohio court specifically held that the value of unexercised stock options (their increase in value from the date they were granted to the date they could have been exercised) is gross income for child support purposes.

- **Schedule E: Real Estate, Royalties, Partnerships, Trusts.** In Schedule E, the taxpayer lists income derived from the sources mentioned. Depending on what's listed, the items here might be the source of significant cash flow that might be used in calculating support. In particular, this schedule may show:

  - **Rental revenue.** Rental property could be a significant source of cash flow. Think about more than just the monthly rent when evaluating this figure for cash flow purposes. For example, if rental property is leased to a business owned by one or both of the spouses, does it rent at market rates? When was it acquired, and how much is owed on it? Was it ever refinanced? If a taxpayer is paying debt service, there will be less cash available for support.

  - **S corporation and partnership income.** S corporations and partnerships do not pay federal income tax. All taxable income, whether distributed or not, must be reported individually by the shareholders and partners based on their ownership percentages and is reflected on what's called a K-1 form. If an S corporation or a partnership is involved, get a copy of the corporate or partnership income tax return, together with a K-1, to understand significant details about what constitutes income and assets.

- **Forms 1099-MISC and 1099-NEC.** These forms list miscellaneous income, such as payments made to nonemployees (for example, consultants or independent contractors) and interest and dividend income reinvested but not actually received. If the income is for services rendered, you may find it on the Schedule C form.

How Long Should You Keep Tax Returns?

The short answer: forever.

As the only official record of your earnings history, the tax return may be your most important financial document, period. It is crucial not only in a divorce but also for other financial purposes, such as setting your level of Social Security benefits.

Some advisers suggest you keep all tax returns for at least five years. That's just plain bad advice. Our strong recommendation: *Never* throw them away. You can store them on a thumb drive or external hard drive so they don't take up a lot of extra space in your home.

What About the Gifts You Gave Me?

It's sad but true that some of the most heated arguments during a divorce center on gifts—whether the gifts are an art collection and silverware, or the bread machine and Tupperware. Determining how to attribute financial gifts from family members, such as money used toward the down payment on the house or to buy a car, can cause a great deal of friction during the divorce.

As a general rule, property acquired by gift or inheritance is the separate property of the spouse who receives it. But it might not always be the case. For instance, in a situation involving one of our clients, a husband transferred real estate holdings to his wife to protect himself against creditors. At divorce, she claimed the property was a gift and her husband had no interest in it. She was dismayed when the transfer was deemed a transfer to defraud creditors. The transfer was voided, and the property was subject to the claims of her husband's creditors.

Financial Facts Checklist

At the end of this chapter is a list of the items you should gather, whether you are doing your divorce yourself or working with an attorney or other legal or financial professionals. It's a good idea to get this information together yourself—you'll save time and money and gain a sense of control over your divorce.

Most of this information should be in your files at home or your office. If you don't have a clue about where to find a particular item, watch the mail. You might be able to glean the names of insurance companies, banks, brokerage houses, and other institutions that you can contact to get information. Your insurance agent should be able to answer questions on policies, and the personnel or benefits office of your (or your spouse's) employer can shed some light on retirement benefits. For information on real estate, contact the agent who sold you the house or the company that holds the mortgage.

Instructions: Financial Facts Checklist. Put a check (✓) in the blanks next to items you have. Enter a zero for items that neither you nor your spouse has—and when you find them, enter a checkmark within the zero. For documents you don't have, make a note about which of you will be responsible for getting them. Some of the terms in the chart may be unfamiliar to you. Don't worry. You will understand them better as you continue reading. For now, use the list to jog your memory—or your accountant's—about what documents to look for.

Questions to Ask an Attorney

1. Is there any hint that my spouse is hiding income? If so, how can we expose that?
2. What documents do I need to prove our real income?
3. What liability do I have if I find our real income is greater than the income we reported on our tax returns?
4. Are there any obvious sources of other income on my spouse's tax return, such as income from passive activities like rentals, business interests, dividends, and capital gains or losses?

Financial Facts Checklist

Tax returns (past five years)

☐ U.S.

☐ State

Pre- or postnuptial agreements

☐ Spouse 1

☐ Spouse 2

Previous divorce documents, including property settlement, alimony and child support orders

☐ Spouse 1

☐ Spouse 2

Wills

☐ Spouse 1

☐ Spouse 2

Trust documents

☐ Spouse 1

☐ Spouse 2

Pay stubs (from January 1 of current year)

☐ Spouse 1

☐ Spouse 2

Bank records

☐ **Checking accounts**
    in whose name:
    account number:
    balance:
    latest statement:
    canceled checks:
    deposit slips:

☐ **Children's custodial accounts**

☐ **Certificates of deposit**

☐ **Savings accounts**
    in whose name:
    account number:
    balance:
    latest statement:
    deposit slips:

☐ **Custodial wallet/cryptocurrency account**
    in whose name:
    account number:
    balance:
    latest statement:

Other accounts (including all accounts closed within past two years)

☐ **Annuities**
    in whose name:
    account number:
    interest/dividends:
    balance:

☐ **Cash management accounts**
    in whose name:
    account number:
    interest/dividends:
    balance:

Financial Facts Checklist (continued)

Other accounts (including all accounts closed within past two years) (continued)

❏ **Brokerage accounts**
    in whose name:
    account number:
    interest/dividends:
    balance:

❏ **Credit union accounts**
    in whose name:
    account number:
    interest/dividends:
    balance:

❏ **Commodities accounts**
    in whose name:
    account number:
    interest/dividends:
    balance:

❏ **Mutual funds**
    in whose name:
    account number:
    interest/dividends:
    balance:

Tax-free investments

❏ **Municipal bonds**
    in whose name:
    account number:
    interest:
    balance:

❏ **Tax-exempt money market accounts**
    in whose name:
    account number:
    interest/dividends:
    balance:

Insurance policies (either spouse)

❏ life
❏ homeowners' or renters'
❏ liability
❏ health
❏ children

❏ motor vehicles
❏ personal umbrella
❏ disability
❏ parents

Employee/group insurance benefits (either spouse)

❏ medical
❏ disability

❏ life
❏ long-term care

Other employee benefits

❏ auto allowances
❏ sick pay
❏ travel benefits
    ❏ frequent flyer miles
    ❏ rental car bonus points
    ❏ hotel bonus points
❏ severance pay

❏ expense account
❏ stock options
❏ salary bonuses
❏ deferred compensation
❏ military/VA benefits
❏ workers' compensation claim/award
❏ vacation pay

Financial Facts Checklist (continued)

Retirement plans

- ❏ money purchase plans
- ❏ ESOPs (Employee Stock Ownership Plans)
- ❏ Keoghs
- ❏ thrift plans
- ❏ IRAs or SEP-IRAs
- ❏ SIMPLE IRAs
- ❏ 401(k) plans
- ❏ TSAs (tax-sheltered annuities)
- ❏ profit-sharing plans
- ❏ defined-benefit plans
- ❏ Roth IRAs

Financial statements

- ❏ net worth—balance sheet or assets/liabilities statements
- ❏ cash flow or income/expense statement
- ❏ records documenting collections—gold, coins, stamps, etc.
- ❏ inheritances (include copy of will or other verification of amount received)
- ❏ gifts received
- ❏ personal injury awards
- ❏ prior court judgments
- ❏ personal loans payable
- ❏ anticipated inheritances/gifts
- ❏ litigation claims
- ❏ loan applications
- ❏ personal loans receivable
- ❏ debts
  - ❏ lists of outstanding debts on date of separation
    - ❏ Spouse 1
    - ❏ Spouse 2
    - ❏ joint
- ❏ credit card accounts
  in whose name:
  account number:
  balance:
- ❏ ticket/subscription rights to sports/cultural events
- ❏ memberships in country clubs, fraternal orders, social/charitable groups

Real estate records

- ❏ current value of home(s)
- ❏ original purchase price(s)
- ❏ property tax statements
- ❏ deeds
- ❏ bills for home improvements
- ❏ original mortgage(s)
- ❏ last monthly statement
- ❏ escrow closing statements
- ❏ appraisals

Financial Facts Checklist (continued)	

Safe-deposit box

❑ location/number/key ❑ inventory and/or copies of contents

Documents identifying other property, such as:

❑ patents ❑ copyrights

❑ royalties ❑ license agreements

Miscellaneous personal property, such as:

❑ boat ❑ furs ❑ jewelry

❑ camper ❑ airplane ❑ artwork

❑ other motor vehicles ❑ motorcycle ❑ wine collection

Information on businesses

❑ filing papers ❑ current list of owners

❑ percentage of ownership ❑ officer/director positions held by spouse/self

❑ tax returns ❑ retirement plan documents

❑ bank statements ❑ loan applications

❑ financial statements (last five years) ❑ business agreements (partnership, buy-sell, etc.)

❑ credit card records ❑ appointment diaries

❑ documents on business-owned real estate (deeds, appraisals, leases, etc.)

❑ credit card records

Household furnishings (attach itemized list)

Miscellaneous personal documents

❑ passport

❑ power of attorney

❑ résumé (for self and spouse)

❑ appointment diaries

❑ bills for living expenses (child care, phone, electric, internet access, cleaning, yard work, laundry, etc.)

❑ check stubs for other payments, such as disability income, unemployment compensation, or Social Security benefits

Any other document that will help establish:

❑ net worth	❑ income	❑ liabilities
❑ Spouse 1	❑ Spouse 1	❑ Spouse 1
❑ Spouse 2	❑ Spouse 2	❑ Spouse 2
❑ joint	❑ joint	❑ joint

Facing the Future: What Must I Plan For?

If you're thinking about a divorce or beginning one, you might believe you see only problems ahead. Nevertheless, you need to begin changing your outlook from "we" to "me"—from being a couple to being on your own.

It's helpful at an early stage to set basic goals for yourself. In most goal-setting exercises, you're asked to think about where you'd like to be in a few years—an effective approach for some people. In counseling divorcing clients, however, it's often helpful to turn the question around. If you have trouble looking at the future, answer this:

*Where **don't** you want to be five years from now?*

Speaking financially, few of us want to be in debt, burdened with property we can't sell, or working two jobs to survive. Yet that could happen to you if you drift through a divorce without planning ahead. By thinking about the kinds of financial problems you'd like to avoid, you can narrow your focus and clear the way for what you *do* want to accomplish.

As an initial planning exercise, use the columns in the chart that follows to jot down the immediate problems you foresee, as well as your goals. (Use the examples to give you ideas about your own needs.)

Once you have a basic idea of where you'd like to go in the future, take a few moments to reexamine where you are now. Use these questions to help you think about your own situation.

Major Upcoming Life Events

You can't predict the future, but certain major upcoming events will affect what you will and will *not* be able to do with your money. Some you've anticipated for years. For instance, if your teenagers will begin college soon, you might need a smaller house and a larger paycheck. Or perhaps you're reaching retirement and must prepare for living on a reduced income.

Other events, although not certainties, also warrant planning. If you're in an industry that's downsizing or a company that's being restructured, consider what it might cost to undertake a career shift or pursue more education. Even if you're young and healthy, you should carry insurance in case of an accident. If you have children, you should map out a support system that will kick in should you die or become incapacitated—consider the finances of these arrangements as well as maintenance of the children's overall well-being.

Whatever your situation, remember that a proactive approach is always better than a reactive one. When you anticipate and prepare for major financial events, you can increase your odds of staying afloat by having a backup plan in place to cover related expenses.

Anticipated Financial Commitments

Take a moment to outline what's happening in your life and your anticipated financial commitments. Your list should include a timeline from start to finish. To whom are you committed and for how long? Have you agreed to support aging parents or another family member? How will you fund your commitments—monthly payments or annual installments? What happens if you can't afford these commitments? What other resources are available to you? Will you need money for a business investment or your educational goals? Do you have an adjustable rate or balloon payment mortgage? These types of game-changer events will challenge your ability to shape your financial future.

By getting this information down on paper, not only will you clarify your financial needs, but you can also reduce the fear factor in your vision of the future. You can determine whether a previous commitment, or one you want to make, is realistic. This is an important step to take when you're making key financial decisions in your divorce.

Once your list is complete, mark your top three priorities, in order. These are the issues that should immediately command your time and attention. It's a good idea to tackle only three items at a time, because while you're working on them, your financial condition is likely to change, and your priorities might shift accordingly. This approach is not a one-shot exercise; you can repeat it any time you feel stuck in deciding what to do next in your divorce.

Major Goals That Will Cost Money

We all have personal goals, such as to lose weight, be great parents, and learn new skills. Here, list the important life goals that are likely to affect your finances—and vice versa. These are big-ticket items like owning your own home, gaining the education necessary to improve your employability, or fulfilling an aspiration that's essential to your happiness and sense of accomplishment.

List those goals and estimate their corresponding costs.

Where You Do/Don't Want to Be in the Future	
In the Next Six Months: **Financial Problems to Avoid**	**Financial Goals to Meet**
Examples: Letting bills become overdue Paying only interest due on credit cards Using credit cards for all purchases Not tracking expenses **Problems to Avoid:**	**Examples:** Pay off credit cards, or at least reduce balances by 50% Create a monthly budget calendar to avoid overdue bills Save 5% of income each month in emergency reserve Start monthly investing into XYZ mutual fund **Your Goals:**

Where You Do/Don't Want to Be in the Future (continued)	
In the Next Year: **Financial Problems to Avoid**	**Financial Goals to Meet**
Examples: Not enough money to pay mortgage Being late on mortgage No medical insurance Borrowing from friends or Mom **Your Problems to Avoid:**	**Examples:** Sell house and prepare to buy my own—set aside $20,000 toward down payment Obtain disability insurance policy **Your Goals:**

What's Happening in Your Life	
Major Upcoming Life Events	**Anticipated Financial Commitments**
Examples: Daughter beginning college in two years Move to new home in three years Job change in spring because of recent layoffs Son's wedding next June **Events in Your Life:**	**Examples:** Pay for Dad's health care New car—$300 per month Remodel kitchen—$15,000 **Your Commitments:**

Major Goals That Will Cost Money	
Major Goal	**Expected Price Tag**
Educational:	
Example: Earn M.B.A.	$50,000 over two years
Example: Earn certificate in computer programming	$3,500 over six months
Your Educational Goals:	
Job:	
Example: Acquire contractor's license	$2,000
Example: Expand catering business by getting second truck	$18,000
Your Job Goals:	
Other:	
Example: Get certified as scuba diver	$1,000
Example: Go on African safari	$5,000
Your Other Goals:	

Where Does the Money Come From?

You've taken a look at what you absolutely *must do* and what you'd *like to do* next in your life. But how are you going to pay for it? And what are the consequences of how you bring money into your household?

> ## During Your Separation, Be Aware of Where Your Money Comes From
>
> While separated, you can get money in the same ways you did while married. Funds are available to you through:
> - a job (salary) or business (income)
> - borrowing/credit
> - selling property or assets
> - your spouse—in the form of temporary alimony, or
> - your spouse's payments of marital debts.
>
> But in this time period—between today and the final settlement—you are in a unique situation. You are setting the stage for the settlement, and you do not want to make financial decisions that could work against you. You must be sure to plan ahead and keep detailed, accurate records.
>
> For instance, a woman who had never worked during her marriage got a low-paying job in a retail store and left her children in her parents' care when her husband filed for divorce. In the final settlement, she received no alimony because she was already working to support herself—even though she wanted to go back to school to get training for a better job. Had she borrowed money to live on instead of getting the retail job, she might have been able to make a strong case for alimony.
>
> As this cases illustrates, you must take care to anticipate the consequences of how you handle your money.

If you borrow or use credit cards. Under normal circumstances, financial planners would not recommend that you go into debt. During divorce, however, you might need to borrow money simply to survive. If you must use credit cards, try to find those with the lowest interest rates possible. If you borrow from family or friends, ask whether they will let you start repaying them when you're back on your feet.

It's crucial for you to document any money spent to support yourself and your children. If you use credit or loans to pay for "common necessities of life"—food, shelter, clothing, or medical care—you might be able to obtain reimbursement for half of the costs. (See Chapter 5.)

If you sell property or assets. Before selling any jointly owned property without your spouse's knowledge or consent, ask your attorney whether you're legally permitted to do so. You will not be able to sell real estate, motor vehicles, or other assets with title documents that need both spouses' signatures. If you do sell any joint assets, be sure to set aside half of the proceeds for your spouse, or keep clear records of the money you received so that your spouse gets similarly valued property in the settlement.

If you need temporary alimony. If you need help paying the bills while the divorce is pending, you can request that your spouse pay temporary alimony. If your spouse is unwilling to do so voluntarily, you will need to file paperwork and request a hearing to have the issue resolved by a judge.

For temporary spousal support, the judge looks at the financial needs of the party making the request—particularly that spouse's current income and expenses—and the other spouse's ability to pay temporary alimony. In most places, court officials have issued guidelines (formulas) for judges to use in setting alimony. (For more information on alimony, see Chapter 18.)

Enforcing—and Making Permanent— Temporary Support Agreements

If your temporary alimony agreement is in writing, but has not been ordered by the court, you might want to take that extra step to obtain a court order. Without a court order, you probably won't be able to enforce the agreement if your spouse doesn't pay.

As explained in Chapter 11, getting a court order is not difficult. If you and your spouse agreed to the amount of temporary alimony, you can put your agreement into writing as a "stipulation." You—or your attorney— can then take a few simple steps to get that stipulation turned into a court order. It involves asking the judge to sign the stipulation and issue a support order. You shouldn't have to appear in court, though you might have to pay a filing fee.

Protecting Against Risks to Life, Health, and Property

If you had no choice but to drive through a snowstorm on a curvy road, you would no doubt put chains on the tires and check the antifreeze. In navigating through your divorce, you must also take precautions if you are to survive financially.

Use this chapter to "check the antifreeze"—that is, to make sure you are doing what you can to reduce risks and protect yourself and your property.

Insurance

Insurance is designed to protect you from financial disaster. But when you divorce, your coverage itself might be at risk. Because policies can make for boring reading, and almost no one thinks about this subject until it's too late, insurance needs are commonly forgotten during divorce.

To demonstrate the importance of insurance in your life, ask yourself: *If I were in an accident or became ill, how would I pay my medical expenses?*

Of course, being aware of what can happen without insurance and doing something about your situation are two different things. Review the steps below, then follow up.

Health Insurance

Find copies of your current health insurance policy. Check with your insurance agent to be certain that you and your children are still covered. Find out how long your current policy will remain in effect and what the costs will be for the next six months to one year.

If you're covered under a group policy, you might need to speak to your human resources representative or a special agent or broker who handles the company's health care insurance. If your family is covered by your spouse's insurance, you will be able to keep your coverage for 36 months after the divorce. (See "Keeping Health Care Coverage Through Your Spouse's Employer Under COBRA," below.)

Keeping Health Care Coverage Through Your Spouse's Employer Under COBRA

If your health insurance is provided through a plan offered by your spouse's employer, and 20 or more people work for that employer, you can continue your health care coverage for a period of time after the divorce. Under the federal COBRA (Consolidated Omnibus Budget Reform Act), divorced spouses of employed medical plan participants can pay for their own coverage for up to 36 months after the divorce is final. Under the law, the premiums you're charged for the COBRA coverage may not exceed 102% of what the employer pays to cover you. But you should check the costs of other health plans before deciding to get COBRA coverage through your spouse's employer. (For more information, contact your local office of the federal Department of Labor and check the department's website, www.dol.gov—choose "Health Plans & Benefits: Continuation of Health Coverage—COBRA," under the "Topics" tab.)

Your spouse's employer must inform you of your right to continue the coverage when your divorce becomes final. Don't leave it to your ex-spouse to notify the employer of that date. You should contact your ex-spouse's employer (probably the human resources department) and request the continued health care coverage as soon as your divorce is final.

Remember, the maximum length of time you can continue the coverage is 36 months. If you are healthy, start looking into individual coverage immediately. It might cost less than the continued group coverage. (Ask whether the provider of your continued coverage offers conversion to individual coverage. Be aware that such plans are usually expensive and limited in benefits.) Also, if you get a new job that provides group health insurance or if you remarry and your new spouse's employer offers group coverage, your continued coverage will usually be terminated.

Even if your ex-spouse's employer has fewer than 20 employees, state law may require the employer to provide COBRA-type benefits. For more information, contact your state department of labor, the personnel office at your spouse's job, your attorney, or your financial adviser.

You can also look for medical insurance under the Affordable Care Act (ACA), also called "Obamacare," and see whether a plan through the ACA would be more cost effective than your options under COBRA.

Parents with custody can get health insurance for their children through the *noncustodial* parent's employment-related insurance program (or other group insurance plan), according to federal law. Neither the noncustodial parent, that parent's employer, nor that parent's insurance company may deny coverage for any of the following reasons:

- The child does not live with the noncustodial parent.
- The child is not claimed as a dependent on the noncustodial parent's federal income tax return.
- The child lives outside of the plan's service area.

One challenge that the parent with custody might face is the noncustodial parent's reluctance to turn over money received for reimbursed medical claims. To avoid this problem, the custodial parent can obtain a qualified medical child support order, known as a QMCSO.

A QMCSO is a court order that provides for health coverage for the child of the noncustodial parent under that parent's group health plan. When this court order is implemented, it requires the noncustodial parent's employer to enroll the child in the group plan. Further, the QMCSO requires that the insurance company reimburse the custodial parent directly for health care expenses incurred by the custodial parent for the child's benefit. This guarantees that custodial parents actually receive reimbursement for out-of-pocket contributions for a child's health care expenses. (For more on QMCSOs, see Chapter 18.)

Life Insurance

When you divorce, you need to reconsider who should be named the beneficiary of any life insurance policies. Often, divorcing people forget to change beneficiaries. Then, years later, when such a person dies, the *ex*-spouse could get all the benefits—even if there is a second spouse or if the deceased spouse wanted someone else, such as a child, to be the beneficiary.

In some divorce settlement agreements, the spouses may identify the beneficiaries of their life insurance policies. In certain cases, the judge might make a similar order. If your settlement agreement or divorce decree says who the beneficiary will be, but you forget to change the policy, the beneficiaries named in the agreement or decree might be protected when you die. But they might also end up in a messy fight with the insurance company or your former spouse's heirs, with no guarantee they will win. Don't rely on the settlement agreement or divorce decree to name the beneficiary.

At the same time, don't automatically remove your spouse from your policy when you separate. You might be prohibited from doing so until after your divorce is final. Also, to provide for your children's support and college education, you may want to either establish a trust or keep your soon-to-be ex-spouse as the beneficiary of your policy. This way, your spouse will receive a lump sum of cash to rear your minor children if you die before they reach adulthood.

RESOURCE
For more on trusts, see *Make Your Own Living Trust,* **by Denis Clifford (Nolo).**

If you are paying alimony, your ex-spouse might insist on being the beneficiary of a life insurance policy. That will keep your ex-spouse from losing the stream of income you provide if you die prematurely.

Sometimes, one spouse might want to name the children as beneficiaries rather than have any money go to the children's other parent. Think carefully before you make such a move. If the children are under 18 when you die, the probate court that oversees the distribution of your assets will require that a guardian be appointed to manage the insurance proceeds—usually in a bank account—until the children reach 18. If the guardian wants to remove money from the account, called a blocked or suspended account, the guardian will need court approval—an expensive, time-consuming, and cumbersome procedure. And even when the money is distributed to the children at age 18, keep in mind that young adults are rarely mature enough to handle large amounts of money.

If you are receiving alimony or child support, don't overlook the importance of maintaining life insurance on your spouse so that these payments are protected. Keep existing life insurance in force or add a new policy on the life of the person paying support. (See Chapter 18 for more on alimony.)

Disability Insurance

Another risk to your income is that you—or the ex-spouse who is paying support—might become disabled. If you're dependent on support, either spousal or child, you might want to consider obtaining disability insurance on your paying spouse. Talk to the benefits department at your spouse's company to see whether disability insurance is available. Or contact your insurance agent to determine the cost of getting disability coverage either for you or for the paying spouse.

Especially if you're a single parent, you might hesitate to buy disability insurance due to the expense and your perceived lack of need. Consider the harsh reality your children would face, however, if you became disabled and unable to work.

Look After Your Life Insurance

Would you want your soon-to-be ex-spouse to benefit from your life insurance? When you divorce, you both must make sure that the disposition of any life insurance policies you own is clearly specified in your agreements. These questions can help you clarify what needs to be done with these policies:

- Who will own the policy if it is transferred?
- To whom may it be transferred?
- Are there any restrictions or conditions of transfer?
- Will the original owner get the policy back at some future time (for example, upon remarriage, termination of spousal/child support, or death of the person to whom the policy was transferred)?

Look After Your Life Insurance (continued)

- Are there any outstanding policy loans? If yes, who will pay these loans?
- Will the policy owner have the right to designate beneficiaries? If yes, are there any restrictions on who is named a beneficiary? Must the policy owner designate a beneficiary (that is, an irrevocable beneficiary)?
- If so, does the restriction end upon a remarriage, termination of spousal support, or a death?
- If the beneficiary is a child, does this designation end when the child support obligation ends?
- If a policy matures during the lifetime of the insured person (as can happen with an annuity or an endowment policy), who will receive the maturity proceeds?
- What other policy rights will be affected by ownership or beneficiary restrictions? (These rights might include cash surrender, policy loans, or dividends.)
- Who will pay the premiums, and for how long?
- What happens if premiums are not paid? (While negotiating your settlement, you may want to require the payer spouse to provide evidence of payment to the other spouse at least ten days before the end of the policy's grace period.)
- Does a policy provision state what will happen if a premium is not paid—for example, that it will be paid via an automatic premium loan, paid-up insurance premiums, or extended term insurance?

If your settlement agreement or judgment makes changes to the life insurance policy, you must notify the insurance company and complete the necessary forms. Ideally, your agreement should give the spouse who will keep the policy until a certain date to complete the forms; if that spouse does not comply, the agreement should permit the court to complete the forms on that spouse's behalf.

(© Northwestern Mutual Life Insurance Company. Reprinted with permission.)

Business Continuation Coverage

Do you or your spouse own a business? Check to see if you have insurance referred to as "key man" coverage. This coverage is designed so that the business can cover its operational costs in the event of the death of the business owner or another key person.

Property and Estate Protection

While the ultimate fate of your property might be unknown at the moment, you should nevertheless protect your interests by double-checking title documents and reviewing your will, trusts, and other documents that dispose of your property at death.

Title Documents

To divide assets and negotiate your divorce settlement, you must know how title (history of ownership) to those assets is legally recorded, regardless of whether that property is ultimately considered your separate property or part of the marital assets. Real estate title documents (deeds) are located at the county records office, usually called the county recorder. If you can't find the deeds at the recorder's office, a title company can help you. The recorder may have a website where you can order a copy of a recorded document (expect to pay a fee). You can also ask a real estate agent for a "property profile" (usually free) that shows how title is held, or ask your mortgage company for loan documents, including any recorded deeds.

You should take a look at all recorded deeds to make sure your spouse has not unilaterally removed your name from property the two of you held jointly. In most states, either spouse can change title held in joint tenancy into tenancy in common, and you want to be sure your spouse hasn't done this without your consent.

Joint Tenancy and Tenancy in Common

Joint tenancy property is owned with each joint tenant having a "right of survivorship." This means that if either joint tenant dies, the other owner automatically inherits the deceased's portion, even if a will or another document states otherwise. To sell joint tenancy property, all owners must agree, or the owner who wants to sell must change title from joint tenancy to a different form of ownership, called tenancy in common, and then sell that share. Tenancy in common does not have the right of survivorship. Either owner can leave—or sell—that owner's share. (For more on joint tenancy property, see Chapter 6.)

Title documents for other types of property—for example, car registration forms and bank account and investment statements—are located in different places. To protect yourself from having your spouse unilaterally change title, you should write to the Department of Motor Vehicles or your bank or stockbroker to ask that no title changes take place until the divorce is settled.

Wills, Trusts, and Other Estate Planning Documents

If you've made a will or living trust or taken other measures to determine what will happen to your property after your death, your divorce most likely alters those plans dramatically.

In many states, a final divorce judgment automatically revokes part or all of your will. It's common for divorce to cancel all parts of your will that leave property to your ex-spouse; in some states, the entire will is wiped out. In any case, you should make a new will.

If you die before your divorce is final, your spouse may be entitled to a share or all of your property—even if your will leaves everything to other beneficiaries. To be certain about the distribution of your property, you can consult a Nolo estate planning publication (see the resource list at the end of this chapter) or a trusts and estates attorney.

CAUTION

Take steps to ensure that your property is distributed according to your wishes. If you don't have a will and haven't arranged to transfer your property by other means (for example, joint tenancy or a living trust), your property will be distributed at your death according to state law. Usually this means your spouse and children will get your property. If you're divorced and have no children, your property will probably go to your parents, siblings, and siblings' children. If that's not what you want, make sure you take the time to make a new will.

Planning for Your Children

If you have children, it's especially important to have an estate plan. At the least, consider:

- who will physically care for your children if you can't
- how your children will be supported if you're not around, and
- who will manage the property you leave them if they are under 18.

In your will, you can name someone to be the personal guardian of your children and have physical custody. And you can name the same person, or someone else, to manage the property your children inherit from you. As for figuring out how to support the children after your death, you may want to consider term life insurance, which provides a preset amount of money if you die while the policy is in force. It's a relatively cheap way to provide quick cash for beneficiaries.

Questions to Ask an Attorney

1. Can I change the beneficiary of my life insurance from my spouse to my children during the divorce? How and when can I do that?
2. Can the divorce settlement include a provision for life insurance on the person who provides support, to protect the support order or alimony?
3. As additional alimony or a separate provision, can the settlement include a provision for health insurance? Disability insurance?

Nolo's Estate Planning Tools

Nolo publishes several books and software products on wills, living trusts, and avoiding probate:

- *Quicken WillMaker & Trust* is interactive software that helps you make a sophisticated will. For example, with *WillMaker* you can choose among three ways to provide property management for children should you die before they are competent to handle property themselves. In addition, *WillMaker* allows you to express your last wishes for your funeral and burial and contains a health care directive (living will) and a durable power of attorney for finances, all valid in your state.

- *Plan Your Estate*, by Denis Clifford, is a comprehensive estate planning book, covering everything from basic estate planning (wills and living trusts) to sophisticated tax-saving strategies (AB trusts and much more).

- *Quick & Legal Will Book*, by Denis Clifford, is a primer for the do-it-yourself-minded who have the confidence and thoroughness to create detailed wills without an attorney's oversight. The book also provides the necessary forms for married and single individuals.

- *Nolo's Online Will* has a similar scope, and also includes tools to ensure that the will meets your state's legal criteria.

- *8 Ways to Avoid Probate*, by Mary Randolph, explains important and frequently overlooked ways to avoid probate, an often lengthy process of certifying a will. It is now possible to avoid probate for many kinds of property without creating a living trust. If you suspect you should be paying attention to probate avoidance, but dread thinking about it, start with this small and thorough book.

- *Make Your Own Living Trust*, by Denis Clifford, explains in plain English how to create a trust yourself, without hiring a lawyer. It contains all the forms you need to create your own living trust with step-by-step instructions for filling them out.

Taxes: How Do I File and Pay?

When you're divorcing, you can't wait until just before April 15 to think about your taxes.

While you don't have to confront every small detail in your tax papers when you're in the midst of a separation, you can and should take basic precautions that might save you money and prevent hassles later.

For instance, suppose you assume that you and your divorcing spouse will file income taxes jointly. At tax time, however, you discover your spouse has already filed separately. How will you pay the IRS for taxes you didn't expect to owe? Better to grapple with the filing question now than to make costly assumptions.

The following guidelines will help you address the income tax questions that are most important at this stage of your divorce. As you move through the rest of the divorce process, you will face more complicated tax issues regarding your property, many of which fall outside the scope of divorce law and this book. When you do face more complex tax law questions, you should consult with your accountant or another tax expert that you trust, but for now, let's stick to the basics.

Get a Rough Estimate of Your Tax Bill

To try and avoid nasty surprises when taxes are due (usually April 15), make a rough calculation of your federal and state taxes. Ask your accountant or tax preparer to help you if need be. Figure out the amount you would pay if you filed separately and the amount you would pay if you filed with your spouse. Even if you haven't done all the paperwork— or don't have all the information necessary to find the exact amount— it's useful to get a tax estimate. The estimate will at least give you a guide for deciding how to file. You'll also be able to use the information if you eventually need to convince your spouse to file jointly.

If possible, discuss the tax filing decision with your spouse, lawyer, accountant, and/or tax adviser. Your goal is to reach an agreement about filing and then document that agreement in writing.

If you don't have access to tax information. Often, one spouse does most of the bookkeeping for a family. If your spouse played that role and doesn't t want to give you the information voluntarily, you might have to get a court order or use legal discovery (evidence-gathering) techniques. For either, you'll probably need the help of an attorney. Consult the appendix for resources. Before hiring a lawyer, be sure to remind your spouse that withholding information will only increase both of your legal bills, and you'll get the information eventually.

You can contact your accountant for copies of previous tax returns, or ask the IRS for Form 4506. By completing the form and returning it to the IRS, you should be able to get the tax returns you need—as long as you signed the return when it was filed. The easiest way to get forms is to visit www.irs.gov. From there, you can link to state tax forms, tax tables, and publications and search for divorce-related tax topics. Upon request, the IRS will send you an account transcript, created from information on your tax returns, from as far back as ten years.

The IRS has several publications that can help during a divorce. The most important are:

- Publication 17, *Your Federal Income Tax (for Individuals)*
- Publication 501, *Exemptions, Standard Deduction, and Filing Information*
- Publication 504, *Divorced or Separated Individuals*
- Publication 505, *Tax Withholding and Estimated Tax*, and
- Publication 555, *Community Property*. If you live in one of the community property states of Arizona, California, Idaho, Louisiana, Nevada, New Mexico, Texas, Washington, or Wisconsin (Alaska allows married couples to opt into a community property system, and spouses in Florida, Kentucky, Tennessee, and South Dakota have the option of identifying property held in trust as community property), many federal tax rules are applied differently than in the other states, which are called "equitable distribution states."

If you have to wait for copies of previous years' returns and financial information, you can work with a tax accountant to estimate the amount you will owe the IRS. You can find out about deductions in several ways. Banks and lenders can tell you how much interest has been paid on a mortgage, and certain charities can give you the dollar amount you or your spouse donated. You can try calling your spouse's employer to verify salary information (although they won't always speak to you), and check copies of any loan applications you have. Chapter 12 will walk you through preparing "Net Worth" and "Cash Flow" statements, which can also help clarify your tax situation.

Which Status Is Better to Use When Filing Tax Returns?

One of the most important decisions you'll need to make is whether to file a joint return with your spouse or to file separately. The table below summarizes the types of filing status available to you and the requirements for each.

When in Doubt, File Separately

If you and your spouse are unable to agree on how to handle your taxes, file separately. Generally, you can amend two separate returns (yours and your spouse's) to file jointly if you change your minds. You cannot, however, amend a joint return after the due date for that return in order to file separately. If you initially file separately, you have three years to amend your returns and file jointly. Note that *filing separately might actually cost more in dollars*, but on the other hand, it could save you some stress and grief.

You will, of course, want to file separately if it will save on taxes—but you should also file this way if your spouse misrepresents income or expenses. If you file jointly, you could be liable for back taxes, interest, and penalties on a joint return. By filing separately, you will lessen your risk and keep your options open. Bear in mind that if you file separately, you give up your right to claim certain tax deductions. These include education credits, child or dependent care expenses in most instances, the earned income credit, and interest paid on student loans.

Except in community property states, if you file a separate return, you generally report only your own income, exemptions, credits, and deductions. If your spouse had no income, you can claim an exemption for your spouse. If your spouse refuses to provide the information necessary to file a joint return, you should file a separate return.

Filing Status	Requirements
Married filing jointly	You must be married up to and including the last day of the tax year (December 31) even if you are living apart.
Married filing separately	You must be married up to and including the last day of the tax year.
Head of household	If you are single: • you must provide more than half of the costs of maintaining your household, and • your household must be the principal home of at least one dependent. If you are married and have lived physically apart since before July 1 of the tax year: • you must file a separate return • you must maintain your home and have your child, stepchild, or other dependent living there for more than half the tax year (temporary absences such as vacations, time in school, and time when a child is absent under a custody agreement do not count as time spent away) • you must be able to claim the child as a dependent or release that claim (provide your spouse with a waiver—see Form 8332), and • you must furnish more than half the cost of maintaining the household during the tax year. (In figuring that cost, include clothing, education, medical treatment, mortgage principal payments, vacations, life insurance, transportation, and the value of services performed in the household by the taxpayer. Exclude property taxes, mortgage interest, rent, repairs, utilities, home insurance, and food eaten in the home.)
Single	You must be unmarried, legally separated, or have your marriage annulled as of the last day of the tax year and be ineligible for head of household status.

Avoiding Liability for Your Spouse's Dishonesty With the IRS

The IRS Restructuring and Reform Act of 1998 provides relief from joint liability when a spouse incorrectly reports items on a jointly filed tax return. The three kinds of relief and the factors influencing them are shown below. Innocent Spouse Relief is for all joint filers. It relieves you of some or all of the responsibility for paying tax, interest, and penalties if your spouse did something wrong on your joint tax return. The Separate Liability Election permits you to limit your liability for any deficiency to the amount that would be allocated to you if you had filed a separate return. Rules for Equitable Relief give the IRS discretion to relieve you of liability when you cannot qualify for relief under the rules for Innocent Spouse Relief or the Separate Liability Election.

Two additional forms of relief are available for spouses in community property states. If one spouse fails to inform the other of community property income, the IRS can force that spouse to pay 100% of the tax due on the income that was kept secret. Also, if a couple has lived separately for an entire calendar year and each spouse has filed a separate return, the community income would be taxed to the person who earns it.

If you believe you may qualify for relief, go to the IRS website, www.irs.gov and search for "innocent spouse relief." The site will guide you through the qualifying factors one question at a time and, if you appear to qualify for the relief, download the appropriate application forms. You can also download Publication 971, *Innocent Spouse Relief*, at www.irs.gov/publications/p971. Before filling out the forms, however, consult your tax adviser and consider consulting a tax attorney who specializes in this area of the law.

Special Rules for Taxpayers Living in a Community Property State

As explained in detail in Chapter 12, married couples in Arizona, California, Idaho, Louisiana, Nevada, New Mexico, Texas, Washington, and Wisconsin live under community property laws. (Alaska allows married couples to opt into a community property system, and spouses in Florida, Kentucky, Tennessee, and South Dakota have the option of identifying property held in trust as community property.)

Although these states' community property laws generally all operate in the same way, there are differences among the states. One significant variation is how they treat income from separate property. Some treat it as separate income, while others consider it community income even though it comes from separate property. (See "Questions to Ask a Tax Adviser" at the end of this chapter.)

Broadly, these rules provide that income earned and assets acquired during marriage are owned 50-50, regardless of which spouse actually brought home the paycheck. Before filing a separate tax return in a community property state, check with a tax adviser. You will probably have to report half of the combined community income and be permitted to take half of the joint deductions, in addition to reporting your separate income and claiming your deductions. As straightforward as this sounds, it's not always clear whether a deduction (expense) is community or separate. It basically depends on whose money was used to pay it and the character of the debt. If you paid an expense out of community funds, you must divide it equally and report half of it on each spouse's return.

Community property laws also affect exemptions for dependents. When community income supports a dependent child, the exemption may be claimed by either spouse, but it can't be divided. If you have two or more dependent children, you can divide the exemptions (each claiming a child), but you can't divide any single exemption in half. If you both try to take the exemption, the IRS will assume that each of you provided exactly half of the support and won't permit either of you to claim the exemption.

A Note on Tax Rates

We can be no more certain than anyone else that the tax rate figures used in this book will be current by the time you read them.

In the interest of sanity and clarity, this book uses all the 2023 rates in the examples and sticks with the current brackets—generally 10%, 12%, 22%, 24%, 32%, 35%, and 37%, with taxes on capital gains at 0%, 15%, and 20% (plus a 1.45% Medicare tax). The planning principles outlined in this book apply regardless of any future rate adjustments, but in the event of new tax laws, you might need to plug new numbers into the worksheets you find here.

The changes to the tax code make advance planning for your tax filings—always a sound strategy—even more important if you are facing the prospect of divorce in the near future.

What to Know If You File Jointly

Filing a joint return is often to your economic advantage. A married taxpayer can claim the child and dependent care credit and the earned income credit (for low-income taxpayers) only on a joint return. In addition, certain deductions—such as the dependency exemption for a spouse and the deduction for a spousal IRA contribution—can be taken only on a joint return.

In deciding whether to file a joint return, you will want to calculate—or talk to your tax adviser about—how each of these factors will affect your tax bill:

- your tax rate
- any deductions or credits you may lose
- tax losses from partnerships or business losses
- tax benefits available by filing a joint return as compared to filing separately, and
- your liability for your spouse's dishonesty in reporting income and taking deductions when you file a joint return. (See below.)

Liability on Joint Tax Returns

If you file a joint return, each spouse is liable for 100% of the taxes due on the return as well as any penalties and interest assessed on that return. Unless you qualify as an innocent spouse (see "Avoiding Liability for Your Spouse's Dishonesty With the IRS," above), you are generally liable for any unpaid taxes, even after your divorce is final. (In some cases, if you sign a joint return under duress or your spouse forges your name, the IRS may not consider you jointly liable, but you should consult a tax attorney experienced in this area of the law.)

If you believe your spouse is being dishonest in reporting income or claiming deductions and credits, file a separate return—even if it is to your economic disadvantage. If it turns out that your spouse was being honest, you can always amend your returns and file jointly within three years of the original due dates. You cannot, however, amend a joint return and file separate returns later.

The federal government increasingly gets involved in collecting past-due child support and alimony payments. If the IRS withheld a tax refund on your joint return because your spouse was behind in child support or alimony payments, you may qualify as an "injured" spouse and be able to recover your share of that refund. There's an easy process for doing this. Simply go to the IRS website, www.irs.gov, download and complete Form 8379, and return it to the IRS.

Additional factors to consider include your responsibility when signing a joint return and liabilities you could incur if your spouse signs your name to a return or refuses to sign the return.

Your Responsibility When Signing a Joint Return

According to the IRS, you may not ignore the information on any income tax return you sign. Legally, you must examine the return and make certain that any transaction of which you are aware is properly reported.

What If Your Spouse Refuses to Sign a Joint Return?

If a spouse refuses to file a joint return and instead files separately, the other spouse must also file a separate return.

One spouse can file a joint return using only that spouse's name if the other spouse meets all the following requirements:

- refuses to file a joint return
- doesn't file a separate one
- had no income or earnings, and
- always filed a joint return in the past.

This works only if it is clear that the couple intended to file a joint return. If the refusing spouse feels the prepared return is fraudulent and won't sign as a result, the other spouse cannot file a joint return without the refusing spouse's signature.

Other Concerns When Filing a Joint or Separate Return

You may have several other concerns regarding your spouse and the IRS, such as the following.

What If Your Spouse Settles a Tax Bill With the IRS?

Suppose one spouse makes an agreement (called an "offer in compromise") to pay the IRS less than the actual taxes due, plus interest and penalties, on a jointly filed return. That agreement doesn't prevent the IRS from collecting money from the other spouse for the balance due. If the ex-spouse who is not covered in the settlement remarries, that person's new spouse also could be subject to unforeseen tax liabilities.

For instance, in one case, a widow had reached a settlement with the IRS to take care of significant tax liabilities that were attributable to her deceased husband. When she remarried, she had not finished paying the amount mandated by the settlement. She also transferred property she received from her first husband's estate to her new husband. The IRS sought to collect the balance of the settlement from the second husband, who tried to argue that he should not be responsible for the payments because he did not participate in the original agreement. The court found, however, that because the property had been transferred to him, the IRS could collect the debt from him as well, and therefore, he had to pay up. (Although this example involved a widow, the same principle would apply had she been divorced and transferred her divorce settlement property to her new husband.)

Will an Indemnity Clause in a Divorce Agreement Protect You From the IRS?

An "indemnity clause" is a section in a marital settlement or separation agreement in which one spouse agrees to pay the tax liability and to hold the other spouse harmless—in other words, ensure that the other spouse doesn't have to pay. This clause, however, isn't binding on the IRS. Except in unusual circumstances, the IRS can grab a joint taxpayer's property even after it has been divided in divorce to satisfy a joint tax debt. In that case, the indemnity clause means that the spouse who ended up paying the debt can collect reimbursement from the other spouse.

What If Your Marriage Is Annulled?

If your marriage is legally annulled, the IRS takes the position that it never existed. If you filed joint tax returns during your marriage, you will have to file corrected returns (as a single person) for the preceding three years. You must do this even if you had no separate income to declare.

Dividing the Joint Tax Liability—or the Refund

Once you have prepared a joint income tax return, you might discover that you owe additional taxes or are due a refund. To avoid animosity and misunderstandings, you and your spouse must find a fair way to share the tax liability or divide the refund.

Of course, you need not do all of this work by yourself; a tax preparer can make these calculations for you. No matter who does the math, plug the numbers into the formula below. To do so, you must first figure out what you each would have owed (or would have received as a refund) if you had filed separately.

Example: How to Calculate Your Share of a Refund on a Joint Tax Return

	Example	You
1. Your individual separate tax liability (married filing separately)	$3,000	
2. Your spouse's individual separate tax liability (married filing separately)	$7,000	
3. Total separate tax liability [Step 1 + Step 2]	$10,000	
4. Joint tax liability on return (married filing jointly)	$6,000	
5. Your share of the total tax liability [Step 1 ÷ Step 3]	0.30	
6. Your spouse's share of the total tax liability [Step 2 ÷ Step 3]	0.70	
7. Your share of joint tax liability [Step 4 × Step 5]	$1,800	
8. Your spouse's share of joint tax liability [Step 4 × Step 6]	$4,200	
9. Total tax payments made by couple	$12,000	
10. Total tax payment made by you [in Step 9]	$3,000	
11. Your share of the refund [Step 10 – Step 7]	$1,200	

Step 1.   Prepare a separate tax return for yourself using the "married filing separately" status to find the amount you would owe individually if you and your spouse filed alone.

Step 2.   Prepare a separate tax return for your spouse using the "married filing separately" status to find the amount your spouse would owe individually if you and your spouse filed alone.

Step 3.   Add together each spouse's individual separate tax liability to determine the total amount of your separate tax liabilities.

Step 4.   Prepare a joint tax return using the "married filing jointly" status to determine your total joint tax liability.

Step 5.   Determine the percentage of the total taxes you owe by dividing your individual separate tax liability by the total separate tax liability.

Step 6.   Determine the percentage of the total taxes your spouse owes by dividing your spouse's individual separate tax liability by the total separate tax liability.

Step 7.   Determine the amount of the total taxes you owe by multiplying your joint tax liability by the percentage of the total taxes you owe.

Step 8.   Determine the amount of the total taxes your spouse owes by multiplying your joint tax liability by the percentage of the total taxes your spouse owes.

Step 9.   Calculate the total tax payments made by each spouse by adding all federal tax withheld, as shown on the W-2 forms, and all estimated tax payments made. If this amount is less than the amount in Step 4, more money must be paid to the IRS; if this amount is more than the amount in Step 4, the IRS will send you a refund.

If you owe more to the IRS:

Step 10.   Subtract the total amount of tax payments made by each spouse (Step 9) from each spouse's separate share of the joint tax liability (Steps 5 and 6).

Step 11.   Send a payment to the IRS for the amount due. The spouse who pays the IRS is entitled to be reimbursed by the other spouse, who must make up the difference between what they have already paid individually (through withholding or estimated tax payments) and that spouse's share of the amount the couple still owes the IRS.

If you are entitled to a refund:

Step 10.   Determine the amount of the total tax payment that should be refunded to each spouse by subtracting each spouse's individual share of the joint tax liability (Steps 7 and 8) from the amount each spouse has already paid to the IRS (through withholding or estimated tax payments).

Step 11.   The spouse who receives the refund from the IRS must reimburse the other spouse as determined in Step 10.

> **(!) CAUTION**
> **If you and your spouse anticipate receiving a tax refund on your joint return, don't forget that this money is likely to be considered marital property.** That means it will be assigned or divided between the spouses as part of the property division upon divorce. For more on dividing up property, see Chapter 12.

Tax Issues Involving Temporary Alimony or Child Support

Often in divorce negotiations or mediation, spouses reach informal agreements about temporary alimony or child support payments. But sometimes they neglect to get the agreement in writing or to get a court order outlining the agreement. Do not make this mistake. (Read Chapter 18 before entering into any agreement to pay or receive alimony or child support.)

Getting a court order is not difficult. If you and your spouse agree on the amount of temporary alimony and/or child support, you can put your agreement in writing as a "stipulation." You (or your attorney) can then take the simple steps needed to get that stipulation turned into a court order. It involves asking a judge to sign the stipulation. You and your spouse should not have to appear in court.

Under former Internal Revenue Code 26 U.S.C.A. Section 215, court-ordered alimony—including temporary alimony—was tax deductible to the paying spouse. The spouse receiving alimony had to report the payments as income.

However, the 2017 Republican tax bill removed the alimony deduction. Under the Tax Cuts and Jobs Act, for any alimony agreements executed after December 31, 2018, paying spouses can't deduct alimony payments on their taxes, and supported spouses no longer have to include alimony as income. Divorcing couples will have to consider these tax rules as they structure or amend alimony agreements.

Child support is neither deductible for the parent paying it nor taxable as income to the parent receiving it. However, regardless of whether you and your spouse are living apart, you will want to make arrangements for child support so that your children are adequately cared for. For more on child support agreements, see Chapter 18.

Get Your Tax Agreement in Writing

Whatever you and your spouse decide to do about taxes, be sure to get the agreement in writing. Have it notarized and have a divorce attorney review it, if you can afford to do so. Be certain, too, to check with an accountant or a financial planner for advice on the tax implications of your divorce.

RESOURCE
For more information on dealing with the IRS, see *Stand Up to the IRS*, by Frederick W. Daily and Stephen Fishman (Nolo).

Questions to Ask a Tax Adviser

1. In my state, is income from separate property considered separate or marital income?
2. What income from separate property is considered to be separate property?
3. If my spouse and I ran a business while we were married, under what circumstances must I report the income and deductions on my own tax return now?
4. Is the income I earned after we separated but before the divorce becomes final considered separate or marital income? ●

Property and Expenses:
Who Owns and Who Owes What?

12

What—exactly—is at stake in your divorce? To answer that question, you must get a handle on your property.

In this chapter, you will learn how to define which property is legally yours and which assets you might have to struggle for in the tug-of-war of divorce. You will also develop a much-needed picture of your cash flow. Finally, you will learn how to use legal discovery procedures if you have any trouble getting the information you need. The financial fact-finding you did in Chapter 8 (you *did* do it, didn't you?) will be immensely helpful here.

By completing the tasks that follow, you will lay the foundation for the analysis and decision making that must be done to reach your final settlement. Think of this stage as developing your database or stocking your pantry with the items you'll need throughout the divorce process.

The four basic issues you must address at this point are covered in the following sections:

- Who Owns What—Marital Property and the Laws of Your State
- Who Knows What—Using Legal Discovery
- Net Worth—What Do You Own and What Do You Owe?
- Cash Flow—Where Does the Money Go?

Who Owns What—Marital Property and the Laws of Your State

Before you begin to negotiate your divorce settlement, you must know what property you own alone or separately—as opposed to what property your spouse owns solely or the two of you own together (jointly). Keep in mind that the rules that follow are general. To get the specific property laws of your state, you'll need to consult a lawyer in your area or do some legal research.

Read this section for an overview of ownership, and then do whatever additional research is needed. Once you have determined which of your property is separate and which is marital, you will list this information in the "Net Worth Statement" in "Net Worth—What Do You Own and What Do You Owe?" below.

Jointly Owned Property

The property that couples accumulate during marriage is called, straightforwardly enough, "marital" property. Depending on which state you live in, however, marital property will take different forms and may also be referred to as "joint" property or "community" property.

Community property: Arizona, California, Idaho, Louisiana, Nevada, New Mexico, Texas, Washington, and Wisconsin. (Alaska allows married couples to opt into a community property system. In Florida, Kentucky, South Dakota, and Tennessee, spouses have the option of identifying property held in trust as community property.) In community property states, all earnings during marriage and all property acquired with those earnings are considered community property the couple jointly owns. Even if one spouse earned a salary during the marriage while the other worked in the home raising the couple's children or maintaining the household, the salaried spouse's earnings are shared equally and considered community income.

In community property states, separate property—that is, property that is not "community"—consists for the most part of money and property that the individual spouses owned before marriage, and gifts and inheritances that either spouse receives at any time, including during marriage.

At divorce, community property is divided equally (50/50) between the spouses. A spouse who contributed separate property funds to the purchase of an item with community funds—for instance, a wife who contributed her $5,000 inheritance toward a $20,000 down payment for the family home—may be entitled to a dollar-for-dollar reimbursement for that contribution. Conversely, a spouse who added community property money to a separate property item belonging to the other spouse may also be entitled to a reimbursement.

In community property states, the default is that community property will be divided equally upon divorce. However, in most community property states, courts have the discretion to divide property equitably (fairly) if dividing the property in half would result in unfairness to one party.

Equitable distribution of property: all other states. In all other U.S. states, family law courts follow the equitable distribution principles that assets and earnings accumulated during marriage are divided equitably (fairly) at divorce. In theory, equitable means equal, or nearly so. In some equitable distribution states, if a spouse obtains a fault divorce, the "guilty" spouse might receive less than a full share of the marital property upon divorce.

Separately Owned Property

In all states, a married person can treat certain types of earnings and assets as separate property. At divorce, this separate property isn't divided under the state's property distribution laws, but rather, the spouse who owns it keeps it.

In community property states, the following is considered separate property:
- property acquired before marriage
- property acquired during marriage with premarital earnings (such as a premarital savings account or income from a pension that vested before marriage)
- property acquired with the proceeds of the sale of separately owned premarital property
- gifts given to only one spouse
- inheritances, and
- property acquired after permanent separation.

In the equitable distribution states, separate property includes:
- property accumulated before marriage
- gifts given to only one spouse, and
- inheritances.

In addition, some equitable distribution states consider wages kept separate from other marital property to be separate property.

Separate Is Separate Unless It's Mixed

In both community property and equitable distribution states, the separate property of a spouse generally remains separate property. However, if separate property becomes mixed or commingled with marital or community property or the other spouse's separate property, you might not be able to keep your separate property separate, unless you can clearly trace the origin of your separate property and show how it was commingled. This means if you want to make sure you can make a claim to your separate property upon divorce, keep it in a separate account. Don't commingle or mix it into other accounts during the marriage, and make sure you can trace your separate property back to its original source.

Debts

Debts incurred during a marriage are usually considered joint debts, and both spouses are legally responsible for them. When a couple divorces, however, responsibility for marital debts is allocated in accordance with the property division laws of the state.

This usually means that the debts are divided equally or equitably (fairly, though not necessarily in half), especially when they were incurred for food, shelter, clothing, and medical care (called "necessities" or "family living expenses"). When assigning debts, courts also consider which spouse is better able to pay the debts (the spouse with the higher income or lower living expenses). If a couple has many debts but also has a great deal of property, the spouse better able to pay the debts may be ordered to assume the payments and also receive a larger share of the property.

Who Knows What—Using Legal Discovery

Chapter 8 describes several ways for gathering financial information during a divorce. Doing it yourself not only keeps lawyer's fees down, but also educates you about your family's finances and prepares you to negotiate from a position of strength.

If you can't find the information yourself, however, and all efforts to collect it informally fail, your lawyer can conduct "discovery." Discovery is the term for formal procedures used to obtain information during a lawsuit. As with all matters in your divorce, remember that your attorney works for you. You should be the one making the decisions about how extensive discovery procedures should be.

If you've never seen the family checkbook and have signed tax returns for years without reviewing them, then your lawyer might have to do a lot of digging to create a picture of your financial life. Likewise, if you have participated in budgeting and bookkeeping, but your spouse owns a cash-and-carry business that you suspect is being used to hide assets, discovery might be worth every penny you spend.

On the other hand, if you and your spouse have few assets and you have a pretty good idea of what you're both worth, then using discovery to ferret out more information might be a waste of money.

Apply the maxim "think financially and act legally." If you do, you should be fine.

In a divorce, the common discovery devices include the following.

Depositions. A deposition is a proceeding in which a witness or party must answer questions orally, under oath, and before a court reporter. In divorces, many lawyers want to take the other spouse's deposition to ask about key issues in the case and potentially hidden assets.

Interrogatories. Interrogatories are written questions one party sends to the other to be answered in writing under oath. Interrogatories are often used to ask a spouse to list all bank accounts, investment accounts, and other assets ever held by that spouse.

Request for production of documents. This is a request to a party to produce certain defined documents. In divorce cases, spouses often request financial documents from each other, including bank statements, profit and loss statements, tax returns, pay stubs, W-2s, and other documents showing earnings, expenses, assets, and debts.

Subpoena and subpoena duces tecum. A subpoena is a court order telling a witness to appear at a deposition (or at trial). A subpoena duces tecum is an order to provide certain documents to a specific party. These devices are commonly used to get documents or testimony directly from banks, insurance companies, stockbrokers, and the like.

Net Worth—What Do You Own and What Do You Owe?

Generally, couples divide marital net worth at divorce. Subtracting what you owe from what you own reveals that net worth. It is important to know that net worth number because if you go to trial the judge will attempt to see that you each end up with your fair share, depending on the laws of your state. But it's also important for you to know specifically—item by item—what there is to divide. If, as is usually the case, you're able to negotiate a property settlement and avoid a court battle (perhaps with the help of attorneys or a mediator), you'll want to know exactly who owns what and how much it's worth. Only by knowing that can you negotiate the fairest deal.

The "Assets and Liabilities Worksheet" in this chapter will help you figure this out. It will also help you complete the "Marital Balance Sheet" in Chapter 19 that will set out your joint property, the equity in it, and its before-tax value. Your home, for example, might have a fair market value of $600,000. But if the loan is $400,000, you have just $200,000 in equity. Further, you or your spouse may have contributed unequal amounts of separate cash for the down payment. That kind of information must be factored in to get a realistic view of what true assets there are to divide.

While it might seem laborious to compile all these facts and figures, your effort will pay off in succeeding chapters. This book refers back to these lists often. Patience and attention to detail now will be rewarded later.

To figure out your net worth, use the worksheets on the following pages. If you can't fill in everything in each category, don't worry. Gather as much information as you can. If you eventually hire someone to help you, you'll still be far ahead and will have saved money by gathering some of the information yourself.

Do You Hate Filling Out Forms?

Almost no one enjoys the task of writing information into small blanks on financial forms. In your divorce, however, you must get your financial facts straight. Any attorney or other professional you consult will want the information you are documenting in your Net Worth and Cash Flow statements. Most important, you will be organizing the information you must have to make the best decisions in your divorce.

Get help or meet with others who are dealing with the same issues so you can assist each other when the work gets tedious. You are not completing these forms as a mere exercise—you are using them to lay the groundwork for your new financial life.

Make copies of these forms so you can use them throughout your divorce and make changes as events change. Also, keep copies of the documents you consulted while you were filling out the forms.

Instructions: Net Worth Statement Assessing Assets

To determine your net worth, you only need to estimate the current value (last column) of each asset you own. Complete the other columns if the information is available. List all marital property—not just the property in which you have an interest. These columns will help you understand as much as possible about your assets so you can make informed decisions when it comes time to divide your marital property.

As you fill in the information, subtotal the amounts in the last (far right) column for various asset categories (such as real estate or personal property). You will then transfer these subtotals to the "Net Worth: Balance Sheet Summary" that follows.

Column 1: Title [or Owner]. List the owner of each item of property, and note how ownership is listed on any title document. You or your spouse may have an ownership interest in an item of property even if title is in the other spouse's name only. This could happen if marital money or labor went toward the purchase of, payments on, or improvements to the property. Several types of property—such as houses, cars, and stocks—come with title documents (the house deed, car registration, and stock certificate). When property is owned jointly, these title documents specify exactly how title is held—meaning how the property is owned. The possible ways to hold title to property are:

- *Joint tenancy.* Co-owners of joint tenancy property own the property in equal shares. When two or more persons own property as joint tenants, and one owner dies, the remaining owner(s) automatically inherits the share owned by the deceased person. This is termed the "right of survivorship." For example, if a husband and wife own their house as joint tenants and the wife dies, the husband ends up owning the entire house, even if the wife attempted to give away her half of the house in her will.

  In most states, a joint tenant can terminate a joint tenancy and change title to tenancy in common at any time, even without a spouse's knowledge. You only need to do this if you don't want your spouse to inherit your share if you die. The easiest way to do this is to write up a deed stating something like the following: *Leslie Matthews transfers her one-half share of the home at 1312 Lincoln Drive from Leslie Matthews joint tenant to Leslie Matthews tenant in common.*

  When such a change is made, the right to survivorship no longer holds—but if you want the property to go to someone else before your divorce is final, make sure you have a will.

- *Tenancy by the entirety.* Tenancy by the entirety is a way married couples can hold title to property in some non–community property states. Tenancy by the entirety is very similar to joint tenancy in that upon the death of one of the spouses, the property automatically passes to the surviving spouse, regardless of contrary provisions in the will. Unlike joint tenancy, however, one person cannot unilaterally sever the tenancy by the entirety. After divorce, former spouses cannot hold title as tenants by the entirety. Instead, title will be tenancy in common unless you specify joint tenancy.

- *Tenancy in common.* Tenancy in common is a way for any two or more people to hold title to property together. Each co-owner has an "undivided interest" in the property, which means that no owner holds a particular part of the property and all co-owners have the right to use all the property. Each owner is free to sell or give away their interest. On death, an owner's interest passes through a will or by the automatic inheritance laws if the owner had no will. Divorcing spouses who plan to own property together after they split usually hold the property as tenants in common. Occasionally, ex-spouses will hold property in joint tenancy.

- *Community property.* Married couples in community property states can take title as community property. Community property is divided equally at the end of their marriages. Property owned jointly after divorce can't be held as community property.
- *Separate title.* Sometimes title will be in only one person's name, even if both spouses own the property. The property will be divided between the spouses if the spouse whose name is not on the title document can prove an ownership interest. For example, if the house is in the wife's name only, but the canceled checks for the mortgage payments are written on the husband's separate account, the property will be divided.

Column 2: Source [of Asset]. Specify where the money to purchase the asset came from. Be sure to note whether the source was separate or marital property or income, and keep copies of all records that show the disposition of separate property.

Column 3: Date of Purchase/Acquisition. Put the date you bought items or received a gift or an inheritance. For items bought over time—such as shares of the same stock—list all dates and the number of shares bought each time. Use a separate sheet of paper if necessary.

Column 4: Current Balance or Fair Market Value. For deposit accounts and similar investments, list the balance from your last statement. Keep copies of each statement.

Fair market value means what you could sell the item for now, not your purchase price or replacement cost. For valuable assets, such as art, jewelry, collections, antiques, furs, china, and silver, list the wholesale value. To determine these values, you might go to pawnshops, antique stores, jewelers, art galleries, auctioneers, or sterling silver replacement firms; you might also visit secondhand sales sites, like eBay, Craigslist, Facebook Marketplace, Nextdoor, or Poshmark, to find similar sales prices online. If you have a collectible or high-end specialty item, you might need to have it appraised. For automobiles, use the *Kelley Blue Book* at www.kbb.com. For household furniture, furnishings, and personal effects, give your best estimate of the garage sale value (generally 50 to 75% off the price you paid or current retail value).

Important: Use these amounts to calculate your subtotals.

Column 5: Debt. How much do you still owe on this item?

Column 6: Equity or Legal Value. Equity is the actual value of the item after the debt is paid off. Subtract Debt from Current Balance or Fair Market Value to get this figure.

Instructions: Net Worth Statement Calculating Liabilities

The other half of determining your net worth is listing your liabilities (that is, what you owe). The Balance Due in the last column on the worksheet shows what you currently owe in each liability category. But you should also fill in the information in the other columns because it will be useful in working on your Cash Flow Statement and in evaluating assets in your settlement negotiations.

Column 1: Original Amount. Enter the amount you originally borrowed. Don't include interest. For your credit cards, put the amount of your purchases or cash advances.

Column 2: Date Incurred. Put the date the debt was incurred. For credit cards, note the various dates you charged items.

Column 3: Interest Rate. List all interest rates. If the rate is variable (as many mortgages and credit cards are), list the present rate and note that it is variable.

Column 4: Loan Term. How many years do you have to repay the loan or debt?

Column 5: Monthly Payment. List the amount you actually pay each month.

Column 6: Balance Due. Enter how much it would cost to pay off the loan in full. Check with the lender or creditor to determine the loan payoff amount. This balance is your current liability. The subtotal for each liability will be the amount you transfer to the "Net Worth: Balance Sheet Summary" chart, which follows.

Net Worth Statement: Assets and Liabilities Worksheet

Assets	Title S1/S2/J/C [1]	Source S/M [2]	Date of Purchase/ Acquisition	Current Balance or Fair Market Value	Debt	Equity or Legal Value
Cash & Cash Equivalents						
Cash						
Certificates of Deposit (CDs						
Certificates of Deposit (CDs						
Checking						
Checking						
Savings						
Credit Union						
Money Market Funds						
Money Market Funds						
Money Market Funds						
Crypto						
Other Liquid Assets						
Cash & Cash Equivalents Total						

[1] S1=Spouse 1, S2= Spouse 2, J=jointly, C=community property

[2] S=separate property, M=marital property

Net Worth Statement: Assets and Liabilities Worksheet (continued)

Assets	Title S1/S2/J/C [1]	Source S/M [2]	Date of Purchase/ Acquisition	Current Balance or Fair Market Value	Debt	Equity or Legal Value
Marketable Assets & Investments						
Life Insurance (cash values)						
Life Insurance (whole life policies)						
Stocks						
Bonds						
Mutual Funds						
Loans/Accounts Receivable						
General Partnerships						
Limited Partnerships						
Liens & Judgments Due You						
Mortgages & Notes Receivable						
Contract Rights						
Marketable Assets & Investments Total						

[1] S1=Spouse 1, S2= Spouse 2, J=jointly, C=community property

[2] S=separate property, M=marital property

Net Worth Statement: Assets and Liabilities Worksheet (continued)

Assets	Title S1/S2/J/C [1]	Source S/M [2]	Date of Purchase/ Acquisition	Current Balance or Fair Market Value	Debt	Equity or Legal Value
Retirement Plan Assets						
Keogh or Self-Employment Plan						
IRA						
IRA						
Roth IRA						
Employee Stock Owner-ship Plan						
Pension/Profit Sharing/401(k)						
Annuity Plan						
Retirement Plan Assets Total						
Real Estate						
Residence						
Vacation Home						
Income Property						
Unimproved Real Property/ Lots						
Real Estate Total						

[1] S1=Spouse 1, S2= Spouse 2, J=jointly, C=community property

[2] S=separate property, M=marital property

Net Worth Statement: Assets and Liabilities Worksheet (continued)

Assets	Title S1/S2/J/C [1]	Source S/M [2]	Date of Purchase/ Acquisition	Current Balance or Fair Market Value	Debt	Equity or Legal Value
Business Interests						
Closely Held Private Stock						
Sole Proprietor						
Other Business Assets						
Business Interests Total						
Equity/Employee Benefit-Based Compensation						
Restricted Stock Awards						
Restricted Stock Units						
Stock Options/ Cash Value						
Life Insurance, purchased through company						
Equity/Employee Benefit-Based Compensation Total						
Personal Property						
Vehicle						
Vehicle/Motor Home						
Motorcycle/Off-Road Vehicle						
Home Furnishings (inc. art, antiques, silver, heirlooms)						
Jewelry/Furs						

Net Worth Statement: Assets and Liabilities Worksheet (continued)

Assets	Title S1/S2/J/C [1]	Source S/M [2]	Date of Purchase/ Acquisition	Current Balance or Fair Market Value	Debt	Equity or Legal Value
Collections/ Coins/Stamps						
Boat/Plane						
Horses/Other Livestock						
Other (specify):						
Personal Property Total						

[1] S1=Spouse 1, S2= Spouse 2, J=jointly, C=community property

[2] S=separate property, M=property

Liabilities	Original Amount	Date Incurred	Interest Rate	Loan Term (mos)	Monthly Payment	Balance Due
Mortgages/Real Estate Loans						
Mortgage						
Mortgage						
Equity Loans						
Mortgages/Real Estate Loans Total						
Vehicle Loans						
Vehicle						
Vehicle						
Vehicle Loans Total						
Other Loans (be sure to note if loans are secured by an asset)						
Bank Loan						
Bank Loan						

Net Worth Statement: Assets and Liabilities Worksheet (continued)

Liabilities	Original Amount	Date Incurred	Interest Rate	Loan Term (mos)	Monthly Payment	Balance Due
Loan Against Retirement Plan						
Loan Against Brokerage Account						
Private Loan						
Student Loan						
Student Loan						
Other:						
Other Loans Total						
Credit Accounts						
Credit/Charge Account						
Credit/Charge Account						
Credit/Charge Account						
Credit/Charge Account						
Credit Accounts Total						
Miscellaneous Debts						
Claims						
Unsettled Damages						
Liens & Judgments Owed						
Leases						
Taxes Owed						
Miscellaneous Debts Total						

Net Worth: Balance Sheet Summary

Instructions: Enter the subtotal for each asset and liability category from the last (far right) column of the Assets and Liabilities Worksheet. Add those figures to get total assets and liabilities. To find your net worth, subtract Total Liabilities from Total Assets.

Summary of Assets (from Assets and Liabilities Worksheet)

Cash and Cash Equivalents Total	
Marketable Assets/Investments Total	
Retirement Plans Total	
Real Estate Total	
Business Interests Total	
Equity/Employee Benefits-Based Compensation Total	
Personal Property Total	
Total Assets:	

Summary of Liabilities (from Assets and Liabilities Worksheet)

Mortgages/Real Estate Loans Total	
Vehicle Loans Total	
Other Loans Total	
Credit Accounts Total	
Miscellaneous Debts Total	
Total Liabilities:	
Net Worth (Assets Minus Liabilities)	

The Difference Between Assets and Income

You've just inventoried your assets and determined how much they're worth. In the next section, you'll examine your income—the stream of money that enables you to pay your expenses.

Does the difference between assets and income matter much? After all, in the end they're both your money, right? Well, when you're divorcing, the distinction is crucial. *Assets* are what get divided your divorce settlement. *Income* is what a court primarily looks at in determining how much alimony and child support you're entitled to, or how much you have to pay.

Some items are considered both income and assets. And both terms cover more things than you might think. Now is the time to be as accurate as possible about what your income and assets are.

You can begin to define income by using the IRS's rules—if you have to pay taxes on it when filing your returns, it's income. The government generally taxes you on your salary and wages, including tips, commissions, bonuses, vacation pay, sick leave, and compensatory time, as well as distributions from retirement or deferred compensation plans, and income from investments. You also owe taxes on income paid for lost wages and salary, such as severance pay, workers' compensation, unemployment insurance, disability insurance, and some disability pensions.

But for purposes of determining the appropriate amount of alimony and child support, income isn't just what the IRS says it is. A judge will consider virtually every possible source of funds in calculating the amount. (For more on the legal, financial, and emotional realities of alimony and child support, see Chapter 18.)

As for assets, certain ones are obvious: cash, house, car, bank accounts, and so on. But others are more obscure and easy to miss. (See Chapter 8 for a rundown of easy-to-forget assets.)

"Sources of Compensation," below, lists various types of compensation and assets—the items of value you're likely to be dealing with when ending a marriage. The table indicates whether each one is treated as income for purposes of determining child and spousal support or whether it is considered marital property that may be divided when the marriage ends. As you know, sometimes an item can be both.

Sources of Compensation

Source	Income for Support Purposes?	Asset Subject to Division?
Capital gains from sale of assets	Yes	Yes
Social Security benefits	Yes	No
Veterans benefits	Yes	No
Military personnel fringe benefits, such as overseas housing allowance	Yes	No
Gifts	Generally no	No
Prizes	Possibly	Usually yes, if won during marriage
Educational grants and loans	No, at least in some states	No
Income of new spouse or partner	No, in most states	No
Reimbursement for employment expenses	Yes, to the extent it reduces cost of living	Yes, if expenses were paid out during marriage
Personal loans from corporations	Yes	Yes
Retained earnings of private corporation	Yes	Yes
Depreciation on equipment	Yes	Equipment is treated as property
Depletion allowance from oil and gas interests	Yes	Interests are treated as property
Personal expenses paid by a business	Yes	Payment increases value of marital business
Voluntary contributions to pension, retirement, and savings plans	Yes	Yes
Voluntary debt reduction	Yes	Yes
Stock options	Yes, whether exercised or not, as long as they are exercisable and have increased in value	Yes, generally
Accrued vacation time or sick time payable in cash	Yes	Yes

Cash Flow—Where Does the Money Go?

Cash flow is how money comes in and goes out. Regardless of how your settlement winds up, a divorce forces *two* households to exist—at least for a while—on the same income that had supported only *one*. So you need to know as precisely as possible what it costs you to live. And, of course, you must take the needs and expenses of your children into account.

The Cash Flow Worksheets on the next few pages outline your sources of income and day-to-day living expenses. While filling out the worksheets, be realistic. And do not worry if you do not have enough information for every line. Do the best you can.

How Much Do Children Cost?

Once you have completed the worksheets, you will have a good idea of your estimated annual expenses. But what proportion of that goes for raising your kids? Knowing that figure could be important as you negotiate child support.

So you need to estimate how much you spend on your kids. To find that sum, do the following simple calculation:

Total monthly expenses	$_____
Subtract total child care expenses (monthly × 12)	$_____
Subtotal	$_____

Now multiply that subtotal by the percentage of your household that's composed of children. (For example, if you have two children living with you, that's 2 out of 3 or 67%; if three out of four residents are children, that's 75%, and so on.)

(Subtotal) _____ × (percentage representing children) _____ = _____

That's the children's pro rata share of non-child-care expenses. Now add back in the amount of child care expenses.

Child care expenses $_____

And your total is the child care expenses plus the children's pro rata share of other expenses.

Total estimated child-related expenses $_____

Instructions: Cash Flow Statement Adding Up Income

Income generally comes from three sources:
- earned salary or wages from your job as an employee
- earnings from your own business as a self-employed individual, and
- miscellaneous other sources, such as job bonuses, interest earned from investments, and income from a disability insurance policy.

Record all sources of income for you and your spouse, completing only those categories that apply. For investments from marital property such as interest income, rental property, and notes and trust deeds, divide the monthly income by two and enter half in your column and half in your spouse's column.

If an investment or asset is not owned 50-50, enter the appropriate percentages that apply. For instance, suppose a second house that produces rental income was bought partially with one spouse's separate property and partially with marital property (the income earned during marriage). In that case, the split might be 75-25 instead of 50-50.

If either you or your spouse holds more than one job or owns a self-run business, total your income from all sources on a separate sheet of paper and enter the total on this worksheet.

Instructions: Cash Flow Statement Estimating Expenses

Designed to create a realistic picture of your cash flow, this worksheet is divided into 15 categories, such Residence, Child Care, Installment Debt, Transportation, and Insurance.

To determine your current expenses, record the actual amount you spent for the past month for each item that applies. Multiply this monthly average by 12 and enter the amount at the bottom of the page. Don't forget to include once-a-year expenses, such as insurance premiums or real estate taxes. Finally, estimate how much of each expense is allocated for your children, and enter it in the box at the beginning of this section.

Certain payments could be listed under more than one category. For example, a car payment could be considered a loan payment under the Installment Debt category, but may also be listed under the Transportation category. To help develop a picture of where your money actually goes, expense items are specified whenever possible—as with the car payment.

Listing Credit Card Expenses

To get a clear picture of your spending, list your various credit card expenditures under appropriate categories. For example, if your Visa bill is $198, with $120 spent for clothes and $78 for meals out, and you pay the bill off in full each month, enter the $120 under clothes and $78 under food expenses. If, however, you carry a balance on your credit card bill—for example, the bill totals $4,000 now and you make monthly payments of $300—enter the amount of the monthly payment under installment debt, and do not list the payment under the specific expense category.

When you complete the worksheet, double-check it to be sure you have not listed the same expenses under more than one category.

Income and expenses must be considered together. If you're spending too much, you've got to reduce expenses or increase your income. Otherwise, you'll find yourself facing serious debt problems.

Questions to Ask an Attorney

1. In my state, does the way title is held determine the disposition of property at divorce? Does it determine whether property is characterized as marital or separate?
2. Does interest income or appreciation on separate property belong to "me" or to "us"?
3. What happens if an asset loses money?
4. Are debts in my spouse's name separate property or marital property?
5. Am I liable for my spouse's credit card debt even though I did not sign the credit application?

Cash Flow: Income and Expenses

Income		Self		Spouse	
		Per Pay Period	Per Month	Per Pay Period	Per Month
Salary & Wages Pay period is: ☐ weekly ☐ biweekly ☐ monthly					
Gross income (including commissions, allowances, bonuses, and overtime)					
Subtract:	Federal & state taxes				
	FICA:-Social Security				
	Other: medical or other insurance, pension, stock plans, union dues, and the like				
Net Income from Salary & Wages					
Self-Employment					
Gross income					
Subtract:	Federal & state taxes				
	Self-employment taxes				
Net Income from Self-Employment					

Cash Flow: Income and Expenses (continued)				
	Self		**Spouse**	
Income	**Per Pay Period**	**Per Month**	**Per Pay Period**	**Per Month**
Other Sources				
Dividends				
Interest income				
Rental property				
Royalties				
Notes and trust deeds				
Annuities, pensions/401(k)				
Alimony				
Child support				
Social Security				
Income tax refund				
Other (miscellaneous)*				
Subtract: any deductions				
Net Income From Other Sources				

* Include income from trusts, disability benefits, unemployment insurance, welfare, and other public assistance programs.

Your Own Net Income from Salary & Wages	
Spouse's Net Income from Salary & Wages	
Your Own Net Income from Other Sources	
Spouse's Net Income from Other Sources	
Total Net Monthly Income From All Sources	
Estimated Net Annual Income (Total Net Monthly Income From All Sources × 12)	

Cash Flow: Income and Expenses (continued)	
Monthly Expenses	**Amount**
Residence (family home and vacation home, if applicable)	
Rent/mortgage	
Property taxes	
Homeowners' insurance	
Renters' insurance	
Savings for repairs	
Maintenance, general repairs, painting	
Lawn/garden service	
Supplies	
Pool care	
Housecleaning	
Pest control	
Homeowners' association fees	
Other (specify):	
Other (specify):	
Other (specify):	
Other (specify):	
Total Residence Expenses	
Clothing	
For yourself	
For children	
Total Clothing Expenses	

Cash Flow: Income and Expenses (continued)

Monthly Expenses	Amount
Medical and Dental Care (expenses not covered by insurance; include children)	
Doctors	
Hospital	
Counseling/psychiatrist	
Prescriptions	
Optometrist/eye care	
Dentist/orthodontist	
Lab costs	
Vitamins	
Other (specify):	
Other (specify):	
Other (specify):	
Total Medical/Dental Expenses	
Insurance (do not include property insurance from Residence Expenses)	
Life insurance	
Disability insurance	
Long-term care insurance	
Personal property insurance	
Umbrella policy	
Other (specify):	
Other (specify):	
Other (specify):	
Total Insurance Expenses	

Cash Flow: Income and Expenses (continued)	
Monthly Expenses	**Amount**
Child Care Expenses	
Babysitter/day care/nursery school	
Preschool	
Lessons (art, sports, music, etc.)	
Allowances	
School tuition	
School lunches	
School transportation	
School books and supplies	
School uniforms/clothing	
Extracurriculars (art, sports, music lessons, etc.)	
Other (specify):	
Other (specify):	
Total Child Care Expenses	
Food at Home/Household Supplies	
Groceries/household supplies	
Liquor/wine	
Other (specify):	
Other (specify):	
Total Food at Home/Household Supplies Expenses	
Food Outside Home	
Restaurant meals	
Socializing outside home	
Total Food Outside Home Expenses	

Cash Flow: Income and Expenses (continued)

Monthly Expenses	Amount
Entertainment Expenses	
Movies	
DVDs/rentals/streaming services	
Plays	
Concerts	
Sports events	
Gym/club dues	
Entertaining/catering	
Music	
Books/magazines/newspapers	
Family trips/vacations	
Hobby supplies	
Other (specify):	
Total Entertainment Expenses	
Transportation/Auto Expenses	
Gas	
Oil/antifreeze	
Repairs/tires	
Car insurance	
Registration/fees	
Auto club	
Parking	
Tolls	
Taxi/train/bus/rentals	
Savings for new car	
Total Transportation/Auto Expenses	

Cash Flow: Income and Expenses (continued)

Monthly Expenses	Amount
Utilities	
Gas and electric	
Water	
Garbage	
Cable TV	
Internet service	
Cell phone	
Home phone	
Other (specify):	
Other (specify):	
Other (specify):	
Total Utilities Expenses	
School/Adult Education Expenses	
Tuition/fees/books	
Transportation	
Lunches	
Total School/Adult Education Expenses	
Laundry and Cleaning	
Dry cleaning and laundry (clothes)	
Dry cleaning and laundry (rugs, drapes, and furniture)	
Housekeeping/cleaning	
Other (specify):	
Total Laundry and Cleaning Expenses	

Cash Flow: Income and Expenses (continued)	
Monthly Expenses	**Amount**
Incidentals	
Pet care (food/veterinarian)	
Gifts (birthdays, holidays)	
Donations and charities	
Personal care (hair care/cosmetics/manicures/massages)	
Stationery (paper/postage/computer supplies)	
Tobacco products	
Bank service charges	
Plants (florist/houseplants)	
Storage	
Church/synagogue contributions (tithes)	
Miscellaneous	
Other (specify):	
Other (specify):	
Other (specify):	
Total Incidentals Expenses	
Installment payments (Important: Include here only charged items not listed in other expense categories. Also note which party acquired the debt.)	
Creditor:	
Creditor:	
Creditor:	
Creditor:	
Total Installment Payments	

Cash Flow: Income and Expenses (continued)	
Monthly Expenses	**Amount**
Other Expenses	
Estimated tax/income tax	
Tax preparation	
Nonreimbursed business expense	
Alimony paid	
Child support paid	
Legal/accounting (nonbusiness)	
Savings and investments	
Support of relatives not living in your home	
Deductible paid for auto accident or other claim	
Other (specify):	
Total Other Expenses	

Cash Flow: Income and Expenses (continued)			
	Category Amount	Monthly Amount	Annual Amount
Estimated Net Annual Income			
Monthly Expenses			
Total Residence Expenses			
Total Clothing Expenses			
Total Medical/Dental Expenses			
Total Insurance Expenses			
Total Child Care Expenses			
Total Food at Home/Household Supplies Expenses			
Total Food Outside Home Expenses			
Total Entertainment Expenses			
Total Transportation/Auto Expenses			
Total Utilities Expenses			
Total School/Adult Education Expenses			
Total Laundry and Cleaning Expenses			
Total Incidentals Expenses			
Total Installment Payments			
Total Other Expenses			
Total Monthly Expenses From All Sources			
Annual Expenses (Total Net Annual Expenses From All Sources × 12)			
Cash Flow (subtract total annual expenses from total net annual income)			

What Will Happen to the House?

If you're a homeowner, a divorce raises some difficult questions. Before making a decision, think through all the available options.

SKIP AHEAD

If you and your spouse don't own a house, skip ahead to Chapter 14.

A home can represent the partnership between spouses, a place where the children grew up, and a refuge from the demands of life. Perhaps your house stands for a connection to the community—or to the future generations of your family to whom you had hoped to bequeath it.

Whatever your house has meant to you, you're threatened with its loss during divorce. But rather than thinking you will "lose" your house, consider at least four basic options available to you:

Option A: Buy out your spouse's share and either keep it or sell it in the future.

Option B: Sell your share of the house to your spouse.

Option C: Sell the house together and split the proceeds with your spouse.

Option D: Continue to own the house jointly with your spouse and either buy your spouse's interest or sell yours in the future to your spouse or a third person.

To ease your anxieties, it helps to look at the numbers to find the true value of your home so you can make an informed choice. In the following sections, we explain the financial factors you need to consider before choosing the best option. Make sure that any property appraisal is current, not an estimate from months or years earlier.

CAUTION

The laws in your state and the circumstances of your particular case may affect your options regarding the house. For example, if you can't reach an agreement concerning the house, judges may presume that a custodial parent will stay in the family home until the children reach maturity. In that case, you wouldn't be able to sell the house and split the proceeds with your spouse (Option C). Rather, the custodial parent would have to buy out the other parent's interest, or you might sell the house some time in the future (Option A or D). If you're unsure of your state's laws regarding custody and the right to sell the house, consult with an attorney before completing the calculations in this chapter.

Financial vs. Legal Realities

To understand your options better, consider homeownership from both legal and financial perspectives.

Suppose that during your marriage, you and your spouse bought a house using income earned from the marriage. You might assume that if you sell the house, the proceeds will be split 50-50. But the following table compares the legal and financial realities.

Legal Reality	Financial Reality
In the 41 states that follow the principles of equitable distribution, it's quite possible that the proceeds of the house won't be split down the middle. The 41 equitable distribution states are all the states except Arizona, California, Idaho, Louisiana, Nevada, New Mexico, Texas, Washington, and Wisconsin. In Alaska, couples can opt into a community property system. And in Florida, Kentucky, South Dakota, and Tennessee, a married couple can elect to designate property as community property when it is within a trust. (See Chapter 12 for a full discussion.) In equitable distribution states, judges are supposed to divide property "fairly." "Fair" doesn't necessarily mean "equal." In reality, "fair" could mean that one spouse receives a greater share of the proceeds.	If you and your spouse can reach your own settlement without going to court, you can each negotiate the best deal for yourself, rather than have a judge impose one on you. Rarely is anyone happy with the settlement a judge carves out. The judge won't factor in most financial consequences of keeping or giving up certain assets. A negotiated settlement, though not always perfect, is usually more palatable.

The House—Keep It, Transfer It, or Sell It? Now or Later?

If you've been in a house any length of time, you're probably accustomed to paying a set amount each month on your mortgage. Many people going through divorce simply focus on that monthly payment, which often looks lower than anything they would have to pay if they moved into an apartment or bought another home.

But looks are deceiving. A low or moderate monthly payment can keep you from seeing many of the other costs of owning a home. Suppose you do keep the house. First of all, a refinancing process may mean that your monthly payment increases, especially if you take cash out to buy out your spouse's share. In addition, will you be able to cover the cost of insurance, property taxes, repairs, cleaning, painting, and the like? What if you decide to sell the house in a few years? Are you prepared to cover the costs of the sale? Can you afford to buy out your partner's share of the house and still have money to live on? Unless you know the true financial costs of keeping a home, you can't answer these questions.

Steps Toward Settling the House

Here's a bit more about the most common scenarios for dealing with the family home at divorce.

Option A: Buy out your spouse's share and either keep it or sell it in the future.

This option can hold the most unforeseen financial risks. Therefore, you'll want to take into consideration as many known factors as possible. You must determine whether you can afford your monthly housing costs. You also want to estimate how much you can expect to make if you sell the house, and recognize the tax implications of a future sale. And, you want to compare what you would receive if you and your spouse sold the house now. Of course, if you plan to keep the house for life, you don't need to worry about future sales costs or income taxes.

A Tax Break on Capital Gains

Before May 6, 1997, the rules for determining the financial value of the family home often made it an asset of questionable value in a divorce settlement, because any profit realized from its sale could ultimately be eaten up in taxes. With changes to the tax code since that time, however, many homes are now sold without incurring capital gains taxes. The key change, for purposes of this discussion, is that capital gains—such as profit from selling the house—are not taxable up to $250,000.

Most capital gains that exceed $250,000 are taxed at a maximum capital gains tax rate of 15%. But for some homeowners, gains between $250,000 and $500,000 are also tax free. To qualify for the $250,000 exclusion, you must have owned and occupied the residence for two of the five years prior to the sale or exchange of the house. (Even if you sell sooner than in two years, you may be able to reduce or eliminate capital gains taxes on your profits under certain circumstances. Those exceptions would include being forced to sell the house for health reasons, a change in your place of employment, or because of an "unforeseen circumstance." The IRS defines the latter as war, human-made or natural disasters, losing your job, death of a spouse, and divorce or legal separation.)

If you are still married (or are remarried) when you sell the house, you and your spouse will owe no taxes on the first $500,000 of gain if you file a joint tax return and all of the following are true:

- either spouse owned the house two of the last five years
- both spouses used the house two of the last five years, and
- neither spouse used the exclusion during the prior two years.

If you hold on to your house and sell it after remarrying, you may have to pay taxes on gains over $250,000 if, for example, your new spouse doesn't live in the house at least two years, or if your new spouse used the exclusion on the sale of a different house during the previous two years.

Option B: Sell your share of the house to your spouse.

To determine whether or not your spouse is making a good offer for your share of the house, you must understand its true financial value. The steps below will help you figure that out.

Option C: Sell the house together and split the proceeds with your spouse.

Before choosing this option, not only do you need to know your current housing costs and equity value—you also need to know the costs of selling the house and the amount of profit you will realize after the taxes are paid.

Option D: Continue to own the house jointly with your spouse and either buy it in the future from your spouse or sell it in the future to your spouse or a third person.

When a divorcing couple holds on to their house, it's usually either because a custodial parent is staying with the children or because the housing market is so weak that the couple doesn't want to sell the house yet. However, owning the house together can be emotionally and legally tricky. If you do it, make sure you have a written agreement ensuring that the out-of-house spouse's $250,000 capital gains exclusion is preserved. This agreement must be pursuant to a "divorce or separation instrument"—meaning a divorce judgment or related document that discusses your arrangement about the home, a written separation agreement, or a decree requiring one spouse to make payments for the support or maintenance of the other.

If the agreement doesn't meet the strict requirements of the Internal Revenue Code, the out-of-house spouse could lose the exclusion. (See "A Tax Break on Capital Gains," above, for a general discussion of the capital gains exclusion.) It is also possible to buy the house from your spouse in the future. But before making such an agreement, ask your tax adviser about the consequences.

STEP BY STEP

Finding the true value of your house will take several calculations.
Follow the steps below to answer these questions:

1. What is your total housing cost per month?

2. What is the current fair market value of your house?

3. What is the legal equity value of your house?

4. How much will it cost to sell the house?

5. What is the tax basis for your house?

6. What would be the financial value (after-sale/after-tax value) of your house if you sell it with your spouse?

7. What would be the financial value (after-sale/after-tax value) of your house if you keep it now and sell in the future?

8. What is your ownership share of the house?

9. Can you afford to purchase the house from your spouse?

10. What is your best option regarding the house?

CAUTION

You might be tempted to skip certain steps, knowing that you favor one option over the others. You are strongly advised to work through each step before making a decision. Completing all of the calculations will give you the most comprehensive picture of your financial choices—and can alert you to factors you may have overlooked.

Is Defaulting on the Mortgage an Option?

During the Great Recession and related foreclosure crisis, millions of home-owners defaulted on their mortgages—that is, they failed to pay their monthly mortgage payments or paid less than the amount due. In some cases, defaulting was a strategy they had chosen; many other times, it was seen as the only way to survive financially. Short term, of course, defaulting will lower your monthly expenses. But long term, it can have significant costs.

For one thing, defaulting on your mortgage can add to the amount you already owe. For example, you'll be charged late fees for nonpayment, and that can add hundreds of dollars to your mortgage bills. Similarly, once you're in default, your loan servicer may charge you for "default-related services" such as property inspections, property preservation services like maintenance, and foreclosure costs, such as attorneys' fees and title searches. In addition, even one late payment will damage your credit scores, affecting your ability to get a loan in the future. (See Chapter 5 for more on credit scores.)

If you are in default, your lender may start the foreclosure process. This process will add to the costs you will need to pay to bring your account current. It's also a matter of public record, meaning it'll be tougher for you to get credit and buy another home in the future.

If you aren't able to bring your account current or work out another solution, your home could be sold at a foreclosure auction. And in many states, you may be held responsible for paying what's called a "deficiency judgment"—the difference between what you owe on the loan and the amount the mortgage holder gets at the foreclosure auction.

Given all of these facts, you want to do everything you can to avoid default and foreclosure. If you're struggling to make your mortgage payments or you're in default, contact your mortgage servicer right away. You might be embarrassed to talk about your payment problems, and you may hope that your financial situation will soon improve. But keeping the lines of communication open is key to resolving your problem. Talk to your servicer about the options, which could include a loan modification (see "Loan Modification Programs," below), a repayment plan, or a temporary reduction or suspension of payments (called a "forbearance"). Even if you're not eligible for any of these options, your loan servicer might be able to help you find a solution short of foreclosure, including a possible short

> ### Is Defaulting on the Mortgage an Option? (continued)
>
> sale—selling the house at a price below what's owed and getting the lender to accept that as payment in full—or a voluntary transfer of the property through a "deed in lieu of foreclosure."
>
> Staying in touch with your mortgage servicer also could save you money. For instance, some may not order property inspections or property preservation work if you let them know each month that you're still living in the home and maintaining it. They're also more likely to delay a foreclosure sale if you're working with them to find a better solution.
>
> If you need help dealing with your loan servicer, you can get free personalized guidance from housing counseling agencies certified by the U.S. Department of Housing and Urban Development. To learn more, go to www.hud.gov/i_want_to/talk_to_a_housing_counselor.

Step 1: What Is Your Total Housing Cost Per Month?

Your mortgage does not represent the entire amount you spend on housing. (And remember, if you refinance the house in order to raise cash to buy out your spouse, you're likely to end up with a larger loan and probably bigger monthly payments.) You must also consider costs like utilities and maintenance to get a true picture of expenses.

Use these steps to find your net monthly housing costs:
a. List your monthly housing costs.
b. Total your gross monthly housing costs.
c. Find your net monthly housing costs by subtracting tax savings from your gross monthly housing costs.

List Your Monthly Housing Costs

List the amount you pay each month for the items on the "Monthly Housing Costs" chart that follows. You already have this information on the "Cash Flow Statement" you completed in Chapter 12. If you don't know the monthly cost of an item, or if you don't incur an expense every month, estimate the amount you spend per year and divide by 12. To estimate what you'll spend on significant repairs and maintenance needs, look around the house and note any major work that needs to be done. Check previous invoices to get an idea of what you'd normally spend on these expenses—or call a plumber, an electrician, or another person who can give you an estimate.

Monthly Housing Costs		
Item		**Your Monthly Costs**
Mortgage		$
Second mortgage (or equity loan payment)		$
Property taxes		$
Maintenance		
General repairs & painting	$	
Lawn/garden service & supplies	$	
Pool care	$	
Housecleaning	$	
Pest control	$	
Homeowners' association fees	$	
Other	$	
Total maintenance		$
Insurance		$
Utilities		$
Major repairs		$
Total gross housing costs per month		$

As this chart reveals, the price of owning and maintaining your house is higher than your monthly mortgage alone. Even if certain expenses aren't being incurred now—or haven't been for awhile—don't be lulled into thinking they no longer exist.

This chart includes the cost of repairs because those repairs will be your sole responsibility if you opt to keep the house. You may be able to get your spouse to split immediate repair costs with you when you negotiate the settlement. But because you don't know for sure that your spouse will agree, figure that you will have to come up with the money yourself.

Total Your Gross Monthly Housing Costs

Once you have filled in the information on the "Monthly Housing Costs" chart, add up all of the items in the "Your Monthly Costs" column. That figure is your gross monthly housing costs. Write that amount here.

$ _____ *Gross monthly housing costs*

Find Your Net Monthly Housing Costs

In considering your monthly housing costs, you should not overlook the tax benefits of homeownership. Homeowners can deduct up to $10,000 of the property taxes they've paid. They can also deduct mortgage interest paid on up to $750,000 on a first or second home, if it was purchased after December 15, 2017. For homeowners who purchased homes on or prior to December 15, 2017, they can still deduct any interest payments made on up to $1 million in home-related debt, including debt incurred for purchasing or building a new home or substantially improving a home, so your actual housing costs may be *lower* than the sum of your gross monthly housing costs. At the end of each year, you'll receive a Form 1099 from the bank or lender who holds your mortgage showing how much you paid in mortgage interest during the year.

If you take out a loan to purchase your spouse's share of the house, interest on that loan won't be deductible unless you use the house as collateral, you are legally liable for repayment, and the mortgage or deed of trust is recorded. Thus, interest on an informal loan from parents or friends may not be deductible, unless you give the lender a secured note and record it.

In addition, you may be able to deduct points (prepaid interest) in the year you purchase a home if you take out a mortgage to buy it. However, points are not deductible if you refinance your house to buy out your spouse's interest. Points on loans for home improvements are deductible in the year in which the loans are taken out. If you refinance the mortgage on your house, your deductions for the points are spread out over the life of the new loan. Additionally, any prepayment penalty you incur because you refinance the mortgage is deductible as interest in the year paid. Any points not previously deducted can be deducted as interest in the year of the refinancing.

To calculate your tax savings, follow these instructions:

a. Add together the total amount of interest paid on your mortgage during the year and the amount you paid in property taxes.

b. Multiply that number by your tax bracket—we assume a 24% federal tax bracket. (Don't forget your state tax bracket if your state allows a deduction for mortgage interest.)

c. Divide this calculation by 12 to get a monthly average.

d. Subtract the monthly average from your gross monthly housing costs to get your net housing costs.

Although the result may not be the exact amount you can deduct, you'll get a pretty close estimate for your housing costs. For precise figures, consult your accountant or tax adviser. The example and step-by-step formula that follow will make it easier for you to find your net monthly housing costs.

> EXAMPLE: Mitch and Candy's house is worth $150,000. Their mortgage is $1,200 per month ($14,400 per year), and they pay $272 a month ($3,264 per year) on a second mortgage. Their annual mortgage payments are $17,664 ($14,400 + $3,264); $14,000 of those payments is interest. They pay property taxes of $2,250 a year. Their federal tax bracket is 24%, giving them an annual tax savings of $4,550 or $379 a month. Assume their gross monthly housing costs equal $2,502.

Annual mortgage interest		$14,000
Annual property taxes	+	2,250
Deduction	=	16,250
Tax bracket	×	0.284
Tax savings	=	3,900
Monthly tax savings	÷ 12 =	325
Gross monthly housing costs		$2,502
Monthly tax savings	–	325
Net monthly housing costs	=	$2,177

To apply this formula to your situation, fill in the blanks below. You will need to know your annual mortgage interest, annual property taxes, and tax bracket.

$ _____ *Annual mortgage interest*

To find your mortgage interest, contact your lender and request a calculation of the annual mortgage interest on your loan. Or, ask the lender for the amortization schedule for your loan. On either document, you will see a monthly listing of how much of the mortgage payment repays principal (your debt or balance due) and how much pays interest on the loan.

$ _____ *Annual property taxes*

To find your property taxes, refer to your federal tax returns, call the county tax assessor, look on the assessor's website, or call your lender if your property taxes are paid through an escrow account with your lender. You can subtract taxes assessed for street, sidewalk, utility, curb, sewer, and other property improvements.

_____ *% Tax bracket*

To find your tax bracket, check the income tax schedules contained in the IRS tax packet or ask a tax adviser to verify your current tax bracket. Or simply use 24%, the federal tax bracket into which most people fall. Remember to use only your anticipated income as a single person, including any alimony you might receive or pay, as the basis for your tax bracket. And your filing status will be either "single" or "head of household." (For help in figuring out which category to use, see Chapter 11.)

Now enter those numbers in the "Net Monthly Housing Costs" chart. Using the formula in the chart, calculate your net monthly housing costs. You will refer to this number later when making your decision on what to do with the house.

Net Monthly Housing Costs		
Annual mortgage interest	=	$
Annual property taxes	+	$
Deduction	=	$
Tax bracket	×	
Tax savings	=	$
Monthly tax savings	÷ 12 =	$
Gross monthly housing costs	=	$
Monthly tax savings	−	$
Net monthly housing costs	=	$

Appraiser Qualifications

In every state, a real property appraiser must meet the minimum national qualifications the Appraiser Qualifications Board (AQB) sets and may be limited in the services the appraiser can provide. Some are qualified to appraise only residential real estate; others are certified general appraisers, whose services may extend to all types of real property.

If you have both residential and commercial property to divide, make certain that the appraisers you plan on using have the necessary credentials to assess all the real property in your possession. While the AQB sets minimum national standards for real estate appraisers across the country, each state may set its own standards, which may be even more restrictive.

Step 2: What Is the Current Fair Market Value of Your House?

The current fair market value of your house is the amount you can realistically expect to get when you list your house for sale on the open market. You can obtain fair market value estimates from real estate agents free of charge. You might want to ask the agent who helped you buy the house originally or an agent who consistently markets in your neighborhood.

You can also get appraisals or opinions of fair market value from a certified appraiser, but be prepared to pay. For a referral to a certified appraiser, ask your banker or lender or contact the Appraisal Institute (www.appraisalinstitute.org, 888-756-4624). If you and your spouse cannot agree on the value of the house, ask your attorney to select an appraiser. This person will testify to the house's value if the issue is contested in court.

Real estate appraisers generally look at a house from several financial angles and take an average of these values to estimate what it is worth. The two primary views they take are:

- what the market will bear—that is, the sales prices of comparable houses in the area, and
- your house's replacement value (the cost of building materials and the like).

 WEB RESOURCE
Real estate sites that may be helpful in determining your home's value:

- **www.realtor.com.** Can help you find a home or neighborhood, learn about home values, find lenders and movers, make calculations, compile checklists, and locate real estate reference materials, and
- **www.zillow.com and www.redfin.com.** Two of the best real estate sites, online real estate services that allow you to quickly access the "value" on your home or others you may be interested in, as well as providing mortgage information.

Once you have a good estimate of the fair market value of your house, write it here:

$ _____ *Fair market value*

Loan Modification Programs

If you're intent on keeping your home after a divorce, but fear that monthly payments will be too high, you should investigate various mortgage modification programs designed to help people stay in their homes during economic hardship.

In a modification, the lender typically agrees to do one or more of the following to reduce your monthly payments:

- lower the interest rate
- convert a variable interest rate to a fixed interest rate
- extend the term of the loan (say, from 30 years to 40), or
- forbear some of the principal balance. ("Forbearing" the principal means setting aside a portion of the total debt before calculating your monthly payment. In most cases, you must pay the set-aside amount in a balloon payment when you sell the property, when you refinance the loan, or when the loan matures.)

Different options are available for borrowers with Fannie Mae, Freddie Mac, FHA-insured, VA-guaranteed, and USDA mortgages. For example, you might qualify for a Fannie Mae or Freddie Mac Flex Modification if you have one of those kinds of loans. A Flex Modification could reduce your payment by as much as 20%.

Lenders are also free to offer their own in-house modification options, called "proprietary" modifications, for borrowers with other kinds of loans.

To apply for a modification, contact your loan servicer's loss mitigation department, sometimes called a "home retention" department.

Remember that the estimates you receive are just that: estimates. The precise value of your house will only be known once the property is sold to a neutral third party—one that has no interest in your divorce. This is why valuation experts often disagree over property values.

In the event you and your spouse both hire appraisers who don't agree on the value of your house, be prepared to ask the professional you've hired a few questions:

- Where are the areas of disagreement?
- What is the estimated value of those areas of disagreement?
- How might the differences be resolved?

Since you will probably have to pick and choose your battles in divorce, you should undertake a cost-benefit analysis of any appraisal disagreements. Try to determine how much you stand to lose in the disagreement and weigh it against the (considerable) fees of litigation, including attorneys' fees, expert witness fees, court costs, recording fees, and any wages you might lose during the process.

Think Like a Buyer

Before paying for an appraiser, you might ask a real estate agent who regularly markets your neighborhood to prepare a comparative market analysis (CMA). This analysis is typically provided at no charge.

After physically inspecting your house, the agent researches the market for recent sales, how long property takes to sell, currently listed homes, pending sales, and expired listings (unsold homes taken off the market).

Don't hesitate to ask more than one agent to provide you with a CMA. In addition to getting a consensus about what your home is worth, you will also learn about the quality of agents with whom you may do business later.

In valuing your house, think like a buyer, not a seller. Specifically, do not rely on the following as indicators of a sales price for your home:

- the amount you spent on improvements (you may have spent more than the home prices in your neighborhood will support)
- the price you paid for your home; (markets are dynamic and the market value of your home may have gone up or down since you purchased it), or
- the assessed value shown on your property tax statement—local tax assessments are often out of date and rarely reflect the actual market value.

Step 3: What Is the Equity Value of Your House?

The equity value of your house is its fair market value (the figure you obtained in Step 2) minus debt connected to the house. Remember—if a court were to calculate each spouse's share of a house, the court would consider only the amount of equity. That number, however, does not reflect the sale costs or taxes—that is, the financial reality of owning or selling a house.

The debt connected to your house equals what you owe to any lenders (first mortgage, second mortgage, or home equity loan or line of credit) plus any liabilities on the house. All liabilities must be paid before any cash disbursements can be made from the sale of a house. Liabilities include income or property tax liens, child support liens, judgment liens (if someone sues you and obtains a judgment, that person can put a lien on your house), or mechanic's or materialman's liens placed by a contractor who did work on your home but wasn't paid.

Ask your lender for the balance on your mortgages and equity loans. The lender should offer you two figures—a principal balance and a payoff balance. The principal balance is simply the amount of principal remaining to be paid on your loan. The payoff balance is the principal balance plus an additional month's interest and any prepayment charges you must pay to close out the loan. Use the payoff balance in calculating the debt on your house.

Possible Debts Against Your House	
Mortgage balance	$
Second mortgage balance	$
Equity loan or line of credit balance	$
Property tax lien	$
Income tax lien	$
Child support lien	$
Judgment lien	$
Mechanic's or materialman's lien	$
Other liens	$
Total current debt on house	$

Now subtract the debt on the house from its fair market value to obtain the equity value.

> *Fair market value (Step 2)* $ _____
>
> *Total current debt on house*
>   *(Step 3, above)*   – $ _____
>
> *Equity value of your house*   = $ _____

You might not be aware of all liens on your property. Tax liens and mechanic's liens, for example, often appear without the owner's knowledge. To find all liens on your house, you'll have to do a title search. You can hire a title insurance company to conduct the search, or you can visit the records office in the county where your deed is recorded. A clerk in that office can show you how to search for any liens on your house.

Step 4: How Much Will It Cost to Sell the House?

To determine how much money it will take to actually sell your house, you can do a quick ballpark estimate, or you can use the calculations that follow to find a more precise figure. To find a precise figure, you'll have to include not only the costs of sale, but also the amount it will take to fix up the house and prepare it for sale.

Quick Ballpark Estimate of Cost of Sale

Take the fair market value figure you determined in Step 2. To get a ballpark amount for the sales cost, multiply that amount by 0.07. Obviously, some sales will yield higher or lower costs of sale, but 7% will do for a rough estimate. Enter that number in the *Total cost of sale* blank, below.

Precise Valuation of Cost of Sale

To obtain a more accurate cost of sale figure, you need to total the following amounts:

> $ _____ *Agent's commission*

This figure represents the amount a real estate agent charges you for selling a house. Generally, it's set at 6% of the final selling price. The fee can sometimes be negotiated down. Also, if you list your house as a FSBO—for sale by owner—you avoid the agent's commission altogether. But be sure to educate yourself about the process before you list your house as a FSBO. You can find information on the topic at www.nolo.com in the "Real Estate" section of the website.

$ _____ *Closing costs*

These costs can include escrow fees, abstract and recording costs, appraisal fees, surveys, title insurance, transfer and stamp taxes, loan charges, and miscellaneous expenses. All this can add up to several thousands of dollars. A lender or real estate agent can help you figure the exact amount.

$ _____ *Attorneys' fees*

In a few states, you will need to hire an attorney to help you "close" the sale of your house. If you paid an attorney when you bought the house, the cost should be similar, though you may need to adjust it upward to account for inflation and the passage of time. Otherwise, ask a real estate agent for an estimate.

$ _____ *Fix-up costs*

Fix-up expenses are not considered when calculating capital gains, but they are a very real expense when selling a home. Estimate here the amount of money you will have to spend to prepare your house for sale. Does it need major repairs or just a paint job? Does the foundation, roof, or plumbing need work? Will you need to have the house inspected? Must you get a termite inspection? (If you need help in getting a handle on what repairs are necessary, the American Society of Home Inspectors' website at www.ashi.com provides a list of inspectors near you, or you can ask your realtor for referrals.)

$ _____ *Total cost of sale*

Add these amounts together to get a reasonably close estimate of what it will cost to sell your house.

What Happens When the House Secures a Spouse's Separate Property Debt?

Generally, a spouse should not keep a house that secures the debts of a soon-to-be-former spouse. Before agreeing to keep a house securing your spouse's separate property debt, be certain your spouse has paid all such debts, and request proof of payment.

A California case underscores the point. The husband forged his wife's signature on a quitclaim deed (giving him sole ownership) and then used the house as security while running up additional debts. His creditors got a judgment against him and attached a lien to the house. At the divorce trial, the court ordered the husband to pay the judgment. The wife chose to keep the house and buy out his share. In calculating the value of the house, however, the court did not reduce it by the amount of the lien. Thus, the wife had to pay the husband one-half of the value of the house—and also pay off the lien plus interest.

Moral of this story: Once a lien, always a lien—until the creditor is paid. A creditor's right to payment is not affected by who is ordered to pay marital debt. If you want to keep the house, deduct all liens, plus interest, when calculating the value. If your spouse refuses, don't keep the house.

If you decide to sell the house together, make sure that all separate property debts secured by the house are identified. Instruct the escrow company to pay each spouse's separate debts out of that spouse's share of the proceeds. For instance, if the net sale proceeds total $100,000 after costs of sale, each spouse is entitled to $50,000. However, if there is a separate property lien of $25,000 against one spouse, the escrow company should issue checks as follows: $50,000 to the spouse without the separate property debt, $25,000 to the spouse with the separate property debt, and $25,000 to the creditor.

Step 5: What Is the Tax Basis for Your House?

The tax basis of an asset is a little-mentioned financial concept that no one thinks about until it's time to sell the asset—or until a divorce.

The tax basis is the dollar amount the IRS uses to determine whether you've made or lost money on an asset. Essentially, your tax basis is the original purchase price plus the cost of any improvements you have made, minus any tax benefits you have realized. Knowing the tax basis lets you calculate your profit to determine whether you'll owe taxes when your house is sold during or after divorce. If the house isn't sold until after the divorce, the person who gets the house gets the tax liability.

To figure your tax basis, enter the appropriate amounts in the blanks below.

$ _____ *Purchase price*

The purchase price should be on the original purchase contract or closing statement—check your files or safe-deposit box. If you still can't find it, call your lender or the escrow company that processed your purchase.

$ _____ *Acquisition costs*

These are costs associated with the purchase, such as recording fees, title insurance, and document fees listed on the escrow statement. Do not include loan principal, interest, or points.

(If you acquired the house before May 6, 1997, check to see whether you filed IRS Form 2119 with your tax return. The "Adjusted Basis of the New House" shown on the form is equal to the purchase price plus the acquisition costs. If you used Form 2119, you don't need to add in the acquisition costs.)

$ _____ *Capital improvements*

Capital improvements are items that add value to your house, such as a new bathroom or den, a security system, or extensive landscaping. The costs of these changes are not fix-up or repair costs. You will need to go through your files to find receipts that document the improvements made to your house.

The following are examples of capital improvements:

- Additions
  - bedroom
  - bathroom
  - deck
  - garage
  - porch
  - patio
  - storage shed
  - fireplace
- Lawns and grounds
  - landscaping
  - driveway
  - walkway
  - fence
  - retaining wall
  - sprinkler system
  - swimming pool
  - exterior lighting
- Communications
  - satellite dish
  - intercom
  - cameras/security system
- Heating and air-conditioning
  - heating system
  - central air-conditioning
  - furnace
  - duct work
  - central humidifier
  - filtration system
- Solar panels
- EV/car stations
- Electrical
  - light fixtures
  - wiring upgrades

- Plumbing
    - water heater
    - soft water system
    - filtration system
- Insulation
    - attic
    - walls
    - floors
    - pipes and ductwork
- Interior improvements
    - built-in appliances
    - kitchen modernization
    - bathroom modernization
    - flooring
    - wall-to-wall carpet
- Miscellaneous
    - storm windows and doors
    - roof
    - central vacuum system

$ _____ *Tax benefits*

Tax benefits refer to the rollover of gain (profit) from homes sold up to August 5, 1999 as well as deductions taken for a home office. To find your tax benefits, refer to your tax returns or call your accountant. *For simplicity's sake, you can calculate the tax basis without subtracting any tax benefits.*

Use the figures you entered earlier in this section to find the tax basis of your house.

Purchase price	$_____
Acquisition costs *(do not include fix-up costs)*	+ $_____
Capital improvements	+ $_____
Tax benefits	+ $_____
*Tax basis of house**	= $_____

*If you have Form 2119, you can use the Adjusted Basis for this figure
  if you add capital improvements.

For Those With Home Office Depreciation After May 6, 1997

Claiming a tax deduction for use of a home office is a growing trend. However, the law allowing you to exclude $250,000 of gain (profit) on the sale of a house does not include the amount attributed to depreciation for home office use. So if you depreciate your house for home office use, the amount of depreciation will be taxed as a capital gain (25%).

The following formula allows you to figure the amount not qualifying for the exclusion:

Total home office depreciation taken since May 6, 1997	= $	_____
× 25% capital gains rate	×	0.25
Taxes not qualifying for exclusion	= $	_____

Step 6: What Will the Financial Value of Your House Be If You Sell It With Your Spouse?

If you profit from the sale of a house, you may exclude up to $250,000 of that profit ($500,000 if you file a joint return) once in a 24-month period. You must consider this exclusion in order to figure out the financial value (after-sale/after-tax value) of your house and analyze your future options concerning house purchases and tax deferrals. Remember, too, that you will need to know your capital gains rate to determine the financial value of the house. As a general rule, if you are in the 24% tax bracket, your capital gains rate is 15%, and if you're in the 12% bracket, your capital gains rate is 5%. (Don't forget that you may owe state taxes as well.)

To find the financial value (after-sale/after-tax value) of your house, enter the following information from the previous steps:

$ _____ *Fair market value (from Step 2)*

$ _____ *Current debt (from Step 3)*

$ _____ *Cost of sale (from Step 4)*

$ _____ *Fix-up expenses (from Step 4)*

$ _____ *Tax basis of the house (from Step 5)*

$ _____ *Taxes to pay from home office use (from Step 5)*

_____ *% Capital gains rate (including state)*

Now take the following steps:

1. Find the amount realized by subtracting the cost of sale from the fair market value.
2. Find the gain or loss on the potential sale by subtracting the tax basis from the amount realized. If you had a loss, use zero as the amount of gain and go directly to Step 5.
3. Find the taxable gain by subtracting your exclusion from the gain. (Taxable gain is that portion of gain exceeding the maximum gain you can exclude.) The maximum exclusion is $250,000 for individuals and $500,000 for many married couples filing jointly. The net gain is the portion of the gain that will be taxed. If your net gain does not exceed the maximum exclusion allowed, go directly to Step 5.
4. Find the taxes on the taxable gain by multiplying the taxable gain by the capital gains rate.
5. Find the financial value by subtracting the current debt on the house, taxes on taxable gain, cost of sale, fix-up expenses, and taxes on home office use from the amount realized.

EXAMPLE:

1. Find the amount realized:

	Your House	Example
Fair market value	_____	*$400,000*
Cost of sale	_____	*$ 28,000*
Amount realized	_____	*$372,000*

2. Find the gain or loss:

	Your House	Example
Amount realized	_____	*$372,000*
Less tax basis	_____	*$100,000*
Gain (or loss)	_____	*$272,000*

3. Find the taxable gain:

		Example
Gain	_____	*$272,000*
Exclusion	_____	*$500,000*
Taxable gain	_____	*$0*

4. Find the taxes on taxable gain:

Taxable gain	_____	*$0*
Capital gains rate	_____	*× 15%*
Taxes on taxable gain	_____	*$0*

5. Find the financial value:

Amount realized	_____	*$372,000*
Current debt on house	_____	*$90,000*
Taxes on taxable gain	_____	*$0*
Taxes on home office use	_____	*$0*
Fix-up expenses	_____	*$6,000*
Financial value	_____	*$276,000*

Step 7: What Will the Financial Value of Your House Be If You Sell It in the Future?

Of all the options you may pursue regarding the house, the choice of selling it in the future can be the most difficult to analyze. Take your time and get help in determining real estate values, if necessary.

No one can predict what will happen in the future to the real estate market or the tax laws. But real estate brokers can make calculated guesses. Assuming you would not keep a house you expected to be worth less in the future, it's important that you know what its future value is likely to be.

A technical aid, the Future Value Factor table, lets you calculate changes in the value of an asset like a house. We've included a Future Value Factor table in the appendix. Use it, along with the formula below, to get an idea of what your house will be worth in the future. But remember that this will be only an estimate.

To use the Future Value Factor chart, you must decide how long you plan to stay in your house (called the holding period), and you must select a rate of inflation. Financial planners often figure an annual inflation rate of 3% or 4% when estimating housing values. Depending on the state of the economy and your local housing market, you might be tempted to use an inflation rate higher than 3% or 4%. Certainly many houses increase in value at a rate substantially higher than the inflation rate. Nevertheless, we recommend that you be conservative when speculating on the future value of your house. It's better to expect less and get more than vice versa.

You will see that the *Future Value Factor* chart lists numbers of years vertically and rates of inflation horizontally. Estimate the number of years you expect to hold on to the house, select an anticipated inflation rate, and find where the selected row and column intersect. That will give you the future value factor. For example, if you expect to hold the house another seven years and you assume inflation won't go above 4% during that period, your future value factor is 1.3159.

To find the future financial value (after-sale/after-tax value), enter the following information for your house:

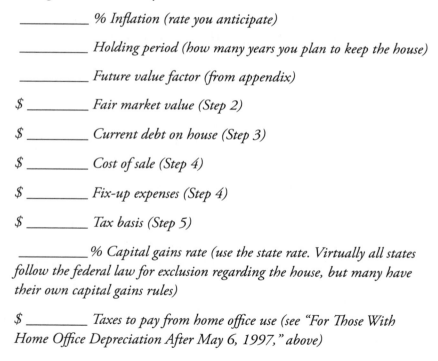

_____ % *Inflation (rate you anticipate)*

_____ *Holding period (how many years you plan to keep the house)*

_____ *Future value factor (from appendix)*

$ _____ *Fair market value (Step 2)*

$ _____ *Current debt on house (Step 3)*

$ _____ *Cost of sale (Step 4)*

$ _____ *Fix-up expenses (Step 4)*

$ _____ *Tax basis (Step 5)*

_____ % *Capital gains rate (use the state rate. Virtually all states follow the federal law for exclusion regarding the house, but many have their own capital gains rules)*

$ _____ *Taxes to pay from home office use (see "For Those With Home Office Depreciation After May 6, 1997," above)*

Now take the following steps:

1. Find the future value factor (see the appendix) by estimating the holding period and the rate of inflation.
2. Find the future sale value by multiplying the fair market value by the future value factor.
3. Find the potential amount realized by subtracting the cost of sale from the future sale value.
4. Find the potential gain or loss on the potential sale of your house by subtracting the tax basis from the amount realized. If you had a loss, use zero as the amount of gain and go directly to Step 7.
5. Find the potential taxable gain by subtracting your exclusion from the gain. Taxable gain is that portion of gain exceeding the maximum gain you can exclude. If you are single, the maximum gain you can exclude is $250,000. (Remember: To qualify for the exclusion, you must own and reside in the home for two of the last five years prior to sale, and you must not have sold or exchanged a principal residence in the two years prior to the sale.) If your taxable gain does not exceed the maximum exclusion allowed you, go directly to Step 7.
6. Find the taxes on the taxable gain by multiplying the taxable gain by your capital gains rate.
7. Find the financial value (after-sale/after-tax value) by subtracting what you expect your debt on the house will be, as well as taxes on taxable gain, cost of sale, fix-up expenses, and taxes on home office use, from the amount realized calculated in Step 3.

EXAMPLE:

1. Find the future value factor—see the appendix.

For the purpose of this example, assume a holding period of five years and an inflation rate of 5%—the future value factor is 1.2763.

2. Find the future sale value

Fair market value	*$400,000*
Future value factor	× _1.2763_
Future sale value	= *$510,520*

3. Find potential amount realized

Future sale value	*$510,520*
Cost of sale	*– 35,736*
Potential amount realized	*= $474,784*

4. Find potential gain or loss

Amount realized	*$474,784*
Less tax basis	*– 100,000*
Gain (or loss)	*= $374,784*

5. Find the potential taxable gain

Gain	*$374,784*
Exclusion	*– 250,000*
Potential taxable gain	*= $124,784*

6. Find the potential taxes on taxable gain

Taxable gain	*$124,784*
Capital gains rate	*× 15%*
Potential taxes on taxable gain	*= $18,717*

7. Find the future financial value

Amount realized	*$474,784*
Anticipated debt on house	*– 90,000*
Taxes on taxable gain	*– 18,717*
Taxes on home office use	*– 0*
Fix-up expenses	*– 6,000*
Potential financial value	*= $360,367*

Now fill in the numbers for your house.

1. Find the future value factor

Enter number from appendix: _____

2. Find the future sale value

Fair market value _____

Future value factor × _____

Future sale value = _____

3. Find potential amount realized

Fair market value _____

Cost of sale − _____

Potential amount realized = _____

4. Find potential gain or loss

Amount realized _____

Less tax basis − _____

Gain (or loss) = _____

5. Find the potential taxable gain

Gain _____

Exclusion − _____

Potential taxable gain $ = _____

6. Find the potential taxes on taxable gain

Taxable gain _____

Capital gains rate _____ × *15%*

Potential taxes on taxable gain = _____

7. Find the future financial value

Amount realized _____

Anticipated debt on house − _____

Taxes on taxable gain − _____

Taxes on home office use − _____

Fix-up expenses − _____

Potential financial value = _____

Step 8: What Is Your Share of the House?

You might have expected your marriage to be a 50-50 proposition, and you might believe that your divorce will be the same—a simple division in which each person gets half. When it comes to the house, however, those percentages might not hold up.

In this step, you must determine what share of the house belongs to you. That number will help you choose your best option regarding the house and inform your negotiation of the final settlement. When you determine the total value of the house under different scenarios, you need to know your share so you can figure out how much of that total value you can expect to receive. For instance, if the total value of your house is $100,000 and you are each entitled to 50% of it, you'd get $50,000. But if you are only a one-fourth owner of that house, you'd be entitled to $25,000, not $50,000.

The laws of your state and the origin of the money used to buy your house determine the amount of your share. Refer to Chapter 12 for an overview of marital and separate property. If one spouse was the sole owner of the house when you entered the marriage, the other spouse may nevertheless be entitled to a share at divorce. In some states, when the nonowning spouse or the marital earnings pay for mortgage payments and improvements (such as additions and renovations), that action usually gives the nonowner some ownership interest.

Once you have determined your estimated ownership share, enter it here.

_____ *% Separate property*

_____ *% Marital property*

Your house can be worth different amounts under different circumstances, depending on your ownership share and the option you ultimately choose. Multiply the percentage of marital property by the equity or legal value and place that figure on the "Marital Balance Sheet" in Chapter 19. Then, using the same process, figure out the amount of the home that is separate property and place that in the "Marital Balance Sheet," noting that that separate-property share must be bought out as part of the ultimate negotiations.

Step 9: What's Your Best Option Regarding the House?

Now look at your options considering your calculations in the previous steps. The advantages and disadvantages of each option are recapped below. If you choose Option A or B and do not think you can afford to buy out your spouse's interest, see the suggestions in Step 10, below.

Option A: Buy out your spouse's share and either keep it or sell it in the future.

Advantages. For the sake of children, or stability in your own life, it might serve you to keep the family home. You can take advantage of the IRS exclusion that lets you sell a house and not pay taxes on the first $250,000 of profit.

　Disadvantages: When you eventually sell the house, you will be solely responsible for costs of sale and for taxes on the profit over $250,000. Also, the real estate market in your area could crash and that the house could sell for less money in the future.

Is this a viable option? _____ *Yes* _____ *No*

Option B: Transfer your share of the house to your spouse.

Advantages. You don't have to pay taxes on the money you receive because the IRS does not tax money received as a property buyout during a divorce.

　Disadvantages. You might not earn enough on the sale of the house to afford to buy a new one. If your income isn't high enough, you might not qualify for financing.

Is this a viable option for me? _____ *Yes* _____ *No*

Option C: Sell the house together and split the proceeds with your spouse.

Advantages. You share the cost of sale and the tax liability with your spouse. Also, you can each take advantage of the IRS provision that lets you exclude up to $250,000 of gain on the sale of the house ($500,000 if you've remarried and meet certain conditions; see "A Tax Break on Capital Gains," above).

Checking Out Sex Offenders

When evaluating a new place to live, you might be particularly concerned with safety, especially if you have children. The Dru Sjodin National Sex Offender Public Website (www.nsopw.gov) is the first national search site that allows parents and other concerned residents to identify sex offenders not only in their neighborhoods but in adjacent communities as well— even if the neighboring community is across a state line. Users may search all, or selected, sex offender registries by name, state, county, city/town, or ZIP code. Coordinated by the U.S. Justice Department, the site connects sex offender lists in all 50 states, the District of Columbia, and Guam. It's named for a University of North Dakota student who was abducted and murdered in 2003 by a convicted sex offender who'd been released by a neighboring state.

Disadvantages. You'd be selling the family home, to which you might have strong emotional ties. Further, the amount you receive from the sale of the house might not be enough for you to afford to buy another house, or you might not qualify for financing to buy another home.

Is this a viable option for me? _____ *Yes* _____ *No*

CAUTION
If you sell the house to a third person during the calendar year before the year in which your divorce is final, and taxes are due on the sale, consider filing taxes using a "married filing separately" taxpayer status. Otherwise, you could be responsible for your spouse's liability if your spouse is dishonest with the IRS (see Chapter 11). Alternatively, you could set up an escrow account to cover potential taxes due.

Option D: Own the house jointly with your spouse and buy it in the future from your spouse or sell it in the future to your spouse or a third person.

Advantages. You (and your children) will continue having a familiar place in which to live. The house may bring a higher price if real estate values rise. You and your spouse will jointly share the eventual costs of sale and taxes. While you're living in the house, your spouse may agree to pay part of the mortgage (in the form of alimony or child support), repair costs, or maintenance costs.

Disadvantages. Major misunderstandings between divorced spouses can arise as to responsibility for repairs, maintenance, improvements, taxes, and the like. Nonresident spouses often are unable to purchase homes for themselves while they're continuing to share responsibility for the family home. As a safeguard, spouses who jointly own a home while one party uses it should make written agreements stating the rules for repairs and other financial contributions. In order for the out-of-house spouse to keep the capital gains tax exclusion of $250,000, the parties must agree in writing, or the court must order, that the in-house spouse have use of the residence.

Is this a viable option? _____ Yes _____ No

Regarding the house, the following option is the best one for me:

☐ *Option A: Buy out my spouse's share and either keep it or sell it in the future.*

☐ *Option B: Sell my share of the house to my spouse.*

☐ *Option C: Sell the house together and split the proceeds with my spouse.*

☐ *Option D: Own the house jointly with my spouse and sell it in the future to my spouse or a third person.*

Continued Homeownership and Estate Planning

If you decide to hold on to your house with your spouse and sell it in the future, you will need to plan your estate and possibly acquire life insurance to cover each spouse's obligations in the event of the other spouse's death.

You should also evaluate how title to the house is held. (See Chapter 12.) For example, couples who currently hold their property in tenancy by the entirety or as community property will no longer have that option after divorce. In addition, if you held your house in joint tenancy while you were married—an arrangement whereby the other automatically inherits if one owner dies—that joint tenancy might no longer be appropriate. In some states, divorce may automatically sever joint tenancy. Converting ownership to tenancy in common would let you leave your share of the house to whomever you wish when you die.

Carrying life insurance on your former spouse provides you with ready cash to purchase the home from the estate if your ex dies before the house is sold. An agreement outlining your rights and responsibilities for co-ownership also can protect you in the event your ex-spouse dies prematurely.

Step 10: How to Purchase the House From a Spouse or Former Spouse

Now that you have chosen an option, you need to face one more financial reality: paying for your choice. Typically, individuals going through divorce don't have sufficient cash to purchase a spouse's interest in the family home. The following suggestions may help you to find a way to finance your best option on the house.

Refinance the house and pay proceeds to selling spouse.

Refinancing the home provides a source of cash to buy out the other spouse. As a practical matter, you may refinance in order to make a buyout happen, so that you become the only holder of the loan. If refinancing does not generate enough cash to buy out your spouse, you'll need another loan (called a second mortgage) secured by the house.

Refinancing a home mortgage can reduce your monthly mortgage payment and lower the amount of interest you pay over the life of the loan. It also may provide an opportunity to lock in a fixed mortgage rate. You generally need three things to qualify for refinancing:

- an adequate income
- a credit score that shows your ability and willingness to handle debt responsibly, and
- some equity in your home.

If you face challenges in meeting those requirements, don't give up. Some refinancing plans offer more flexibility, so it pays to shop around. Talk to lenders, mortgage brokers, and credit unions about what programs they offer. If you don't qualify for refinancing now, make an effort to find out what you'll need to do to qualify in the future. If you do qualify, explore whether a 15-year mortgage would make sense. If you can afford the higher monthly payment, you'll build up equity significantly faster than with a 30-year loan.

When looking for the best refinancing deal, be sure to shop, compare, and negotiate. Contact several lenders—commercial banks, mortgage companies, and credit unions—to be sure you're getting the best price. Specifically, ask about:

- **Rates.** Is the quoted interest rate fixed or adjustable? Is it the lowest available? What's the full annual percentage rate (APR)? This takes into account not only the interest rate but also other charges expressed as a yearly rate.
- **Points.** These are fees paid to the lender or broker and are often linked to the interest rate—usually the more points you pay, the lower the rate. Ask for the points to be quoted to you as a dollar figure.
- **Fees.** The broker or lender should be able to give you an estimate of fees, which can include loan origination or underwriting fees, broker fees, and settlement or closing costs. Some are paid when you apply; others are paid at closing, and many are negotiable. Often you can include the money to pay these fees in the loan, but that will increase your loan amount and total costs. Ask for an explanation of any fee you don't understand.

Sell the nonresident's interest to a third person.

If you're going through a divorce, a relative or friend might be able to help you acquire your home while also getting a tax benefit. Your relative or friend would purchase your spouse's interest in the house under what is called "an equity share financing arrangement." You would then co-own the property with that person and probably would pay rent. If you were to sell the property, the two of you would share in any profit.

You and your relative or friend will need an agreement spelling out your respective rights and responsibilities. To be sure the agreement complies with IRS rules and that you will both obtain available tax benefits, see a tax adviser.

Sell to a spouse using an installment loan.

Spouses often agree, and some courts order, that the custodial parent will continue to live in the family home with the minor children. The custodial parent could purchase the home from the other, in exchange for a secured installment note with payments over a fixed period of time. An installment note secured by the home allows the buyer to deduct interest and protects the seller in case the buyer defaults.

Keep the house in exchange for a release of alimony.

If an ex-spouse would be entitled to a sizable amount of alimony, consider exchanging it for the house. This would be accomplished with a lump sum payment of alimony. Courts might not allow all future support payments to be waived; check with an attorney on this point.

Keep the house in exchange for other assets.

Most often, couples trade assets and debts depending on needs and affordability. If you choose this option, see "Tallying Your Marital Balance Sheet" in Chapter 19.

Borrow from your retirement plan to finance the buyout.

Consider your retirement plan account as a possible source of financing for a home purchase. The costs of borrowing from a retirement account are usually lower than borrowing from a traditional lender. And because you are borrowing from yourself, loan payments are credited to your retirement account. Plus, loan processing is often quicker than with a traditional lender.

However, if you don't repay the loan within a reasonable time period, it is considered a distribution from your retirement plan. In addition to having to report the withdrawal as income on your tax return (and pay ordinary income taxes on it), you'll be subject to a 10% IRS early withdrawal penalty unless certain conditions are met. (See Chapter 14 for details on retirement plans.)

You can only borrow the money if both of the following apply:
- the loan provides for both principal and interest payments, and
- you agree to repay the money within a "reasonable" time, generally assumed to be five years.

To be able to deduct the mortgage interest paid, the loan must be secured by your residence.

You will not be able to deduct the mortgage interest if either of the following is true:
- the loan is secured by your employer's contributions to your retirement plan, or
- you are considered a key employee of the company, which means you:
  - are an officer or the employer
  - are one of the ten largest owners
  - own more than 5% of the company during the current year or preceding year, or
  - own more than 1% of the company and earn more than $150,000 per year.

Questions to Ask an Attorney or Financial Adviser

! CAUTION
The issue of the house raises several important legal and financial questions. Below are some important questions for you to ask an attorney or research at your local law library, as well as questions for a financial adviser.

Attorney Questions

1. Is a portion of the house considered separate property? How does the court treat a separate property interest in the family home in my state?
2. Am I entitled to a credit for mortgage payments I make while my spouse lives in the family home after we separate? Is this credit reduced by the value of tax benefits received from the mortgage interest deduction?
3. What happens if the bank forecloses on this loan?
4. What is my income tax liability, if any, if the title to the house transfers to me and there is a foreclosure?
5. If there is a foreclosure, can the lender get a judgment against me for any difference between the foreclosed value of the house and the mortgage balance that I owe?
6. Should I get divorced before or after the house sells?
7. If we continue to hold the house as joint tenants, does the right of survivorship continue after the divorce?
8. If we want to defer sale of the house, what are the consequences for me? What steps would we need to take?

Financial Adviser Questions

1. What penalties apply for prepayment of our mortgage?
2. Do we have any unamortized points from our existing mortgage?
3. Am I adequately insured?
4. If our house sells and we are still married, should we file a joint tax return?

5. If we own it jointly and then I buy out my spouse's share, how do I report this for tax purposes?

6. Who gets the mortgage interest deduction and the property tax deduction if the title is held as tenants in common? If it's held as joint tenants?

7. If I refinance the mortgage, will the interest and points, if any, be deductible? ●

Retirement Benefits: Who Gets What?

Whether your retirement benefits come from your own job, your spouse's job, or other retirement plans, those benefits must be divided when you divorce.

SKIP AHEAD
If neither you nor your spouse has a retirement plan, skip ahead to Chapter 15.

Under the best of circumstances, planning for your retirement is difficult. You might not have given much thought to retirement planning, hoping it would somehow take care of itself. But it won't. You've got to give some serious consideration to when you will retire, how much income you'll need during retirement, the sources for that income, and how you will divide retirement benefits with your ex-spouse.

Retirement planning is a relatively new concept. Generations ago, few people had to worry about late-life security because most just didn't live that long. Today, an entire industry has emerged to provide retirement planning services. The pressure to create sound retirement plans can be intense, and divorce adds another layer of complexity.

In most states, retirement plans are treated as property to divide at divorce. Naturally, you might be emotionally attached to the retirement benefits that you worked so hard to earn or feel that you're entitled to as part of your commitment to the marriage. Take heart. Retirement benefits can serve as significant bargaining chips when spouses trade assets in the final property settlement.

RESOURCE
The concept of retirement planning is only introduced in this chapter. For more information, see *IRAs, 401(k)s & Other Retirement Plans: Strategies for Taking Your Money Out,* by Twila Slesnick, and John Suttle (Nolo).

Planning for Your Retirement

No matter how you and your soon-to-be ex-spouse divide the retirement benefits, it's important now to plan for your own retirement. Here's why, and what you'll need to do:

- Americans are living longer. You should plan for an income stream through at least age 90.
- The responsibility for providing retirement income is being shifted slowly but surely by employers onto the shoulders of employees. Take advantage of any and all retirement plans available to you now through your employer. Once your credit cards are paid off, contribute more—the maximum allowed if possible.
- You have more investment choices now than ever before in 401(k) plans and self-directed plans. Learn what you need to know about available mutual funds, as well as their objectives and performance, so you can make intelligent decisions.
- If you are not part of the "triple-squeeze" generation—supporting an aging parent, putting a child through college, and trying to save for your own retirement simultaneously—you might be soon. Be sure to consider these factors as you make your decisions about splitting retirement plans in divorce.

Understanding Retirement Plans

Almost every book and expert on the subject of retirement planning uses a different system to categorize plans. In the pages that follow, this book separates plans into several major categories and provides a table that gives detailed information on the various retirement plans. Once you've determined which plans you and your spouse have, you can focus on the sections in this chapter that apply to you.

The table also specifies how, under the law, particular plans may be divided at divorce. To divide some types of plans, you must get a special kind of court order called a QDRO (pronounced "quadro")— a Qualified Domestic Relations Order (see below). Other retirement assets can be divided by a court order or judgment other than a QDRO. And some kinds of retirement assets can't be divided at divorce.

This chapter distinguishes between defined benefit plans and defined contribution plans. In defined benefit plans, also called pension plans, an employer provides a fixed amount to an employee at retirement, usually in monthly payments that continue until the employee's death. In defined contribution plans, which include 401(k) plans, the employee— and often the employer—contributes money into the employee's retire-ment account, which grows over time. IRAs—or Individual Retirement Accounts—are similar to defined contribution plans, although dividing the assets at divorce doesn't require a QDRO.

If you or your spouse has a defined benefit plan, it's difficult to deter-mine just how much the plan is worth today. That's because the plan is designed to pay out in the future, and inflation causes today's dollars to have a different value than they'll have 20 or 30 years from now. It takes an expert, such as an actuary, to find the current value of this kind of plan. That makes dividing the asset a complicated task, as you'll see. It's a lot easier to tell how much a defined contribution plan or an IRA is worth today: As the account grows, the current value is reported to the account holder in regular statements.

 WEB RESOURCE
The internet is a terrific resource for gathering additional information.
Sites such as www.morningstar.com and www.finance.yahoo.com offer valuable insights into and analysis of many different types of retirement funds. Be sure to check whether your retirement plan has information available online. Many company and government plan sponsors provide up-to-date account values and information through their websites or through automated phone systems.

Employer-Sponsored Defined Contribution Plans

Type of Plan	Description	Type of Order Necessary to Divide Plan
Salary Savings/401(k), 403(b), and 457 Plans	Employee contributes a portion of salary on a pretax basis, which may be matched in full or in part by the employer. The most an employee may defer (meaning contribute) to one of these plans is up to $22,500 annually in 2023 or $30,000 if age 50 or older. Employer contributions are on top of that limit.	QDRO
Thrift Plan	Employee contributes a portion of salary on an after-tax basis, which may be matched in full or in part by the employer. Because the employee's contribution is made on an after-tax basis, distributions (payouts) may be partially tax free.	QDRO
Profit-Sharing Plan	Employer contributes to the employee's account only if company is profitable. Amount of contribution is based on either a fixed or a discretionary formula.	QDRO
Money Purchase Plan	Employer contributes a fixed percentage of salary to employee's account every year. Employer contribution is mandatory, regardless of whether company makes a profit.	QDRO
Employee Stock Ownership Plan (ESOP)	Contributions are a percentage of salary and are used to purchase company stock. The stock is held in trust for the employee, who receives the accumulated interest in the plan at termination of employment in the form of stock or cash. The plan provisions define the rights of the employee to exercise stock options.	QDRO
Tax-Sheltered Annuity (TSA)	TSAs are a retirement vehicle allowing teachers, public school system employees, and employees of nonprofit organizations to contribute a portion of salary into the annuity. If your TSA is through the Teachers Insurance and Annuity Association–College Retirement Equities Fund (TIAA-CREF), you can get detailed information, including account values, on the Web at www.tiaa.org.	QDRO

Employer-Sponsored IRAs		
Type of Plan	Description	Type of Order Necessary to Divide Plan
Simplified Employee Pension IRA (SEP-IRA)	SEP-IRAs are retirement plans in the form of IRAs. An early withdrawal penalty of 10% applies to SEP-IRAs as well as traditional IRAs and Roth IRAs. The maximum contribution an employer can make to an employee's SEP-IRA can't exceed the lesser of 25% of the employee's compensation or $66,000 for 2023. (Note: Elective salary deferrals and catch-up contributions are not permitted in SEP plans.)	A regular court order or judgment divides these plans.
Salary Reduction– Simplified Employee Pension IRA (SAR-IRA)	These retirement plans were available prior to 1997 and included a salary reduction agreement in which the employee could elect to have a portion of salary contributed to a SEP-IRA on a pretax basis. For the plans still in operation, a participant's elective deferral contributions are limited to $22,500 in 2023. The overall contribution limit (including both employer and employee contributions, but excluding catch-up contributions) is the same as the SEP limit, above.	A regular court order or judgment divides these plans.
SIMPLE (Simplified Incentive Match Plans for Employees) IRA	A SIMPLE IRA involves a written salary reduction agreement between the employee and employer that allows the employee-participant to reduce compensation and have the employer contribute the difference to a SIMPLE IRA on the employee's behalf. (Employees may elect not to contribute.) The employer makes matching contributions or nonelective contributions. Nonelective contributions are made for each eligible employee, even if the employee does not elect to contribute. For 2023, the total annual employee salary reduction contributions (elective deferrals) are limited to 2% of compensation or $15,500 total. For employees age 50 or over, a $3,500 catch-up contribution is also allowed. The employer's matching contribution is the lesser of the employee contribution or 3% of the employee's annual salary. The distribution rules applicable to a traditional IRA also apply to a SIMPLE IRA, except that if the employee withdraws money prematurely within two years after beginning participation, the 10% penalty is increased to 25%. In addition, during the first two years of plan participation, a rollover (transfer of funds) can be made only to another SIMPLE IRA plan. A SIMPLE IRA cannot be designated as a Roth IRA.	A regular court order or judgment divides these plans.

Government-Sponsored Retirement Plans

Type of Plan	Description	Type of Order Necessary to Divide Plan
Government/ Military Pension	These defined benefit plans are offered to civil service workers, government employees, and military personnel. (Veterans can get additional information on their benefits at www.va.gov.)	Specific governmental regulations and procedures apply for implementation of a court order to divide these plan benefits between spouses.

Personal Retirement Plans/Personal Annuities

Type of Plan	Description	Type of Order Necessary to Divide Plan
Deferred Annuity	A deferred annuity is an annuity contract in which an insurance company promises to make payments at some future date. Taxes on appreciation are deferred until the money is withdrawn.	A regular court order or judgment divides these plans. Most insurance companies have forms that permit the transfer of ownership.
Traditional IRA	Individuals may contribute up to $6,500 per year for 2023 ($7,500 for workers over age 50). Withdrawals before age 59½ are subject to a 10% withdrawal tax penalty, unless an exception applies (see www.irs.gov/retirement-plans/plan-participant-employee/retirement-topics-tax-on-early-distributions). The early withdrawal penalty does not apply to a withdrawal because of disability or a withdrawal for certain medical insurance premiums, educational expenses, or first-time homebuyer or builder expenses up to a maximum of $10,000. The account value is untaxed until funds are withdrawn.	A regular court order or judgment divides IRAs.
Roth IRA	Individuals may contribute up to $6,500 per year for 2023 (workers over age 50 are allowed to contribute another $1,000 per year). Contributions are not deductible when you make them, but qualified distributions of the contributions and earnings are tax free when withdrawn. In general, you can take tax-free withdrawals if, after holding the account for five years, you meet certain conditions. You must be at least 59½, disabled, or using the money (up to $10,000) toward the purchase of your first home, qualified educational expenses, or medical expenses or health insurance. If you do not meet any of these conditions, you may be subject to a 10% early withdrawal tax penalty.	A regular court order or judgment divides IRAs.

Miscellaneous Retirement Benefits		
Type of Plan	Description	Type of Order Necessary to Divide Plan
Nonqualified Deferred Compensation Plan	A small percentage of executives and key upper-level employees have deferred compensation plans. Generally, such a plan provides that a portion of the employee's compensation is deferred until the future. Agreements to participate in the plans are made directly between the employer and the employee, which makes requesting documentation from the employer important. (For more on these plans, see Chapter 16.)	Often the plans do not permit the asset or income to be divided, making them legally complicated. In such a case, the court might order the employee spouse to pay the nonemployee spouse when the employee spouse receives the benefit. Because the employee spouse pays taxes upon receipt of benefits, the order should include a provision that the employee spouse will deduct the nonemployee spouse's share of taxes on the benefit.
Social Security	If you are divorced, you can receive benefits at age 62 based on your former spouse's earnings if the marriage lasted at least ten years, you are unmarried, and the benefit based on your own earnings is not greater than 50% of your former spouse's benefit. If your former spouse is at least age 62 and not receiving benefits but can qualify for them, you can still receive benefits if you have been divorced for at least two years and meet the other requirements. To apply for benefits on your former spouse's record, you will need either the spouse's Social Security number or date and place of birth and parents' names. Your benefits as an ex-spouse do not reduce or otherwise affect benefits available to your former spouse. You can find out about Social Security benefits by calling 800-772-1213 or visiting www.ssa.gov. For more on Social Security, see Chapter 5.	Social Security benefits are generally not considered marital property and are not divisible at divorce.

Retirement Plans Are Not Created Equal

Retirement plans vary tremendously. Even if two plans look equal on paper, fine-print plan provisions can make one plan more valuable than another. For instance, one plan may allow for a lump sum payout upon retirement, while another may not. Getting your retirement dollars in a lump sum may provide more flexibility than getting monthly payments in dollars whose value erodes over time or disappears entirely if the plan becomes insolvent in later years.

Retirement plans must comply with federal regulations, but the way they are apportioned at divorce may differ from state to state. One state may define retirement benefits as marital property (an asset to be divided at divorce), while another may rule that benefits are income (and not to be divided). Be sure to ask your lawyer how your state treats retirement benefits upon divorce. (In a worst-case scenario for the employee spouse, a state may regard retirement benefits as both marital property and income, allowing "double-dipping" for the nonemployee spouse.)

Some Plans Promise Better Tax Breaks Than Others

One major attraction of most retirement plans is that you defer paying income taxes on the money that accumulates in the plan. In some plans, though, you must pay income taxes on the money before it's deposited. One task during your divorce will be to determine the tax position of your benefits. Normally, you want to defer paying the taxes until you withdraw the money from the plan and presumably are in a lower income bracket or have a lower annual income.

Divorce Leads to Division Decisions

Will you split the retirement money now or later? A present division means you divide the value of the plan now, at divorce. A future division means the plan is divided at retirement or at the point in the employee spouse's career when the benefits would normally be paid out. When and how you divide the plan depends on the type of plan you have, payout provisions, valuation methods, and other factors. Your division decision at divorce has a direct impact on your future financial security, so do not make this choice lightly.

Qualified Domestic Relations Orders

QDROs, interim QDROs, and other kinds of court orders are used to divide various kinds of retirement plans.

QDRO

QDRO stands for Qualified Domestic Relations Order. It is an order from the court to the retirement plan administrator spelling out how the plan's benefits are to be assigned to each party in a divorce. It's critical that your QDRO be complete and accurate, because any assets or items that the order omits, even accidentally, cannot be reinstated later.

What Constitutes a QDRO

For a document dividing a retirement plan to be considered a QDRO, it must specify:

- the name and last known mailing address of the employee spouse (the participant)
- the name and mailing address of the nonemployee spouse (the alternate payee)
- the amount or percentage of the participant's benefits to be paid to the alternate payee, or the manner in which the amount or percentage is to be determined
- the number of payments or the period to which the order applies, and
- the name of the plan, such as the Walton Company Pension Plan, to which the order applies.

A QDRO cannot:

- require a plan to pay any benefit or option not otherwise provided by the plan
- require a plan to provide benefits that exceed the value of the participant's interest as determined by an actuary
- require the payment of benefits to an alternate payee if those benefits are already payable to another alternate payee (that is, another ex-spouse) under a previous qualified order, or
- specify who will be responsible for payment of taxes.

Retirement Plan Lingo

Before making decisions, familiarize yourself with the terms you'll hear regarding retirement plans. You have a better chance of getting answers to your questions if you know what to ask for:

- **Account balance.** For plans such as IRAs and defined contribution plans, you'll want to know "the balance," which simply means the amount in the account.
- **Accrued benefit.** The amount that is earned (or accrued) in a retirement plan as of a particular date.
- **Annuity contracts.** A contract between a life insurance company and the investor or annuity owner. Typical provisions include the amount of interest (both the guaranteed minimum and the current), surrender charges (fees for ending the contract prematurely), and penalties and options at retirement.
- **Defined benefit plan.** The employee's retirement benefit is fixed, based on a specific formula.
- **Defined contribution plan.** The employee and sometimes the employer contribute to a retirement account, often at regular intervals.
- **Employee benefit statement.** A summary telling you the amount of benefits (in dollars) that have accumulated in your name or your spouse's.
- **Full plan.** You might or might not need a copy of the full plan, depending on how well the summary plan description (see below) is written. Don't hesitate to ask for the full plan if you have questions.
- **Procedures and model orders for division.** Many companies have written procedures for dividing up company retirement plan benefits. Request a copy of these materials.
- **Qualified plan.** A retirement plan that qualifies for certain benefits described in Section 401 of the U.S. Tax Code; also known as an "ERISA" plan.
- **Summary plan description.** Employers are required to issue a description (annually in most cases) outlining the status and terms of retirement plans.
- **Trust/custodial agreement.** A document spelling out specific provisions of the retirement plan and the agreements between the legal owner of the plan, usually the plan administrator (called the "trustee"), and the employee (the beneficial owner). These agreements are particularly important with IRAs because they describe the costs of establishing, maintaining, and terminating IRA accounts.

Plans subject to QDROs include:

- qualified plans
- defined contribution plans
- defined benefit plans, and
- tax-sheltered annuities (TSAs).

Plans that QDROs do not cover include:

- deferred annuities
- traditional IRAs
- Roth IRAs
- SEP-IRAs
- nonqualified deferred compensation plans (government and church plans)
- plans administered by a plan participant (you or your ex-spouse), and
- plans under which you do not receive benefits from your ex-spouse's retirement plan.

Sometimes an order concerning the retirement plans is in a document called a Domestic Relations Order, Marital Settlement Agreement, or Divorce Settlement Agreement. These kinds of orders are not QDROs.

Interim QDROs

If you are not ready to divide the retirement plan assets and prepare a QDRO, you can still protect your rights to survivor benefits under your spouse's retirement plan by filing what is called an interim QDRO. Later, when retirement assets are divided, you can get a final QDRO. If you divorce before dividing your property, it's very important to have an interim QDRO prepared and signed by a judge, simultaneous with the judgment that changes your marital status to legally separated or divorced. Here's what an interim QDRO accomplishes:

- It treats the nonemployee spouse as a surviving spouse. Even if the employee remarries, the former spouse's interest in survivor benefits is paid before the new surviving spouse receives anything.
- It prohibits the employee from electing to receive retirement plan benefits without permission of the former spouse or a court order, except for any minimum required distribution.
- It sets the former spouse's rights at 50% of the community portion of the employee's benefit.

An attorney should be able to advise you on filing an interim QDRO. But don't wait very long to obtain the actual QDRO. A delay can mean a loss of benefits. Be sure the QDRO is accepted by the employee spouse's plan administrator. A divorced ex-spouse without a QDRO does not have the same protection available under the plan during marriage.

> ## CAUTION
> You should *always* consult a lawyer when you need a QDRO, and make sure the lawyer is comfortable preparing a QDRO or uses a reputable specialist to outsource the work. This task is not something you can do yourself; even some very experienced attorneys find QDROs painfully complicated.
>
> If you're representing yourself, you'll need help protecting your right to share in retirement plans. This might require filing papers to "join" the retirement plan as a party in your divorce, and other important paperwork. Make sure you get the help you need to do it right.

The Legal Value of Your Retirement Plans

As this book often stresses, the value of an asset as recognized by a court may be vastly different from what the asset is worth outside the courtroom. So it is with retirement plans. Normally, the value of a plan as determined by the court—its "legal value"—is the following:

- For defined contribution plans, personal annuities, and IRAs, the legal value is the amount that appears on your statement as the current value of the account, less any loans outstanding.
- For defined benefit plans, the legal value is what the plan administrator or an actuary tells you it's worth.

You need to know the legal value because it is often the only dollar value lawyers and judges will take into consideration. This value represents the amount you and your spouse will argue over if you disagree about the value of the benefits. However, the legal value does not account for important financial realities: taxes, early withdrawal penalties, early termination fees, and other assessments.

Benchmarks to Retirement

Most people think of age 65 as the standard retirement age. But other birthdays are also important in preparing for the after-work years. By noting these key ages ahead of time, you may be able to minimize taxes and maximize benefits.

Be sure to review your company's retirement plans. Each plan has its own rules about the age at which retirement benefits can begin. In some circumstances you may choose to receive your retirement benefits early, but your monthly benefit will be lower. Your benefits administrator can give you more information on what retirement benefits are available to you and the ages at which you can begin receiving these benefits. Most employers also provide employees with a statement showing an estimate of retirement benefits at early and regular retirement ages. Ages to note include:

Age 55 If you retire, quit, or are fired and are age 55 or older, you may receive benefits from an employer-sponsored qualified plan without having to pay a 10% penalty. This exception does not apply to either personal or employer-sponsored IRA distributions.

Age 59½ You are allowed to withdraw funds from personal and employer-sponsored IRAs and retirement plans without paying the 10% penalty.

Age 60 Widows and widowers become eligible for Social Security benefits.

Age 62 You may be eligible to receive Social Security benefits, but benefits will be less than if you retire at age 65.

Age 65 Retirees qualify for Medicare benefits.

Age 67 Full Social Security benefits are available for anyone born in 1960 or later. The actual age at which full Social Security benefits are available depends on the year in which you were born. For those born before 1938, full Social Security benefits are available at age 65. For those born later, the retirement age is between 65 and two months and 67, depending on your birth year.

Age 70 Full Social Security benefits are available, even if you continue to work full-time.

Benchmarks to Retirement (continued)

Age 70½ You're required to begin taking distributions from IRAs (except Roth IRAs) by April 1 of the year following the calendar year in which you reach age 70½. For other employer-sponsored qualified retirement plans, distributions must begin by April 1 of the year following age 70½ or the year of retirement, whichever is later. If the participant is at least a 5% owner of the business, distributions must begin at age 70½.

Defined Contribution Plans, Personal Annuities, and IRAs

If you have a defined contribution plan, a personal annuity, or an IRA, determining the legal value is simple. The plan statement gives the value. If you can't find the information you need, consult the plan administrator or get a copy of the annuity contract.

Defined Benefit Plans

If you have a defined benefit plan, you'll need to do some work to find its legal value. Because these plans promise a payment in the future, they are harder to value in the present.

The legal value of a defined benefit plan is the plan's present or actuarial value. The plan administrator or the company might be able to give you this value. Another option is to hire an independent third-party actuary to calculate the plan's present value. This option should be relatively inexpensive—perhaps $300 to $500. The bill could run higher if your spouse hires a separate actuary to argue that your actuary's assumptions about the future are wrong, and you find yourself having to call the actuary as an expert witness to testify in a court trial. Disputes can arise because the value of these plans lies in the future and is therefore speculative.

After you get the actuarial value for each plan, you will need to determine what percentage of the plan qualifies as marital property to be divided at divorce. (Some actuaries will do this at the same time they establish the value of the plan.)

Determining the Marital Portion

To simplify the process of calculating the marital portion of your retirement plan, use the marital interest percentage method (total months of participation while married divided by total months of plan participation). This method is generally used in dividing defined benefit plans.

The problem with using this method is that it does not accurately value the higher contributions made during the later years of employment. In the early years of plan participation, the contribution is smaller because contribution is based on salary, which is likely to have increased over time. For a more precise calculation, you may need to talk to your actuary, CPA, financial planner, or pension administrator.

How the Separation Date Can Affect a Retirement Plan's Value

A doctor in California asked the pension plan administrator of his medical group to tell him the value of his plan. The doctor had separated from his wife four years earlier, and they were ready to divide the retirement plan. The administrator valued the plan currently at $225,000. Wanting a second opinion on this obviously valuable asset, the doctor went to an actuary for another valuation of the plan. The actuary valued the plan at only $175,000. Why the difference? Under California law, the marital period of the doctor's retirement plan stopped on the day of separation four years before. The doctor's wife was entitled only to a portion of the amount that had accrued from their wedding day to the date they separated. By contrast, the plan administrator had calculated the entire value of the plan, including the four-year period that the couple had been separated. Different states define the applicable period differently.

For more on the significance of the separation date, see Chapter 5.

The Financial Value of Your Retirement Plans

The financial value of a retirement plan is almost always lower than its legal value. Financial value encompasses everything from unexpected bonuses (a cash settlement upon divorce) to nasty surprises (a penalty from the IRS).

Although retirement benefits are often years away from being paid out and you may not see the financial return for some time, you nevertheless want to compare all assets on similar terms during your divorce. Just as you may be contemplating a sale of the family home, so, too, must you assume the "sale" (or liquidation) value of a retirement plan. When negotiating the overall settlement, you'll want to be able to compare each asset's legal value and financial value.

To find the financial value of your retirement plans, you'll have to look at income tax consideration as well as charges and penalties. Below is an overview.

Tax Brackets and State Income Taxes

Throughout this book, we assume that you fall into the 24% federal income tax bracket. Because some states tax a percentage of IRA deposits and other retirement plans (thrift plans and employee stock ownership plans), you'll need to ask a tax adviser whether you might owe state taxes on your benefits. You won't owe state income taxes in Alaska, Florida, Nevada, South Dakota, Texas, Washington, or Wyoming, states that impose no income taxes. (New Hampshire and Tennessee tax only interest income and dividends.)

Income Tax Considerations

Uncle Sam does not let you simply accrue money for retirement and then use it, without receiving his share sooner or later. Your job is to find out when taxes on benefits are paid—either before the money goes into the retirement plan or when it comes out during retirement. The plan will contain this information.

How Can a Pension Worth Hundreds of Thousands Later Be Worth So Little Now?

Actuaries commonly look at several factors when calculating the present value of retirement plans. For example, plans often assign benefits based on the highest three years of earnings. But during divorce, current salary is used in the calculation.

Similarly, calculations of the future worth of a plan will differ if a person anticipates retiring at age 62 rather than age 65. They will also vary with the rate of inflation that's predicted and how the payouts are structured. Some plans include a COLA—cost of living adjustment—that affects the plan's value. And, finally, some actuaries assume a consistent rate of growth— say, 5% of retirement plan investments—and others use a different figure.

For example, take the case of John and Andrea. An actuary tells Andrea that the marital portion of John's plan will pay out about $100,000 during John's retirement but is worth only about $38,000 in today's dollars. So if she and John divide the plan equally at divorce, she will get one-half, or $19,000. If she waits until John retires, she could get $50,000. Andrea, understandably, wants to know why something supposed to be so valuable tomorrow can be worth so little today.

Here's why. John's pension plan shows that he will get $10,000 per year during retirement. He's supposed to retire at age 65 and, according to actuarial tables, live ten years after that. In theory, then, he will receive $100,000.

John, however, is only 45 and won't be retiring for another 20 years. Assuming an inflation rate of 4%, the $10,000 he will be paid in the first year of his retirement is equivalent to $4,564 today. The second year of his retirement (21 years from now) is worth even less.

The "Present Value Factors" chart in the appendix compares time value with inflation and can help you make a rough estimate of the value of benefits. The left-hand column on that chart represents years, while the percentages across the top of the page are rates of inflation. Follow the 20-year line (the number of years after which this example assumed John would retire) to the 4% predicted rate of inflation and you find the present value factor of .4564. Multiply $10,000 by .4564 and you get the "value today" of $4,564. You can follow the rest of the 21- to 30-year lines to see how the rest of the value of John's plan was calculated.

Suppose your ex-spouse offers to keep the house but to give you all the retirement plan benefits—your own and your spouse's. Should you take the deal? You cannot answer that question unless you know what income tax you will owe when the benefits begin paying out.

At first glance, your share of the retirement benefits and your share of the house might equal the same dollar amounts. But those amounts probably reflect legal reality only. You might have to pay substantial income taxes when you begin receiving the retirement benefits, while your spouse could take the house and possibly avoid any tax liability.

When dividing plans at divorce, look to keep the plan in which the contributions—or at least some of the contributions—were made with after-tax dollars. When plans are funded with after-tax dollars, part of the money you withdraw at retirement will not be taxed.

Qualified plans—such as defined contribution plans and defined benefit plans—must meet certain IRS regulations for employers to get tax benefits. Tax-sheltered annuities (TSAs), although not considered qualified plans, tend to be affected by the same regulations.

In determining the taxability of money contributed to a retirement plan, the IRS asks two questions:

- Did the employer contribute money? If the answer is yes, when you begin collecting your retirement benefits, you'll have to pay taxes on the amount your employer contributed and the interest earned on that contribution.
- Was the contribution made with pretax or after-tax dollars? Retirement plans are sometimes referred to as contributory or noncontributory. Contributory plans are those to which the employee makes a contribution, and employers often make a matching contribution. For instance, some employers chip in 50 cents for every dollar the employee contributes. Some even match the employee contribution dollar for dollar, often to a limited amount, such as $1,000.

The IRS might seem harsh, but it doesn't intend for you to pay taxes twice on your income. If you are currently reporting as income the money you are contributing to your plan, you will not have to pay taxes on those contributions when the money comes out of the plan at retirement.

If you do not know the percentages of your retirement plan contributions made with pretax dollars and after-tax dollars, you can:

- contact the plan administrator, personnel manager, or benefits coordinator and ask for an accounting of pre- and after-tax contributions, or
- check the annual benefits statement, which should break down pretax and after-tax contributions.

The income taxes you will have to pay on retirement benefits are based on a number of factors: your tax bracket, the tax basis of the plan, your status as either the plan participant (employee) or the alternate payee (spouse of plan participant), and the type of plan you or your spouse has.

The tax basis of a retirement plan consists of money contributed that's already been taxed as income—that is, contributions for which you weren't permitted to take a deduction when you filed your taxes. Most employer contributions, plus interest earned on all contributions—from both employer and employee—are not included in basis because those dollars are not taxed until they are paid out. The plan administrator should be able to help you find the tax basis.

For IRAs and deferred annuities, special tax considerations apply.

IRAs. When you deposit money into a traditional IRA, you do not report that money as income—that is, you pay no taxes on it. This assumes that neither you nor your spouse is an active participant in a qualified plan. If both of you are active participants in qualified plans, you can deduct your $3,000 IRA contribution if your income falls within specified limits.

Roth IRA. Unlike with regular IRAs, money you contribute to a Roth IRA is not tax deductible. But you receive the benefits tax free when you collect at retirement. This makes Roth IRAs particularly valuable to retain in a divorce.

In general, you can also take tax-free withdrawals if you have held the account for five years or more and are under age 59½, become disabled, or use up to $10,000 toward the purchase of your first home or for qualified education or medical expenses.

Until recently, you could convert your traditional IRA to a Roth only if you had an adjusted gross income of less than $100,000. But now anybody—even spouses filing separately—can convert retirement assets to a Roth IRA, though they'll owe taxes on the amount converted.

Deferred annuities. The money put into a deferred annuity usually comes from your savings or from income on which you have already been taxed. The tax basis of your annuity is the total purchase price less unpaid loans and any other tax-free amounts you received. You will pay taxes on the difference between the current account value and the tax basis. From the standpoint of income tax liability, the Roth IRA and deferred annuities are similar. Both will have a tax basis, because contributions were made with after-tax dollars.

Charges and Penalties

Participants in retirement plans often face charges and penalties when there is an early withdrawal—that is, when money is taken out before a certain date. Check your plan documents carefully or ask your plan administrator to see if these charges or penalties apply, to be sure you don't unknowingly incur them.

If a participant in a qualified retirement plan takes money out before retiring, the IRS may assess an early withdrawal penalty (also called an excise tax) as high as 10% of the amount withdrawn. There may be a state tax penalty in addition to the federal penalty.

The holder of an IRA or an annuity who withdraws money before reaching age 59½ will pay a 10% tax penalty to the IRS unless certain exceptions are met.

Insurance companies and some investment companies impose surrender charges to discourage participants from withdrawing funds before the date specified in the contract. These can take the form of deferred sales charges on mutual funds, surrender charges on annuities, early withdrawal charges on CDs, and brokerage or transaction costs.

Another tax wrinkle concerning IRAs: If the participant spouse transfers all or part of an IRA to the other spouse, neither will owe taxes on the transfer. If the participant spouse cashes out the IRA and transfers the money to the other spouse, however, the participant spouse will owe taxes on the money withdrawn. It's therefore crucial to be sure that the money goes directly from one account to another in what's called a "trustee-to-trustee" transfer or "assignment of ownership."

The 10% early withdrawal penalty tax does not apply to any distribution to an alternate payee pursuant to a QDRO, regardless of the alternate payee's age when he or she receives it and whether the alternate payee is the spouse, former spouse, child, or other dependent. However, once the distribution is rolled over into an IRA, it becomes subject to the penalty if a later distribution occurs. (Note: An IRA is not a qualified plan and is not subject to a QDRO.)

Pros and Cons of Early Distributions

It is becoming increasingly common for employees to break into retirement accounts early or take out loans on them. When there is a real economic necessity—such as a medical emergency or buying a first home—this might be a prudent decision. As pointed out in Chapter 13, it also can make sense to take out a loan on your 401(k) to purchase a share of your house. The 10% tax on early distributions is sometimes waived for this purpose (visit www.irs.gov to research exceptions to the early distribution rule).

That said, early withdrawal penalties and taxes can severely diminish the value of a 401(k). If you and your spouse are considering an early distribution as you move forward in a divorce settlement, be certain that you do the math to determine what your account will be worth. If you're in your 40s or 50s, the consequences of losing value of your retirement plan in a taxable—and avoidable—event can be devastating.

Calculating the Financial Value of Plans

Again, any retirement plan has a financial value different from the legal value that a court assigns it. The financial value takes into account real-world factors like tax consequences and early withdrawal penalties. Doing the calculation that follows and entering it into the chart may seem complicated. But knowing the financial value of a plan will help you make a better-informed decision about where the assets should go in your divorce settlement.

The calculation is different depending on whether the plan is a defined benefit plan or a defined contribution plan, a TSA, or an IRA.

Defined Contribution Plans

For each defined contribution plan, TSA, or IRA plan, follow the steps below to complete the chart that follows this calculation:

1. In Column A, enter the total number of months you or your spouse participated in the plan.
2. In Column B, enter the number of months in which you or your spouse participated in the plan while married.
3. In Column C, enter the marital interest percentage by dividing the number in Column B by the number in Column A. For example, if you participated in a plan for 120 months and were married 72 months while participating in the plan, you would have a marital interest percentage of 60% ((72 ÷ 120) × 100).
4. In Column D, enter the current dollar value of the account. (The amount should be on your statement.)
5. In Column E, enter the marital portion of the account by multiplying the amount in Column D by the percentage in Column C.
6. In Column F, enter the amount of any loans you and your spouse have taken against this retirement account. (The amount should be on your statement.) Do not include any separate loans.
7. In Column G, enter the legal value of your retirement plan by subtracting the amount in Column F, if any, from the amount in Column E.

8. In Column H, enter the tax basis of the retirement plan—the after-tax contributions, including nondeductible contributions made to an IRA.

9. In Column I, enter the marital portion of the tax basis by multiplying the figure in Column H by the percentage in Column C.

10. In Column J, enter the financial value of this account. You do this as follows:

Marital account value (Column E less Column I)	$_____
*Early withdrawal penalty**	– $_____
Taxes due on distribution (marital account value × your tax bracket)	– $_____
Other surrender charges or penalties	– $_____
Financial value	$_____

* The early withdrawal penalty is the amount in Column D × 10%, or × 25% for employer-sponsored SIMPLE IRAs you have participated in for two years or less. Be sure to add any state early withdrawal penalties.

Defined Benefit Plans

For a defined benefit plan, follow the steps below to complete the chart that follows:

1. In Column A, enter the total number of months you or your spouse participated in the plan.

2. In Column B, enter the number of months in which you or your spouse participated in the plan while married.

3. In Column C, enter the marital interest percentage by dividing the number in Column B by the number in Column A. For example, if you participated in a plan for 120 months, and were married 72 months while participating in the plan, you would have a marital interest percentage of 60% (($72 \div 120) \times 100$).

4. In Column D, enter the actuarial value of the plan. (You'll need to consult with the plan administrator or an actuary for this information.)

5. In Column E, enter the marital portion of the account by multiplying the value in Column D by the percentage in Column C.

6. In Column F, enter the amount of any loan you and your spouse have taken against this retirement account. (The amount should be on your statement.) Do not include any separate loan.

7. In Column G, enter the legal value of your retirement plan by subtracting the amount in Column F, if any, from the amount in Column E.

8. In Column H, enter the tax basis of the retirement plan—the after-tax contributions.

9. In Column I, enter the marital portion of the tax basis by multiplying the figure in Column H by the percentage in Column C.

10. In Column J, enter the financial value of this account. You do this as follows:

Marital account value (Column E less Column I) $_____

Taxes due on distribution (marital account value × your tax bracket)   – $_____

Other surrender charges or penalties   – $_____

Financial value $_____

Once you have completed the steps above for each retirement plan, add all the numbers in Columns D, E, F, and J and enter these results in their respective columns on the "Total" line. Then, be sure to transfer the totals to the "Net Worth: Assets and Liabilities Worksheet" in Chapter 12.

Also transfer the legal value to the "Marital Balance Sheet" in Chapter 19. Any separate property (including a separate property loan) should be entered in the appropriate section on the "Marital Balance Sheet."

Rolling Over Your Distribution From Your Ex-Spouse's IRA

Under IRA rules, any money you withdraw from an IRA prematurely (before age 59½) must be reinvested (referred to as a "rollover") within 60 days or it will be subject to an IRS early withdrawal penalty.

You can defer the income tax liability on the distribution by rolling over the distribution to another IRA within 60 days of the divorce. If you decide to roll over the distribution, keep in mind the following:

- You cannot roll over any portion of the distribution that is attributable to after-tax contributions of the plan participant. In other words, any nondeductible contributions that your ex-spouse made to an IRA can't be rolled over into your account. But if part of the distribution is attributable to after-tax contributions and part is attributable to before-tax contributions, you will be able to roll over a portion of the distribution.
- If you take possession of funds from your ex-spouse's IRA and *then* roll them over into your own IRA, 20% will be withheld for taxes.
- However, if the plan distribution goes directly to the new plan, then you avoid the 20% withholding on the distribution.

Even if you have someone else managing your account, it is still your responsibility to see that it is done correctly. In one case, a trustee was handling a taxpayer's account. The trustee mistakenly transferred a rollover distribution to a brokerage account instead of an IRA. When the trustee discovered the mistake, the amount was transferred to a qualified plan, but the 60-day limit had expired. The IRS ruled that the distribution was not rolled over within the 60 days, and therefore the distribution was taxable even though the taxpayer was not at fault.

The lesson here is that it's your responsibility to follow up on how your accounts are handled. Trustee mistakes can and do occur. Failure to properly time your rollover can lead the IRS to assess penalties.

Additional Financial Factors Affecting Retirement Plan Divisions

Often, spouses keep their own retirement benefits in exchange for other assets. As a simplified example, if each spouse's share of the house is $75,000 and the nonemployee spouse's share of the other's retirement plan is $75,000, then the employee could keep the retirement plan while the other spouse would take the house.

Fairly dividing assets during a divorce, however, is not as simple as the above example. To truly exchange assets of equal value, you must take a variety of financial factors into account. Consider the following factors before you make a proposal about dividing retirement benefits with your spouse.

Vesting

One retirement plan concept that is especially important at divorce is vesting. You've probably heard people say they'll be "fully vested" after a certain number of years or that they'll "be vested in another year." Vesting means that you are entitled to the retirement benefits your employer has contributed to the plan for you. Even if you quit your job or are fired, you are entitled to those benefits.

Being fully vested means that you are entitled to all the benefits your employer has contributed. Being partially vested means that if you were to begin receiving the benefits from your employer's contribution to the plan, you'd be entitled to only a particular percentage. If the plan paid $1,000 a month upon retirement and you were 30% vested, you'd receive $300.

Vesting affects only the portion of your benefits that your *employer* contributed toward your retirement plan and its earnings. The contributions you make to your plan, and the earnings attributable to those contributions, always belong to you.

Calculating the Financial Value of Plans										
Type of Plan	A: Months of Plan Participation*	B: Months of Marriage During Plan	C: Marital Interest	D: Dollar Amount of Account	E: Marital Portion of Account	F: Marital Loans Against Account**	G: Legal Value	H: Tax Basis	I: Marital Portion of Tax Basis	J: Financial Value***
Employer-Sponsored Retirement Plans										
Qualified Plans—Defined Contribution Plans										
Business or Corporate Defined Benefit Plans										
Salary Savings or 401(k) Plan										
Thrift Plan										
Profit-Sharing Plan										
Money Purchase Plan										
ESOP										
TSA										
Employer-Sponsored IRAs										
SEP-IRA										
SAR-IRA										
SIMPLE IRA										

*Check state laws to determine the date retirement plan benefits become separate property.
**If separate, do not include balance here, but be sure to include separate property loan balance on the "Marital Balance Sheet" in Chapter 19.
***If your state awards unvested benefits, you might want to subtract the unvested portion.

Calculating the Financial Value of Plans (continued)

Type of Plan	A: Months of Plan Participation*	B: Months of Marriage During Plan	C: Marital Interest	D: Dollar Amount of Account	E: Marital Portion of Account	F: Marital Loans Against Account**	G: Legal Value	H: Tax Basis	I: Marital Portion of Tax Basis	J: Financial Value***
Qualified Plans—Defined Benefit Plans										
Business or Corporate Defined Benefit Plan										
Government-Sponsored Retirement Plans										
Government Plan or Military Pension										
Personal Retirement Plans										
Deferred Annuity										
Personal IRA										
Traditional IRA										
Roth IRA										
Total										

*Check state laws to determine the date retirement plan benefits become separate property.
**If separate, do not include balance here, but be sure to include separate property loan balance on the "Marital Balance Sheet" in Chapter 19.
***If your state awards unvested benefits, you might want to subtract the unvested portion.

If you are not fully vested, consider consulting an attorney to determine whether your state characterizes nonvested retirement benefits as marital property. If it does not, then division of your plan in that state is not affected by vesting. If the state does characterize the benefits as marital property, however, and you divorce before you fully vest, you could face the awful prospect of paying your spouse a portion of the retirement benefits even though you might *never* receive them yourself. If you are not fully vested and might encounter this costly dilemma, be sure you know your rights and obligations before negotiating over your retirement plan as part of your divorce settlement. (See "Questions to Ask an Attorney," below.)

For example, in a state where nonvested benefits are considered marital property, the total value of your retirement plan is calculated and that amount is divided. If you want to keep the retirement plan, you might have to buy out your spouse's share or exchange it for another asset. If you're fired or change jobs, you might not receive your employer's contributions to your retirement plan, even though you paid your spouse for them.

To reduce these risks, carefully consider whether to divide your plan in the future or in the present (see "The Division Decision: Now or in the Future," below).

If you are fully vested (and therefore entitled to your employer's contribution and required to divide all retirement benefits at divorce), double-check the details of your benefits package to be sure you know about any provisions that could be affected by divorce or death. In some cases, when a single (unmarried or divorced) employee dies before the age of 55, that person's estate may not be entitled to the benefits even though the person is fully vested.

Benefits in Payout Status

Even after pension benefits vest, the employee may still have to wait before actually receiving the benefits. Usually, vested pensions do not pay out ("mature") until the worker reaches a certain age, such as 65. Some employees choose to continue to work even after their pensions mature because pension payments increase the longer an employee works past the maturity date. But if you continue to work to prevent your ex from getting matured benefits, a court may order you to retire (or to pay your former spouse the amount the ex would receive if you did retire).

Double Payments

Be aware of the risk of double payments. You should not have to pay your spouse twice for the retirement benefits you receive as income. If your spouse is given a portion of your retirement benefits as part of the property settlement, you don't want your retirement benefits to be considered part of your income available for support when alimony is calculated. To protect yourself against this type of "double-dipping," remember the following: You can divide the plan or divide the stream of income, but do not divide both.

This double-dipping of payments is one of the most common ways in which retirement benefits are lost at divorce. Don't let it happen to you. One way to protect yourself is to include a provision in your settlement exempting your retirement payments from being considered income for the purposes of alimony. Check with an attorney to discuss your options.

Cost of Living Adjustments

Cost of living adjustments (COLAs) are provisions in retirement plans that provide for an increase in benefits based on your life expectancy and the formula by which benefits are paid out. A plan with a cost of living provision is usually more valuable than a plan without one. Check with the plan administrator to see whether your retirement plan or your spouse's includes a cost of living provision.

Access to Cash

In getting cash out of a retirement plan at divorce, the alternate payee (nonemployee spouse) holds the advantage. If you are the alternate payee, you can request that the QDRO provide for a payout when a marital property settlement becomes final. The plan administrator must withhold 20% of the amount distributed to you to offset some of the income taxes you will owe, even if you deposit the money into an IRA or any other qualified pension plan within 60 days of receiving it. If the plan administrator directly rolls over the plan assets into your IRA (or another qualified plan), however, the 20% mandatory withholding rule does not apply.

If money is tight (as it often is during divorce), you might want to open a savings account with all or part of the money you receive from a retirement plan distribution. Although you'll have to pay taxes on this money, you will have easy access to the funds should you need them. Most important, you won't be hit with the 10% early withdrawal penalty that would apply if you put it into an IRA and then needed to withdraw money to live on.

If you are the plan participant (employee spouse), you probably won't get an early payout from your plan even though your spouse may. Your divorce does not change your status with respect to your benefit payments. It's rare that you will be able to get to your benefits before the date on which the plan specifies you are to receive them. The exceptions are if you become disabled, if you quit your job or get fired, or if the plan itself ends.

Tax Consequences in Dividing Benefits

When dividing matured benefits in a divorce, the employee spouse must be aware of the tax risks. Many divorce settlements specify that the nonemployee spouse gets a share of the other spouse's retirement benefits when the employee spouse retires. Usually, the pension plan administrator sends a check to the ex-spouse. But this means that only the retired employee pays income taxes on the benefits.

To reduce your tax burden, make sure the QDRO orders the pension plan administrator to send two checks—one to you and one to your ex-spouse. Each person pays income taxes on the benefits that person receives. If your plan is not subject to a QDRO, it may be possible to reduce your tax liability by using the Domestic Relations Order, Marital Settlement Agreement, or Divorce Agreement to specify how the benefits and taxes are to be paid.

The Division Decision: Now or in the Future

Taking into account all the financial factors that can affect your retirement benefits, you are ready to move on to the division decision itself. Generally, you can divide a retirement plan or take a payout in one of the two following ways.

Present division. You divide the value of the plan now, at divorce, instead of later, at retirement.

Future (deferred) division. You divide the value of the plan at retirement or at that point in the employee's career when benefits would normally be paid out. Future divisions are most common with defined benefit plans, which promise payment in the future and are difficult to place a current value on.

Remember—no matter which approach you take, everything must be spelled out in the QDRO.

Survivor Benefits

A defined benefit (pension) plan must offer survivor benefits to the spouse of a vested participant employee who dies before retirement age. The surviving spouse is entitled to payments known as a qualified preretirement survivor annuity. An ex-spouse can be treated as the participant's current spouse for the purpose of receiving these survivor benefits. But a provision to that effect must be included in the QDRO, or the benefits will be lost.

If the participant dies prior to retirement, the preretirement survivor annuity begins paying out to the survivor at the point when the participant would have reached the earliest retirement age provided for in the plan.

Debts and Retirement Benefits After Divorce

After a divorce, some former spouses find it necessary to file for bankruptcy to discharge their debts. With a QDRO, retirement benefit payments are made directly from the plan to the nonemployee ex-spouse. This eliminates the risk that the employee might be able to avoid the obligation to pay retirement benefits to the nonemployee ex-spouse by filing for bankruptcy. If, however, there is no QDRO, then the obligation to pay retirement benefits is a personal obligation, and the employee may be able to avoid it by filing for bankruptcy.

Even if a former spouse doesn't need to file bankruptcy, it's easy to fall behind on support obligations. While money can't be forcibly taken from most retirement plans to pay support, some courts have ruled that IRA funds are not insulated if an ex-spouse or the IRS seeks to collect unpaid alimony or child support.

Furthermore, once divided, retirement plan assets are not insulated from the IRS if taxes are due on a joint return. That's true even if the parties agreed that one spouse was liable for payment of those taxes.

Here are some pros and cons of dividing the most common types of retirement plans either at the time of the divorce or later at retirement age. You'll see that the considerations can vary depending on whether you're the alternate payee (nonemployee spouse) or the plan participant (employee spouse).

IRAs

IRAs are not subject to QDROs and can be divided any way the court orders. They can also be transferred from one spouse to another.

Distributing the proceeds from an IRA, however, triggers a 10% early withdrawal penalty for those under age 59½. The proceeds are also fully taxable to the participant spouse.

Transferring an IRA to a spouse without a divorce or separation agreement or a court order creates tax liability for the participant spouse. The only way to avoid the tax is for the court to order a direct transfer of the IRA from one plan to a new one for the receiving spouse.

I would like to divide the IRA as follows:

_____

_____

_____

_____

Defined Contribution Plans, 401(k)s, and TSAs

Splitting these kinds of plans now has advantages, and the advantages are the same whether you are the alternate payee or the plan participant. If you divide the benefits now, you'll cut an economic tie to your spouse and won't need to worry about it later. In addition, consider that:

- Deferred divisions are difficult for the court to supervise.
- Each spouse gains control over a share of funds.
- It's obvious how much the plan is now worth—you don't need an actuary to figure out its future value.

But there are also advantages in waiting before you divide the plan. For both the plan participant and the alternate payee, waiting allows time for any unvested benefits to become vested. Additionally, if you have insufficient property or cash to buy out your spouse's share, deferred division may be the only way to even up a property split. Also, because the plan participant won't receive money from the plan until later anyway, why divide it early? If you have unvested benefits and you divide now, you may end up paying more to your spouse than you receive from the plan.

I would like to divide the defined contribution plan, 401(k), or TSA as follows:

_____

_____

_____

_____

Questions to Ask an Attorney

Retirement plans raise many legal and financial questions. Below is a list of important questions for you to ask an attorney or research at your local law library.

1. Does my state treat retirement benefits upon divorce as marital property to be divided or as income that may belong only to the earner? (Benefits treated as income could affect the amount you pay or receive in alimony or child support.)

2. Is a nonqualified deferred compensation plan considered income or property subject to division?

3. What is the marital portion of our retirement benefits?

4. Must I (or my spouse) be fully vested to receive my (or my spouse's) employer's contribution to a retirement plan?

5. Does my state consider nonvested retirement plans to be marital property?

6. Does my state consider disability pension benefits to be income or property subject to division?

7. How much experience do you have in writing Qualified Domestic Relations Orders? Do you use another firm to write them? (Some firms specialize in this area.)

8. Does my spouse's pension plan direct the distribution of assets upon my death in the event I die before receiving all of the benefits?

9. Will the divorce deprive me of any medical benefits currently covered under my spouse's retirement package? (This is particularly pertinent if the spouse is/was employed by a federal, state, or municipal government.)

To get details on retirement plans held by your spouse, speak with the employer and, if it's a large company, the head of the human resources department. That person may refer you to the plan administrator or the trustee/custodian of the plan. The plan administrator keeps the books and records on the retirement plan, and the trustee/custodian is authorized to administer the plan assets. Begin by writing a letter to your spouse's employer. A sample is below.

Sample Letter to Spouse's Employer

Re: Marriage of _____

        Case No. _____

        Court Name: _____

        Employee's Name: _____

        Employee's Social Security #: _____

        Employee's Date of Birth: _____

To Whom It May Concern:

This letter is to serve as notice that I am pursuing an interest in any retirement or other deferred compensation plans available through your organization or its successors for the benefit of employees belonging to _____.

At your earliest possible convenience, I would appreciate receiving the following:

1. Summary of all deferred compensation plans or stock plans that are available to employees, directors, officers, or other personnel of your company and in which my spouse is eligible to participate, regardless of whether my spouse participated in the plan.

2. A copy of the full text of all plans for which my spouse was eligible, regardless of my spouse's participation therein.

3. A copy of all benefit statements for my spouse for the last five years.

4. Documentation of all stock or stock options owned by or held for the benefit of my spouse.

5. Acknowledgment that your organization has received this Notice. An acknowledgment for the Plan Administrator is below.

6. A copy of your written procedures used in determining your requirements for a Qualified Domestic Relations Order.

7. The formal names of the plan or plans.

8. The names and addresses of all plan administrators.

9. Any other documentation or information that you believe may be of assistance in order to establish a Qualified Domestic Relations Order.

To save everyone the cost of formal discovery, I ask that you respond as soon as possible.

If you have any questions, please feel free to contact me at your convenience.

Sincerely,

[_____ _your signature_ _____]

I consent to the release of this information.

Date: _____

Employee/Plan Participant Spouse: _____

[_name of your spouse_]

ACKNOWLEDGMENT OF RECEIPT OF NOTICE OF ADVERSE INTEREST

I, _____, hereby acknowledge receipt of the letter dated _____, from _____ , which claims an interest in any retirement, pension, or other deferred compensation plan or accounts of _____.

Dated: _____

Title: _____

Organization: _____

_____

If you don't get the answers you need from this letter, write to the plan administrator, company president, or anyone else who could help you get the information. You might engage the services of an attorney if you can't get through to anyone or aren't getting a response. However you do it, persist until you get what you need. Retirement plans are too complex not to leave a "paper trail," so don't let your spouse or spouse's attorney intimidate you into thinking that the information you need doesn't exist. ●

Financial Investments:
How Do We Divide the Portfolio Pie?

When you divide the investments you and your spouse made during marriage, it's doubtful you'll get exactly what you want—but you should get what you need.

SKIP AHEAD

If neither you nor your spouse has investments, skip ahead to Chapter 16.

The first step in dealing with financial investments is to analyze your portfolio objectively—that is, the stocks, bonds, mutual funds, real estate investments, gold, collectibles, and the like that make up your investment holdings. Then work to get the assets that can put you in the best position to build toward your future after divorce.

How do you know which investments will serve you best? Ask a dozen financial planners and you'll get the same answer: "That depends."

Choosing the investments that will serve you best depends on several factors—your future plans, current age, risk tolerance, income needs, and investment experience. You should aim for investments that meet your individual needs, allow you to sleep at night, and keep your taxes to a minimum.

As you read this chapter and evaluate your investments, keep in mind the following two questions:

- Is the investment performing well?
- Is the investment appropriate for me?

Whether you are a novice or veteran investor, use the formulas and tips in this chapter to select the investments that will best support you after the divorce. Even if you are completely unfamiliar with the investments you and your spouse share, you don't have to be intimidated—if you do your homework.

In some instances, you might need to consult with financial experts before making decisions, because certain investments can carry complications due to tax laws or illiquidity (not being able to sell an investment at a reasonable price), and because of today's uncertain market and economic downturn. Tax advisers, stockbrokers, and financial planners might be particularly useful. Whether you get help from experts or not, you can save time and money by doing some groundwork and gathering information.

Concepts to Consider

To get started, here are a few basic investment concepts to help you.

An Investment From Marriage May Make Little Sense When You're Single

While married, the two of you might have chosen certain investments because they met your shared goals—such as a mutual fund to help save for the down payment on a house or an annuity to increase the retirement kitty. Once you divorce, however, your goals, tax bracket, and ability to withstand losses could change. Perhaps as a couple you could afford to hold on to a stock with great potential, even when its value fell. As a single person, however, such a stock might be totally unsuitable if you're looking for stable income. Similarly, a spouse in a high-income tax bracket might not want to keep an investment that generates substantial taxable interest.

Don't Take an Investment You Can't Live With

Does the mere mention of S&P 500 or Nasdaq give you the jitters? Can you bear to sit by and watch what happens to the bond market? Do you have the time, energy, and interest to keep up with your investments' performance? Think about these questions carefully as you look at each asset. You should only keep an investment if you can stand living with it. Don't take an asset if you don't understand its risks.

Use Your Divorce to Cut Your Losses

When it comes to investments, no one likes to admit to making a bad call or a poor decision—especially if your spouse warned you not to buy the loser in the first place. But you wouldn't fight to keep the awful picture Aunt Lucille gave you for a wedding present, would you? Why hold on to investments that are not doing well? Because of the emotional distress of divorce—or simple "investment inertia"—some people hang on to investments they should sell. Divorce is the perfect time to review *all* of your investments and unload those that drain your portfolio value or don't meet your long-term financial goals.

No Investment Is Risk Free

No capital investment comes with a 100% guarantee of success. Whether you're working with banks, hedge funds, brokerage firms, or investment companies or buying U.S. government–issued bonds, everything carries risk.

The booms, busts, and investment scandals and swindles of the last three decades should be enough to bury the notion of a "risk-free" investment. Yet, this great illusion of the American marketplace lives on. You should not be taken in, no matter how persuasive an argument seems. The fact is, regardless of what you might see, hear, or want to believe, every investment carries risk. (Even what were once the most trusted places for money—banks, savings and loans, and insurance companies—have shown this to be true.) Ignoring risk is common among today's investors who have been hit by a virtual avalanche of new financial products, each promising rewards that might or might not materialize. Take time to ask questions about the downside of any investment you plan to keep as part of your settlement. Keep in mind one general rule: *The greater the potential for gain, the greater the risk.*

Never keep an investment that carries a greater risk than you can afford. Doing so increases the risk of loss, because you will probably sell the investment when its value drops rather than ride out its ups and downs.

EXAMPLE: In the property settlement, Cheryl received 300 shares of WOW Mutual Fund, a fund investing in virtual currency blockchain companies. The fund had a high return of 22% in the prior year. Her husband, Jim, convinced her that with the $14,000 worth of WOW shares, she would make more money than with the lower-return Treasury bonds he was taking as part of the settlement. Cheryl quickly learned, however, that the greater the potential for gain, the greater the risk; her $14,000 investment dropped to $8,700 the next year.

Who Do You Trust to Handle Your Investments?

It's common for people to seek help and financial advice in their community and social networks. But as many investment scandals have made clear, financial fraud often hinges on the victims' trust and vulnerability. When you're in crisis—such as during a divorce—it's easy to put your faith in someone who seems wise and caring, but might not be.

For your protection and peace of mind, you should engage a third-party financial adviser to help handle your investments. If you house your investments with a third-party custodian—and you should—it's easier to monitor the health of the investment and access advice from a reliable source. Check with your local bank or an established investment management firm to see how you might work with a financial adviser.

Trust, but verify, is a sound approach when you're allowing someone else to handle your investments.

Asset Options: Sell Now, Keep It Forever, or Take It for a Loss

"Assume sale." Those two words sum up the best advice you can follow when deciding what to do with assets at divorce. So often, cherished investments you thought you would keep forever end up on the auction block after divorce. Ideally, you should keep only those investments that financially fit your goals and needs—and you should sell or transfer to your spouse those that do not. If you sell the investment at divorce, you share the selling costs and potential tax bite with your soon-to-be ex-spouse. Waiting until after the divorce to unload assets means you incur all those expenses yourself.

Too often, divorcing couples overlook the simple fact that an asset they are eventually planning to sell can be sold *prior* to the divorce. They get caught up in making trade-offs to reach a quick or supposedly fair property settlement and accept assets they don't want or intend to keep. If, however, you assume sale, you're forced to consider taxation and other costs. Then your negotiations can be based on the real cost of keeping the asset and not an illusory value. And if you do keep the asset, you know what it's truly worth.

Losers Can Be Winners

When you incur a capital loss at sale, remember that this loss can offset capital gains. If your capital loss exceeds $3,000, you can carry over the excess losses until they are used up, either by offsetting capital gains or by taking the maximum $3,000 deduction from your gross income.

Gains and losses on jointly owned or community property are generally divided equally between spouses upon the divorce judgment or settlement. This is important because a loss greater than $3,000 will have tax implications in years after you and your spouse divorce. If one spouse has a greater need to declare such losses, then they become an item of value in negotiation, and an agreement for their division should always be included in the final divorce settlement or judgment.

An investment asset may provide you with a tax loss when you sell it. If it would, and if you have another asset on which you expect a gain, it might make financial sense to take the loss-producing asset in the settlement. Then you can sell the "loser" after the divorce to offset the tax gain from the sale of the other asset, and reduce your overall tax liability. It pays to know which stocks, bonds, or mutual funds carry a tax loss with them. For example, limited partnerships and rental real estate, which produce a loss because of depreciation, actually increase your tax liability. Be sure to consult a tax adviser before taking one of these items that show a loss.

> EXAMPLE: Suppose you bought a stock for $2,000 and sold it for $1,500. Your loss is $500. If you had another stock you bought for $1,500, held for 12 months, and then sold for $2,500, your gain is $1,000. If you didn't sell the first stock, you'd pay a capital gains tax of $150 on the $1,000 gain. If you sold both assets, however, the loss partially offsets the gain and your tax liability would be 15% of $500, or $75.

Sell Now

Elliot accepted his wife's offer of their coin collection even though he did not particularly care about the coin market and didn't really want the collection. Nevertheless, he accepted it with the illusion that by making this concession to his wife, he would speed up the settlement. Not only did the settlement proceedings drag on, but after the divorce, when he sold the collection, Elliot paid a hefty sales commission and substantial taxes on the gain—which meant Elliot received an asset of lower value than he thought he was getting. Coin collections and other collectibles did not get the benefit of a reduced capital gains rate under the Taxpayer Relief Act of 1997 and are still taxed at 28%.

Balance Security, Income, and Growth

Your investments should give you more than headaches. In fact, a portfolio should balance three financial needs over your lifetime: security, income, and growth.

During your divorce, analyze whether or not your investments meet these needs—and in what proportions. The degree to which you need security, income, and growth will change depending on what phase of life you're in. Generally, you will want more growth than income while you are young and more income than growth when you get older.

Security. Conventional wisdom among financial advisers holds that you should have an emergency fund in place before you even consider investing. This fund should equal three to six months of your cost of living expenses such as mortgage, rent, utilities, and food. It should be readily available in a money market fund or short-term bond fund. Disability or life insurance can also provide important sources of income or cash in the event of an emergency. Once your emergency needs are met, you can consider investments for income or growth.

Income. Income investments pay monthly, quarterly, semiannual, or annual dividends or interest to supplement your salary or provide an income during retirement.

Growth. These types of investments should "make your money work for you," offering steady growth beyond what you would earn from conservative vehicles like certificates of deposit or money markets. Growth investments include individual stocks, equity mutual funds, and real estate.

If You Don't Know the Tax Basis, the Tax Bill May Shock You

"Buy low and sell high." That cliché of the marketplace leaves out an important piece of information: When you sell high, you owe Uncle Sam taxes on the profit. Just how much you owe is determined by the amount of profit you realized on the investment. That profit can be determined once you know the tax basis of the investment.

For your mutual funds and stock investments, your tax basis is the original purchase price plus the value of any dividends you reinvested in the funds or stocks, minus any commissions you paid to purchase. The tax basis for real estate is the original purchase price plus the cost of improvements you made to the property, minus any tax benefits received. Specific formulas for finding the tax basis are given throughout this chapter.

Income vs. Growth Needs

Susan, a young executive, had just received a raise when her husband decided he wanted a divorce. Being a conservative investor, her husband had invested their money in a large number of utility stocks, which provided a steady but small flow of dividends. Because Susan's salary increase gave her a more than adequate income, she wanted cash for her share of the stocks rather than the stocks themselves. With cash in hand, she invested in several high-tech stocks that paid no dividends (and therefore did not increase her tax liability for ordinary income), but gave her what she wanted and needed: potential for appreciation or growth.

EXAMPLE: Leslie bought 100 shares of stock at $12 per share in May and another 100 shares of the same stock in December for $30 per share. Three years later, when the stock soared in value to $80 per share, Leslie decided to sell it, after holding all of the stock more than 12 months. Assuming a 15% capital gains tax rate, here's what Leslie's tax bill would look like:

May Stocks		December Stocks	
Sell 100 shares @ $80	$ 8,000	Sell 100 shares @ $80	$ 8,000
Bought 100 shares @ $12	− 1,200	Bought 100 shares @ $30	− 3,000
Gain	$ 6,800	Gain	$ 5,000
(times capital gains tax rate)	× 0.15	(times capital gains tax rate)	× 0.15
Taxes due	$ 1,020	Taxes due	$ 750

The tax basis for the stocks purchased in May is the $12 per share price. Upon sale of these stocks, there is a greater gain, which in turn creates a bigger tax bill. For the stocks purchased in December, with the $30 per share purchase price, the gain is lower, and so are the taxes. If Leslie had to sell half of the shares, she would be better off selling the December stocks than selling those she purchased in May. By doing so, she saves $270 in taxes ($1,020 − $750 = $270).

Suppose Leslie's spouse offers to split the 200 shares of stock. Should Leslie take the May stocks or the December stocks? Leslie would be better off taking the December stocks, on which the taxes owed are lower. The fairest settlement would be for each spouse to take 50 of the May stocks and 50 of the December stocks. Another possibility would be to sell the stocks and split the tax bill equally. In that case, the calculations would look like this:

200 shares sold @ $80 per share,		
held more than 12 months		$16,000
Tax Basis		
100 shares @ $12	=	$1,200
100 shares @ $30	=	$3,000
	–	<u>4,200</u>
Total Gain	=	$11,800
Capital Gains Tax Rate	×	<u>15%</u>
Total Taxes on Gain	=	$1,770
Each Spouse's Share of Taxes Due	=	$885
Each Spouse's Share of Proceeds		
From Sale of Stock	=	$5,015

Keep in mind that losses and gains are netted to determine the final tax liability, and commissions paid to brokers reduce the final tax liability. This example assumes that this was the only asset Leslie and her spouse sold this year.

Beware of Inflation and Inflated Claims

Nothing takes the fun out of investing faster than losing money. Yet investors often overlook the simple factor of inflation, which constantly erodes the value of their holdings. To determine the true amount of return you earn from an investment, you must consider not only taxes, but inflation as well. Over the last year, the United States has experienced a roller coaster of inflation rates, reaching as high as 8% at one point. However, at the time of writing this edition, to prevent a recession, the Federal Reserve Board has stepped in again and cut the federal interest rate down to somewhere between 5% and 6%.

With that in mind, we can take the simple example of a $10,000 certificate of deposit (CD), which is currently paying approximately 5% interest at a time when inflation is running at 5.5% annually. At the end of a year, the CD would seem to be worth $10,500 (the $500 earned via the 5% interest payment).

Assuming a federal tax bracket of 25%, the amount due the government would equal $125, reducing the $10,500 to only $10,375. Now factor in inflation. The $10,000 loses $550 (inflation of 5.5%) a year. At the end of a year, instead of $10,500, the CD really has the purchasing power of only $9,825 ($10,375 − $550), for a stunning loss of almost 2% on the original $10,000.

Be on guard, too, for inflated or misunderstood claims. Quite commonly, investors consider only one dimension, such as the interest rate an investment pays. They often forget about the numerous other factors that affect value, such as inflation, sales charges, management fees, dividend payments, and other unforeseen risks.

Look to Total Return, Not Yield

The commonly misunderstood differences between yield and total return illustrate the problem of one-dimensional analysis. *Yield* represents income in the form of dividends and interest. *Total return* is the yield plus the percentage of appreciation (growth) or loss in the per share value of an investment.

> EXAMPLE: Ron saw an advertisement for a mutual fund offering a yield of 9%. Later that day, his broker called to tell him about another fund with a 5% yield. Which should he buy?
>
> Ron must look beyond yield to total return. The yield represents only the dividends or interest he'll receive on his shares. The total return takes into account both the yield and the percentage increase (appreciation) or decrease (loss) in the value of the shares.

Ron's broker explained that the shares in the fund yielding 9% decreased in value by 20% the previous year, meaning the total return was minus 11% (9% − 20%). The shares in the fund yielding 5%, on the other hand, increased 8.3%, for a total return of 13.3%. Note that the higher-yield fund actually produced a lower total return.

Tax Basis and the IRS

When spouses divorce, information concerning the tax basis of an asset must be given to the spouse who receives the asset when title (ownership) changes. Because tax consequences are so fundamental to the selection of an asset, however, you should know the tax basis before you divide your assets, not after.

Steps to a Settlement

Now that you have an overview of the concepts to consider when making investment choices, it is time for a plan of action for reaching decisions. Answer these questions to formulate your plan:

1. What investments do you and your spouse hold?
2. Who owns each investment?
3. What is the legal value or fair market value of each investment?
4. What is the financial or after-tax/after-sale value of each investment?
5. Which assets should you keep?
6. How will you and your spouse divide the investments?

To answer these questions, complete the "Investment Chart" that follows. Begin by listing your investments in the far left column, using suggestions offered in Step 1, below. As you move on through Steps 2, 3, and 4, you will find detailed instructions on how to fill in the remaining columns. Finally, when you reach Step 6, you will return to the chart to show how you want to divide assets with your spouse.

Investment Chart						
(1)	**(2)**	**(3)**	**(4)**			
Investments	**Title** *	**Legal or Equity Value** (Fair Market Value – Debt)	**Financial** (After-Tax/After-Sale) **Value**	**I Keep**	**Spouse Keeps**	**Sell and Split Proceeds**
Cash and cash equivalents						
Bank checking accounts						
Bank savings accounts						
Certificates of deposit						
Money market funds						

* S1=Spouse 1, S2=Spouse 2, J=jointly, C=community property

Investment Chart (continued)

	(1) Investments	(2) Title *	(3) Legal or Equity Value (Fair Market Value – Debt)	(4) Financial (After-Tax/After-Sale) Value	I Keep	Spouse Keeps	Sell and Split Proceeds
Mutual funds							
Personal notes payable to you							
Cryptocurrency or virtual currency							
Other							
Stocks and bonds							
Common stocks							

* S1=Spouse 1, S2=Spouse 2, J=jointly, C=community property

Investment Chart (continued)

(1) Investments	(2) Title *	(3) Legal or Equity Value (Fair Market Value – Debt)	(4) Financial (After-Tax/After-Sale) Value	I Keep	Spouse Keeps	Sell and Split Proceeds
Preferred stock						
Mutual funds						
Treasury bills						
Government bonds (such as Ginnie Maes)						
Municipal bonds (include mutual funds, unit trusts, and individual bonds)						

* S1=Spouse 1, S2=Spouse 2, J=jointly, C=community property

Investment Chart (continued)

Investments	(1)	(2) Title *	(3) Legal or Equity Value (Fair Market Value – Debt)	(4) Financial (After-Tax/After-Sale) Value	I Keep	Spouse Keeps	Sell and Split Proceeds
Corporate bonds							
EE U.S. savings bonds							
Zero-coupon bonds							
Other							

* S1=Spouse 1, S2=Spouse 2, J=jointly, C=community property

Investment Chart (continued)

	(1)	(2)	(3)	(4)			
Investments		**Title** *	**Legal or Equity Value** (Fair Market Value – Debt)	**Financial** (After-Tax/After-Sale) **Value**	**I Keep**	**Spouse Keeps**	**Sell and Split Proceeds**
Real estate							
Income or rental properties							
Real estate investment trusts (REITs)							
Raw land							
Other							
Insurance investments							
Cash value of life insurance policies							

* S1=Spouse 1, S2=Spouse 2, J=jointly, C=community property

Investment Chart (continued)

(1) Investments	(2) Title *	(3) Legal or Equity Value (Fair Market Value – Debt)	(4) Financial (After-Tax/After-Sale) Value	I Keep	Spouse Keeps	Sell and Split Proceeds
Annuities						
Other						
Limited partnerships						
Real estate						
Oil and gas						
Equipment leasing, etc.						
Other						

* S1=Spouse 1, S2=Spouse 2, J=jointly, C=community property

Investment Chart (continued)						
(1)	**(2)**	**(3)**	**(4)**			
Investments	**Title***	**Legal or Equity Value** (Fair Market Value – Debt)	**Financial** (After-Tax/After-Sale) **Value**	I Keep	Spouse Keeps	Sell and Split Proceeds
Collectibles						
Gold and silver						
Coins, jewelry, art, and other valuables						
Other						
* S1=Spouse 1, S2=Spouse 2, J=jointly, C=community property						

Step 1: What Investments Do You and Your Spouse Hold?

Using Column 1 of the "Investment Chart," list all investments owned by you, your spouse, and the two of you together. If you're unsure of certain investments, check old tax returns, or call your financial planner, stockbroker, brokerage firm, accountant, or other tax adviser. You should also check online, if you or your spouse has used electronic brokerage services.

Step 2: Who Owns Each Investment?

Under "Title" in Column 2, show whether the investment is owned by spouse 1 (S1), spouse 2 (S2), or jointly (J). Investments owned jointly—except those that are separate property—are divided at divorce. Remember: The name of the person on the investment does not necessarily determine who owns it. Most states divide marital property during divorce, even when assets are only in one spouse's name.

List the investments owned separately by you and your spouse even though they won't be divided in the settlement. As you negotiate the settlement, it is possible that your or your spouse's separate investments will be considered in terms of income needs or for alimony.

If you need more information on what constitutes separate and marital property, see Chapter 12.

Step 3: What Is the Legal (Equity) Value of Each Investment?

With investments, the equity or legal value basically equals the fair market value or face value—that is, the amount the investment is worth, less any debts. (For cash or cash-like assets—such as CDs or money market accounts—the legal value is the same as the account balance.) The legal value is generally the dollar amount attorneys use when discussing investments in trying to settle your divorce. In Steps 4 and 5, below, you will take a closer look at the financial value of your investments.

To find the legal or equity value of your investments, you often need to do no more than place a phone call.

You might, however, run into problems determining which date to use in valuing the account. As mentioned in Chapter 5, many states value portfolio assets, like houses, as close to the *date of divorce or settlement* as possible, not the *date of separation*. You'll need to find out your state's practice.

Even if your state legally values assets at the date of separation, you and your spouse can agree to another date—and you should. Stocks, bonds, mutual funds, and other liquid assets, particularly, should be valued as close as possible to the date you take control of them. Otherwise, if you value assets as of the date of separation, but then don't transfer them until months or years later, you may incur losses because of market forces.

Ultimately, to get through your divorce, you will probably need to find the account balance at different times. But you can begin by filling in the current amounts for the legal value of investments in Column 3 of the "Investment Chart." Use the following information to help you calculate or locate the legal value for each investment. Some of this information may be listed on your "Net Worth Statement" from Chapter 12.

Cash and cash equivalents. Most people use online banking for savings, checking, money market accounts, and the like. So, start online for current values. Look at your most recent statement, download a PDF version, and print it out if you plan to bring it to a settlement conference. The same goes for any cryptocurrency. Go online to your custodial wallet. Download and print out your most recent statement. If you aren't using online banking, then for your bank checking and savings accounts, certificates of deposit, and money market funds, call the bank or look at your statement. For money market mutual funds, call the fund manager or administrator. The value of personal notes will probably be found among your personal papers. Find out whether the account is pledged as security for any debt. Be sure to investigate your spouse's business, if any, and any personal loans.

Stocks and bonds. For most stocks and bonds, you can check with your broker, your discount brokerage firm, or an online service. If you call a brokerage firm, ask for the trading department to check the current price of stocks or mutual funds. You can also look at the business section of the newspaper. For stocks, look in the stock market tables for the price in the column labeled "Close." That's the price at which the stock was selling when the market closed the day before. Multiply this number by the number of shares you own to get a ballpark value. Get an estimate of bonds by calling a broker or discount brokerage firm. Banks can give you the value of savings bonds. For mutual funds, look in the business section of the newspaper in the column labeled "NAV," the Net Asset Value.

Real estate. For income or rental property, you will probably need an appraiser. (See Chapter 13.) For the value of real estate investment trusts (REITs), ask a broker or brokerage firm or check the published values in a newspaper. To find the value of raw land, check the purchase price and ask a few real estate agents to find out whether land values have gone up or down in your area. It's also helpful to know whether there is a balance due on the mortgage or whether the property is free and clear of debt.

> **CAUTION**
>
> **Two identical pieces of property can have different values if the rents charged in one building are not the same as the rents charged in the other.** Rent control laws can also affect (bring down) the value of property. A spouse trying to artificially lower the value of rental property might rent units at below-market rates on a month-to-month basis, and then raise rates (and the property's value) after the divorce. If you suspect this is happening, check previous tax returns to see what rents were charged, and ask realtors or check online rental sites to see how much rent is charged for comparable units in the area.

Insurance. Contact the insurance company or broker and ask for the policy's current value and surrender value. If you're not the owner of the policy, the insurance company may refuse to give you the information. Call your spouse, or have your attorney call your spouse's attorney to get what you need.

Limited partnerships. Investments in businesses that operate as limited partnerships are more difficult to value than, say, investments in stocks or bonds. That's because, unlike stocks, there is no conventional trading market for interests in limited partnerships.

Certain "secondary markets," however, do buy and resell limited partnership interests. But these markets may assign widely divergent values to limited partnership interests. Ask a stockbroker or financial planner for the names of several secondary market firms. In your survey, ask for the price at which the partnership shares could be sold and whether additional costs would be incurred.

What secondary markets say the partnership interest is worth and the amount you will actually realize from its sale will probably be different. And your original purchase price and what you could sell it for now will have an even larger difference. Generally, these markets buy partnership shares at a deeply discounted price from the amount you originally paid or might receive if held until maturity. Use the amount the firms give you to fill in the "Investment Chart."

Limited partnerships can be complicated investments, especially when you're attempting to value and divide your interests. For additional discussion, see below.

Collectibles. Gold and silver values are listed, per ounce, in the daily newspaper. Coins, jewelry, art, and collectibles must be appraised. Be sure to find the wholesale or resale price, not the retail price. You might need to hire an experienced appraiser to help you value high-end and/or unique collectibles.

Step 4: What Is the Financial (After-Tax/After-Sale) Value of Each Investment?

Remember: You will need to know the tax basis of your investments to calculate gains, losses, and your potential tax liability when you sell. In addition, the IRS requires that when you transfer property at divorce, you must provide tax basis information to the party who will keep the asset. If you are in the dark about investments, you might need to press matters with your spouse to get the information to figure the tax basis.

You can't make informed decisions about which investments to accept or sell in the settlement unless you know your potential tax liabilities *before* any property transfer takes place.

Knowing the tax basis will help you find the financial value (or after-sale/after-tax value) of your investments. For most investments, you will probably enlist the services of a professional tax adviser, but the following formulas and tips should help you get a ballpark estimate of your taxes and other costs.

After calculating the financial value of each investment, enter that value in Column 4 of the "Investment Chart." But first, talk to a broker or financial planner or another investment professional to find out whether your investments carry any additional or hidden costs. If they do, subtract those amounts from the financial value before entering the values in Column 4. Be on the lookout for:

- **Account charges.** An amount charged for maintaining an account with a broker, brokerage house, or firm.
- **Redemption fees.** What you pay to redeem or sell the investment.
- **Trading fees.** A commission for buying or selling stocks or bonds. **Early withdrawal penalties.** Penalties incurred for early withdrawals on CDs, life insurance annuities, and other investments.

Cash and Cash Equivalents

Because the tax basis of cash and cash equivalents is essentially what you will liquidate them for, no taxes are due when you cash them in. To the extent that you earn interest on checking accounts, savings accounts, money market accounts, or certificates of deposit, you must report that interest as income and pay taxes on the interest the year you earned it. To estimate the interest you will earn this year, call your banker. Then simply use the legal value as the financial value, and write that amount in Column 4 of the "Investment Chart."

Stocks, Bonds, and Mutual Funds

Calculating taxes and other costs associated with stocks and bonds will require you to do some tedious paperwork. You will have to gather old statements or look them up online to reconstruct past trading activity (perhaps, even, over several years). Only you can decide whether it's worth it to do that work yourself rather than hiring someone else for the job. No matter who does it, if you sell stocks and bonds you will need this information to complete your tax return. Some good software packages and websites are available to help you make this calculation. Several investment calculators can be found at www.bankrate.com. Some brokerage or financial planning services companies may be able to determine this figure for you using their own specialized software programs.

Bonds

See an accountant or a tax adviser to analyze the tax aspects of bonds. The Internal Revenue Code has numerous complicated rules depending on when the bonds were purchased and the type of bonds you own. For instance, some bonds, such as municipal bonds, are tax exempt, meaning their interest is free from taxes. But if you bought them at a discount, when you redeem them or they mature you will have to pay capital gains tax on the difference between the purchase price and maturity value.

Also keep in mind these general rules:

- **EE U.S. savings bonds.** You can pay taxes on the interest generated on EE bonds each year, as with most investments, or when you redeem the bonds. You can defer paying taxes on the interest if you roll the bonds forward into HH bonds.
- **HH bonds.** With these government bonds, you pay interest semiannually.
- **Zero coupon (corporate or municipal) bonds.** On corporate bonds, you must pay taxes on interest earned each year even though you don't receive the interest payment until the bond matures.

Once you talk to an accountant or other tax adviser about your bonds, enter their financial value in Column 4. This value can be determined using the formula for stocks and mutual funds, below. But keep in mind that the value of bonds fluctuates with interest rates. If interest rates in the United States have risen since you purchased your bond, the value will be slightly less than when you bought it. If interest rates have declined, the opposite will be true: Your bond, if you sell it, will be worth more than when you bought it. Check your monthly statement from your brokerage account or ask your broker for the amount you will get if you liquidate your bond or bonds.

Stocks and Mutual Funds

Use the following formula and instructions to find the financial value for your stocks and mutual funds. To complete the calculations, you will need to know the following:

$ _____ *Purchase price*

Check your confirmation statement or call your broker. Be sure to include the initial investment plus any subsequent purchases you made.

$ _____ *Dividends reinvested*

These should be shown on your monthly statements from the brokerage firm or mutual fund company. You can also look on tax Form 1099, sent annually to you from the company, showing dividends or interest earned each tax year.

$ _____ *Commissions and transactions fees*

These are fees paid when you purchase stocks and mutual funds unless the mutual fund is a "no load" fund, meaning it has no commission. The amount is on your confirmation statement; if it's not, call your broker or discount brokerage firm. For "load" mutual funds, the commissions, which are automatically charged, are reflected in the purchase price. Ask your broker whether the fund has a redemption charge or surrender charge, a fee you pay when the fund is sold.

$ _____ *Equity value*

Enter from Column 3 of the "Investment Chart."

$ _____ *Tax rate*

You will need to know your income tax bracket and how long you have held the investment to know what to put here. If you held the stock or mutual fund for more than 12 months, enter 15% as your tax rate. If you held it less than 12 months, check with your tax preparer for your tax bracket.

To find the financial (after-sale/after-tax) value of stocks and mutual funds, use the following formula:

1. Find the tax basis by adding the purchase price, reinvested dividends and commissions, and transaction fees (paid at purchase).
2. Find the adjusted sales price by subtracting commissions and transaction fees (to be paid when you sell) from the fair market value.
3. Find the gain (or loss) by subtracting the tax basis from the adjusted sales price.
4. Find the taxes due (or tax refund) by multiplying the gain (or loss) by the capital gains rate based on your tax bracket.
5. Find the financial value by subtracting the taxes due (or adding the tax refund) from (or to) the adjusted sales price.

EXAMPLE: Let's assume you bought 100 shares of XYZ at $10 per share and it has grown to $22 per share.

1. Find the tax basis by adding the purchase price, reinvested dividends, and commissions and transaction fees (paid at purchase).

Purchase price		$1,000
Dividends reinvested	+	60
Commissions & transaction fees	+	65
Tax basis	=	$1,125

2. Find the adjusted sales price by subtracting commissions and transaction fees (to be paid when you sell) from the equity value.

Equity value		$2,200
Commissions & transaction fees	–	68
Adjusted sales price	=	$2,132

3. Find the gain (or loss) by subtracting the tax basis from the adjusted sales price.

Adjusted sales price		$2,132
Tax basis	–	1,125
Gain (or loss)	=	$1,007

(If you incur a loss on this asset, you can net it against a gain on another asset to reduce your capital gains tax liability.)

4. Find the taxes due by multiplying the gain by the capital gains rate based on your tax bracket.

Gain		$1,007
Capital gains tax rate	×	15%
Taxes due	=	$151

5. Find the financial value by subtracting the taxes due from the adjusted sales price.

Adjusted sales price		$2,132
Taxes due	−	151
Financial value	=	$1,981

To apply this formula to your situation, fill in the blanks below. Copy this page to use as a worksheet or to calculate the value of additional investments.

1. Find the tax basis by adding the purchase price, reinvested dividends, and commissions and transaction fees (paid at purchase).

Purchase price		$ _____
Dividends reinvested	+	$ _____
Commissions & transaction fees	+	$ _____
Tax basis	=	$ _____

2. Find the adjusted sales price by subtracting commissions and transaction fees (to be paid when you sell) from the equity value.

Equity value		$ _____
Commissions & transaction fees	−	$ _____
Adjusted sales price	=	$ _____

3. Find the gain (or loss) by subtracting the tax basis from the adjusted sales price.

Adjusted sales price		$ _____
Tax basis	−	$ _____
Gain (or loss)	=	$ _____

4. Find the taxes due by multiplying the gain by the capital gains rate based on your tax bracket.

Gain		$ _____
Capital gains tax rate	×	$ _____
Taxes due	=	$ _____

5. Find the financial value by subtracting the taxes due from the adjusted sales price.

Adjusted sales price		$ _____
Taxes due	−	$ _____
Financial value	=	$ _____

Keep in mind that the above formula calculates only federal income taxes. In most states, you will have to pay state taxes as well.

Dividing Stocks, Bonds, and Mutual Funds: Consider the Tax Basis. As noted at the beginning of this section, the IRS requires that you give information about the tax basis of an asset to the person receiving it at the time of transfer. It's very important for you to understand the tax basis of an asset. If you don't, you could decide to keep investments that give you a higher tax burden than those your spouse will carry. At the least, you ought to share the tax burden equally.

Once you know the tax basis, you can calculate the taxes that would be due if you were to sell the assets. Knowing the potential tax liability enables you to compare the true value of investment assets and other assets. This knowledge will also influence your tax strategy after the divorce, as you consider whether to sell or keep the investments.

The IRS allows three different methods to calculate the taxes. In these examples, a gain is assumed. If you have experienced a loss on your investments, the investment might be of value if you have a gain elsewhere—but only if you sell the asset immediately.

First in–first out. If you've purchased shares of stock over several years at different prices, this method lets you sell the first batch you bought. For example, Mindy and Ryan bought 300 shares of stock at $13 per share in 2014 and another 300 shares of the same stock at $20 per share in 2016. The stock is now worth $25 per share. They decide to sell 300 shares before they divorce. But which 300?

Using the first in–first out option, they would sell the 300 shares bought in 2014. They would have to pay taxes on the gain of $12 per share ($25 fair market value – $13 purchase price = $12 gain). Had they sold the 2016 shares, they'd owe taxes on a gain of only $5 per share ($25 fair market value – $20 purchase price = $5 gain). But by selling the shares that will give them a larger profit, they can split the taxes owed.

As an alternative to selling shares before the divorce, Mindy and Ryan consider splitting the 600 shares in half. It's fair on the surface. If one spouse keeps the 2014 shares, and the other keeps the 2016 shares, however, the division becomes unfair because the tax liabilities differ. They could even things up again if they divide other property to cover the tax difference, or if they each take half the 2014 shares and half the 2016 shares.

Document Dividends and Reinvestments

When Evelyn divorced in 2018, she got $5,000 worth of shares in a mutual fund as part of her settlement. A savvy investor, she sold the shares in the last week of September 2022 for $10,000. Initially, it appeared Evelyn would pay taxes on the $5,000 gain: $10,000 (sales price) – $5,000 (original price) = $5,000 (gain).

But Evelyn had kept records showing that she reinvested all the dividends she received. In adding up each reinvestment, she found that she had reinvested total dividends of $1,600 into the fund. This finding lowered her tax liability. Remember: Her tax basis is the original purchase price plus reinvested dividends. Her original $5,000 investment, plus the dividend reinvestments of $1,600, totaled $6,600. The amount of gain she had to pay taxes on, therefore, was only $3,400, not $5,000.

Specific identification. This time, assume that Mindy and Ryan bought their 600 shares at various times paying prices ranging from $13 to $20 per share. If they decide to sell 300 shares before their divorce and use the specific identification option, they would pinpoint precisely which 300 shares to sell—perhaps 100 bought at $13, another 100 bought at $18, and the final 100 purchased at $20 per share.

If they split the shares as part of their divorce settlement, they should consider the tax liability for the shares bought at each price. If Mindy wants 300 of the $20 stocks—leaving Ryan with all of the stocks purchased at $13 and $18 per share—Ryan will pay more in taxes than Mindy.

Average basis. Mindy and Ryan's third option is the average basis. As the name implies, this option lets them take an across-the-board average tax basis on all the shares of stock, no matter when purchased and at what price per share. They would simply take the total amount paid (and dividends reinvested) and divide it by the total number of shares owned.

Because of the difficult calculations and the fact that supporting documentation regarding reinvestments and commissions is often missing, many divorcing couples use the average basis to divide stocks and mutual funds. Before settling on it, however, compare it to the first in–first out and specific identification options. Incorporate the calculations from this section on tax basis options with financial values when you read Steps 5 and 6, below.

Real Estate

In valuing real estate investments, you can consider many of the factors raised in Chapter 13, assuming you own a family home. If you haven't read that material, refer to it for basic formulas and an explanation of real estate terms.

Unlike the family home, investment properties can be hard to value. The local economy, rental vacancy rates, rent control or stabilization laws, property management, and other market forces affect the property's value. Nevertheless, you can estimate the financial (after-sale/after-tax) value of your real estate investments by using these guidelines.

$ _____ *REITs (real estate investment trusts)*

A real estate investment trust company invests in a variety of holdings, which can range from apartments and hotels to office buildings and shopping centers. Because most REITs are publicly traded, their value is easily identified. Refer to the stock tables in the newspaper, or ask your broker for current values. To find the financial value, subtract any commissions or fees from the fair market value.

$ _____ *Raw land*

Real estate agents and appraisers normally base the value of raw (undeveloped) land on current comparables, that is, the amount at which comparable parcels of land are currently selling. Other factors to consider in determining the real financial value of raw land are:
- how land may be affected by a city's general plan
- the kind of building permits that have been issued in the area, and
- how land surrounding your land may be used.

Real estate agents can help you answer these questions. Also, talk with the county building permit office and the city office regarding permits and future land use. Then, make your best estimate of the financial value.

$ _____ *Income or rental properties*

For most income-producing property, use the formula in Chapter 13, Step 6, to determine the financial value. With rental property, you must also consider total depreciation: the amount you've deducted in taxes to account for the declining value of the property.

If you own real property, such as a residential rental, know that there is an exception to the lower capital gains rates that went into effect under the Taxpayer Relief Act of 1997. Not all the net capital gain that you have on this kind of property will qualify for the lower rate of 15%. Instead, to the extent that you have taken depreciation on the property, your gain will be taxed at a maximum rate of 25%.

> EXAMPLE: Jim and Carol own a rental property, which they bought in 2013 for $100,000. Over the years, they have taken $15,000 in depreciation deductions, so the property's adjusted tax basis is now $85,000. They sell the property in 2018 for $150,000, realizing a $65,000 long-term capital gain

($150,000 – $85,000 = $65,000). Assuming Jim and Carol are in the 35% tax bracket, $15,000 of their gain (the amount of the depreciation they have taken) will be taxed at 25%. The rest of their gain ($50,000) will be taxed at the lower rate of 15%.

To find the financial value of rental real estate, you will need to know the following:

$_____   *Fair market value*

Single-family homes are somewhat easier to value than commercial, industrial, or multifamily dwellings. For single-family residential real estate, you can ask several real estate agents or appraisers for current comparable values. With other types of rental units, however, you will need to consult an appraiser or a broker who specializes in evaluating the type of property you have. See Chapter 13 for information on finding an appraiser.

An appraiser will use one—or a combination—of these three recognized calculations.

Cost approach. The fair market value equals the amount it would cost to replace a building, plus the land's value. This approach usually applies to single-family dwellings.

Market data approach. Also used with single-family dwellings, this approach compares properties that all provide similar cash flows to determine the fair market value.

Income approach. The fair market value is based on the cash flow a building currently generates plus an estimate of the amount it will generate in the future. Commercial, industrial, and multifamily dwellings are often appraised with this approach.

Ask the appraiser which approach is being used to value your rental property—and why. Just as a retirement plan can be worth different amounts when appraisers use different assumptions, so too can real estate values vary when different approaches are used. Avoid disputes by making sure everyone agrees on what basis is being used to value the property. When you know your properties' fair market value, use the chart below to keep track of those values. Write the address or the description by which you and your spouse will refer to the property in the first column, and the fair market value in the second column. The remaining columns will be addressed as you continue reading this section.

$_____   *Debt on property*

The debt connected to real estate equals what you owe to any lenders (mortgages and lines of credit) plus any liabilities (liens) on the house. All liabilities must be paid before any cash disbursements can be made from the sale of real estate. The mortgage due is sometimes called the "payoff balance." To find the current debt on the house, talk to your lender and check the property's title for any liens you're unaware of. (See Chapter 13.) List the debt in Column 3 of the "Real Estate Values" chart.

$_____   *Total capital improvements*
                          or depreciation

To find total capital improvements made or depreciation taken on rental properties, check your records or previous tax returns, or talk to your accountant or tax adviser. List the totals in the fourth and fifth columns of the "Real Estate Values" chart.

$_____   *% Your tax bracket*

By now, you have probably established your tax bracket, by either checking income tax schedules or talking with your accountant. You will need this information in the upcoming formula.

$_____   *Cost of sale*

You can do a quick ballpark estimate of what it will cost you to sell your rental property or you can follow these steps to find as precise a figure as possible. To find this number, you'll have to include not only the costs of sale, but also the amount it will take to fix up the property and prepare it for a sale.

To get a ballpark estimate of the sales cost, multiply the fair market value by 0.07, an accepted estimate of what it costs to sell a house. Obviously, some sales will yield higher or lower costs of sale, but 7% will do.

Real Estate Values				
Property Address or Description	Fair Market Value	Current Debt on Property	Total Capital Improvements	Total Depreciation Taken
Rental house 323 Third St, Rye, NY	$100,000	$60,000	$20,000	$40,000
Duplex Sun Court, Surf City, CA	$280,000	$100,000	$0	$32,000
	$	$	$	$
	$	$	$	$
	$	$	$	$

To obtain a more accurate cost-of-sale figure, total the following amounts:

$ _____ *Agent's commission*

The amount a real estate agent charges you for selling property, this generally averages 6% of the final selling price. This fee can sometimes be negotiated down.

$ _____ *Closing costs*

Included in these costs are escrow fees, recording costs, appraisal fees, and miscellaneous expenses that can add up to thousands of dollars. A lender or real estate agent can help you figure the exact amount.

$ _____ *Attorneys' fees*

In a few states, you will need to hire an attorney to help you "close" the sale of real property. If you used an attorney when you bought the property, base your figure on that amount, taking into account the fact that most lawyers raise their fees over time. Otherwise, ask a real estate agent for an estimate.

$ _____ *Fix-up costs*

Estimate here the amount of money you will have to spend to prepare the property for sale.

Now add all of these figures and fill in the cost of sale.

To find the financial or after-tax/after-sale value of rental real estate, use this formula:

1. Find the equity by subtracting the debt from the fair market value.
2. Find the tax basis by adding total capital improvements to the purchase price and then subtracting total depreciation taken.
3. Find the adjusted sales price by subtracting the cost of sale from the fair market value.
4. Find the gain (or loss) on the potential sale of the property by subtracting the tax basis from the adjusted sales price. If you experienced a loss, you may have no tax liability and you can probably offset other gains with your loss to reduce your taxes due.
5. Determine the portion of gain related to depreciation taken. That portion will be taxed at 25%, while the remainder of the gain will be taxed at either 15% (if you are in a tax bracket above 15%) or 5% (if you are in the 15% tax bracket).
6. Find the financial or after-tax/after-sale value by subtracting costs of sale from the equity and then subtracting the taxes due.

EXAMPLE:

1. Find the equity by subtracting the debt from the fair market value.

Fair market value		$100,000
Debt	–	60,000
Equity	=	$40,000

2. Find the tax basis by adding total capital improvements to the purchase price and then subtracting total depreciation taken.

Purchase price		$50,000
Total improvements	+	5,000
	=	55,000
Total depreciation	–	12,500
Tax basis	=	$42,500

3. Find the adjusted sales price by subtracting the cost of sale from the fair market value.

Fair market value		$100,000
Cost of sale	–	7,000
Adjusted sales price	=	$93,000

4. Find the gain (or loss) on the potential sale of the property by subtracting the tax basis from the adjusted sales price.

Adjusted sales price	=	$93,000
Tax basis	–	42,500
Gain (or loss)	=	$50,500

5. Find the taxes due by multiplying the depreciation by 25%, subtracting total depreciation from the gain, and then multiplying that number (remaining gain) by 15% (assuming you are in the 24%+ tax bracket). Total these numbers for the taxes due.

		$12,500
	×	25%
Gain from depreciation	=	$ 3,125
Gain on sale		$50,500
	–	12,500
Remaining gain	=	$38,000
	×	15%
	=	$5,700
		$3,125
	+	5,700
Taxes due	=	$8,825

6. Find the financial or after-tax/after-sale value by subtracting the cost of sale from the equity and then subtracting the taxes due.

Equity		$ 40,000
Cost of sale	–	7,000
Taxes due	–	8,825
Financial or after-tax/after-sale value	=	$ 24,175

To apply this formula to your situation, fill in the blanks below:

1. Find the equity by subtracting the debt from the fair market value.

Fair market value		$ _____
Debt	–	$ _____
Equity	=	$ _____

2. Find the tax basis by adding total capital improvements to the purchase price and then subtracting total depreciation taken.

Purchase price		$ _____
Total improvements	+	$ _____
	=	$ _____
Total depreciation	–	$ _____
Tax basis	=	$ _____

3. Find the adjusted sales price by subtracting the cost of sale from the fair market value.

Fair market value		$ _____
Cost of sale	–	$ _____
Adjusted sales price	=	$ _____

4. Find the gain (or loss) on the potential sale of the property by subtracting the tax basis from the adjusted sales price.

Adjusted sales price		$ _____
Tax basis	–	$ _____
Gain (or loss)	=	$ _____

Who Pays the Rent

If you or your spouse moves from the family home, you can make temporary arrangements for paying the mortgage and other bills. But what if you own rental property and the renters move? Who will pay the mortgage? Or suppose you and your spouse decide to sell the property. Who will pay for repairs? Who will be reimbursed for capital improvements to the property? You must settle these questions. If you pay these costs alone, keep good records of every expense so that you will have a chance to get reimbursed as part of the final settlement.

5. Find the taxes due by multiplying the depreciation portion of the gain by 25% and the remaining gain by 15% (assuming you are in the 24%+ tax bracket). Total these numbers for the taxes due.

		$ _____
	×	_____ 25%
Gain from depreciation		$ _____
		$ _____
	−	$ _____
		$ _____
	×	_____ 15%
Remaining gain		$ _____
		$ _____
	+	$ _____
Taxes due		$ _____

6. Find the financial or after-tax/after-sale value by subtracting cost of sale from the equity and then subtracting the taxes due.

Equity		$ _____
Cost of sale	−	$ _____
Taxes due (or tax refund)	−	$ _____
After-tax/after-sale value	=	$ _____

Insurance

Buying more insurance than you need and paying too much in insurance premiums are common mistakes. At divorce, you have the opportunity to take a good look at your policies and correct these mistakes if necessary.

Whole life or universal life insurance not only provides income in the event of someone's death, but also has some investment benefits, although these benefits might be minimal compared with other investments. As you pay your premiums, a cash reserve builds up. This reserve increases over and above the premiums you pay because you earn interest on your premiums. The reserve also grows because the expenses, such as commissions paid to brokers, decrease over time. Be aware, though, that the cash value decreases if you borrow money against the policy.

Term policies, on the other hand, provide death benefits only. They have no cash buildup and therefore have no growth potential.

Keep only those policies you truly need for insurance. Never surrender an essential policy or let it lapse without having replacement insurance, but do get rid of unnecessary policies. Life insurance companies select policyholders with care. If you have to apply for insurance in the future, you may be denied coverage because of an as-yet-unknown health problem. If you surrender policies with cash value—that is, you turn them in and collect the cash—you will have to pay taxes on the interest earned. You figure the interest by subtracting the total premiums paid and the surrender charges from the cash value. The difference is the interest, and that amount is what you'd have to report to the IRS as income.

Annuities

Annuities are investments, offered by insurance companies, that are meant to provide income at retirement. Annuities are discussed in Chapter 14.

Cash Value Policies

Any policy with a cash value is often called, logically enough, a "cash value policy." If you decide that your policy is not the most cost-effective for you, you can use the cash value to purchase another insurance policy that is more suitable. The benefit of buying another policy rather than taking the cash out of your current policy is that you can defer the taxes you would owe on the accrued interest. (I.R.C. § 1035.) The only drawback is that you will have to pay a commission when you purchase the new policy, and these costs will decrease the initial cash value of the new policy.

To quickly estimate the financial value of your insurance (a detailed analysis is not necessary), you need to obtain the following:

$ _____   *Cash value*

Take a look at the most current policy statement and see if it shows the cash value. If it doesn't, ask your insurance agent.

$ _____   *Surrender charges*

Again, this information should be on the current policy, or you can get it by checking with your agent.

$ _____   *Premiums paid*

Check the most current policy statement or ask your agent.

Following the example in the "Value of Insurance Policy" chart, below, use the formula shown to find the financial or after-tax/after-sale value on cash value insurance policies.

Value of Insurance Policy		
	Example	**Your Policy**
Cash value	$ 10,000	
Surrender charge	– 500	
Cash surrender value	$ 9,500	
Premiums paid	– 6,000	
Gain (or loss)	$ 3,500	
Tax bracket	× 0.24	
Taxes due	$ 840	

Cash surrender value	$ 9,500	
Taxes due	– 840	
Financial or after-tax/after-sale value	$ 8,660	

Limited Partnerships

You might have difficulty finding an accurate value for your interests in a limited partnership. It's often hard to tell how much was invested and how much has been received in tax benefits (write-offs). This book doesn't provide detailed information on figuring the financial value of limited partnerships. Instead, consult your accountant to get an understanding of the value of these assets and to ask your broker for information on companies that specialize in secondary market sales of limited partnership units.

Also, call the general partner (and any other limited partners) to find out everything you can about the partnership, especially its economic health. Be alert to these potential problems with limited partnerships:

- You might not be able to divide your interest. General partners might not be willing to divide the investment in the limited partnership between you and your spouse. If you can't divide your interest, and neither of you wants to give up your interest to the other in exchange for other property, be sure you and your ex-spouse have a carefully written agreement about how taxes, bookkeeping, and distribution checks will be handled after the divorce.

- A limited partnership can generate taxable income that you never receive, called phantom income. Ask the general partner whether phantom income is expected and how much of this income will be taxable.

- Some limited partnerships make requests for additional investments (called capital calls) from the limited partners. Before keeping a limited partnership, check the original investment document, contact your accountant, or ask the general partner whether you may be liable for additional investments.

- All limited partnerships are risky investments, because the general partner has almost complete control over the assets of the partnership. A general partner's decision to sell an asset or allow a foreclosure can create a tax liability for you. You might call your broker or the general partner to determine when the sale of assets in the partnership is anticipated and what the tax consequences would be.

- Bookkeeping can be difficult. When the partnership sends out its IRS reporting form (K-1) each tax year, it sends only one form to each investor. The partnership usually sends only one distribution check as well. If you and your spouse are unable to divide the partnership interest, then only one of you will receive the form and the check. You need to agree on who that will be and how you'll handle it—for example, what the deadline will be for the spouse who receives the check and information to pass along the other spouse's share.

Unless you've been lucky, limited partnerships are more trouble to keep after divorce than they are usually worth.

Collectibles

Your biggest problem in determining the financial value of collectibles (like art, special plates, or even baseball cards) will be finding a valuation on which you and your spouse can agree. You might hear any number of conflicting values depending on who is making the appraisal.

To find the financial value of collectibles, first list the following:

$ _____ *Purchase price*

Check original receipts, look at old tax returns, or consult with a broker.

$ _____ *Acquisition costs*

Did you drive to a distant city to buy the piece? Stay overnight in a hotel? Pay admission to an antique fair? All of these could add to the taxable cost basis of the antique, meaning you'll owe less tax when you sell it.

$ _____ *Improvements*

Did you restore the piece or do anything to it—such as reupholstering, refinishing, or refurbishing—that increased its value?

$ _____ *Selling price or wholesale value*

Ask a dealer, an auctioneer, or a consignment shop to give you an estimate of the wholesale value of your holdings. Many people mistakenly assume that some items, such as diamonds, are worth a great deal because they consider only the retail value. But jewelers buy loose diamonds at wholesale prices and will not pay you more than that price when they buy from you.

$ _____ *Commissions*

Talk with a broker, a wholesaler, or anyone familiar with the market for your item. With collectibles, the commission can be as high as 30% of the sale price.

_____ *% Tax bracket*

Consult an accountant or previous tax schedules.

To find the financial or after-sale/after-tax value of collectibles, use this formula:

1. Find the tax basis by adding commissions (paid at purchase), acquisition costs, improvements, and purchase price.
2. Find the adjusted sale price by subtracting commissions (due at sale) from the selling price or wholesale value.
3. Find the gain (or loss) by subtracting the tax basis from the adjusted sales price.
4. If you incur a loss on this asset, you can net it against a gain on another asset to reduce your capital gains tax liability.
5. Find the taxes due by multiplying the gain times the capital gains tax rate of 15%.
6. Find the financial value by subtracting (or adding) taxes due (or tax benefit) from (or to) the adjusted sale price.

EXAMPLE: Janet and Tom purchased a painting during their marriage that they now wanted to sell. It had gone down in value, so they had a loss they could net against other gains.

1. Find the tax basis by adding commissions (paid at purchase), acquisition costs, improvements, and purchase price.

Purchase price		$10,000
Acquisition costs	+	250
Improvements	+	250
Commissions	+	500
Tax basis	=	$11,000

2. Find the adjusted sale price by subtracting commissions (due at sale) from the selling price or wholesale value.

Selling price or wholesale value		$ 7,000
Commissions	–	500
Adjusted sales price	=	$ 6,500

3. Find the gain (or loss) by subtracting the tax basis from the adjusted sales price.

Adjusted sales price		$ 6,500
Tax basis	−	11,000
Gain (or loss)	=	$(4,500)

4. Find the taxes due by multiplying the gain times the capital gains tax rate of 15%.

Gain (or loss)		$(4,500)
Capital gains tax rate	×	15%
Taxes due (or benefit)	=	$(675)

5. Find the financial value by subtracting the tax benefit from the adjusted sale price.

Adjusted sales price		$ 6,500
Taxes due (or benefit)	−	($675)
Financial value	=	$ 7,175

If loss is not netted against gains, you can only use up to $3,000 in losses in one year. So you would carry forward the $1,500 ($4,500 loss − $3,000 = $1,500) to the next year.

To apply this formula to your situation, fill in the blanks below:

1. Find the tax basis by adding commissions (paid at purchase) and purchase price.

Purchase price		$ _____
Commissions	+	$ _____
Tax basis	=	$ _____

2. Find the adjusted sale price by subtracting commissions (due at sale) from the selling price or wholesale value.

Selling price or wholesale value		$ _____
Commissions	−	$ _____
Adjusted sales price	=	$ _____

3. Find the gain (or loss) by subtracting the tax basis from the adjusted sales price.

Adjusted sales price		$ _____
Tax basis	–	$ _____
Gain (or benefit)	=	$ _____

4. Find the taxes due by multiplying the gain times the capital gains rate of 15%.

Gain		$ _____
Capital gains tax rate	×	*15%*
Taxes due (or benefit)	=	$ _____

5. Find the financial value by subtracting the taxes due or benefit from the adjusted sale price.

Adjusted sales price		$ _____
Taxes due	–	$ _____
Financial value	=	$ _____

Step 5: Which Assets Should You Keep?

Once you know the financial (or after-tax/after-sale) value of investments, you have a starting point for negotiating with your spouse. The values are useful whether you want to sell your assets to the person you're divorcing, buy them for yourself, sell them to a third party, or divide them between you.

The ultimate decision to keep or sell an investment depends on many factors including your age, risk tolerance, income needs, and investment experience. Asking yourself the following simple questions will help you make sound decisions about your investments.

1. *Has this investment performed well?*
   If Yes, go to Question 2.
   If No, consider these options:
   - Sell the asset before the divorce so you and your soon-to-be ex-spouse share the costs of sale, taxes, and other expenses.
   - Take the asset for yourself, but only if it provides you with the benefit of a tax loss. That is, it can offset a gain you may have on another asset. You should consult a tax expert to determine whether you need to take any losses.
   - Offer to sell the asset to your spouse in the divorce settlement.
2. *Is this investment appropriate for me—is it providing the income, growth, liquidity, or security I need?*
   If Yes, how long do you plan to keep it?
   - Long-term—buy out your spouse's interest and keep this investment.
   - Short-term—consider selling before your divorce becomes final, sharing the proceeds, taxes, and other costs with your spouse, and then using the proceeds to purchase a similar investment.

   If No, consider these options:
   - Sell before your divorce is final, sharing the proceeds, taxes, and other costs with your spouse.
   - Buy out your spouse and sell immediately to take advantage of tax losses.
   - Let your spouse buy out your share or interest in the investment.

Step 6: How Will You and Your Spouse Divide the Investments?

You are now ready to prepare your position for negotiating over investment assets. Look at the "Investment Chart" you completed earlier in this chapter and use it to show how investments will be handled in your divorce. For each investment listed in Column 1, put a checkmark in one of the last three columns to show whether you intend to keep the asset, have your spouse keep it, or sell it and split the proceeds. If you have cash value life insurance or rental property, be sure to read the sections that follow before making a final decision about these assets.

Special Problems With Cash Value Life Insurance

The financial value of the policy isn't the only consideration with cash value life insurance. Be sure to consider the following before choosing to keep this asset in your divorce:

- What is the quality of the insurance company? You might be able to evaluate the quality of an insurance company by checking its ratings by one of the three main rating services, Standard and Poor's, Moody's, and A.M. Best. But these ratings provide no guarantees. Before it folded in 1990, for example, Executive Life received an A+ rating from Best, considered the top rating company.
- What interest rate are you receiving on the premiums accruing as your cash value? Would alternative—yet safe—investments, such as corporate bonds, municipal bonds, or federal government bonds, yield you more?
- Are there any loans outstanding on the policy? If so, the amount paid at death will be reduced by the outstanding loan. Before taking this asset at divorce, be sure the loans are paid back so the full amount is paid, or be prepared for the death benefits to be reduced.

Special Problems With Rental Property

The financial value of the property isn't the only consideration with rental property. Be sure to ask yourself the following questions before choosing to keep this asset in your divorce:

- Where is the property located? Is it on a busy street? On the beach? Given its location, what is its potential for appreciation?
- What is the quality of the neighborhood? Is it improving or deteriorating?
- How will the property be affected by changes in the local economy?
- Are newer and nicer buildings directly competing for your renters?

- Are your rents above or below market?
- What does it cost to maintain and manage the property?
  Is your cash flow positive or negative? Can you afford the property
  when renters vacate and the income is down?
- What are the tax incentives or disincentives to keeping the property?
- What would it cost to improve the property?
- How much income can you expect the property to generate?
- When might you sell? Can you determine your rate of return over
  that time?
- What is the vacancy rate?
- What kind of loan do you have—fixed or adjustable rate?
  If it's adjustable and interest rates rise, can you still afford it?

Your answers will help you reach one of three conclusions:

1. The property has strong potential (the location is great, it has
   little rental competition, and operating costs and vacancy rates
   are low) and it should appreciate faster than other investments
   I could make using the same amount of money.

   It would be a good asset to keep.

2. The property has some potential, but it's uncertain. Other investments using the same amount of money might outperform this one.

   We should probably sell now and split the proceeds,
   or my spouse can take it.

3. This property has little potential (operating costs are high,
   the location is bad, and/or vacancy rates are high) and other
   investments have a higher probability of meeting my needs.

   We should probably sell now and split the proceeds,
   or my spouse can take it.

Now review all your investments—stocks, bonds, rental real estate,
limited partnerships, and others—and write your decisions on the
"Investment Chart" at the beginning of this chapter. ●

Evaluating Employee Benefits and Stock Options

As companies get more creative in compensating their employees, the stakes are raised in the divorce process.

Today's employees receive more than what shows up on the pay stub or tax form. Benefits such as stock options, restricted stock units, insurance, retirement plans, rent or hotel stays, travel, housecleaning, wellness programs, miles, cars or transportation, and other perks and fringes are forms of compensation.

For divorce purposes, the key question is whether to classify various types of employee compensation as:

- **income**—a continuing source of money that can affect decisions about alimony and child support
- an **asset**—property of some sort that can be apportioned between the spouses in the settlement
- **neither income nor an asset,** or
- **both income and an asset.** (For more on the distinction between income and assets, see Chapter 12.)

This chapter looks at different forms of employee compensation in light of their value to you and your spouse in the divorce process.

Employee Benefits

Employee benefits (also known as nonwage compensation) have mush-roomed in recent years as companies and nonprofit organizations have sought to attract and retain employees. Startup businesses, especially, use nonwage compensation because they may not yet generate the cash to pay competitive salaries. In addition, more and more companies are beginning to recognize that providing socially conscious employees perks and access to employee programs that benefit employees and their families will not only keep employees healthy and happy, but will foster continued loyalty among their workforce.

Nowadays, common employee benefits include retirement plans—both pension plans and deferred compensation plans; insurance coverage; disability and death benefits; employee assistance plans; virtual therapy;

educational assistance and paid training programs; ergonomic assessments, workstation assistance, electronic stipends for home office expenses, and work from home programs; travel, health club memberships, mindfulness and other wellness programs; and discounts at stores or hotels.

Courts can and do disagree about how to classify these types of employee benefits at divorce. Many of these benefits are not worth much to anyone other than the employee and would not move the needle in terms of income available for support, but others are certainly more valuable. For example, one court may say that use of a company car and internet stipends lower an employee's living expenses, freeing up more money for spousal and child support; another might not. So it's important to talk to your attorney about the role that employee benefits may play in your case.

Various types of retirement plans, employer sponsored and otherwise, are explained in Chapter 14. The following sections provide an overview of other common employee benefits and how they could affect your divorce settlement. The question that's usually at issue is whether a particular benefit can be considered taxable (or gross) income. If so, a court may take it into account in setting child or spousal support. In other instances, a benefit may be regarded as a marital asset—something that gets allocated between spouses at the time of divorce.

Health Insurance

The employee benefits that most affect day-to-day living are in the insurance area. Medical insurance, especially, is one of the most important benefits that are subject to a divorce court's powers. Health insurance can also cover prescriptions, therapy, dental and vision care, and the like.

Many health insurance plans provide benefits through an insurance company or a health maintenance organization (HMO). Other plans are paid directly by the employer (known as "self-funded" or "self-insured" plans).

An employer's contributions for health insurance are *not* considered taxable income to the employee. Nor does an employee report as taxable income amounts paid by the insurance company for covered medical expenses.

A court may order a parent to provide health coverage for children as part of a child support order (see Chapter 18). But this benefit is not considered an asset to be divided at divorce.

Disability Plans

These plans protect employees against the risk that illness or injury will interrupt their ability to work. Typically, the employer offers coverage for disability under an accident or health plan.

Usually, the employer's contribution is excluded from the employee's gross income on the tax return. In the event of disability, however, amounts the employee receives are included as gross income.

Employer-sponsored disability insurance is not an asset to be divided between spouses at divorce. But a contribution paid by the employer may be factored into the court's calculation of child and spousal support.

Group Term Life Insurance

This is an insurance policy carried by an employer to provide death benefits for employees and, occasionally, for retirees. Unless an employee is upper management, this insurance is generally available only during the term of employment.

The employee generally excludes from taxable income the employer's contribution to the premium up to $50,000. In the event of death, the beneficiary is not taxed on the death benefits received.

Group term life insurance is not an asset that a court divides. However, the court may order a party to maintain all employer-provided life insurance, naming a former spouse or children as the beneficiary (see Chapter 10).

Accidental Death or Dismemberment Insurance

Again, employer contributions to premium payments and insurance proceeds the employee received are excluded from the employee's income. If the employee pays the premium, the amount paid may be a factor the court considers in a child support order; however, the policy itself is not an asset to divide.

Health Savings Accounts

A health savings account (HSA) is a tax-advantaged medical savings account to which contributions may be made by employers, employees, or both. Funds in an HSA account may be invested in a manner similar to a 401(k) account or an IRA. Those funds can later be withdrawn tax free for qualified medical expenses, such as deductibles; coinsurance; dental, vision, and chiropractic care; and other items not necessarily covered under a traditional health insurance plan.

Each HSA account must be combined with a separate catastrophic health insurance policy with a high deductible. Medical expenses must hit $1,350 for an individual and $2,700 for a family before coverage kicks in. Once the deductible is met, the insurance usually covers 100% of health care costs. The idea is that Americans will consume less care and be more vigilant about health care costs if they see a relationship between medical costs and their bank accounts.

Unused funds can be rolled over into the next year's account. (HSAs, which were launched in 2004, effectively replace medical savings accounts, or MSAs, because employers of all sizes can offer HSAs while MSAs were limited to employers of 50 or fewer workers.)

Some controversy exists about whether HSAs favor high-income individuals, and there is some dispute over how quickly employers are adopting HSA plans. But there's no doubt that payments the employer makes to the plan are not included in the employee's gross income, and if an employee contributes, that contribution is deductible from gross income on tax returns. So, these accounts have the potential to accumulate significant balances over years of contributions and investment gains.

The employee spouse gets to keep all amounts in the HSA account on the date of separation or divorce. The employee spouse can be ordered to pay existing marital medical expenses with money on deposit. (See Chapter 10 for a discussion of retaining health care coverage through a spouse's employer.)

Dependent Care Assistance Programs

Dependent care programs provide child care or related services for employees who need this help in order to work. Frequently, employers offer child care benefits as a choice under a cafeteria plan (see below). The program may offer direct payments to the employee, or it may involve an employer-sponsored child care center.

The employee's gross income doesn't include amounts the employer contributed. This benefit is not subject to division as an asset. But the court may consider the program's value as compensation and may order an employee to provide this benefit as part of a child support order.

Cafeteria Plans

Cafeteria plans offer participants a choice of certain benefits—such as medical insurance, group term life insurance, disability insurance, and child care—or cash. Employees may also be given the option under a cafeteria plan to use, sell, or buy additional vacation days.

Typically, in a cafeteria plan the employee elects before the beginning of the year to take a salary reduction. The amount of the reduction is then applied to the employee's share of the insurance premium or to cover other expenses such as child care.

The value of the benefits the employee receives is excluded from the employee's gross income. But any cash the employee receives under the plan is included in gross income.

Severance Plans

Severance involves payments made to an employee who the employer terminated. Whether written or informal, severance plans have two goals: to reward an employee's past service and to help the employee make ends meet during retraining or a job search. Sometimes an employer offers severance pay in exchange for the employee's promise not to sue for wrongful termination.

Severance plans, where they exist, vary from employer to employer. Some offer one week's pay for each year of service. Others have a more generous "golden parachute" policy, typically for executives. Eligibility for severance and the amount received often depend on the employee's position in the firm as well as length of service.

Severance may be paid in a lump sum, periodic payments, or a combination of the two. Generally, severance payments are included in gross income.

Educational Assistance Programs

These programs reimburse employees for tuition, fees, and attendance at outside educational programs or institutions or provide tuition and fees for in-house seminars. Courses don't have to be related to a person's work. Such expenses an employer paid for aren't included in an employee's gross income.

Group Legal Services

These plans offer employees low-cost legal services such as referrals, advice, and representation. They allow a group to use its collective purchasing power to negotiate lower rates from lawyers.

The employer and/or the employee pays for the cost through union dues or payroll deductions. Participation may be automatic or voluntary, and a plan may be offered independently or through a cafeteria plan.

The benefits received under group legal services plans used to be excluded from employees' income. That's no longer the case; employees must now pay taxes on any such benefits received.

Employee Assistance Programs

These programs cover a variety of services for employees and their families, including help for drug and alcohol abuse, stress, anxiety, depression, family problems, money and credit problems, and legal problems. Usually, employers contract with a third party to provide counseling and referral services with a social worker or family counselor.

Benefits or reimbursements an employee receives under an employee assistance program may or may not be included in gross income, depending on the nature of the benefit and the employee's income level. Employers should be able to provide information on the tax consequences of benefits offered under their program.

Stock Options and Nonqualified Deferred Compensation Plans

SKIP AHEAD
If neither you nor your spouse has stock options, stock incentives, or nonqualified deferred compensation plans (a kind of benefit usually reserved for upper management), skip ahead to the next chapter.

Stock options and other kinds of corporate incentive and compensation programs present a challenge for divorcing spouses who are trying to sort out and take control of their finances—not just because the plans themselves can be complicated, but also because there's still a lot of uncertainty over how to deal with them in the divorce process.

This section provides an overview of different kinds of plans and explains some key terms that come up in this area. If you or your spouse has such benefits, questions to keep in mind are:

• How much is the benefit worth now?
• Is the benefit something that can be divided between spouses?
• Can the benefit be transferred from one spouse to the other?
• Is the benefit considered income?
• If the benefit is income, will a court take it into account in calculating alimony and/or child support?

Many cases have no sure answers. But you need to be aware of these issues so that you can discuss them with an attorney and factor them into your negotiations.

SEE AN EXPERT

If you or your spouse has stock options or other types of compensation covered in this section, you should talk to your divorce lawyer as well as a tax attorney or certified public accountant. Many tax considerations can be involved.

Types of Stock Options

Stock options are an important part of the compensation program of many corporations. The aim, in addition to compensating employees, is to encourage employees to work hard to achieve success for the firm and thus increase the value of the company's stock.

Stock options have been common perks for senior management for many years. But in recent years, stock options have become part of the compensation package of many rank-and-file workers. It's been estimated that in publicly traded companies, between a quarter and a third of all employees own stock options; in technology companies, the percentage likely tops 50%. Yet, other studies have shown that large numbers of these workers do not understand the stock options they hold—or their tax implications.

A stock option is a right granted to an employee to purchase a certain number of shares in the company's stock at today's price sometime in the future. The stock purchased can be sold later, when the market value might be higher.

Usually, the employee can't exercise the right to purchase and sell stock as soon as the option is received. Instead, the employee must remain with the firm for a minimum period before the options vest (that is, become exercisable). When they do vest, the stock's market value presumably will have risen, thus giving the employee an automatic profit in return for having stayed with the firm through the vesting period.

As a result, employees can find themselves with potential wealth tied up in an employer's option plan. In fact, options nationally are said to represent about $1 trillion in unexercised wealth. But there is also great risk in unexercised options. That's because while the expectation is that the value of the stock will go up, sometimes it goes down quickly and significantly.

Stock Option Documents You Need to Get

To determine what kind of stock options are involved in your case, you should obtain as much information on the options as possible. Much of this information can be obtained from the employer that granted the options. Important documents include:

- the original stock option plan statement and all amendments
- grant agreements between employer and employee (one for each grant)
- employer's letter of intent to employee offering a stock option contract
- an option summary statement reflecting the status of each grant, including vesting, exercise, and sales as well as changes in the number of shares resulting from stock splits (generally, the employer provides such statements annually or quarterly)
- a list of the company's monthly stock prices and dividend payments (if it's a publicly traded firm), and
- all Securities and Exchange Commission Form 10-K filings, annual proxy statements, or other filings with any governmental or regulatory agency during the term of employment. (These often are available at the EDGAR website at www.sec.gov; look under the "FILINGS" heading. EDGAR stands for Electronic Data Gathering Analysis and Retrieval, an information system of the Securities and Exchange Commission.)

Thus, while stock options are an increasingly common marital asset and often an item in contention in a divorce, they can entail substantial losses as well as gains. A divorcing spouse might have to pay additional support when options go up in value, but receive no relief if they go down.

Option plans are complex, and they differ from company to company. What's more, divorce courts differ greatly on how to value options, what portion—if any—of them should be characterized as marital property, and how to treat them for purposes of support.

There are various kinds of stock options, discussed below. However, they all have these similarities:

- Options may be exercised (the shares may be purchased) during a specified period of time and at a fixed price.
- After the vesting period, an employee can wait to exercise the option until—and if—the stock's market value exceeds the price at which the employee can buy it, thus guaranteeing a profit.
- The employee has no risk during the vesting period because there's no obligation to buy the stock and no money invested yet. If the value of the stock declines, the employee simply elects not to exercise the option.

Now let's look at the two broad categories of stock options: statutory and nonstatutory (also known as nonqualified stock options, or NQSOs).

Statutory stock options are so called because they are subject to a strict set of regulations under federal statutes. For example, to qualify for a favorable capital gain tax rate, an option holder must either exercise the option within two years after the employer grants it, or hold on to the stock for at least a year after exercising the option.

The two types of statutory stock options are *incentive stock options* (ISOs) and *employee stock purchase plans*. A written plan the company's board of directors and stockholders have approved governs ISOs. The plan lists the employees who are eligible and the number of shares available for these employees.

When an employee is granted an ISO, that's not considered income on which the employee can be taxed. Nor is it taxable income when it's exercised. After the employee sells the stock, the profit is considered a capital gain and is taxed at that rate.

Can the employee transfer the ISO to an ex-spouse upon divorce? The law says that the option itself—the right to buy the stock—can't be transferred. If it is, the option becomes a "nonqualified" option (see below). However, if the employee exercises the option first, the ISO stock the employee has bought can be transferred to the employee's spouse.

Stock Option Lingo

Even to the most sophisticated investors, stock options can be confusing. Here are simple definitions of some of the key concepts:

- **Stock option.** A contractual right, not an obligation, to buy a certain number of shares (exercise the option) at a point in the future (the vesting date) at a specific price (the grant price).
- **Grant.** The issuance by an employer of the right to acquire stock at a specific time in the future at a predetermined price.
- **Grant price.** The price at which the shares are purchased when the option is exercised, regardless of their market price when exercised. Also known as "strike price," "option price," or "exercise price."
- **Vesting.** The time that must elapse before the employee acquires the right to exercise an option or a percentage of the option granted (for example, 25% of all total options granted over four years).
- **Exercise.** The exchange of an option for actual shares of the company. The employee must pay the grant price as well as the payroll taxes associated with the exercise. And when the employee sells the stock, the employee may be taxed on the profit made (capital gains) on the difference between the grant price and the sale price.
- **Exercise date.** The date after vesting when the employee purchases shares at the predetermined price under the terms of the option agreement.
- **Holding period.** The period of time that an employee is required to keep the stock after purchasing it and before selling it. The holding period begins on the exercise date and ends on the day before the stock is sold.
- **Expiration date.** The last day the employee can exercise the option under the terms of the contract.
- **Cashless exercise.** This occurs when the employee simultaneously exercises an option and sells the stock just acquired, covering the cost of the options and the taxes due. The employee takes the remainder in cash instead of stock shares.
- **Spread.** The difference between the grant price and the market value on the exercise date.
- **Gain.** The difference between the grant price and the market value on the day the stock is sold.

Besides an ISO, the other type of qualified option is an employee stock purchase plan. Such a plan allows an employee to set aside money from regular paychecks to purchase company stock, either at a discount or at market value on the date of the grant. The stock is held in trust for the employee, who receives the holdings in stock or cash when employment ends. As with an ISO, the option to buy stock under an employee stock purchase plan cannot be transferred from one divorcing spouse to another.

Nonstatutory (or nonqualified) stock options have fewer restrictions, and the tax consequences for the employee are not as favorable. When an employee exercises an option and makes money by buying stock at lower-than-market rates, that money is subject to federal income tax as well as FICA, Medicare, and state and local taxes.

An NQSO can be transferred from an employee to an ex-spouse at divorce. The ex-spouse exercising the option is liable for income tax just as the employee spouse would be.

Restricted stock and restricted stock units (RSUs) are stock options that fall outside the statutory and nonstatutory categories because of how they're taxed. Rather than the date when the stock is exercised or sold, it's the *vesting schedule* that determines the tax consequences for these types of employee stock. Both have become more popular in recent years as companies try harder to tie compensation to work performance by creating a vested interest in the health of the company's stock.

Restricted stock is typically granted to executives who have detailed, or "insider" knowledge of their companies. As such, these options are subject to Securities Exchange Commission regulations. Employees generally receive these stocks up front, but are subject to forfeiture rules until fully vested.

RSUs represent an agreement, which promises that amounts of stock will pass into the employee's possession at some date(s) in the future. The number of shares in each unit varies from agreement to agreement.

In divorce, the value of restricted stock and RSUs may depend on whether they are defined as compensation or as an asset, which may have vested during the marriage or will become fully vested after the divorce is finalized. It is important to remember that in both cases, you can't guarantee that the employee will receive these stock options until they are fully vested.

What Are Stock Options Worth at Divorce?

How can stock options be valued and apportioned among divorcing spouses? That question presents complex problems for family lawyers and courts, as well as for divorcing spouses.

Among the issues: Are stock options property or income, or both? Are options that vest after the couple's separation date considered marital property? If the employee spouse doesn't exercise the option until years after the divorce, does the ex-spouse deserve a portion? Is there a formula courts can use for dividing options? Should a court be able to raise levels of alimony and child support if the value of the stock increases, and reduce the support if the value falls? If an employee's option hasn't yet vested because the employee hasn't worked at the company long enough, how does that affect the value of the option?

There's not a lot of legal precedent to go on, and no hard-and-fast rules apply to all stock option plans in all states.

There are, however, some broad guidelines. Stock options granted to an employee spouse before the separation date generally are seen as marital property. Those granted after separation tend to be viewed as separate property of the employee spouse. In a series of California cases, the judges found that options that were granted and exercised before the separation date were community property—whereas options that were granted during marriage but not exercised until after separation entitled the ex-spouse to a partial interest, based on the amount of time elapsed. About half the states have followed these general principles.

Courts have also generally held that recurring capital gains—including profits from exercised stock options—are income and can be used for calculating support.

What about potential income from *unexercised* options? Some courts have said that unexercised options are part of gross income and therefore can be used to help determine support payments. Courts have also said that an item can be considered both income for support purposes and property for purposes of equitable distribution. If an option is both unexercised and *unvested*, that raises more valuation questions that have no clear answer.

Courts have developed various methods for apportioning options. Sometimes, as we've seen, options can be transferred. Some courts have required the parties to hold stock options as tenants in common (for more on tenancy in common, see Chapters 6, 10, and 12).

Still other courts have applied other methods to determine the options' present value, then ordered one spouse to give the other assets from the estate to offset the value of the options. The risk here is that later the stock's value can either fall or skyrocket, leaving each spouse feeling blessed or chagrined.

How stock options are handled in divorce depends on many factors, including the laws in your state. There is no guarantee your situation will be treated the same as someone else's or that the court will come to the same conclusion in your case as it has in other cases or as courts have in other jurisdictions. You might need to talk at length with a lawyer about stock option issues in your case. See "Points to Include in the Options Agreement," below, for some key points that should be covered in any settlement reached by you and your spouse.

 WEB RESOURCE
Several websites offer information and resources on stock options. Among them are:

- **www.mystockoptions.com.** This comprehensive site includes articles, a glossary, a tax guide, a tax calculator, and answers to frequently asked questions.
- **www.stockopter.com.** While primarily a site for financial professionals, it includes a useful glossary and explanatory articles under the "StockOpter University" tab.

Points to Include in the Options Agreement

While few firm rules cover how to handle stock options in divorce cases, any agreement between you and your spouse should cover certain points. Here is a checklist of issues to include in your analysis:

- **Identify the grants.** Make sure you have all paperwork pertaining to the options as furnished by the employer, specifying the terms of the grant, the grant price, key dates, and all rules that apply.
- **Decide who will bear the exercise fees.** An employee typically pays a fee when an option is exercised. At divorce, whoever exercises the option usually pays the fee, whether that's the employee or the ex-spouse.
- **Agree to follow court orders and employer conditions.** Both spouses should agree that the options must be exercised in a way that adheres to both the judge's ruling and the employer's terms.
- **Clarify when options change or terminate.** The agreement should be clear about the duration of options periods and what happens to the options if the employee leaves the company. The employer should be responsible for providing information to the parties about any changes in conditions or timetables for exercising options.
- **Protect personal identification information.** Do not include in any court order personal information, such as address, date of birth, or Social Security number. Such information should be provided to the employer and other parties by mail, certified with return receipt requested.

Nonqualified Deferred Compensation Plans

Nonqualified deferred compensation is one method by which companies have traditionally rewarded their highest-ranking executives. Far less common than stock options, these plans are generally found only in large corporations and are limited to a few executives, such as the chief executive officer, chief financial officer, president, and vice presidents.

Under such a plan, the employer defers part of an executive's income now—thereby reducing the executive's current tax burden—and provides the income later, when the executive will presumably be in a lower tax bracket. Like stock options, these plans are legally complex and difficult to value and divide at divorce, or even to evaluate to determine what is income available for support.

There are many kinds of nonqualified deferred compensation plans. Some look like 401(k)s, some resemble defined benefit plans (see Chapter 14), and others are merely promises by the employer to pay income to the employee in the future. A common type of plan is the SERP (Supplemental Executive Retirement Plan), or "top hat" plan, which provides additional retirement benefits to a select group of high-level managers through the use of various formulas.

If you are divorcing a spouse with a nonqualified deferred compensation plan, you or your lawyer will want to request documentation from the employer. This might include the plan summary, full plan documents, an employment contract, and an actuarial analysis.

Two factors reduce the value of these plans in divorce. Because such plans are often unfunded, there is a risk that the employee will never receive the benefits if the company goes bankrupt, reorganizes, or is taken over by another company. Also, the benefit cannot be split between divorcing spouses under a QDRO. (A QDRO assures direct payment of certain benefits to the nonemployee spouse. See Chapter 14.)

Questions to Ask an Attorney or a Tax Specialist

1. How do our state courts treat all our employment benefits? As property? As income?
2. What do our state courts have to say about how stock options should be valued and apportioned in divorce?
3. After my divorce, will I be entitled to any medical benefits I would have received under my spouse's retirement plan had we stayed married? (This is especially likely if your spouse is or was employed by a federal, state, or local government agency.) ●

How Will We Divide Debts?

When you divorce, you divide not only property but debts as well.
It's crucial that you and your spouse reach an agreement about how
debts will be handled.

f you are willing to assume a debt, you might ask for something in
return. You might be able to make trade-offs—perhaps getting the
car or the piano in exchange for paying off credit card debts.

Before negotiating your agreement, you'll want to know what your state
laws have to say about who is responsible for what debts. You also need to
be aware of the possibility that your spouse will declare bankruptcy, default,
or fail to live up to your agreement in some other way. Use this chapter to
investigate your legal and financial position on debts and divorce.

General Rules on Who's Responsible for Debt

Some general rules for separated, divorced, and married people having
financial problems follow. Study these rules to understand which debts you
are obligated to pay and which property you risk losing if you don't pay:

- In non–community property states, a person is responsible for
  paying only the debts that person incurred during marriage—that
  is, you can't be forced to pay the bills your spouse runs up—except
  that both spouses are usually responsible for paying debts incurred:
  - with joint accounts
  - where the creditor was looking to both spouses for repayment
  - for the family's necessities, such as medical care, food, clothing,
    and shelter, and
  - for the children's education.
- While your spouse's creditor might not be able to come after you
  directly, the court will take the debt of both parties into account
  when dividing property, so you might end up paying indirectly.
- Usually, debts incurred after the separation date but before the
  divorce is final are the responsibility of the spouse who incurred
  them, and that person must pay them. An exception to this general
  rule is that both spouses are responsible for paying debts for the

family's necessities and the children's education, regardless of who incurred them.

- A spouse generally isn't responsible for paying the debts a mate incurred before marriage or after the divorce became final.
- If either you or your ex-spouse agreed to pay certain joint debts as part of a divorce settlement—or if a divorce decree signed by a judge requires that one spouse pay the joint debts—the agreement or decree is binding only on you and your ex. Because you were married when the joint debts were incurred, the creditor has a right to collect from both of you, and no agreement between you and your spouse can change that. If you pay bills your ex-spouse was supposed to pay, whether voluntarily or involuntarily, your remedy is to try to get your ex to reimburse you. Complaints to the creditor will get you nowhere.
- A creditor usually can't take the separately owned property of one spouse to pay the separate debts of the other. Separate property of one spouse can be taken to pay debts you incur together, and separate property of one spouse is always available to pay that spouse's separate debts. (Separate property is property owned prior to the marriage, property accumulated after divorce, and property received any time, including during marriage, by one spouse only, by gift or inheritance. In a few equitable distribution states, separate property also includes wages a spouse earned during marriage.)

Be Aware of Medical Expenses

State statutes often expressly state whether one spouse is liable for the necessities of the other. Are medical expenses always considered necessities? The issue of liability for a spouse's medical debts commonly arises in court these days. And there's no clear answer. About half the courts say neither spouse is responsible for the other; the other courts say that both are responsible to each other.

If You Live in a Community Property State

The community property states are Arizona, California, Idaho, Louisiana, Nevada, New Mexico, Texas, Washington, and Wisconsin. In Alaska, married couples can opt into the community property system. In Florida, Kentucky, South Dakota, and Tennessee, spouses can identify property held in a trust as community property. In the community property system, property acquired and debts incurred during the marriage—called "community property" and "community debts"—are joint. In most instances, both spouses are liable for all debts incurred by either, subject to some exceptions. Here are the rules:

- Both spouses are generally liable for all debts incurred during marriage, unless the creditor was looking to only one spouse for repayment or the purchase in no way benefited the "community." For example, if on a credit application a spouse who bought a kayak claimed to be unmarried or stated that the other spouse's income would not be used to pay the debt, the spouse would not be liable to pay for the kayak if the borrowing spouse defaults. Similarly, if a spouse charged a trip to the Bahamas with a lover, the spouse who stayed at home would not be liable, as this debt does not benefit the community.

- Spouses are generally not liable for the separate debts their mates incurred before marriage or after permanent separation. But a court order dividing debt between the parties at divorce *cannot* affect the rights of the creditor without the creditor's consent. Where the divorcing parties have joint credit, a creditor may collect from either party.

- Community property includes all property acquired and all income earned during marriage, except for income earned on property owned before the marriage. This category would include revenue from an income-generating piece of property or payments from a vested pension.

- Separate property is limited to property owned prior to the marriage, property acquired after divorce (after separation, in a few states), and property only one spouse received by gift or inheritance at any time, including during the marriage.

Listing Your Debts

Below is a chart on which you can list all your debts—yours, your spouse's, and your joint (marital) debts. The liabilities worksheet, which you filled out as part of your "Net Worth Statement" in Chapter 12, should contain all this data.

Using the examples as a guide, list in Column 1 all current debts you and your spouse are responsible for paying. This information can be taken from the "Assets and Liabilities Worksheet" in Chapter 12. In Column 2, write the balance owed on each debt. In Column 3, note whether the debt is your separate debt, your spouse's separate debt, or a marital (joint) debt. In Column 4, write in the name of the person who will assume responsibility for paying the debt. Only in unusual circumstances will one of you be responsible for the other's separate debt. You will need to divide the marital debts, however.

You might want to make several copies of this chart in the event you negotiate back and forth about who will be responsible for paying which debts.

Marital Debts and Bankruptcy

For many couples, debts and divorce go together the way love and marriage once did. Unmanageable debts might serve as a catalyst for the ending of the marriage in some cases. Other couples feel the pinch as their expenses double when one spouse moves out—they maintain two households, yet their incomes stay the same.

For couples or recently divorced individuals overwhelmed by their debt burden, declaring bankruptcy might provide a way out. In some cases, bankruptcy lets you erase your debts in exchange for giving up certain property. Every state declares specific assets, such as clothing, certain equity in a home, certain equity in a car, and several other items to be exempt. You get to keep exempt property when you file for bankruptcy.

Spousal Debt Chart

Debts—Example	Balance	Spouse 1, Spouse 2, or Joint	Who Will Pay
Car loan	$ 8,000	Joint	Spouse 2
Franklin Bank Visa	$ 1,800	Spouse 1	Spouse 1
Marshall Bank Visa	$ 2,300	Joint	Spouse 1
Personal loan	$ 5,000	Joint	Spouse 1
Student loan	$ 10,000	Spouse 2	Spouse 2
USA MasterCard	$ 4,000	Joint	Spouse 1

Debts	Balance	Spouse 1, Spouse 2, or Joint	Who Will Pay

What to Do If You Are Facing Bankruptcy

Bankruptcy is a serious step that should never be considered until all other options are exhausted. For one thing, a bankruptcy could show up for ten years on your credit reports for Chapter 7 and seven years for Chapter 13, potentially affecting your ability to get a loan or a job, or even to rent an apartment.

Instead, understand that, in some cases, a bankruptcy, if absolutely needed, can help out both spouses if they file jointly. It can effectively wipe out many types of debt, such as credit card balances, personal loans, and medical bills, leaving fewer obligations to divide during the divorce. But that will require cooperation and compromise.

If you're motivated to explore the bankruptcy option, consider these steps and alternatives:

1. **Get a handle on what you owe.** Set aside time to gather all your bills and tally how much they're costing you each month and what interest rates you're paying. Include secured debts, such as your home and car, and mandatory incidentals like power, phone, groceries, and insurance. Then tally those you want but could live without, such as cable TV, gym memberships, dinners out, and other optional purchases. Typically, you should pay the mortgage and the car loan first and keep them current. But beyond that, be tough. If things are so tight that you're considering bankruptcy, it's time to wield the axe ruthlessly.

2. **Work with your spouse, if at all possible.** A joint filing can lessen the pain. If you can find the inner resources to work as a team, you'll save yourself money and grief.

3. **Put yourself on a strict allowance.** Take only a minimal amount from your paycheck in cash and, of course, keep the credit card under wraps.

4. **Sell assets.** Get rid of things that have cash value but not sentimental value, such as some antiques, old clothes, or collectibles. Selling them at garage sales, on eBay, or at consignment stores can free up cash for living expenses. Keep track of your spending, because a bankruptcy trustee may ask you to explain where the money went.

What to Do If You Are Facing Bankruptcy (continued)

5. **Seek a second or part-time job.** Even flipping burgers might get a little more money coming in and keep a bad financial situation from getting worse. (If you plan on filing for bankruptcy, talk to a bankruptcy lawyer to find out how this might affect your case.)

6. **Try credit counseling.** Set up an appointment with the local affiliate of the National Foundation for Credit Counseling (www.nfcc.org) and work with them to draft a budget and consider a payback plan (a "debt management plan") with your creditors. Entering into a credit counseling agency's debt management program is similar to filing for Chapter 13 bankruptcy. However, this approach to dealing with your unsecured debts has one distinct advantage: You won't have a bankruptcy in your credit files.

But a debt management program also has several major disadvantages compared to Chapter 13 bankruptcy. If you miss a payment, a Chapter 13 bankruptcy protects you from creditors who could otherwise immediately start collection actions, like filing a lawsuit against you. A debt management plan doesn't protect you from suits. Also, creditors can refuse to participate in the plan. In addition, debt management plans usually require you to pay unsecured debts in full, though some creditors will agree to waive certain fees and reduce interest rates as part of the program. In Chapter 13 bankruptcy, the amount you must pay depends on your disposable income and the value of your nonexempt property. You might only have to pay a small percentage of your unsecured debts. Or you might not have to pay anything.

Also, because major creditors, including department stores, credit card companies, and banks, often provide funding to nonprofit credit counseling agencies, the agency might try to convince you to enter into a debt management plan rather than filing for bankruptcy. That way, you fully repay the debts. If you're considering signing up for a debt management plan, also talk to a bankruptcy lawyer to make sure you get the full picture. You can also ask the attorney if you qualify for a Chapter 7 bankruptcy, which could potentially discharge (wipe out) many of your debts.

What to Do If You Are Facing Bankruptcy (continued)

Or you can try your hand at negotiating. A delayed repayment plan or settling debts for less than you owe may negatively affect your credit reports, but not as much as a bankruptcy would. (However, be aware that settling a debt for less than what's owed might have tax consequences.)

7. **Get help if your spouse files.** If your spouse files for bankruptcy, immediately contact a bankruptcy lawyer. Failing to act promptly might leave you without relief.

Married couples can file for bankruptcy jointly. Married persons can also file individually, and single people can file on their own. Before deciding on filing as an individual or a couple, you must understand what the different outcomes will be.

If a married couple files for bankruptcy together, they can eliminate all separate debts of both spouses, and all jointly incurred marital debts.

Some debts can't be erased (discharged) in bankruptcy. These include student loans, restitution for a crime, most recently incurred income tax debt, and in many cases, debts obtained by fraud.

Support-related debts (such as child support and alimony) owed under a marital settlement or a divorce decree are also protected from bankruptcy discharge. Not only are child and spousal support debts not dischargeable, but they actually go to the head of the line, taking priority over the need to repay almost every other kind of debt besides the bankruptcy trustee's fees. So if you are filing jointly with your spouse, any support-related debts that you or your spouse has from a previous marriage will remain even after your bankruptcy discharge. Although property division debts as part of a divorce proceeding cannot be discharged under Chapter 7, they can be discharged in Chapter 13 bankruptcy.

And if you find yourself in the situation where your spouse is filing for bankruptcy alone, you will be protected under the law—at least for support-related debts. However, a successful bankruptcy can shift some other debts from the ex-spouse who assumed them under the marital settlement agreement and place them on the nondebtor ex-spouse—but not before the nondebtor ex-spouse gets a chance to object to the discharge of certain debts.

Here's some background on how this all works. Family law is a matter for the state courts, but federal laws govern bankruptcy. When those issues overlap—for example, when one spouse files for bankruptcy before, during, or after a divorce settlement—the issues can be complex and confusing. The bankruptcy court's job is to allow the debtor to have a fresh start after bankruptcy while at the same time protecting the rights of the nondebtor spouse and any minor children.

When one spouse files for bankruptcy, the family court can continue to hear and decide issues relating to establishing amounts for child or spousal support (alimony). But it can't split up the family home, apportion investments, or distribute other property unless it receives permission from the bankruptcy court. So if a debt is classified as a support obligation, it must be paid. But if it's judged to be a property settlement claim, it can remain owed in Chapter 7, but be dischargeable in a Chapter 13 case.

After a divorce, an ex-spouse who's assigned responsibility for paying joint debts may file for bankruptcy. If the petition is successful, the bankruptcy court may release that ex-spouse from having to pay the assigned debts. The creditor can no longer collect from the person who filed for bankruptcy—but can still seek payment from the other spouse even though the latter was supposed to be excused from responsibility for those debts under the marital settlement agreement. This innocent spouse can't do much to avoid having to pay, or to get reimbursement from the defaulting ex-spouse. If you find yourself in this situation, you have three bad choices:

- You can file for bankruptcy yourself.
- You can refuse to pay your ex-spouse's debt, and take the hit to your own credit record.
- You can pay the debt and chalk it up to experience.

However, you should consult with a family law attorney to find out if you have any other potential remedies, for instance, asking the family law court to find that your ex-spouse breached the terms of your marital settlement agreement.

Fortunately, with some planning during your divorce, you can reduce the likelihood of facing this unfortunate set of choices. Structure your separation agreement—and, ultimately, your divorce judgment—to take the possibility of bankruptcy into consideration. If you believe there's any chance that your spouse might file for bankruptcy protection, be sure to discuss it with your attorney during your divorce and before you sign any settlement agreements.

The simplest way to prevent a problem is to assign debt responsibility by account holder. Each spouse assumes responsibility for the debt in their name only. If the debt—such as credit card debt—is "jointly and severally" owed, it should be paid off using marital property. For instance, if you don't retire your credit card debt when you sell your marital home or other assets, and one spouse files for bankruptcy, the credit card company will go after the other spouse for payment of jointly owned cards. The credit card companies don't care if this is fair; they care about getting what's owed them.

Don't assume that your soon-to-be ex-spouse will pay the credit card debts assigned by the divorce decree. That's doubly true if a bankruptcy is added to the mix. Any property settlement should contain provisions that address how credit card debt will be handled if one spouse files for bankruptcy.

If there's a sale of the marital home, credit cards can be paid off at the closing. In fact, in some cases, credit card companies will accept a reduced amount if the obligation is paid in one lump sum. If you do that, make sure you get a settlement letter from the credit card firm or collection agency, confirming the terms of the settlement. (However, be aware that in some cases, the IRS considers forgiven debt to be taxable income.)

Also, you won't want to leave any loose ends when it comes to property division. For instance, it isn't a good idea to agree to allow a spouse to take more property and pay you for it over time. This is the type of property division that an ex-spouse can discharge in Chapter 13 if you don't file a costly action and win. The bankruptcy-proof approach would be to sell the property and each take half of the proceeds.

A lawyer can ask for a clause in your property settlement or divorce judgment that limits the impact of a bankruptcy, for example, by giving a nonbankrupt spouse the right to reopen the case if the other spouse files for bankruptcy. But again, keep in mind that such a clause merely gives you the opportunity to raise an issue. You'll have to pay to raise the issue in family court, hope you win, and collect from your ex-spouse. Such issues are best avoided in the first place.

Filing for bankruptcy as a married couple before finalizing a divorce can be a great way to dispose of marital debt. It leaves less to divide between the two of you. Not only will it stop the property division in family court (this is true if one spouse files for bankruptcy, too) so you won't be able to move forward and divide the marital estate in the divorce, but it can be tricky if one spouse owns more property than the other. Why? Because the bankruptcy trustee has the right to ensure that the creditors receive all they're entitled to under bankruptcy law, and the bankruptcy laws are more stringent than state family law. Property that you thought was yours alone might be considered property of the bankruptcy estate, so if one spouse has separate property, it likely won't be a good idea to file for bankruptcy—at least not before consulting with a bankruptcy attorney.

Terms to Know

This brief glossary may aid your understanding of the ins and outs of bankruptcy law.

Automatic stay. An injunction (order) that automatically stops lawsuits, foreclosures, garnishments, and all collection activity against the debtor as soon as a bankruptcy petition is filed.

Bankruptcy estate. All property in which the debtor has an interest at the time of the bankruptcy, including property owned or held by another person and property the debtor acquires or becomes entitled to acquire within 180 days after filing as a result of a settlement agreement or divorce decree.

Chapter 7. This chapter of the Bankruptcy Code provides for prompt liquidation of assets and distribution of the proceeds to creditors. Generally, Chapter 7 is limited to individuals who earn less than the median income in their state and who take an approved course in financial management before the debts are discharged. The debtor must pay in full all domestic support obligations that come due after the bankruptcy is filed.

Chapter 11. Most often used by businesses, this form of bankruptcy seeks to keep the business alive and pay creditors over time. Individuals can also seek a Chapter 11 bankruptcy, but it's an expensive and complex path.

Chapter 13. Under this chapter, the debtor retains property owned and must pay the debts over time, usually three to five years. The debtor must pay in full all domestic support obligations that come due after the bankruptcy is filed.

Discharge. The release of a debtor from personal liability for certain debts. The discharge also prevents the creditors to whom the debts are owed from taking any action against the debtor to collect.

Domestic support obligation. The Bankruptcy Code defines this term broadly. It includes child or spousal support, as well as obligations of one spouse or ex-spouse to the other in a property settlement or divorce decree.

A Carefully Worded Agreement May Protect You From an Ex-Spouse's Bankruptcy

To increase your chance that marital debts won't be discharged in the event your ex-spouse files for bankruptcy, your marital settlement agreement, order, or judgment should characterize the debts as "additional child support," "alimony," or "in the nature of support." This characterization will provide guidance to a bankruptcy judge who is asked to determine whether or not the ex-spouse can avoid having to pay the debts. The language of the agreement won't be binding on the judge, who looks behind the agreement to the true nature of the debts, but it will be evidence to the judge that you and your ex-spouse intended the debts to be nondischargeable.

Exemptions/exempt property. Certain property that the law allows the debtor to keep from unsecured creditors. For example, in some states, the debtor may be able to exempt all or a portion of the equity in a home or some or all of the tools that contribute to the debtor's livelihood. State law governs the amount and availability of exemptions.

Means test. A test of a debtor's financial viability to determine eligibility to file for Chapter 7. If the debtor is determined to be not eligible, the petition for bankruptcy may be dismissed or converted into a Chapter 13 filing.

Nondischargeable debt. A debt that can't be eliminated in bankruptcy. Examples include a home mortgage, alimony and child support, certain taxes, government-backed student loans, and criminal restitution owed.

Types of Bankruptcies

The two most common types of bankruptcy are called Chapter 7 and Chapter 13, after the sections of the law that are being followed. Chapter 7 bankruptcy allows you to discharge all or most of your debts and be free of them forever. Chapter 13 is a "reorganization" bankruptcy where you pay some amount of each of your debts, in an order set by the court.

Being broke got tougher under the Bankruptcy Abuse Prevention and Consumer Protection Act of 2005. Previously, about two-thirds of those seeking bankruptcy protection opted for Chapter 7 instead of Chapter 13 because the former allows you to discharge all debts. But the 2005 law made it more difficult to get a Chapter 7 discharge.

How so? For one thing, a complicated means test, administered by your attorney, will determine whether you'll be allowed to discharge your debt under Chapter 7. If your income is above your state's median income, you must file under Chapter 13 unless the bankruptcy court rules your circumstances are extraordinary. Even those who earn less than the state's median income must file for Chapter 13 if they can make a meaningful payment toward their unsecured debt over the next five years.

How to Choose a Credit Counselor

Whether you're facing bankruptcy or just need help with overwhelming debt, you can use these tips to help choose a reputable credit counseling agency.

Avoid promises of a quick fix. It probably took you many years to build a large debt. Significantly reducing it also can take time. Don't sign up for any plan until you have all the specifics in writing and understand what's being offered.

Do your homework. Shop around by talking to at least two or three agencies before deciding which one to use. Look for a company accredited by the Council on Accreditation (COA) or the International Organization for Standardization (ISO). Consider using a member of the National Foundation for Credit Counseling (NFCC) (www.nfcc.org). All NFCC member agencies must be COA-accredited. Ask how much training their counselors receive and whether they've passed a certification exam in areas like counseling, budgeting, credit and consumer law, debt management, and bankruptcy.

Avoid agencies that provide only a debt management program, which typically involves the counselor's negotiating a payback and paying your bills for you in exchange for a fee. Select one that offers a variety of services that include things like face-to-face help with budgeting and savings.

Beware of high or up-front fees. Carefully read all documents and ask for a clear explanation about the cost for the services. You should not be asked for an up-front fee. Legitimate credit counseling agencies offer financial help for free or at a minimal charge. If the counselors receive a commission for enrolling customers in a debt management plan, go elsewhere. You should also verify with the IRS that the agency is a nonprofit. But remember, just because an organization is nonprofit doesn't mean it's affordable or even legitimate. Check it out with the Better Business Bureau, your state attorney general's office, and local consumer protection agencies.

Ask about the impact on your credit. A bankruptcy will stay on your credit report for up to ten years (Chapter 7) or seven years (Chapter 13), raising the interest rates you're charged for loans and possibly affecting your job prospects. Just undergoing counseling or coming up with a

How to Choose a Credit Counselor (continued)

debt management plan through a credit counselor should not. (However, if you enroll in a debt management program, your credit reports will likely have a note about it.) But be sure to ask. Also, if you make on-time payments as part of a debt management program, your credit might actually improve.

Consider do-it-yourself negotiation. Remember, you have the ability to contact your creditors yourself to negotiate delays in payment or discounted rates if you're facing extreme hardship. While you may get a deeper discount if you work with a credit counselor, make sure you take into account that you'll also be paying a fee to the counselor.

Be wary of pitches about consolidating your debts. While consolidating bills into one large loan can lower monthly payments, don't do it if you might be tempted to use the money you save each month to go on another shopping spree. By stretching out the term of the loan, you'll pay far more total interest.

The law also requires debtors to take a credit counseling class before a bankruptcy can be filed, and a personal financial management class before a bankruptcy is complete. Both involve a nominal fee the debtor must pay.

In addition, a wide range of other provisions make filing for bankruptcy more difficult than it was in the past. For instance, miss one filing deadline and your bankruptcy case could be dismissed.

Bankruptcy isn't for everyone. A Chapter 7 bankruptcy stays on your credit record for ten years, although you can take steps to rebuild your credit and probably obtain credit in two or three years after filing. Nonetheless, a Chapter 7 bankruptcy discharge might be a possibility for you or your spouse, unless you've already filed within the last eight years. If your debt burden is overwhelming, don't immediately discount bankruptcy as an option. If your spouse assumes a large share of the marital debts or owes you a large sum to even up the property division, be on the lookout for a bankruptcy filing, especially if your ex starts to complain loudly about being broke.

Make sure your divorce agreement doesn't leave you vulnerable. Promissory notes, especially unsecured notes (notes that don't give you a lien on property), are almost always wiped out in bankruptcy. You might have a little more protection with secured notes—but you'll have to take proper steps to record it. You might be able to protect yourself by specifying in the settlement agreement that the promissory note or other payments are made in lieu of alimony. If you want to file for bankruptcy, be sure you know what's involved, and whether or not you can wipe out your debts. What's most important is that you get sound legal advice from a bankruptcy attorney or other bankruptcy resources available to you.

RESOURCE
See *How to File for Chapter 7 Bankruptcy,* by Cara O'Neill and Albin Renauer, *Chapter 13 Bankruptcy: Keep Your Property & Repay Debts Over Time,* by Cara O'Neill, or *The New Bankruptcy: Will It Work for You?* by Cara O'Neill, all from Nolo. The first book gives all the information necessary to decide whether to file and the forms for filing a Chapter 7 bankruptcy case. A chapter on nondischargeable debts has information on when marital debts can and cannot be wiped out. The second book contains the same information for Chapter 13 bankruptcy cases. The third will explain the new bankruptcy rules and help you assess whether bankruptcy is appropriate for your situation.

Dividing Debts at Divorce

In Chapter 12, you had the chance to complete "Net Worth" and "Cash Flow" statements. If you skipped that material, you might want to go back and fill the charts out now. If you have already completed the "Net Worth" and "Cash Flow" statements in Chapter 12, use this opportunity to update them. You might leave many items blank on these statements, but at least you'll get an idea of what you actually own and owe, and how much it costs you to live. This information is crucial when you divide your debts at divorce.

You have four basic options in allocating your marital debts:

- You and your spouse can sell joint property to raise the cash to pay off your marital debts.
- You can agree to pay the bulk of the debts yourself; in exchange, you get a greater share of the marital property or a corresponding increase in alimony.
- Your spouse can agree to pay the bulk of the debts; in exchange, your spouse gets a greater share of the marital property or a corresponding increase in alimony.
- You and your spouse can divide joint property equally and divide the debts equally—that is, each of you gets half of the property and each of you agrees to pay half of the debts.

From your perspective, the first two options are much less risky than the second two possibilities. Remember the caution given throughout this book: *When you're connected to someone financially, you're at risk.* What happens if your spouse agrees to pay all or even half of the debts and then gets fired, refuses to pay, or files for bankruptcy? Your credit rating will be damaged, or you will be stuck with paying debts. The likelihood of getting reimbursed or getting a share of the marital property originally given to your spouse will be slim or nil. So if possible, sell your joint property and pay your joint debts, or agree to pay the debts yourself.

Dividing Debts When There's Nothing to Fight Over

As your financial picture gets clearer, you may come to the unhappy conclusion that your bills and liabilities far outweigh your assets and income. Don't feel alone. Not only do most Americans live beyond their means, but many people going through divorce find they simply do not have enough money to make ends meet. Unlike the bitter battles for property that have stereotyped divorce cases on television, you and your partner may admit in despair that there's "nothing to fight over."

If you're in such a position, it's critical for you to take an honest look at your needs and protect your own interests. Even if you have to borrow money to get through your divorce, it could be well worth it to prevent problems later. Hiring a lawyer or financial professional now to review your situation could cost less than a huge tax bill or other debts in the future.

Extensive information on debts and creditors can be found in *Solve Your Money Troubles: Strategies to Get Out of Debt and Stay That Way*, by Amy Loftsgordon and Cara O'Neill (Nolo).

Questions to Ask a Divorce Attorney

Debts and the fear of bankruptcy can cause you to lose sleep during divorce. Ask your attorney the following questions so that you know the best ways to protect yourself financially:

1. Who will be legally responsible for paying which debts?
2. What can be done legally to make sure my spouse pays debts according to our agreement?
3. Am I entitled to reimbursement or credit for our money spent on educational training and expenses, child and spousal support obligations from another relationship, payment of joint debts after filing for divorce, improvement or additions to my spouse's separate property made without my consent, or my spouse's gambling, drug, or alcohol expenses, including rehab?
4. If my spouse makes noise about filing for bankruptcy before our divorce becomes final, should I file, too?
5. How can I stop my spouse from spending marital assets until the divorce is final?
6. If only my spouse signed loan documents while we were married, is that still my debt?
7. If just my spouse signed the loan documents, does the creditor have a right to come after my assets once we're divorced?
8. If I believe my spouse is going to file for bankruptcy, what can I do to protect my child and spousal support?

Questions to Ask a Bankruptcy Attorney

If you do find yourself in a bankruptcy situation, whether it's you or your spouse who's filing, consider asking a bankruptcy attorney these questions:

1. What's the effect of filing for bankruptcy before, during, or after divorce?
2. Which assets are exempt from a bankruptcy estate? Which are included?
3. What debt is included in a bankruptcy estate? Which debts are not discharged?
4. How can I protect myself if I don't want to file for bankruptcy?
5. If my spouse files for bankruptcy after our divorce is final, would our property settlement protect me?

WEB RESOURCE

Many good sites, government and private, provide information about debt, credit, and other consumer issues. Typically, they include search mechanisms that allow you to home in on the issue most relevant for you. These sites include:

- **www.ftc.gov** (Federal Trade Commission)
- **www.aba.com** (American Bankers Association)
- **www.bankrate.com**, and
- **www.marketwatch.com.**

Child Support and Alimony: What Might I Pay or Receive?

Child support and alimony payments can be the most hotly contested issues in a divorce. These payments are often necessary when the money that used to support a single household must stretch to support two.

Unemployment checks and insurance claims can help a couple survive the loss of a job or damage to a house. But who pays the bill when the financial disaster of divorce strikes?

Somehow, household expenses must be paid. Someone must come up with the "alimonia"—a Latin word for "food" or "support." Today, the word is "alimony," although in many states it's called "spousal support," "spousal maintenance," or "rehabilitative support." The names differ depending on where you live, but the impact seems to be universal: The payer feels the amount is far too much, while the recipient knows it's not enough.

Both parties might be right.

Breaking one household into two costs more than anyone thinks it will. Besides doubling the basics—mortgage or rent, utilities, cable, internet, streaming services, and phone bills—divorcing couples must admit that the choices they made as a couple might no longer be realistic. A spouse who left their job to care for the children can't retrace their steps and cover the ground lost after dropping out of the workforce. A husband who refused a transfer so his spouse could pursue entrepreneurial ambitions might be stuck in a dead-end job that he can't leave without jeopardizing his pension. When you are "fired" from the job of spouse, no one offers you an unemployment check. Is it any wonder, then, that alimony often becomes a major battleground in divorce?

If you have children, the struggle to make ends meet can be even more draining. Whether you will pay or receive child support, you'll need to know what it costs. But how can parents put a price tag on their children?

This chapter first takes you through the legal, financial, and emotional realities of alimony and child support, and then outlines your steps to a settlement.

SKIP AHEAD

If you have no children, skip ahead to the section on alimony.

Protect Your Parental Rights

Before making any legal moves that affect your children, make sure you are informed about your rights as a parent. Ask an attorney about what can happen when custody is disputed. Make sure you know when and where all hearings or mediation sessions will take place. Better to ask too many questions than to lose time with your children because you misunderstood the consequences of your actions. Further, because the court will examine your custody arrangements, be prepared for any stunt your spouse might try to pull in the courtroom. But remain calm and collected when you respond. Don't be lulled into a false sense of security because of informal agreements you've made with your spouse. And never move out of the family residence without a written agreement about custody. For more about parenting and custody rights, see *Nolo's Essential Guide to Divorce*, by Emily Doskow.

Child Support—Legal, Financial, and Emotional Realities

Your children's experience of your divorce can have a major effect on your emotional state, but the most important thing is that you make sure that your emotional state doesn't affect your children's experience. On all issues concerning your children—child support, custody, and visitation—you and your mate need to stay focused on what's best for your children.

Be aware of your own behavior, and don't get caught up in a power struggle or try to use the children to get back at the other parent. You will end up causing more damage to the children than to your spouse.

Legal Realities

All parents have an obligation to financially support their children, no matter what the status of their adult relationships may be. Suppose one parent has primary custody, traditionally called "physical custody," and the other has secondary custody, or "visitation rights." (See "Legal Language Alert: Custody by Any Other Name … ," below.) The parent with less custody time is usually ordered to pay some child support to the custodial parent. It is assumed that the custodial parent is supporting the children by providing their day-to-day care and paying for their living expenses when with them. For parents with joint physical custody, the support obligation of each is based on a number of factors, such as the ratio of each parent's income to their combined incomes, the percentage of time the child spends with each parent, and who pays necessary expenses for the child.

While divorcing spouses can make decisions about virtually all the terms of their divorce without court intervention, the court will insist on examining the child support arrangements. If the judge approves of the arrangement, the court will include it in the judgment. Some of the factors evaluated by courts in setting child support include:

- the child's needs
- each parent's income and/or ability to earn and pay support, and
- the amount of time the child spends with each parent.

Legal Language Alert: Custody by Any Other Name …

Traditionally, terms such as "custodial parent" and "noncustodial parent" have been used by courts and among people in general when talking about parent-child relationships after a divorce. In light of changing family patterns, however, courts are beginning to recognize shared parenting styles and other such arrangements. Legal language is therefore changing, and terms such as "primary custody," "secondary custody," and "parenting time" are being used. For the time being, however, this book will continue to refer to "custodial" or "noncustodial" parents.

Unfortunately, some noncustodial parents disregard their child support obligations: They might skip a month, pay late, pay too little, or just stop paying altogether. Society has become far less tolerant of these "deadbeat" parents than it used to be. State and federal legislatures have passed laws aimed at helping families establish and enforce support orders.

The consequences for the failure to pay child support can be very serious. States have different enforcement tools at their disposal, but the following are some of the most common:

- Wage deductions—child support is taken directly out of the parent's wages.
- Federal income tax intercepts—the state can intercept a parent's tax refund.
- License suspension—the state can suspend or revoke driver's licenses and professional licenses.
- Passport restrictions—the U.S. Department of State can deny passport renewals.
- Liens—courts can issue liens on property to cover child support.
- Civil warrants and jail time—a state court can issue a civil warrant for arrest and order jail time if the noncustodial parent is found in contempt of court for disobeying the child support order.

In addition, if state or federal prosecutors get involved in a child support case, they can issue criminal warrants. These and other enforcement methods will be discussed in more detail further along in this chapter, under "Dealing With Unpaid Child Support."

Financial Realities

Any legal award of child support is probably going to be less than the actual amount necessary to meet the needs of growing children, meaning that you will have to devise strategies for finding the rest of the money you need to live on.

Even if you receive an adequate child support award, financial reality demands that you recognize the possibility that your ex-spouse won't pay. If you're the parent receiving child support on behalf of your child (the recipient), what will you do when the check never arrives or comes late? The section below that deals with enforcement tools for child support orders will be helpful.

And if you're the paying parent, the financial reality is that you're obligated to pay child support to help cover your child's living expenses; this payment isn't optional. It is more than likely that your ex-spouse is also working and covering your part of your child's living expenses. Your obligation to help out doesn't stop simply because you and your spouse decided to divorce. So, you must plan for your child support obligation by keeping steady employment and paying on time. If you fail to pay, you might end up with your paycheck suddenly being garnished—or worse, threatened with contempt of court or jail time for your failure to pay.

Emotional Realities

Unfortunately, some parents can't see past their own selfish needs or anger and use their children as emotional pawns during a divorce. One parent might express their resentment by degrading the other parent in front of the children. Don't be that parent. Put your children first, even if you can't stand your ex. The decisions you make during your divorce will affect your children for their lifetimes and can influence their own relationships in the future as well. Your children didn't ask to be a part of your divorce, so it's your duty to shelter them as much as possible from this devastating loss. If you can't do this for your children, do it for yourself; if a judge finds you've been disparaging your ex to your child or talking to your kids about child support, custody, or other inappropriate topics, the judge can order you to attend parenting classes as a requirement for seeing the kids or, even worse, can limit your time with your children.

As difficult as it sounds, try to keep your emotions in check. You don't have to hide your feelings about your divorce from your children, but you also shouldn't take your anger out on your kids. Instead, try to include them in the process in constructive ways and reach out for help if you need it. Many divorce support organizations, such as Kids' Turn (https://safeandsound.org/for-parents/family-support/kids-turn), facilitate workshops for children and parents going through parental separation and divorce. A multitude of age-appropriate books are available that you can read to your children about separation and divorce to help them understand the changes their family is going through. A good one for younger kids (ages three to eight) is *Dinosaurs Divorce: A Guide for Changing Families,* by Laurene Krasny Brown and Marc Brown.

We also urge you to avoid a long, expensive fight about custody and support. Fighting scares children and makes them feel guilty. It also wastes time, money, and resources that could have been spent more positively on your children. By maintaining a healthy emotional attitude about the divorce around your children, you'll be better equipped to deal with the legal and financial realities of child custody and support.

> **RESOURCE**
> **Lots of good books are available to help you deal with the emotional realities of parenting during divorce.** Check any of the websites listed in Chapter 1 for resource lists. Below are a few titles to get you started.
>
> *Building a Parenting Agreement That Works: Child Custody Agreements Step by Step,* by Mimi Lee (Nolo), helps you negotiate and prepare a parenting agreement with your spouse.
>
> *Mom's House, Dad's House: Making Two Homes for Your Child, revised edition,* by Isolina Ricci, Ph.D. (Simon & Schuster), is the classic text on dealing with shared custody.
>
> *Helping Kids Cope With Divorce the Sandcastles Way,* by M. Gary Neuman, L.M.H.C., with Patricia Romanowski (Random House), helps parents understand what their kids—of any age—are experiencing during divorce and offers practical advice for communicating with children.
>
> Many books on the market are written specifically for children of divorcing parents. Ask a local bookseller or visit online book forums for recommendations. You won't be lacking for choices, no matter what the age of your children. Take the time to find titles that speak best to your child's interests and reading abilities.

The Dos and Don'ts of Parenting During Divorce

Do:

Initiate the child's contact with the other parent on a regular basis by phone, letter, audio, Skype, FaceTime, email, and other forms of communication.

Maintain predictable schedules.

Be prompt and have children ready at exchange time.

Avoid communication that may lead to conflict at exchange time.

Ensure smooth transitions by assuring the children that you support their relationship with the other parent and trust the other parent's parenting skills.

Allow the children to carry important items such as clothing, toys, and security blankets with them between the parents' homes.

Follow similar routines for mealtime, bedtime, and homework time in each home.

Handle rules and discipline in similar ways in each home.

Support contact with grandparents and other extended family so the children do not experience a sense of loss.

Be flexible so the children can take advantage of opportunities to participate in special family celebrations or events.

Give as much advance notice as possible to the other parent about special occasions.

Provide an itinerary of travel dates, destinations, and contact information when children are on vacation.

Establish a workable, businesslike method of communication.

Plan vacations around children's regularly scheduled activities.

The Dos and Don'ts of Parenting During Divorce (continued)

Don't:

Make your child choose between parents.

Question your child about the other parent's activities or relationships.

Make promises you do not keep.

Argue with or criticize the other parent when your child is present or can hear you.

Discuss your personal problems with the child or where the child can hear you.

Discuss child custody, child support, or court dates with your child.

Use your child as a messenger, spy, or mediator.

Withhold visitation because of the other parent's failure to pay support.

Get professional help from an attorney or a mental health practitioner, court services mediator, domestic abuse agency, or social services agency if there are issues of:
- child abuse or neglect
- serious mental or emotional disorders
- drug or alcohol abuse or criminal activity
- domestic violence, or
- continuous levels of very intense conflict.

Steps to a Settlement

As you move through your divorce, you will find that your choices about child support are controlled by local financial guidelines. Answering the following questions may help you prepare to understand these guidelines and understand what's probable in terms of paying or receiving child support:
- Who will have custody of the children?
- What does it cost to raise your children?

- How much child support do you need—or can you afford to pay?
- What are the guidelines for child support in your state?
- What is your bottom-line decision regarding custody and child support?

Who Will Have Custody of the Children?

The two types of custody are the legal authority to make decisions about the medical, educational, health, and welfare needs of a child (legal custody), and physical control over a child (physical custody). In most states, courts now tend to award joint legal custody, which lets divorced parents share in making decisions about their children's health, education, and welfare. The most common arrangement is to share legal custody, with one parent having primary physical custody and the other secondary physical custody or liberal visitation.

You can work out whatever arrangement you want regarding custody. If you can't agree, you might be able to use mediation to work things out. Mediation is a nonadversarial process in which a neutral person (a mediator) meets with parents to help them resolve problems. To reach a mediated solution, both parents must agree. The mediator can't impose a solution on the parties. Many states require parents to participate in mediation before bringing a custody dispute to court. If you still can't agree and you leave the custody decision to the court, the legal standard the court will use is "the best interests of the child." The factors courts consider in determining the best interests usually include:

- the child's age, sex, maturity, temperament, and strength of attachment to each parent
- special needs of the child and parents
- the child's relationship with siblings and friends
- the distance between the parents' households
- the flexibility of both parents' work schedules and the child's schedule
- child care arrangements
- transportation needs
- the ability of the parents to communicate and cooperate
- the child's and parents' cultural and religious practices

- the willingness of a previously uninvolved parent to provide adequate supervision
- each parent's ability and willingness to learn basic caregiving skills such as feeding, changing, and bathing a young child, preparing a child for day care or school, or taking responsibility for helping a child with homework, and
- each parent's ability to care for the child's needs.

What Does It Cost to Raise Your Children?

Mentioned in this section are items you should consider in figuring the cost of rearing children. As you review these items, calculate the average amount you spend each month. You can make this calculation by totaling the three most recent months and then dividing by three. Check the monthly expenses column of your "Cash Flow Statement" (see Chapter 12), look back through your checkbook, or make an educated guess to find your monthly outlays.

After filling in each number, total the expenses at the end.

$ _____ *Child care*

If both parents work, child care costs may be significant. If you have relied in the past on informal babysitting arrangements with friends or relatives, you can't and shouldn't consider those arrangements permanent. If you don't know the going rate for child care in your area, investigate. You must factor the cost of competent care into your children's future. The court will order that child care expenses be shared by the parents to allow the custodial parent to work outside the home.

$ _____ *Education or college funds*

Even after divorce, it's possible for parents to work together to realize the joint goal of providing for a child's private schooling or college education. It takes planning and cooperation, but it can be done. Besides college, your children might want to receive special training for a profession or the arts. These costs can sometimes be staggering. It's necessary to anticipate them now, before your settlement is negotiated.

Agreements between divorcing spouses about post-high-school education should include:

- acceptable schools, location, and accreditation
- what GPA is expected of the child in high school and college
- what contributions each parent will make to the student's living expenses—such as allowances, car expenses, and traveling-home expenses—and whether money will be paid directly to the student, to a third party, or to the custodial parent
- student's application for financial aid
- academic load (full-time or part-time)
- whether the student will be required to work while in school, and
- methods to resolve disagreements about postsecondary education.

$ _____   *Emergency savings*

Financial planners make a standard recommendation that you have an emergency cash reserve equal to three to six months of fixed expenses. Be sure that reserve includes your children's normal expenses. You can also make your postdivorce life easier if you include a cash cushion for the emergencies that children can create.

$ _____   *Health and dental care*

Divorce affects your children's health care coverage. You and your spouse must reach an agreement as to who will carry the children on a health plan, who will buy coverage, and how you will pay for medical expenses not covered by the plan or copayments and deductibles. If you can't agree, a court will make the order for you. Some states mandate that if neither parent has insurance covering the children, one parent must pay for reasonable medical insurance. Also be aware of what benefits are covered and how long they last. For more details on health care coverage for youngsters, see "Are There Alternatives to Paying or Receiving Monthly Alimony?" below.

$ _____   *Hobbies*

Are your children involved in sports, music, or ballet? Do they act in community theater? Do they want to go to summer camp? Do they expect to as they grow older? Check how much you've paid for special lessons and hobbies, or talk to parents whose children are involved in similar pursuits to get an idea of future costs. You will want your agreement to indicate who will pay for which activities and hobbies.

$ _____   *Birthdays and holidays*

Do you splurge on special occasions and birthdays? Do your children have high expectations about gifts? These costs can add up. You might need to readjust your budget and let your children know about the change. Under the best circumstances, you and your soon-to-be ex-spouse might agree to a spending limit so that one partner does not use gifts to curry favor.

$ _____   *Total expenses for children*

Rising College Costs

If you're already calculating how much it'll cost for your child to attend college, don't forget inflation. Tuitions have skyrocketed over the past few decades, often doubling the general inflation rate. But, even if they held steady for a decade, inflation means that the dollar you save today will be worth less by the time your child enrolls in college.

Tallying the impact of inflation can be a shock. Suppose tuition currently averages $10,000 annually, not including books and on-campus room and board (private and out-of-state institutions are much higher). If inflation is 4% a year and your seven-year-old enrolls as a freshman in ten years, you will need $16,010 of today's dollars to pay that $10,000 tuition.

You must also consider the fact that college tuition itself has become much more expensive in recent decades. Suppose tuition increases at 7% per year: You will need $19,672 to cover freshman year a decade from now. There's much debate about how tuition might be reined in, but you shouldn't count on that happening. You will need to put your child's college funds in an investment vehicle that grows at a rate faster than inflation. Don't forget about grants, scholarships, public education, and other alternatives that may help defray the cost of a college degree.

Checklist of Issues to Consider When Negotiating Child Support

When you sit down to talk seriously about child support, you will need to take into account all of the considerations listed above, and you'll also need to look at factors that might cause a court to deviate from the standard support guidelines. Here's a checklist that will help you remember to cover all the bases when looking at child support issues. Consider things like:

☐ children's special needs, including physical, emotional, and mental health needs, educational needs, or day care costs

☐ shared physical custody arrangements

☐ support obligations of either parent to a former household, including alimony

☐ an extraordinarily low- or high-income parent

☐ the intentional suppression, reduction, or hiding of income

☐ other support, such as lump sum payments, use of a separate property residence, payment of a mortgage or medical expenses, or provision of health insurance coverage

☐ a parent's own extraordinary needs, such as unusual medical expenses

☐ deferred sale of family residence, in which the rental value exceeds the mortgage payments, homeowners' insurance, and property taxes

☐ travel expenses required for custodial time

☐ how child support will be secured, including a requirement of life or disability insurance

☐ employee benefits, including medical savings plans, cost and quality of medical, dental, and life insurance, and

☐ other fairness factors.

Health Insurance Coverage

You might be worried about how your children's health care needs will be covered after your divorce. It might help you to know that a federal law (P.L. 103-66, Omnibus Reconciliation Act of 1993) allows custodial parents to obtain a court order for children's health insurance coverage through the noncustodial parent's employment insurance plan (as long as the plan isn't self-insured). Coverage can't be denied by the noncustodial parent, that parent's employer, or the insurance company simply because the child does not live with that parent, is not claimed as a dependent, or lives outside of the plan's service area.

The court order for health care for your children is called a QMCSO, a qualified medical child support order. A QMCSO can require that:

- an employee's child be covered under an employer-provided health care plan
- the premium be deducted from the employee's paycheck
- reimbursements be made directly to the nonemployee parent if that parent pays the provider
- the nonemployee parent receive information regarding the health care plan and reimbursements, and
- other health coverage be provided as specifically directed.

You will want to use a QMCSO when:

- the employee parent is or might be a recalcitrant payer
- the employee parent's regular medical plan determines that the children are ineligible for dependent coverage if they are living with the other parent
- the custodial parent prefers to deal directly with the plan administrator for information, forms, and reimbursement
- the employee parent selects a medical plan that is not suitable for the child—for example, if the employed parent chooses a plan with a very high deductible (not appropriate when you have children who will inevitably visit the doctor) the QMCSO gives the other parent the option of selecting a plan with a very low or no deductible, or
- the employee parent wants to take advantage of favorable "family coverage" premiums.

To qualify as a QMCSO, the medical support order must:

- create the child's right to receive benefits under the group plan
- specify the employee parent's name and last known mailing address and also that of each child covered by the plan
- specify each plan and time frame to which the order applies, and
- not require any additional benefits not actually provided in the plan.

While the QMCSO can be valuable in making sure your children's health care is protected, it may include some of the following:

- limited coverage for a child residing outside the area served by the plan—although the plan cannot deny coverage for this reason, it can limit the coverage it offers, and
- limits on a child's ability to obtain medical coverage different from the coverage provided by the employee parent.

If you elect to use a QMCSO, the custodial parent should obtain copies of the following:

- a medical plan and summary plan description
- election forms highlighting the possible elections and open enrollment periods
- information on current beneficiary designations, and
- written material concerning plan requirements for terms of a QMCSO.

A sample QMSCO appears at the end of this chapter.

How Much Child Support Does Your Child Need—or Can You Afford to Pay?

In figuring out how much support your child needs or what you can afford to pay, you will consider the same items you considered with alimony—income and ability to pay, financial needs, taxes, and payment practicalities.

Income Needs

The difference between legal reality and financial reality defines your income needs for child support. Legal reality means the amount your state's child support formula sets. This amount is the guideline amount that you are likely to pay or receive on your child's behalf. Your lawyer or local agencies can help you determine this figure (see "What Are the Guidelines for Child Support in Your State?" below).

The financial reality is the actual cost every month of raising your children.

For recipients. If your actual child-raising costs are higher than the amount in the legal guideline and you have no way to make up the gap, you'll have to negotiate for a higher amount. If your spouse is aware that the guidelines are lower than the amount you're asking for, you might have little leverage. Nevertheless, you can still attempt to push up the amount of support.

For payers. Recognize that the gap between what it costs to raise your children and what you have to pay has to be closed somehow. If your child's other parent has no other source of revenue, keep in mind that you might need to consider paying more than guideline support. You and your spouse might be able to save yourselves time and trouble by negotiating child support from a realistic financial base right from the start. Often, divorcing couples find there is simply not enough money to meet these costs, and both spouses have to pare down their lifestyles.

Taxes

Child support payments have no tax consequences. They are neither deductible to the payer nor taxed as income to the recipient.

Children, however, have plenty of tax consequences. First and foremost, they are considered dependency exemptions. Parents must decide who will claim the children at tax time. Often, the noncustodial parent claims the children in exchange for paying higher support. The custodial parent must relinquish claim to the dependency exemption by signing IRS Form 8332, *Release/Revocation of Release of Claim to Exemption for Child by Custodial Parent.* When the parents have joint physical custody, they may each claim a child (if they have more than one) or they may alternate the claim year to year. No matter who claims the children as dependents, both parents must list the children's Social Security numbers on their tax returns so the IRS knows that only one parent is claiming the children.

The following tax benefits are among those available to parents to offset the cost of raising children:

- earned income credit
- child care credit
- medical expense deductions

- head of household filing status
- dependency exemption
- child tax credit (for three or more children)
- deduction for interest on qualified education loans
- American Opportunity and Lifetime Learning credits for tuition costs, and
- education IRAs.

Not all of these benefits are available to all parents, but you need to be aware of these potential tax benefits as you make your custody and child support agreements.

Only a custodial parent is entitled to claim the child care tax credit. In general, an employed custodial parent of a dependent child under the age of 13 is eligible for the credit for child care expenses incurred so that the parent can earn an income. As the custodial parent's income increases, however, the credit phases out. Keep in mind the availability of the tax credit when negotiating your agreement about who will pay child care expenses.

Any taxpayer can claim a deduction for medical expenses actually paid, but only if those medical expenses exceed 7.5% of the taxpayer's adjusted gross income. If your total medical expenses are high enough, you may want to allocate them to the lower wage earner so that parent can take the deduction.

Only a parent who has physical custody more than half the time can file as head of household. If the parents have joint legal and physical custody (and physical custody is divided 50-50), neither can file as head of household, because the dependent child resides with neither parent for more than 50% of the year.

If you have more than one minor child and share physical custody, you can specify your arrangement as 51% for one child with one parent and 51% for the other child with the other parent. Because each parent has a dependent child in the home more than 50% of the year, each parent can file as head of household.

What Are the Guidelines for Child Support in Your State?

The Family Support Act of 1988 required all states to adopt a statewide uniform child support formula. Parents might be able to agree on a child support amount different from that required by the state formula, and as long as the parents can show that the children's needs will be met by the below-guideline payments, courts will generally approve the amount the parents have agreed on. However, neither the court nor the children are bound by the agreement if it is for less than the state minimum. Remember: *All* parents are obligated to support their children, and a custodial parent cannot give up permanently *the child's* right to receive support.

What If Your Spouse Takes a Lower-Paying Job to Reduce the Child Support Obligation?

Courts are displaying little tolerance for parents who voluntarily quit jobs or take lower-paying jobs than those for which they are qualified to avoid paying child support. When faced with this situation, a court may base child support on "imputed income"—a higher amount of income than the parent is actually earning. Also, to determine support payments, a court may factor in benefits from deferred compensation, fringe benefits, and certain depreciation deductions for the purpose of determining business income. California and New York courts lead the way in making it difficult for individuals to play games with income in order to reduce alimony or child support payments.

Methods of Computing Child Support

Courts use two primary methods to compute child support. Which one applies to you depends on where you live. The two methods are called "income shares" and "percentage of income," and are discussed in more detail below. If you want to find out which formula is used where you live, check with a local family law attorney or check one of the websites or support calculation programs described below.

The Income Shares Method

The income shares method calculates support by evaluating the proportional income of each parent and considering the cost of work-related day care and premiums for the children's medical insurance, among other factors.

The income shares model aims to provide the child with the same proportion of parental income—and thus the same lifestyle the family enjoyed —that the child would have received as a member of an intact household.

How to Find and Use an Online Support Calculator

Many states have state-sponsored websites that use the state's guidelines to help you to make ballpark child support calculations for free. Numerous commercial websites for specific states can help you make the calculations for a fee.

Often, a website specifically designed for your state that says it is the "official" one courts use in your state is available. Now that courts are required to have statewide guidelines for support, judges use computer programs to calculate support—and often you can find the same system, simplified for a layperson to use, online for a fee.

The fee that the websites charge will vary from about $3 to $10 per calculation. Some might offer a monthly fee, but most sites will charge you per calculation. You might think that you only need to do one calculation, but often you will want to do more—for example, if you aren't yet sure how much time your kids are going to spend with each parent, you'll need to do a calculation for each of the different possibilities for time sharing, which can affect support.

To use the support calculators, you'll need to know each parent's gross and net income, deductions, and exemptions—it helps to have a copy of a recent pay stub for each parent. Most calculators will ask for information that will allow for adjustments based on child care expenses, extraordinary medical or educational expenses, and other special circumstances.

For more on how to find state-sponsored websites and other resources relating to child support calculators, check out *Nolo's Essential Guide to Divorce*, by Emily Doskow.

The Percentage of Income Model

The percentage of income model requires that either a flat percentage or varying percentage of the noncustodial parent's gross or net income be paid to the custodial parent.

Under the *flat percentage* model, the percentage of income devoted to child support remains constant at all income levels. Under the *varying percentage* model, however, the percentage of income devoted to child support varies according to the level of income, with the support percentage decreasing as income increases. Under either variation, the percentage to be applied is determined by the number of children and, in some states, by the ages of the children.

Calculating Support

Whichever system your state uses, the easiest way to get a general idea of what your support obligations will be is to ask a lawyer who is familiar with your financial situation. But if you want to get an idea of what you might have to pay, or what you will be owed, or if you are representing yourself, in most states there are websites—either state sanctioned or commercial—that will help you calculate an estimate. See "How to Find and Use an Online Support Calculator," above.

The results you get from a support calculator will be estimates, but they will generally be in the ballpark, and you can use them to negotiate about support. If you have a dispute, though, the court will have the final say, using its official computer program.

Payment Practicalities

The practical matter of getting child support payments from one person to the other can create highly charged problems. Below are questions and suggestions to help prevent these problems. Whether you deal with these items during your negotiations or in the final settlement, use the spaces provided to jot down your ideas. You can refer to these points when needed. Put a checkmark in front of the question once it is resolved.

How and When Child Support Will Be Paid

_____ *How will child support be paid?*

_____

_____

_____

_____

You and your spouse can agree that support will be paid in the form of a monthly check sent directly by the payer to the recipient. The court, however, might want to set up a different process. All child support orders automatically contain a wage withholding provision. An automatic wage withholding order works quite simply. When the court orders you to pay child support, the court—or your child's other parent—sends a copy of the court order to the payer's employer. The custodial parent's name and address are included with this order. At each pay period, the employer withholds a portion of the pay and sends it on to the custodial parent. Only if both parents agree—and the court allows it—can you avoid the wage withholding and make payments directly.

If you don't receive regular wages but do have a regular source of income, such as payments from a retirement fund, an annuity, or Social Security, the court can order the child support withheld from those sources of income. Instead of forwarding a copy of the order and the custodial parent's name and address to an employer, the court sends the information to the retirement plan administrator or public agency from which you receive your benefits.

Mandatory wage withholding operates differently among the states. In Texas and Vermont, for example, all current orders include automatic wage withholding, regardless of the parent's payment history. The rationale is that by not distinguishing between parents with poor payment histories and parents who have paid regularly, no parent is stigmatized.

A few states have set up other mechanisms to collect child support as it becomes due. For example, a judge may order a noncustodial parent to pay child support to the state's child support enforcement agency, which in turn pays the custodial parent. This program is often used where automatic wage withholding is not in effect. It may also be used for noncustodial parents without regular income (the self-employed) or when parents agree to waive the automatic wage withholding.

Some other states let judges order noncustodial parents to make payments to court clerks or court trustees who in turn pay the custodial parents.

_____ *On what day of the month will payments be made?*

_____

_____

_____

_____

Most noncustodial parents find it convenient to pay child support shortly after being paid themselves. If you are a recipient, and payments will not arrive until after your child's monthly child care bill or health insurance premium is due, you'll need to make different arrangements. Try saving money from the previous month or contacting the creditor and negotiating a new payment schedule. Try to get your payments in sync with your cash flow. You don't need to tell the creditor you're waiting for your child support check. Creditors may be surprisingly cooperative when you contact them in advance and honestly negotiate so they are assured of getting their payments.

_____ *How long will child support payments be made?*

_____

_____

_____

_____

You must pay child support for as long as your child support court order says you must. If the order does not contain an ending date, in most states you must support your children at least until they reach age 18. A few states, however, extend the time and require you to support your children:

- until they finish high school
- until they reach 21 (for example, this is the requirement in New York)
- until they complete college, or
- if they are disabled, for as long as they are dependent.

Your child support obligation will end, however, if your child joins the military, gets married, or moves out of the house to live independently, or if a court declares your child emancipated.

Child support obligations extend beyond the death of the paying parent —if that parent leaves an estate, the estate must continue paying support.

If you failed to make some of your child support payments and you owe unpaid support, it doesn't go away when your child turns 18 (or whatever age you are no longer liable for support). Many states give a custodial parent ten or 20 years to collect back child support—with interest.

_____ *How will you handle child support modifications?*

_____

_____

_____

_____

A court retains the power to make orders involving child support. If a noncustodial parent can't afford the payments, that parent must take the initiative to change the child support order. Or, if a custodial parent can't live on the current payment, it's that parent's responsibility to ask for more. As a first step, the parent wanting the change should call the other parent and try to work out an agreement. If you reach an agreement, be sure to get it in writing. You'll then need to get a judge's signature.

If you can't make satisfactory arrangements with your ex-spouse, the parent wanting the change will have to file papers with the court, schedule a hearing, and then show the judge that the support amount is too little to live on—or too much to pay. The court won't retroactively decrease child support, even if the noncustodial parent was too sick to get out of bed during the affected period. Once child support is owed and unpaid, it remains a debt until it is paid.

To get a judge to change a child support order, you must show a substantial change of circumstance since the last order. What constitutes a substantial change depends on your situation and your state's laws. Generally, the condition must not have been considered when the original order was made, and must affect your—or your child's or the other parent's—current standard of living.

Changes that qualify for a *noncustodial* parent to seek a reduction in support include:

- your income has substantially decreased
- you have increased expenses, such as a new child
- a raise you expected—which was the basis of the last order—didn't materialize
- the custodial parent received a large inheritance, an increase in compensation, or income-producing assets, or
- your child's needs have decreased—for example, she is no longer attending private school.

Changes that qualify for a *custodial* parent to obtain an increase in the support amount include:

- you have a substantial decrease in income
- you have increased expenses, such as a new child
- the noncustodial parent received a raise, large inheritance, or income-producing assets, or
- your child's needs have increased—for example, ongoing counseling.

Dealing With Unpaid Child Support

_____ *How will you handle nonpayment of child support?*

_____

_____

_____

_____

Unpaid child support (sometimes referred to as "being in arrears") accumulates when the parent doesn't pay what is owed. A parent who is owed a great deal in arrears can ask a judge to issue a judgment for the amount due.

As mentioned above, states' child support enforcement agencies, custodial parents, judges, and district attorneys use several different methods to collect child support.

Court hearings. Failing to follow a court order is called "contempt of court." A parent who is owed child support can schedule a "show cause" hearing before a judge. The other parent must be served with a document requiring attendance at the hearing, and then must explain why the support hasn't been paid. If the noncustodial parent is a no-show, the court can issue an arrest warrant, which could lead to a night or two at the county jail.

If the noncustodial parent attends the hearing, the judge can still require jail time for violations of the support order. To stay out of jail, the parent must first show why the money wasn't paid and then explain what prevented the parent from requesting a modification hearing.

Federal law mandates that all states provide for wage withholding for child support orders.

Interception of tax refunds or lottery winnings. One of the most powerful collection methods available is an interception of the payer's federal income tax refund, state income tax refund, or sales tax refund. The custodial parent can ask the district attorney to call the Treasury Department for help. States also intercept tax refunds to satisfy child support debts. Also, many states with lotteries let custodial parents apply to the state for an interception of the other parent's winnings.

Property liens. In some states, a custodial parent can place a lien on the payer's real or personal property. The lien stays in effect until the payer pays up, or until the custodial parent agrees to remove the liens. The custodial parent can force the sale of the noncustodial parent's property, or can wait until the property is sold.

Posting bonds or assets to guarantee payment. Some states allow judges to require parents with child support arrears to post bonds or assets, such as stock certificates, to guarantee payment.

Reports to credit bureaus. If the custodial parent owes more than $1,000 in child support, that information may find its way into a credit file that a credit bureau maintains. Federal law requires child support enforcement agencies to report known child support arrears of $1,000 or more. Many child support enforcement agencies automatically send information about the child support order to credit bureaus, even though payments are current.

Reporting to "most wanted" lists. States are encouraged to come up with creative ways to embarrass parents into paying the child support they owe. Most states now publish "most wanted" lists of parents who owe child support.

Refusal to renew professional licenses. Some states will not renew contractor's or professional licenses of people behind on child support. These may include business, recreational, personal, and professional licenses, such as attorney, cosmetologist, doctor, or hunting or fishing licenses. Without a license, the payer can't legally practice the profession in the state.

Refusal to renew or suspension of driver's license. Parents in some states are not allowed to possess a driver's license if they have not met child support obligations.

Wage and property garnishments. Child support arrears can often be collected by a wage garnishment. A wage garnishment is similar to a wage withholding—a portion of the noncustodial parent's wages is removed from the paycheck and delivered to the custodial parent. They differ, however, in one way: the amount withheld. The amount of a wage withholding is *the amount of child support ordered each month.* The amount of a wage garnishment is *a percentage of the payer's paycheck.* The amount the payer was originally ordered to pay is irrelevant.

If the wage garnishment does not cover what's owed, the custodial parent may try to get other property to cover that debt. Common property targets include bank accounts, cars, motorcycles, boats and airplanes, houses and other real property, stock in corporations, and accounts receivable. It's also possible that unemployment compensation can be withheld in some states.

The federal government now requires states to set up agencies to oversee this collection. If the parties use such an agency, the employer of the paying parent makes the child support payment to this state agency, which then writes a check to the custodial spouse.

District attorney assistance. In most states, a local D.A. will help—and in some states is required to help—a custodial parent who hasn't received child support.

Federal prosecution. On the federal level, the Office of the Inspector General (OIG) investigates criminal child support cases. If a parent owes at least $5,000 in child support for a year or more, a federal task force can prosecute, and parents found guilty of criminal nonpayment may face fines and imprisonment.

Passport denial. In cases where arrears exceed $2,500, the nonpaying parent may lose passport privileges.

Finding a Missing Parent

It's hard to collect back (or current) child support when you can't find the person who owes it to you. If your ex-spouse is missing, start by contacting your state child support enforcement agency (or the family support division of the district attorney's office). Be prepared to provide the following information about the missing parent:

- name, address, Social Security number, date of birth, physical description, father's name, and mother's maiden name
- names of friends and relatives and names of organizations to which the missing parent might belong
- name and address of current or recent employer, and
- information about the parent's income and assets, pay stubs, tax returns, bank accounts, investments, or property holdings.

Tapping Pension Plans to Pay Spousal and Child Support

A Qualified Domestic Relations Order (QDRO, pronounced "quadro") is a court order to the administrator of a retirement plan spelling out how the plan's benefits are to be assigned to each spouse in a divorce. (See Chapter 14 for details.) A QDRO can be used to collect child support or alimony payments from the funds in a retirement plan under certain conditions.

A QDRO is most useful when the payer is self-employed and has rights to benefits from a prior employer, or when the payer changes jobs a lot. If the payer is not yet eligible for benefits, you might be able to secure payments from a defined contribution plan, such as a profit-sharing or 401(k) plan. These plans are a particularly good source for support arrears because the plan administrators normally want to make lump sum payments, not series of monthly payments.

If your spouse's pension plan qualifies, you can use the QDRO to collect child support and alimony payments. The QDRO must clearly specify how much will be paid, to whom, and for how long, and the benefits must be currently available to an alternate payee (nonemployee spouse) under the terms of the plan.

If the retirement plan currently pays benefits, the QDRO operates like a garnishment of wages—that is, the money is removed from the benefits check and sent directly to the recipient. If retirement benefits are not yet being paid, the structure of the QDRO depends on the situation. If the payer is eligible to receive benefits under the plan (but has chosen to continue working), the QDRO could require that the plan make the monthly support payments. If the payer is still working, however, it is usually easier to use a wage garnishment.

Tax Problems With Using a QDRO

Child support is not taxable. Using a QDRO to collect child support from a pension plan, however, makes it taxable income to the recipient, because the tax code requires that any payments from a QDRO to a former spouse be taxed. To compensate, you can try to get the child support payments increased to allow for withholding of taxes. Otherwise, do not use this option unless no reasonable alternative exists to collect the payments.

You'll also need to give the enforcement agency the following information about yourself and the child(ren) who are owed support:

- children's birth certificates
- child support order
- divorce decree or separation agreement
- records of past child support received, and
- information about your income and assets.

For more information about collecting past-due child support or locating a parent, go to the website of the Office of Child Support Services (OCSS) at www.acf.hhs.gov/css. Click "Parents," then click "Help for Parents," and click on the link for "How It's Enforced" under "Understanding Child Support."

What Is Your Bottom-Line Decision Regarding Custody and Child Support?

By this point, you've worked through questions on custody and child support. Use the space below to record your decision by writing out what you want to accomplish regarding custody and support in the settlement negotiations.

_____

_____

_____

_____

_____

_____

_____

_____

_____

_____

Alimony—Legal, Financial, and Emotional Realities

It helps to think of alimony as a separate issue, distinct from your property settlement (except if your property earns income). Before reviewing the steps toward a settlement, take a few minutes to read about the legal, financial, and emotional realities surrounding alimony.

Legal Realities

Until the 1970s, alimony was a natural extension of the financial arrangement in traditional marriages, where the husband was the bread-winner and the wife stayed home, caring for the house and children. The amount of alimony was determined by a number of factors—the needs of the spouses, their status in life, their wealth, and their relative "fault" in ending the marriage. For example, if a husband was committing adultery or treating his wife cruelly, he would pay a relatively large amount. If the wife was having an affair or treating her husband cruelly, she would receive little or no alimony.

Today, the following factors are generally considered in determining alimony:

- the recipient's needs
- the payer's ability to pay
- the age, health, and standard of living of the spouses
- the length of the marriage
- each spouse's ability to earn
- the recipient's nonmonetary contributions to the marriage
- the recipient's ability to be self-supporting, and
- tax advantages and disadvantages.

Except in marriages of long duration (usually ten years or more) or in the case of an ill or ailing spouse, alimony today usually lasts for a set period of time, with the expectation that the recipient spouse will become self-supporting and eventually no longer need it.

In an effort to make alimony awards more uniform, some individual counties have adopted financial schedules to help judges determine the appropriate level of support. Of course, spouses can make arrangements outside of court that differ from the schedules. However, if you can't agree on the amount, a judge will decide how much alimony will be awarded. Leaving such a decision to a judge may create a far different result from what you anticipated.

In some states, especially non–community property states, the division of property can affect how much alimony is awarded. For example, if one spouse gets a house with no mortgage, plus rental properties that produce a good income, a court is not likely to award a high amount of alimony. You will have an opportunity to examine the interplay between alimony and your property division in Chapter 19.

Financial Realities

Generally, court-ordered alimony does not provide adequate money to live on. Often there's a big gap between the amount that's needed to live on and what the recipient actually gets.

To understand the financial reality of alimony, you must know what it really costs for you to live. Then you need to develop strategies for making up the difference between true living expenses and the amount you will receive in alimony. As you work through this section, you will look at the tax consequences of alimony as well as practical matters such as when, where, and how payments should be made. Remember, alimony income is risky. It can be stopped, reduced, or increased by the court any time circumstances change.

Emotional Realities

Since the advent of no-fault divorce, fewer couples vent their anger in knock-down, drag-out fights in court. That doesn't mean the anger isn't there; it just manifests itself differently. That repressed anger might lead to fights over alimony, an item directly tied to a person's survival. You could be moving along nicely in the negotiations only to find that when you get to the alimony, your spouse suddenly makes unreasonable demands or starts playing tricks. Focusing on the legal and financial questions below will help you guard against emotional sabotage.

Steps to a Settlement

As you move through your divorce, you might find that your choices about alimony are guided by the local court's financial guidelines and schedules. For instance, if a schedule shows that a person in your situation should get $500 a month in alimony, your spouse will probably use that number, at least as a starting point.

While you need to be aware of any schedule used in your area, don't rely on those figures in determining the amount you will pay or receive. By answering the following questions, you can analyze the financial consequences of paying or receiving alimony:

- How much do you need to live on?
- What, if any, are the financial schedules for alimony in your area?
- How much alimony do you need—or can you afford to pay?
- Are there alternatives to paying or receiving monthly alimony?
- What is your bottom-line decision on paying or receiving alimony?

How Much Do You Need to Live On?

If you've completed the "Cash Flow Statement" in Chapter 12, you have already tracked your living expenses. If not, go back now and use the statement to outline these costs. Whether you will pay or receive alimony, your goal is to get a realistic picture of your household expenses. If your spouse demands more than you feel you can afford to pay—or offers less than you feel you need to live on—you will have to document the cost of your lifestyle. Yes, that lifestyle will probably change after divorce, but for now you need to establish a baseline for expenses.

While you're documenting your own cost of living, estimate your spouse's expenses as well. You will need this information when you are negotiating. If you can't settle, the court will require that you each submit documentation of your income and expenses at trial.

Check the monthly average figures from your "Cash Flow Statement" in Chapter 12 and other documentation containing your marital costs to estimate the following:

$ _____   *My personal monthly expenses*

$ _____   *My spouse's monthly expenses*

What, If Any, Are the Financial Schedules for Alimony in Your Area?

As mentioned previously, a number of counties have adopted financial schedules to help judges—and spouses—calculate and set alimony payments. Be sure to ask your lawyer whether your county follows a financial schedule or guideline. These schedules and guidelines are commonly used for temporary alimony (that is, the amount of alimony you receive during the divorce).

If your county doesn't use a schedule, or you're dealing with ongoing or postdivorce alimony, it will most likely be determined based on the factors listed above. In addition, courts tend to consider the following as well:

- If a marriage lasted less than five years and the couple has no children, many courts will deny alimony altogether, or award only short-term alimony.
- If there are very young children, (typically) below school age, most courts will order some alimony.
- If a child of the marriage has special needs that make it difficult for a stay-at-home parent to work outside of the home, a court may award alimony to that spouse.
- In marriages that lasted at least ten years, most courts will award alimony indefinitely, or at least until the recipient dies, remarries, cohabits, or becomes self-supporting and no longer needs support.

Based on those factors, judges—and attorneys who regularly appear before those judges—estimate the amount of alimony. No universal formula or rule applies. The amount of an alimony award, perhaps more than any other decision a judge can make, is seldom subject to challenge but often leaves ex-spouses very angry.

To get an estimate of the amount of alimony you might have to pay or are likely to receive if the issue is presented to a judge for decision, you will need to speak to an attorney or a mediator to determine local practice and custom. And remember, if you and your spouse can't agree, you leave your fate to a judge whose decision might not meet your expectations.

How Much Alimony Do You Need—Or Can You Afford to Pay?

Figuring out how much alimony you need or can afford to pay centers on the following—income needs, taxes, and payment practicalities.

Income Needs

Only a hard look at the income-alimony gap can reveal potential problems. If you come to terms with this gap, you have a better chance of closing it. Here are a few suggestions if you, like many divorcing people, find that you run out of money before the end of the month:

- Cut expenses to reduce your debt load as much as possible.
- Do not use credit cards to finance your lifestyle.
- Take on a second job.
- Rent out part of your home to offset mortgage costs.
- Sell an asset and use the money to pay off debts.

Calculate how you would fare today if you had no option other than to pay or receive the alimony amount mandated by local custom or financial schedule. Then brainstorm about possible plans for resolving any budget problems you might face. Write your answers below.

Don't despair. In negotiating the overall settlement, you might get enough property or other assets to replace the loss of income caused by the divorce. You can explore this possibility in Chapter 19.

Alimony Recipients	
Monthly expenses:	$
Estimated alimony I will receive and my other net income (after taxes):	$
Difference:	$
How I will make up any shortfall:	

Alimony Payers	
Monthly net income:	$
Estimated alimony I will pay and my monthly expenses:	$
Difference:	$
How I will make up any shortfall:	

Taxes

Under former Internal Revenue Code 26 U.S.C.A. Section 215, court-ordered alimony was tax deductible for the paying spouse and taxable as income to the supported spouse.

However, the 2017 Republican tax bill removed the alimony deduction. Under the Tax Cuts and Jobs Act, for any alimony agreements executed after December 31, 2018, paying spouses can't deduct alimony payments on their taxes, and supported spouses no longer have to report alimony as income. Divorcing couples will have to consider these new tax rules as they structure or amend alimony agreements.

Payment Practicalities

If you will receive or pay alimony, you must be careful not to overlook the details involved in continuing a financial connection with your ex-spouse. Below are questions and suggestions to cover payment practicalities. Whether you deal with these items as your negotiations progress or wait until the final settlement, use the spaces provided to jot down your ideas, which you can refer to later when needed. Put a checkmark in front of the question once it is resolved.

_____ *How will alimony payments be made?*

_____

_____

_____

_____

If you're the recipient, you basically have four choices:
- You can wait for the proverbial "check in the mail."
- You can ask your ex to use a money transfer app like Venmo or Zelle.
- You can set up a wage deduction through your ex's employer, then have that money automatically deposited (through direct deposit plans) into your bank account.
- You can set up a voluntary account deduction through your ex's bank, then have that money automatically deposited into your bank account.
- You can have your lawyer prepare a QDRO (Qualified Domestic Relations Order) specifying that payments come directly from your ex's retirement plan.

Some recipients wait for the check, but it is becoming more common for courts to order wage assignments or garnishments, especially when the payer is also paying child support. Whatever you arrange, be sure the details are clearly outlined in writing.

_____ *On what days of the month will alimony payments be made?*

_____

_____

_____

_____

Payers usually find it most convenient to pay alimony shortly after receiving their salary checks or other income. If you are a recipient and payments won't arrive until after your mortgage, rent, or some other large monthly bill is due, you'll need to rearrange your budget. Try to manage your cash flow so there's some money left over from the previous month. If that won't work, contact the lender and ask that your payment date be pushed ahead to correspond with your cash flow—you don't need to tell the lender you're waiting for your alimony check unless the lender pushes the question. Most lenders will make arrangements to accommodate payments.

_____ *How long will alimony payments be made?*

_____

_____

_____

_____

It's becoming uncommon for alimony payments to be ordered permanently. And even in indefinite arrangements, alimony almost always ends if the recipient remarries or the paying spouse retires.

It usually ends if the payer dies, too. Sometimes, alimony lasts for a set number of years—often for the length of time it takes for the supported spouse to get training and reenter the workforce or, sometimes, to allow the recipient to stay home with young children long enough until they are more independent and in school full time.

Whatever your arrangement, pay close attention to the termination date. Suppose you are to receive alimony until September 30 of a certain year, based on the assumption that you will return to school, graduate in June of that year, and use the summer to find a job. What will you do if your education and career path don't work out as planned? You can usually go back to court and ask for an extension of the alimony, *but only if you make your request before the scheduled termination date.* If you wait until after the September 30 termination date, you're probably out of luck, because the court will have "reserved jurisdiction"—kept the power to make decisions—only until September 30 of that year.

When there is no termination date, alimony is generally modifiable upward or downward depending on a former spouse's continued ability to pay and the other spouse's need.

> *How will you handle future economic changes,*
> _____ *such as inflation or salary increases?*

_____

_____

_____

_____

If your alimony payment does not change, the amount it can actually buy year to year is sure to decrease. That's inflation. It's possible to take inflation into account in your alimony agreement with a COLA—cost of living adjustment—clause. Some couples tie COLA increases to the rise in the Consumer Price Index (CPI); others simply choose a specific dollar amount or percentage.

Records to Keep When You Pay or Receive Support

You must keep adequate records if you are paying or receiving alimony. This point cannot be overemphasized. Frequently, after a divorce, the spouses dispute, or the IRS challenges, the amounts that were actually paid or received. Without documentation, the payer under a pre-2019 alimony order may lose the alimony tax deduction and be ordered to pay back support if the other spouse makes a claim in court. This will not apply under the new tax laws that removed the alimony deduction for agreements and orders entered after December 31, 2018.

Payer

Here are suggestions of records to keep:

- a list showing each payment (for example, date, check number, place where sent)
- original checks used for payments, bank copies of your canceled checks showing both the front and the back (keep in a safe place, such as a safe-deposit box), or statements showing electronic payments—be sure to note on each check (before you send it) the month for which the support is being paid, and
- a receipt signed by the recipient, if you pay in cash.

Be sure to keep these records for at least three years from the date you file the tax return deducting the payments. You might want to keep them even longer, if, for example, your ex-spouse has more than three years to sue and claim that you owe back support.

Recipient

Make a list that shows each payment received. Include the following information:

- date payment was received
- amount received
- check number or other document identifying the number (for example, the number of the money order)
- account number on which any check was written
- name of bank on which check is drawn or money order issued, and
- a photocopy of the check or money order, and a copy of any signed receipt for cash payments.

Similarly, couples can avoid extended bitterness over alimony arrangements if they face the question of salary increases in advance. Will the recipient get a share of the payer's raise? Will the recipient's raise mean the alimony payment decreases? Be sure you know ahead of time how these questions will be handled.

What life or disability insurance policies will cover your ex-spouse?

_____

_____

_____

_____

_____

If you are dependent on someone else for your income, what will you do if that person becomes disabled or dies? If you will be receiving alimony, you'll want to make sure that adequate insurance covers your ex-spouse. You could purchase a life insurance policy on your ex. Or your ex could buy life and disability insurance—naming you as the beneficiary—to protect your income stream.

What will happen if the payer tries to modify the alimony payments or stops paying altogether?

_____

_____

_____

_____

_____

If you are the payer and you can't afford the amount of alimony you've been ordered to pay, you must file a request for a modification (change) of the order with the court. At your hearing, you must show a material change in circumstances since the last court order that would justify reducing the amount of support. Your ex-spouse's cohabitation with someone might qualify, for example.

Another common reason for changing alimony is your decreased income. Where you have voluntarily decreased your income, however—for example, you quit your job as a doctor to work in a pastry shop—the judge may consider your ability to earn, not your actual earnings.

If you are the supported spouse and your ex stops paying, you will need to go to court. Most likely, you will have to schedule a hearing in which your ex-spouse is ordered to come to court and explain why your payments aren't coming. You can also ask the court to grant you a judgment for the amount owed, or the "arrears." You can then use judgment collection methods, such as wage attachments and property liens, to try to collect the arrears.

Alimony and Bankruptcy

Alimony can't be erased in bankruptcy. If your ex owes a substantial amount and tries to have it wiped out in bankruptcy, you will be protected so long as you follow bankruptcy laws and procedures. For more on bankruptcy and divorce, see Chapter 17.

Are There Alternatives to Paying or Receiving Monthly Alimony?

While financial schedules and legal guidelines help establish the amount of alimony, they don't require any particular payment arrangement. Although alimony is traditionally paid monthly, it is possible to pay it in a lump sum, periodically, or together with child support.

Lump Sum Alimony

A lump sum settlement of alimony upon divorce is sometimes called an "alimony buyout." Before agreeing to a buyout, consider its pros and cons.

For the Recipient

Accepting a lump sum settlement has several major advantages:
- You reduce the risk of depending on someone else—who could default, become disabled, or die—for income. Reducing the risk of depending on someone who could default is important—alimony default rates exceed 50% in many places.

- You can use the lump sum for a down payment on a house or other purposes, such as paying bills.
- If you have no children, you can terminate any further contact with your ex-spouse.

A buyout also has disadvantages:

- You lose a steady flow of income.
- Once you accept a lump sum payment, you can't go back to court to reinstate alimony.
- You might receive less than you would have in monthly payments. You and your soon-to-be ex-spouse might agree on a lower amount just to get rid of each other. Also, had you written a COLA (cost of living adjustment) clause into your settlement, your payments would have risen over time, a consideration usually not factored into a lump sum payment.
- You run the risk of losing some or all of the lump sum payment through bad investments or other unforeseen circumstances, such as a debilitating illness.

For the Payer

Making a lump sum settlement has the following advantages:

- Because writing a monthly alimony check to a former spouse can be a grating experience that creates resentment and ill will after the divorce, a lump sum might be easier emotionally.
- If you have no children, you can end the marriage with a strong sense of finality.
- Because a buyout compresses all future payments into one present payment, the total is often discounted for taxes and is less than what would have been paid over a set number of years. For example, Mitch agrees to pay Sara $1,000 per month for the next five years, for a total of $60,000. Mitch figures inflation is around 4%, and in today's dollars, $60,000 is worth only $54,480. Mitch offers that amount less taxes in a present-day lump sum settlement.

A buyout also has disadvantages:

- You have to come up with a large sum of money.
- Under standard alimony plans, payments cease if the recipient dies, remarries, or, in some cases, cohabits with a new partner. You could pay a lump sum at divorce only to watch your ex remarry in a year.
- Because a buyout can't be renegotiated, you could end up paying more in the lump sum than might have been required. For instance, if your ex obtains a high-paying job or your income drops a great deal, you might have been able to reduce the monthly alimony payments.

Transferring Assets to the Recipient in Exchange for Alimony

Certain assets, such as the house, stocks, or a pension plan, could be given to your spouse in exchange for a release from the obligation to pay alimony. You might want to consider this option if you don't relish the idea of making monthly alimony payments or if you're strapped for cash and the payments would make your budget tighter.

You might also consider this option if you don't want to hold assets on which you may have to ultimately pay capital gains taxes, or if you want to sever all financial ties with your soon-to-be ex-spouse.

Family Support

Sometimes, alimony and child support are combined into one monthly payment called "family support."

Recipients of family support enjoy one advantage if a payer defaults. In that situation, the recipient has numerous child support collection techniques available even though part of the amount being collected is alimony. If the payer defaults on alimony payments, the only collection method in most states involves taking the payer to court. Be warned, however, that a growing number of courts are disallowing family support, not wanting to burden the child support collection bureaus with collecting what is really alimony.

Sample Qualified Medical Child Support Court Order

A. _____[*Name of party*]_____ is ordered to maintain in full force and effect all health insurance coverage, including medical, dental, hospital, and health maintenance, available at reasonable cost through employment and/or other group health insurance plan, and to pay premiums on that coverage.

_____[*Name of party*]_____ is also ordered to maintain the minor child(ren) _____[*specify*]_____as alternate recipient(s), entitled to enroll in the group insurance plan, until such minor child(ren) attain majority, are emancipated, die, or marry, or until further order of this Court.

B. In the event that such health insurance coverage is not available at the entry of this judgment but subsequently becomes available at no cost or reasonable cost to _____[*name of party*]_____, _____[*name of party*]_____ is ordered to notify the Court and opposing party and to apply for that coverage.

C. The group health insurance plan that is the subject of this order is available through _____[*employer or other group*]_____. Coverage is provided by _____[*name of insurance company*]_____and coverage is for _____[*description of the type of coverage provided by the plan*]_____.

D. The employer of the plan participant (if the group health insurance is available through employment) is ordered to enroll the child(ren) as alternate recipients in the group health plan.

E. The insurance company is ordered to provide coverage to the child(ren) of the plan participant as alternate recipients even if the child(ren) were born out of wedlock, do not live with plan participant, are not claimed as dependents on the plan participant's federal income tax return, or live outside of the plan's service area.

F. The insurance company is ordered to reimburse the custodial parent directly for covered medical expenses paid by the custodial parent on behalf of the alternate recipients. The insurance company shall not pay such reimbursement to the plan participant.

G. The name and last known mailing address of the party ordered to maintain health insurance (the "plan participant") are:

_____

_____

H. The name and mailing address of the alternate recipient(s) are:

_____

_____

What Is Your Bottom-Line Decision on Paying or Receiving Alimony?

You might have little choice about the amount of alimony payments, but you must nevertheless make decisions about alimony. Will you negotiate for a lump sum buyout? Will you use alimony as leverage in negotiating for other assets? Use this space to describe your bottom-line decision on alimony payments so you can easily refer to this information in Chapter 19 when you bring all your decisions to the negotiating table.

_____

_____

_____

_____

Questions to Ask an Attorney

1. What conduct might jeopardize my right to custody of my children? Am I permitted to move away if I have custody? If I don't have custody and my ex-spouse wants to move with the children, can I fight for custody or block the move?
2. What formula is used to calculate child support in my state?
3. Does child support in my state cover all child-related expenses, including medical, clothing, allowances, and child care? If not, what expenses does child support cover, and who pays for the other costs?
4. What will I do if my spouse falls behind in child support or alimony?
5. How does the court enforce child support and alimony orders?
6. Is it wise to arrange for family support payments instead of child support?
7. How will alimony or child support be affected if a parent receives government welfare benefits?
8. If my ex-spouse remarries or takes a new partner, does that affect the obligation to pay or receive child support or alimony? ●

Negotiating and Finalizing the Best Possible Settlement

Until this stage of the divorce, you have focused on your personal, individual decisions—that is, the things you "want" in your divorce. But how will you get what you want? Through negotiation.

Negotiating a divorce settlement is a process of offers and counteroffers. You and your spouse may be able to compromise and reach a settlement easily, or your demands and those of your spouse might run headlong into each other. Some couples state their terms and reach a settlement in hours, while others go through years of bitter fighting.

Your settlement negotiations will probably bear an uncomfortable resemblance to the dynamics of your marriage. If your spouse has been rigid and demanding throughout your relationship, don't expect that you'll suddenly encounter flexibility and reasonableness in a settlement conference. Similarly, an uncommunicative mate will probably give you the silent treatment as you attempt to complete the settlement. Anticipating your spouse's most likely behavior can make it easier for you to accept and move through the negotiations.

Your decisions—and actions—become crucial in this phase, because you are playing for keeps. Once the settlement is final, it is costly, time consuming, and almost impossible to modify it. Better to make changes to the settlement before you complete it, rather than try to change it later.

In this chapter, you'll address three basic issues regarding negotiating the settlement:

- Have you done your financial homework?
- How are offers and counteroffers made?
- How do you finalize the settlement?

Remember that negotiation is the middle step in a longer process. You must communicate your needs and preferences clearly before negotiation begins, and you must be willing to compromise. Your negotiation should be guided by the acceptance that no settlement is perfect, for you or for your spouse. Your goal is a settlement you can live with.

Have You Done Your Financial Homework?

Imagine walking into a room and sitting across a table from your spouse and your spouse's attorney. The attorney smiles while going through a long list of items that your spouse is prepared to "give" you if you will simply forfeit any claim to the items that are on your spouse's much shorter list.

The attorney points out that the dollar amounts on the bottom line of both lists are equal. Surely you should agree to such a fair and equitable offer.

But should you?

You can't know whether or not the offer is fair unless you've done your homework. If you've worked through the previous chapters in this book, you should be able to accept or reject your spouse's offer relatively quickly. If you haven't read the prior chapters—analyzing your assets and debts, evaluating tax consequences, and understanding alimony and child support—you're likely to accept an offer that's a bad financial deal for you, regardless of how "equal" the dollar amounts on the bottom line appear to be.

You must know where you stand financially before you negotiate the settlement. This point can't be stressed enough. If you have not already done so, read the material relevant to your divorce from Chapters 12 (property and expenses), 13 (house), 14 (retirement plans), 15 (investments), 16 (employee benefit plans), 17 (debts), and 18 (alimony and child support). Even if your spouse has made an offer—or is preparing to counter an offer you've made—take no further steps until you have analyzed the financial consequences of any proposed settlement.

Tallying Your Marital Balance Sheet

In Chapter 12, you filled out the detailed "Assets and Liabilities Worksheet." Now, as you reach the crucial point of your negotiations, that attention to detail will pay off.

You can now devise your "Marital Balance Sheet," a key tool in arriving at a settlement. With the information you've assembled, achieving a fair division of the assets and debts—the goal of every divorce proceeding—should be infinitely easier.

Refer back to the "Assets and Liabilities Worksheet" in Chapter 12. Make note of what property is jointly owned or owned by the spouses individually. Note also the equity or legal value in the last column. Then enter that information in the appropriate columns below. This task will be a bit of a chore, but it's important. This is what you've been working toward.

Once you've entered that information, take a moment to study the overall picture. Think about which assets you want to keep and which ones you want to be rid of or are willing to give up. Bear in mind that what each person gets will also be an important element in deciding what, if any, amount of child support and alimony is ordered.

Begin by preliminarily dividing the property as you would ideally like to see it divided. First, consider which property each spouse would prefer to have and "deserves" to have. For example, if the equity or legal value of your house is $150,000, and you and your spouse each contributed an equal amount of separate property for the down payment, you would logically have a 50-50 share of the equity, or $75,000 apiece before taxes. But if you contributed unequal amounts for the down payment, that figure might need to be adjusted. Similarly, try to determine the stake each of you has in other assets based on who acquired them and with what funds.

The assets and liabilities listed in Chapter 12 are very detailed and specific. Here you're going to be grouping them—investments, collections, real estate, and so on—to get an overall sense of how they could be divided. Inequities will naturally develop. Allocate enough of the value of joint property to the spouse with the shortfall to roughly equalize the respective values. Your negotiations will determine who actually gets what. This exercise will help prepare you for those negotiations.

Look at specific items of jointly owned property to identify those that can be transferred from joint names into the sole name of one party to equalize the values. Consider trading property interests of similar value—say, the wife's interest in the husband's pension for the husband's interest in the family home.

When you get to the bottom of each portion of the "Marital Balance Sheet," check how close you've come to having equal allocations. Make note of any equalizing payment that would be required to bring the allocations into balance.

Dividing Miscellaneous Property

The bulk of your divorce may focus on splitting the miscellaneous items, such as furniture, books, electronic equipment, appliances, kitchenware, tools, and the like. The easiest way to divide these items is to make a list of *everything you jointly own*—including wedding gifts and joint inheritances—and write your name or your spouse's name next to each item. Give the list to your spouse. Ask your spouse to note those items on which they disagrees with your assignment of ownership. Then sit down together and review the items in dispute. If you can't resolve your differences, here are three suggestions:

- Flip a coin. The winner gets first choice of the disputed items. Alternate selecting until the list is exhausted.
- Put the disputed items on your settlement chart and divide them as you negotiate the settlement.
- Find a mediator to help you divide what's still on the list.

This property might not be worth the time you spend fighting over it. Don't let the issue of dividing the silverware and the Funko Pop collection interfere with your negotiations over more financially significant assets, such as the house or retirement plans.

Marital Balance Sheet		
Division of Jointly Owned Property		
Equity or Legal Value (from Chapter 12)	**Allocation to Spouse 1**	**Allocation to Spouse 2**
Assets:		
Marital home		
Rental house		
Real estate		
Investments		
Stock account		
Savings		
Checking		
Crypto		
Money market fund		
Mutual funds		
CDs		
Automobile 1		
Automobile 2		
Furnishings		
Art works		
Collections		
Debts:		
Credit cards		
Credit line		
Bank loan		
Family loan		
Other debt		
Jointly Owned Property Divided		
Equalizing payment, if any		
Spouse 1's Property Divided Equity or Legal Value (from Chapter 12)	**Allocation to Spouse 1**	**Allocation to Spouse 2**
Spouse 1's property		
Equalizing payment, if any		
Spouse 2's Property Divided Equity or Legal Value (from Chapter 12)	**Allocation to Spouse 1**	**Allocation to Spouse 2**
Spouse 2's property		
Equalizing payment, if any		

Summary of Property Division		
Equity	To Spouse 1	To Spouse 2
Joint property		
Spouse 1's property		
Spouse 2's property		
Total division		
Overall equalizing payment, if any		

When Not to Keep the House

After Janet divorced, she found herself paralyzed, though not physically. Because of decisions she made during her divorce, she could not afford to move from her home.

Janet owed $60,000 to her uncle—he lent her the money so that she could buy out her husband. If Janet were to sell the house, she'd first have to pay her uncle. Then she'd have to pay taxes on any profit from the sale that exceeded $250,000. Janet wants a small condo worth less than her house. Between payments to her uncle, taxes she would owe on the profit, the lower market price of her house due to slumping real estate values in her area, and high mortgage rates, she would have barely enough left for a down payment on a new place and might not even qualify for a loan.

Janet's goal is to keep her monthly house payment low. In her current home, she pays only $950 per month. After Janet repays her uncle and puts money aside for the taxes, she will have a little money left over from the sale of the house that she can use as a down payment on the condo. She'll still have to finance the deal. If she took a new 30-year loan at 7.5% interest, her monthly payment would be $1,250—$300 more per month for housing than she pays now. And she simply can't afford it on her current salary.

"It's ironic," Janet now muses. "I fought so hard to keep this house, and now I have to keep it whether I want to or not. I'm so busy at work that I hardly have time to mow the lawn, and I've had to rent out two rooms just to keep everything going. If I had it to do over again, I'd have sold the house during the divorce and started fresh."

How Are the Offers and Counteroffers Made?

Once you have a good grasp of your "Marital Balance Sheet," you can begin the negotiations. In many settlements, the spouses will agree on several issues. To resolve the remaining issues, the couple—perhaps with the help of a mediator or their attorneys—meet or correspond until all issues are settled. Once the details are settled, they are recorded in a settlement agreement. The settlement agreement is then taken to the court for a judge's approval. Unless an agreement contains a clause leaving the children unsupported, a judge will approve the agreement as a formality.

Don't Be Discouraged

Even after doing your financial homework and the hard work of preparing for settlement negotiations, you might still go through numerous settlement conferences in attempting to hammer out an agreement. Some cooling-off time might be needed between offers and counteroffers because of charged emotions. Take the time you need and don't give in just because you never want to see your ex again.

Your settlement might not follow the scenario described above exactly. Here are several other possibilities:

Scenario 1

You and your spouse agree to terms ➤ *file your own papers with the court* ➤ *a final decree of divorce is issued* ➤ *the marriage ends.*

This kind of simple divorce usually takes place after a short marriage with no children or major assets to divide. If you fall into this situation, check to see whether there's a good do-it-yourself divorce book written for your state. (See the resources below.)

Scenario 2

You and your spouse agree to terms on some issues ➤ meet with a mediator to resolve remaining issues ➤ file papers with the court on your own or using an attorney, attorney-mediator, or typing service ➤ a final decree of divorce is issued ➤ the marriage ends.

Mediators are discussed in Chapter 7. Remember that a mediator is not an advocate, but a person who helps you and your spouse arrive at a settlement you can live with. Once you settle the issues, a mediator will probably not help you file your court papers unless the mediator is also an attorney. You (or your spouse) can use an attorney for this, but make sure you find a lawyer who will respect the mediation process and your decisions. Otherwise, the attorney might want to get more involved— find out all the issues of your case, figure out why you settled it as you did, and possibly even counsel you to resolve it differently. This can mean you end up starting over.

Scenario 3

You and your spouse—with your attorneys—agree on certain issues ➤ through your attorneys' meeting or corresponding, you resolve remaining issues ➤ your attorneys file papers with the court ➤ a final decree of divorce is issued ➤ the marriage ends.

If you and your spouse can't settle your case, you'll probably turn to the services of attorneys. The cost will rise and the issues might seem more complicated, but your interests could be better protected. Nevertheless, it is imperative that you retain absolute control over your case. Having come this far in this book, you understand the financial realities of keeping certain assets, assuming (or having your spouse assume) debts, and paying or receiving alimony or child support. Be clear with your attorney as to what is an acceptable and unacceptable settlement. Give your lawyer a copy of the "Marital Balance Sheet" you completed in this chapter.

Understand What You're Getting

Judy and her husband went through an arduous negotiation process. When they couldn't agree on how to divide their property, they scheduled a trial. A few minutes before they were to go before the judge, they settled the issues in the courthouse cafeteria. Their attorneys initialed papers stipulating the terms of their agreement.

When Judy received her copy of the stipulations, she noticed that her husband's attorney had added language describing her husband's equalization payment—money owed for receiving a greater share of marital property—as a distribution of retirement benefits subject to a Qualified Domestic Relations Order (QDRO). Instead of receiving tax-free payments, Judy would be getting the payment in the form of a fully taxable distribution from the retirement plan. Judy could roll the money into an IRA to defer taxes, but she did not want a taxable asset when she and her husband had already agreed that she would receive the nontaxable equalization payment.

Fortunately, Judy reviewed the settlement agreement carefully and asked her attorney about it. Judy then demanded—and got—a correction. The equalization payment was separated from the retirement benefits, as was originally intended. Her alertness saved her almost $40,000 in taxes.

Scenario 4

You and your spouse—with your attorneys—agree on certain issues ➤ *through your attorneys' meeting or corresponding, you resolve some, but not all, remaining issues* ➤ *your attorneys prepare for trial* ➤ *a trial takes place; the judge makes rulings* ➤ *a final decree of divorce is issued* ➤ *the marriage ends.*

Throughout this book, you've been warned against letting a judge decide your fate and letting your marital assets be eaten up in lawyers' fees. If, however, all else fails and you must go to trial, then be prepared. Don't be afraid to ask your lawyer what will happen—and how much the lawyer's bill will be. And don't forget that you'll probably have to pay experts—actuaries, appraisers, financial planners, and the like—if you're disputing asset values. If you can't agree on custody, you'll probably need to bring counselors, psychologists, and others into court to testify. Be prepared for these bills.

If You Must Go to Trial

In some divorces, all attempts at negotiation break down and couples end up going to court. Before a trial, you will want to:

- Ask your attorney about the pros and cons of your position and what other courts have decided in cases like yours.
- Ask which judge you will most likely get and what biases that judge tends to hold.
- Reevaluate the financial and tax implications of your options.
- Reconsider the proposals your spouse made. Think through their merits and drawbacks.
- Think about the benefits of settling without going to court, such as saving vast legal fees, court costs, and other expenses. What if you pay these expenses and lose anyway?

RESOURCE
You can find useful divorce-related information in *Nolo's Essential Guide to Divorce,* **by Emily Doskow (Nolo).**

How Do You Finalize the Settlement?

As mentioned earlier, once the issues are resolved and reduced to a settlement agreement, a judge must approve the agreement. Unless it leaves the children unsupported, a judge will typically sign the agreement.

Tips for Negotiating Your Settlement

Here are several tips to bear in mind during your negotiations:

- You might not get what you deserve, but you can get what you negotiate.
- Know the least you are willing to get, the most you are willing to give, and the bottom line you are willing to agree on.
- Answer questions clearly and concisely—and without blame.
- Put yourself in your spouse's position and ask what you'd do if you were your spouse.
- Don't give in to pressure for the sake of an immediate response.
- Release tension during negotiation sessions; take deep breaths and let them out slowly.
- When difficulties or conflicts arise, use phrases that can help move things forward:

  "I appreciate what we've done so far … ."

  "I'd like to settle this on the basis of principle, not power … ."

  "Help me understand how you reached that conclusion … ."

  "I'm trying to see the point you are making; would you mind clarifying it for me?"
- Deliver minor concessions early to set a positive tone. Focus on making immediate compromises that are easy for you and that your spouse might find valuable.
- Clearly label all major concessions, saying something such as "This is going to cost me dearly, but I'm giving this to you because … ." This may encourage reciprocity.
- Prepare as if this negotiation is very important. Because it *is*.

Usually, when you take your marital settlement agreement to court, you also bring your final divorce papers, requesting that the judge terminate your marital status. Before that, generally, only the complaint or petition requesting that the marriage end—and an answer or response from the other spouse—has been filed. Once the couple resolves the property, debt, custody, alimony, and child support issues, they also usually end their marriage. In some cases, however, you may actually be divorced before you conclude your settlement. In these cases, the divorce process is "bifurcated"—divided in two parts—so that the part ending the marriage is resolved first, and then the issues of property division, debt allocation, custody, alimony, and child support are settled later.

Bifurcation is usually used when one party wants to remarry and doesn't want to wait the many months or years it might take to settle the unresolved issues in the divorce. Our experience is that couples who bifurcate their divorce have little incentive to untangle their finances. Financial discussions tend to drag on, and making a clean break and planning for your own financial future might become more difficult.

Don't expect a grand parade announcing the end of your marriage. All you're likely to receive is a notice from the court. After all the drama of divorce, the end can be nothing more than an anticlimactic notice in the mail. You might even need to call your attorney's office or the courthouse to make sure the marriage is really over.

You can, of course, throw yourself a divorce party to mark the occasion.

Divorce Ceremonies

Some couples hold beautiful and touching divorce ceremonies to end their marriages and begin their lives anew. An important part of any divorce ritual is to have the leader or clergyperson help guide the ex-spouses in expressing gratitude for the best parts of their marriage. They recognize aloud what was good about the marriage and about each other. They may speak with pride and joy. Children in attendance can tell their parents how they feel about them and what their expectations are for the future. Friends can express their support and care for both spouses.

Though it might not be for everyone, a divorce ceremony can be a powerful experience because it offers an opportunity to provide closure on the past and look forward to the future. ●

After the Divorce:
How Do I Get From "We" to "Me"?

Congratulations … you've made it. Your divorce is over, and it's probably a tremendous relief. As far as your financial life is concerned, however, the watchword after divorce is caution—not celebration.

J ust as it was important to avoid spending sprees during the divorce, it's wise to keep your expenses down once the divorce is final. You need time to adjust to your new life. The last thing you want to do is run up big bills that you can't pay.

Similarly, don't let your guard down while you wrap up the details and get ready for life as a single person—or single parent. First, you must be sure to follow through—or see that your spouse follows through—on the settlement you've worked so hard to secure. Be on the lookout, too, for people who try to pressure you into investing your money one way or another. Sit tight. You'll have plenty of time to decide what to do once you've made sure there are no loose ends from your divorce that could trip you up in the future.

How Do I Finish the Business of Divorce?

Forgetting to follow through on details after divorce is one of the easiest things to do. It's also one of the costliest.

During the divorce, you were under tremendous stress. Now, you might be more exhausted than you realize, and that can lead you to overlook important tasks. Even if you're feeling exhilarated instead of exhausted, that state of excitement can lead to overconfidence and a lack of focus.

You could literally lose the property you fought to keep because of simple errors in divorce paperwork. One man lost his vacation home to his ex-wife when she sold it before the deed transferring ownership to him was recorded. Another woman had to pay off debts her ex-husband incurred because she forgot to close a joint account.

Even after the judgment is entered, you must take steps to implement the provisions of the divorce decree and make sure your newly single status is reflected in your financial and legal dealings. Not all items on the following checklist will apply to everyone, but read it all carefully and attend to all the ones that do apply to you.

Checklist: Required Postdivorce Actions

Name change

_____ See that your name is removed from any debts or loans that are no longer your responsibility.

_____ Contact the Social Security Administration by filing Form SS-5 at a local office or downloading the form from the agency's website, www.ssa.gov. It usually takes two weeks to verify the change. (A mismatch between a name on a tax return and a Social Security number could increase a tax bill or reduce the size of a refund.)

_____ Tell your employer, including the human resources department and retirement plan administrator or custodian.

_____ Notify all your creditors.

_____ Apply for credit in your new name.

_____ Change the name on your bank accounts and checks, or open new accounts in your new name.

_____ Apply for a name change on your passport; the application is available online at https://travel.state.gov/content/travel/en/passports/have-passport/change-correct.html.

_____ Notify medical care providers, insurers, the registrar of voters, utilities, the post office, and the state department of motor vehicles.

A Rose by Any Other Name ...

You may feel by now that you've gone through enough changes in your divorce. But one item that you might not mind changing is your name. Changing your name as part of the divorce process can be more efficient—and less expensive—than waiting to do it later, when you will probably have to pay court fees. You can use your birth name, use a name from a prior marriage, or, in some cases, simply make up a new name altogether.

Real estate and cars

Divide the property as set forth in the divorce decree. Specifically:

_____ Execute a quitclaim deed to transfer title to real estate, as the decree requires. New deeds must be recorded at the county recorder's office. Contact your tax assessor's office for forms to sign to keep property taxes from increasing because of the transfer.

_____ Fill out new registration forms changing title to cars, boats, motor homes, or other vehicles and file with the state department of motor vehicles. (Failure to do so could result in trouble or expense for you if the vehicle no longer belonging to you is later involved in a mishap or receives a citation.)

_____ Notify your auto insurer of any changes in automobile drivers, ownership, and addresses. (Also, if needed, apply for a new driver's license with your new name and address.)

_____ Remove your former spouse's name from your mortgage or lease.

Insurance

Review your health, dental, vision, life, and disability policies. Be certain you and your children have adequate coverage. In addition:

_____ Make sure the beneficiaries named in your policies are who you want them to be and are consistent with the divorce decree.

_____ Execute all necessary COBRA documents to ensure continued health insurance coverage, and make sure that your ex-spouse has done the same. You can also check to see if the plans offered through the Affordable Care Act are less expensive.

Estate planning

During your marriage you may have drafted a will, created a trust, or taken other steps to determine who will receive your property after you die. Review those and change them to reflect your new status. Also, create a new power of attorney for health care, naming the person you want to make medical decisions if you become incapacitated.

Debts

Verify that all joint accounts are closed and that you have paid or have a plan to pay all debts you agreed to cover. At the same time, contact the creditors your ex-spouse agreed to pay and make sure they're receiving payments.

(If they aren't, you might want to minimize damage to your own credit by paying those bills and then seek reimbursement from your ex-spouse.)

Deposit accounts

Check your deposit accounts—checking, savings, money markets, certificates of deposit, and Treasury bills—to make sure the names on, and the amounts in, the accounts are consistent with the decisions reached in your settlement.

Changing Joint Deposit Accounts

To change joint deposit accounts, write to the financial institution where you have your account. Here's some sample language to use:

"Please be advised that as of _____[date]_____ , account number _____ , in the names of _____ , is to be closed. All assets from that account are to be transferred into a new account in the name of _____ ."

You and your ex-spouse must sign this form. Some banks and brokerage firms may ask for a copy of your divorce decree, but do not send it unless you're specifically requested to do so.

Investment accounts

Check investment accounts to see that ownership of stocks, bonds, and mutual funds is properly listed.

Children

If you share custody of children, you should have access to their school reports, medical records, and other information. Also, make sure you understand your custody and child support agreements and that you fulfill your obligations. Specifically:

_____ Pay all support when due. Keep detailed records of each payment made or received.

_____ Keep your scheduled visitation times with your children.

_____ If you change jobs, notify your former spouse and your new employer. (Do what's right, even if a judgment or order doesn't require it.)

Tips for Completing the Business of Divorce

Here are a few tips for tying up the loose ends:

- **Review settlement details.** A few days after your divorce is final—after you've recovered from the euphoria or the exhaustion—meet with your lawyer or financial advisers to go over the details of your settlement. Make lists of the items that you, your attorney, your ex-spouse, or others are responsible for completing. Don't leave these items to memory. Make sure the Qualified Domestic Relations Order (QDRO) is entered and implemented, if the divorce decree requires it.

- **Keep records of all payments you make or receive—for alimony, child support, or property exchange.** Make copies of all checks you send or receive. Also, use a calendar or log book to show payment amounts and the date payments are made or received. You need to record these details in case you ever go to court to raise or lower support payments or to collect unpaid support.

- **Make copies of your final judgment and settlement agreement and record appropriate documents.** Get at least one certified copy of your final judgment and settlement agreement. Make copies as needed. In addition, ask your attorney: "What documents do I need to record if my spouse owes me child or spousal support or money to equalize our property division?" Then record those documents with the county. Put the originals in a safe place, such as a safe-deposit box.

- **Start a postdivorce file for essential papers.** Keep your payment records and the duplicate of your final judgment and the settlement agreement in the file. If you experience problems, or need to refer to divorce papers for investment or tax purposes, everything will be located in an easy-to-find spot. On an emotional level, hunting for divorce documents can be frustrating. Avoid triggering old angers and reduce stress by keeping these documents within easy reach.

Can I—or My Ex-Spouse— Change the Settlement?

Your settlement agreement contains several clauses. The main ones probably deal with property division, debt allocation, alimony, child support, and custody. You might be wondering whether you can change any of those provisions, or whether your spouse might try the same. The two of you can *voluntarily* change the terms of your agreement. Any change should be in writing, signed by both parties, dated, and preferably notarized. (Changes agreed to verbally might be unenforceable if you later have different memories about what you decided. In such cases, the courts generally rely on whatever is in writing.) But if your ex-spouse won't cooperate with a change you want, you will have to go to court. Ask your attorney for the specific rulings in your state and what's likely in your case, but below are some general guidelines.

Property division. It's highly unusual for a court to approve one ex-spouse's request to change the terms of the property division after the divorce. A court might approve such a request if the ex-spouse who is asking to change the settlement agreement can show that the other ex-spouse hid assets—such as accounts receivable that should have been used to value a business. The ex-spouse will have to file a motion, schedule a court hearing, and then provide convincing evidence at the hearing of the other party's wrongdoing.

Debt allocation. If your ex-spouse doesn't pay debts according to your agreement, you will no doubt need the court's assistance. You can file a motion and ask the court to order your ex to pay—and to ensure that you're paid, ask the court to have your ex turn money over to the court. To avoid damaging your own credit, however, you should go ahead and pay the bills if you can, and ask the court for an order requiring reimbursement from your ex. The court can order the reimbursement by changing any equalization payment or property distribution that hasn't yet taken place. The court might also order a wage garnishment from your ex's paycheck, or require that other funds belonging to your ex be turned over to you.

Get It in Writing

When you want to change an existing court order—whether it pertains to alimony, child support, custody, visitation, or any other provision—you can ask your ex-spouse to agree to the changes informally first before heading to court. If you're able to reach an agreement, it's important that you put the change in writing, have both parties sign it, and have the signatures notarized. You should also take the agreement to court and ask the judge to issue a new court order based on the agreement. Failure to do so could result in a later finding that the modification wasn't valid.

Alimony. If you knowingly gave up alimony, you usually can't go back to court and try to get it. Once it's waived, it's gone forever. If you are receiving or paying alimony, pay careful attention to the termination date. If you are the recipient and need money beyond that date, you can usually go back to court and ask for an extension of the alimony, *but you usually must make your request before the scheduled termination date.*

If you are the payer and you can't afford to pay the amount you've been ordered to pay in the settlement agreement, you must file a motion for modification with the court. See Chapter 18.

Child support. Child support is always subject to modification by a court because the court retains power over child support until the children reach at least age 18 or 21 (in some states). If you are the payer and can't afford the payments, or if you are the recipient and you can't live on the current payment, you must file papers with the court, schedule a hearing, and show the judge that you can't afford to pay— or to live on—the current support. See Chapter 18.

Custody or visitation. Like child support, custody and visitation are always subject to the court's modification. The parent wanting to change custody or visitation must file papers with the court, schedule a hearing, and show the judge a significant "change of circumstance" since the original order. Changing custody is usually a difficult and emotionally draining process. The court uses the standard of the "best interests of the child" and does not like to change the status quo. Unless you can show that the current custody arrangement is detrimental to your children—for example, their grades are suffering or they are depressed—you are not likely to win your court hearing.

What Do I Want to Do With My Life?

When your divorce is over, it's more crucial than ever to reassess where you're going financially. Rarely does anyone's postdivorce life resemble predivorce expectations. You need to adapt to changes you didn't expect.

If you have used goal-setting tools throughout your divorce, you might simply need to make minor adjustments to your basic plans. If, however, your financial position after divorce is drastically different from what you had anticipated, you might need to reevaluate your objectives, scale down your spending, or take a crash course on investing wisely. Whatever your situation, don't jump into risky ventures with your share of the settlement.

If You Have Money to Invest

Unless you're already a successful investor, it's best to put your money in a safe parking place until you get established—personally and professionally—in your new life. It's ideal to have three to six months' worth of cost-of-living expenses in a money market fund as an emergency fund before you do any investing.

When you feel you have your postdivorce life under control and your future plans are relatively clear, you can move some of your assets into investments where your money can work harder for you—that is, earn more return than from a money market.

You may start slowly with "dollar cost averaging." With this method, you put the same amount of money into an investment on a regular basis over a long period of time. For example, you might put $200 a month into a mutual fund. Your money will buy more shares when the market is down and fewer shares when the market is high. Over time, your average cost per share will be less than your average price per share, and you'll come out ahead.

If Money Is Tight

No matter how well you've planned, you might find yourself with limited resources following your divorce. Cutting costs, then, will be your major priority. Some recently divorced people find it easier to make ends meet by pooling resources. You might be able to connect with others in similar circumstances by contacting groups sponsored by religious or community organizations. Setting up a babysitting exchange or bartering for other services with members of the group can help everyone lower expenses.

Also consider buying groceries in bulk or purchasing necessities from consumer cooperatives or warehouse distributors. To lower your housing costs, you might rent out a room or part of your home.

Avoid taking cash advances or running up the balance on credit cards if you can help it. Most credit cards carry high interest charges—and that interest is not tax deductible.

You can also try to raise cash.

Borrow From Family or Friends

Don't feel discouraged if you have to borrow money from family or friends. Many people find they need short-term loans to get them through this transition period. In times of financial crises, some people are lucky enough to have friends or relatives who can and will help out. Be sure to give them a promissory note for the loan specifying the amount, interest rate, and payment schedule.

Sell a Major Asset or Many Minor Items

One of the best ways you can raise cash and keep associated costs to a minimum is to sell a major asset, hold a garage sale, or sell household items, clothing, or electronics on online marketplaces such as Facebook Marketplace, Nextdoor, or Craigslist. Few people realize how much money may be lying around their house. Selling a hardly used car you were saving until your oldest child turns 16 or a computer you no longer use could help you through a rough period.

RESOURCE

Find the forms you need. For promissory notes, bills of sale, and even child care agreements, look to *Law Forms for Personal Use*, by the Editors of Nolo (Nolo).

Cash in a Tax-Deferred Account

If you have an IRA or other tax-deferred account into which you've deposited money, consider cashing it in. You could have to pay the IRS a penalty—10% of the money you withdraw unless you qualify for the exceptions to this penalty. (See Chapter 14.) In addition, you'll owe income taxes on the money you take out. But paying these penalties to the IRS may be better than struggling to get by.

Get a Home Equity Loan

Many banks, savings and loans, credit unions, and other lenders offer home equity loans, also called second mortgages. Lenders usually lend between 50% and 80% of the market value of a house, less what is still owed on it. Home equity loans have advantages and disadvantages. Be sure you understand all the terms before you sign up for one.

Advantages

- You can obtain a closed-end loan—you borrow a fixed amount of money and repay it in equal monthly installments for a set period. Or you can obtain a line of credit—you borrow as you need the money, drawing against the amount granted when you opened the account, and repay according to your agreement.
- Federal law requires that interest rates on adjustable rate home equity loans be capped—meaning that the rate can increase only a set amount each year as well as over the life of the loan.

Still Having Serious Trouble Paying Your Bills?

If you're getting dunning notices (collection letters) from creditors or are beginning to hear from debt collectors, you may be worried about losing whatever assets you managed to hold onto. If so, you need to take firm steps to deal with this potential crisis.

Develop a budget. Begin by listing all your expenses, both fixed (such as mortgage, car, and insurance payments) and those that vary, such as entertainment and clothing. (You might want to use updated figures from your portion of the "Cash Flow: Income and Expenses" statement in Chapter 12.) Writing down all your expenses will help you track your spending patterns, identify necessary expenses, and prioritize the rest. The aim is to make sure you can make ends meet on the basics, such as housing, food, and health care.

Contact your creditors. Tell them why you're having difficulties and try to work out a modified payment plan. Don't wait until your creditors turn your accounts over to debt collectors. If your creditors already have assigned your accounts to debt collectors, familiarize yourself with the Fair Debt Collection Practices Act, the federal law that details how and when debt collectors may contact you. Go to the Federal Trade Commission website at https://consumer.ftc.gov/articles/debt-collection-faqs to learn more.

Consider credit counseling. If you're not disciplined enough to create a workable budget and stick with it and you aren't able to work out a repayment plan with your creditors, you might want to contact a credit counseling agency. Many are nonprofit and have certified counselors who will advise you on managing your money and debts. But beware: Scams abound in the "credit repair" industry. Ask for referrals from your bank, local consumer protection agency, or friends and family, or go to the National Foundation for Credit Counseling site at www.nfcc.org.

Study debt consolidation. You might be able to lower your cost of credit by consolidating your debt through a second mortgage or a home equity line of credit. But remember that these loans require you to put up your home as collateral. If you can't make the payments, or make them on time, you could lose your house. Also, check the cost—in addition to interest on a debt consolidation loan, you may be asked to pay "points"— each point being one percent of the amount you borrow. Unsecured

> ### Still Having Serious Trouble Paying Your Bills? (continued)
>
> consolidation loans are also available. But these loans come with downsides too, such as high interest rates, and the loan term might be longer than the debt obligations you consolidated, resulting in you paying more interest.
>
> **Bankruptcy.** Personal bankruptcy should be considered the debt management option of last resort. It stays on your credit reports for up to a decade depending on the type of bankruptcy filed and can make it difficult to obtain credit, buy a home, get insurance, or even get a job. Still, it's a legal procedure that can offer a fresh start for a debtor who receives a "discharge"—a court order that exempts the debtor from repaying certain obligations. You must clear some hurdles even before filing for bankruptcy. For instance, you must get credit counseling from a government-approved organization within six months before you file for bankruptcy relief. See Chapter 17 for more about bankruptcy.

Disadvantages

- You are obligating yourself to make another monthly or periodic payment. If you are unable to pay, you might have to sell your house or, even worse, face the possibility of the lender foreclosing. Before you take out a home equity loan, be sure you can make the monthly payment.
- You might have to pay an assortment of up-front fees for such costs as an appraisal, credit report, title insurance, and points, which can run to $1,000 or more. In addition, many lenders charge a yearly fee of $25 to $50.

Get Your Tax Refund Fast

Sometimes, getting a tax refund quickly will help you through a cash flow crisis, especially if the IRS owes you a lot. Numerous electronic filing procedures are available for you to use to help the refund process go much faster, so take advantage of them if you can.

Postdivorce Financial Planning Tips

Financial planning strategies are often based on the idyllic picture of a couple who moves from struggling to make ends meet in their 20s to a happy retirement in their 60s. This picture hardly resembles the norm for divorced people who must redesign their plans. Below are a few tips to help you do that.

Update Your Net Worth and Cash Flow Statements

Your net worth and cash flow have changed because of the property you received or exchanged during the divorce and payments you now make or receive that you didn't before. You can't realize your financial goals in the future unless you know where you're starting from. Update the "Net Worth" and "Cash Flow" statements you completed in Chapter 12 to reflect your new status.

Organize Your Bill-Paying Procedure

Pay off all debts you agreed to cover as part of your divorce settlement as quickly as possible. Create a payment schedule to match your pay periods. If you're paid on the first and 15th of the month, pay your bills then. Consider keeping all bills in a folder. On the first of the month, take out only those bills that you will pay; write your checks and mail the bills (or pay them electronically). Then put the folder away until the 15th. Then do the same on the 15th. By using this system, you won't constantly think about your debts.

Make Sure You Have an Emergency Fund and an Emergency Plan

As we've recommended, you should have an "emergency fund" representing three to six months' worth of cost-of-living expenses. Make sure you can get to this money when you need it.

You might also want to make a contingency plan that takes into account your nonfinancial resources. Could you move in with friends or relatives—including your adult children—if you had to? Knowing you have some kind of cushion of support makes it easier to face life. Once you've been divorced, you might find yourself dwelling on the "worst case" you can imagine. Having a contingency plan can dispel fears and let you move on.

Reevaluate Your Insurance

Most people fall into one of two extremes—either they have too little insurance or they have too much of the wrong kind. Now that your divorce is over, reevaluate your insurance coverage. Read consumer publications and check with several agents to get a good overall update on your insurance position. Consider what your new needs are with respect to health, life, disability, auto, homeowners' or renters', and personal liability coverage. If you are receiving alimony or child support, be sure to consider getting life insurance on your ex-spouse.

Keep Up With Changes in Your Tax Status

When your marital status changes, so does your tax status. Not only might you be in a different tax bracket, but tax laws themselves may change. If you're in a higher tax bracket, you need investments that provide tax-deferred or tax-free income. More likely, however, you are in a lower tax bracket and will want to take advantage of two of the best tax planning opportunities most people have: owning a house and contributing to an IRA or a 401(k) through your work.

Reevaluate Your Retirement Program

How much will it cost you to maintain your current lifestyle once you retire? If you and your ex-spouse divided retirement plans during divorce, be sure to do the follow-up work to secure any payments you are supposed to receive. If you have no retirement plan, go to a brokerage house and ask for a retirement projection. Do not let yourself be pushed into any investment you are not ready to make. Once you have an accurate calculation of postretirement living costs, investigate several types of plans before choosing one that is right for you.

Plan Your Estate

Many people mistakenly assume that they do not have enough property to plan their estates. If you do not plan, however, the state will do it for you after you die. And estate planning encompasses quite a few issues beyond just giving away your property at your death, including medical directives, guardianships, and beneficiary statements. It's important to deal with all of these after your divorce. You will want to:

- Prepare a new will. You might need only a simple will, or you might want to investigate a living trust. Not everyone writes the ex-spouse out after divorce, but it's important that you decide whether you want to or not, and make a new will either way. If you die without a will, the state government will provide a standard one according to its laws, and that might be quite different from what you intended. Make sure your new will doesn't include property that you no longer have after your property settlement.

- If you have minor children, name a guardian for them in your will or be sure the one you previously named is still appropriate. Be sure to talk to potential guardians before naming them; they might be reluctant to accept the responsibility. And designate an alternate in case the guardian you select can't serve.

- Change the beneficiary statements on your retirement plans, brokerage accounts, and insurance policies. These are independent of the wishes expressed in your will.

- Make a new durable power of attorney for financial matters—that is, naming someone to handle your money if you cannot. This precaution can avoid prolonged, costly court proceedings should you become incapacitated.

- Prepare a medical directive, also known as a living will even though it has nothing to do with giving away property at death. The medical directive declares your preference for medical treatment if you become seriously ill. It's often accompanied by a durable power of attorney for health care, which authorizes a trusted person to make the critical decisions if you're near death.

RESOURCE

Nolo publishes a number of books and software programs that can help you take care of your estate. These products are described in Chapter 10.

Setting Goals After Divorce

Right now is the perfect time to look at your financial goals for the short and long term. Use the chart titled "Setting Goals," below, to open up ideas about where you'd like to go in the future.

If You Find a New Love, Protect Your Old Assets ... and Your Alimony

For some people, going through a divorce leads them to swear off the institution of marriage altogether. For others, however, a divorce represents the freedom to be with the person they truly love. If you fall into that category, be sure that you don't let Cupid distract you from the financial realities that you will face. Read the next two sections if you are considering living with or marrying someone new.

Cohabitation Can Be Costly

Once the divorce is over, you might be thinking about moving in with your new partner. Cohabitation, or living together without legally marrying, has risks and it's important that you understand them. Obviously, you will have to deal with the emotional side of your own and possibly your children's reactions to such a move. But you must recognize that you are taking legal and financial risks as well.

First, your settlement agreement may state that if you begin cohabitating with someone else and are the supported spouse, your alimony will automatically stop. Check your settlement agreement and divorce decree before you decide to move in with your new partner.

In addition to the effect living with someone might have on your alimony payments, here are a couple of cautionary tales that will further illustrate why it's important to be financially aware before you decide to live with someone new.

One couple cohabited for four years in Minnesota. During that time, the man used his money to purchase the home in which they lived. The title to the home was taken in "joint tenancy," which means that if one owner died before the other, the survivor automatically inherited the deceased's share of the property, even if a will or trust said something else. (See Chapter 6.) When the couple split up, the woman sued for half the home. The man showed that he used his money to buy it. The woman claimed that he gave her a gift of half the house. The court ruled against her, stating that the house was his unless a written contract stated otherwise.

In a California case, a woman met and moved in with a new man while she was divorcing her first husband. She and her new companion bought a condominium together using joint funds. To avoid complications while negotiating her divorce property settlement, she and her companion put the title to the condominium in his name only. After her divorce was final, the woman married her companion and they moved into a larger home, renting out the condominium—for which title remained in her second husband's name alone. Twenty-seven years later, they were divorcing. The judge ruled that the condo was the property of the second husband, because title was in his name only and she could not prove any ownership interest.

The moral of these stories is: if you and your new love acquire any assets together, be sure the title document (deed or registration) properly reflects your intentions.

In addition to getting property titled the right way, remember that one companion could sue the other for a share of the assets or for alimony-like support. Given these legal and financial realities, it is in your interest to ask a lawyer's advice regarding cohabitation laws in your state before moving in with someone. It's also a good idea to draft an agreement that details your understanding of your respective ownership in the property. You can incorporate this understanding into a prenuptial agreement if you later marry.

> **CAUTION**
> **In many states, you can lose your alimony if you move in with someone new.** Several states presume that someone who cohabits with a person has less need for alimony. Now that same-sex marriage is legal and recognized in all states, same-sex cohabitation will also likely terminate alimony.

Prenuptial Agreements

Many couples marrying for the second time (or more) consider a prenuptial agreement before taking the plunge. A prenuptial contract can be a valuable planning tool if one spouse has sizable wealth and wants to preserve it for their children from a prior marriage. While such agreements have a reputation for being unromantic, they can actually prevent a great deal of heartache.

Engaged couples use prenuptial agreements to define the terms of their financial agreements, rather than letting state law control those terms. They might use a prenup to protect a family business, or to state the nature of certain assets brought into the marriage or to be acquired in the future. Couples can also use prenuptial agreements to ensure that the laws of the state where they were married will govern in the event of a divorce, no matter where they live in the future.

If a couple gets a divorce but doesn't have a prenuptial agreement, assuming they can't otherwise agree, their assets will be divided in accordance with state laws. This means that in community property states, marital property will be divided equally; in equitable distribution states, property will be split "fairly" according to the dictates of the court. If your new spouse contributed to the appreciation of assets that belonged to you alone prior to the marriage, those assets could ultimately be considered marital property subject to division at divorce.

In some cases, prenuptial agreements are challenged by unhappy spouses and struck down in court. This can happen if the terms are too favorable to one spouse or if the agreement was signed under what the court considers unfair circumstances. If you are considering a prenuptial agreement, it is more likely to stand up if it meets these conditions:

- The terms are fair.
- It is in writing (some states require acknowledgment and attorney certification as well).
- It has a clause stating that if any provision of the agreement is invalidated, the rest of the agreement still remains in effect.
- The agreement has a listing attached showing each spouse's assets and liabilities.
- Each spouse has had a separate lawyer review the agreement.
- It includes a clause stating that all agreements between the prospective spouses are included in the prenuptial agreement.
- Each spouse had a reasonable amount of time to review the agreement prior to the wedding.

In addition to a prenuptial agreement, you can protect your separate property through more sophisticated legal tools including an irrevocable trust, revocable living trust, or family limited partnership. For more information on these and other estate planning tools, see one of the many Nolo estate planning publications listed in Chapter 10.

RESOURCE
If you are considering remarrying and want to prepare a prenuptial agreement, check out *Prenuptial Agreements: How to Write a Fair & Lasting Contract*, by Katherine F. Stoner (Nolo).

How Can I Move Beyond the Divorce?

By the time your divorce ends, you might not be sure who won or who lost. You need to give yourself time to reassess what has happened in your life. You might be so tired of the divorce process that you don't want to hear another word about money. Worse, you may feel bitter or gun-shy about moving forward. As discussed throughout this book, you must manage your money and your emotions well if you are to end the relationship with your spouse successfully.

Once you've followed up on the legal and financial details of your settlement, check your emotional state to determine what unresolved feelings you are carrying with you as you move into singlehood. If things are not what you anticipated, don't spend time and money in a continuing connection with your ex-spouse. Recognize your gains and cut your losses so you can get on with your new life.

These questions are designed to help you sort through the emotional and economic fallout of ending a marriage. Figuring out your answers can help you move on.

What changes in my financial life did I not anticipate before the final settlement?

_____

_____

_____

_____

_____

What will be different in my children's lives now that the divorce is over?

_____

_____

_____

_____

_____

_____ *What regrets do I still have about the divorce?*

_____

_____

_____

_____

What financial steps do I feel good about,
_____ *and what could I have done differently?*

_____

_____

_____

_____

How can I continue to expand the positive
_____ *steps I've taken?*

_____

_____

_____

_____

What can I do to avoid repeating the financial
_____ *mistakes I made?*

_____

_____

_____

_____

Setting Goals

*Instructions: Use this matrix to write your short- and long-term goals. Begin now to focus on the future—**your** future—and the memories of the past will begin to fade.*

My professional goals are:

Next six months:	Next one year:	Next five years:

My educational goals are:

Next six months:	Next one year:	Next five years:

My recreation-travel-entertainment goals are:

Next six months:	Next one year:	Next five years:

Setting Goals (continued)

My plans for my children are:

Next six months:	Next one year:	Next five years:

My retirement goals are:

Next six months:	Next one year:	Next five years:

My other goals are:

Next six months:	Next one year:	Next five years:

Appendix

This book helps you through the divorce process by giving you strategies for evaluating your assets and debts and your likelihood of paying or receiving alimony or child support. But you might need help beyond this book. The two best sources of legal help are a law library and a lawyer.

Before discussing additional resources in detail, here's a general piece of advice: Make all decisions yourself. By reading this book, you've taken on the responsibility for getting information necessary to make informed decisions about your legal and financial affairs. If you decide to get help from others, apply this same self-empowerment principle—shop around until you find an adviser who values your competence and intelligence and recognizes your right to make your own decisions.

Law Libraries

Often, you can handle a legal problem yourself if you're willing to do some research in a law library. Here, briefly, are the basic steps to researching a legal question. For more detailed, but user-friendly, instructions on legal research, see *Legal Research: How to Find & Understand the Law*, by the Editors of Nolo (Nolo).

Finding a Law Library

To do legal research, find a law library that's open to the public. Public law libraries are often housed in county courthouses, public law schools, and state capitols. If you can't find one, ask a public library reference librarian, court clerk, or lawyer.

Finding a State Law That Affects Your Divorce

This book occasionally refers to laws that state legislatures have passed. To find a state law, or statute, you need to look in a multivolume set of books called the "state code." State codes are divided into titles. States divide their titles by number or by subject, such as the civil code, family code, or finance code.

To read a law, find the state codes in your law library, locate the title you need, turn to the section number, and read. If you already have a proper reference to the law—called a "citation"—finding the law is straightforward. If you don't have a citation, you can find the law by referring to the index in the code you're using.

After you read the law in the hardcover book, turn to the back of the book. There should be an insert pamphlet (called a "pocket part") for the current or previous year. Look for the statute in the pocket part to see if it has been amended since the hardcover volume was published.

Finding Laws Online

For some people, it might be easier to do legal research online. To find your state's laws online, search for "[your state] statutes" or "[your state] laws." Make sure you're reading the most recent, official laws. Often, when it comes to official statutes, the URL will end in ".gov" or the statutes will be on an official state legislature webpage. (If you're looking for federal laws, you might want to visit the Library of Congress's legal research website at https://guides.loc.gov/law-library.)

Once you find a collection of the laws, you can browse through the various levels of subject headings. They're usually organized by numbered title, article, chapter, and section.

Going Beyond State Laws

If you want to find the answer to a legal question, rather than simply looking up a law, you will need some guidance in basic legal research techniques. Resources that may be available in your law library (or you can buy them online) are:

- *Legal Research: How to Find & Understand the Law*, by the Editors of Nolo (Nolo)
- *Legal Research in a Nutshell*, by Kent C. Olsen and Morris Cohen (West), and
- *Finding the Law*, 12th edition, by Robert Berring and Elizabeth Edinger (West).

Using Background Resources

If you want to research a legal question related to family law but don't know where to begin, one of the best resources is the *Family Law Reporter,* published by the Bureau of National Affairs (BNA). This very thorough, four-volume publication covers all 50 states and the District of Columbia, and is updated weekly. It highlights and summarizes cases, new statutes, and family law news. It also includes a guide to tax laws affecting family law, a summary of each state's divorce laws, and a sample marital settlement agreement.

Most law libraries will have the *Family Law Reporter.* If you can't find it, however, you will need to look at materials written specifically for your state. Ask a law librarian for help.

Lawyers

A lawyer can provide you with information, guidance, or legal representation.

Finding a Lawyer

Before explaining how to find a lawyer, let's first eliminate the types of lawyers you are not looking for:

- the expensive, flamboyant lawyer who grandstands but fails to deliver promised services and passes your case on to a recent law school graduate who works in the office
- the associate or partner at a giant law firm that represents big businesses. These lawyers charge high fees, and few know much about divorce cases or keeping costs down, or
- the lawyer who won't keep you informed about plans for your case and who wants to make all decisions without consulting you. These lawyers are annoyed—and intimidated—by clients who know anything about the law. What they want is a passive client who doesn't ask a lot of questions and pays the bill on time each month.

What you do want is a dedicated, smart, and skilled lawyer who regularly handles family law and divorce cases. The lawyer should understand that your input must be sought for every decision. This being said, here are several ways to find a lawyer.

Personal referrals. This approach is the most common. If you know someone who was pleased with the services of a lawyer, call that lawyer first. If that lawyer doesn't handle divorces or can't take your case, ask for a recommendation to someone else. Be careful, however, when selecting a lawyer from a personal referral. A lawyer's satisfactory performance in one situation does not guarantee that the person will perform the same way in your case.

Group legal plans. Some unions, employers, and consumer action organizations offer group plans to their members or employees, who can obtain comprehensive legal assistance free or for low rates.

Prepaid legal insurance. Prepaid legal insurance plans offer some services for a low monthly fee and charge more for additional work. Participating lawyers may use the plan as a way to get clients who are attracted by the low-cost basic services, and then sell them more expensive services. If the lawyer recommends an expensive course of action, get a second opinion before you agree.

But if a plan offers extensive free advice, your initial membership fee may be worth the consultation you receive. You can always join a plan for a specific service and then not renew.

There's no guarantee that the lawyers available through these plans are of the best caliber; sometimes they aren't. Check out the plan carefully before signing up. Ask about the plan's complaint system, whether you get to choose your lawyer, and whether or not the lawyer will represent you in court.

Lawyer referral panels. Most county bar associations will give out the names of attorneys who practice in your area. But bar associations often fail to provide meaningful screening for the attorneys listed, which means those who participate may not be the most experienced or competent.

Lawyer directories. Most divorce websites have lists of attorneys. Nolo's lawyer directory at www.nolo.com has detailed profiles that let you see a lawyer's background, education, and fee structure. You should do a little research on any lawyer you're thinking of hiring. Check their state bar number on the state bar association website to make sure they don't have any complaints filed against them. Although you should take online reviews with a grain of salt, especially with divorce cases, the reviews can provide helpful information.

What to Look for in a Lawyer

No matter what approach you take to finding a lawyer, here are three suggestions on how to make sure you have the best possible working relationship with your attorney.

First, fight the urge you may have to surrender your will and be intimidated. You should be the one who decides what you feel comfortable doing about your legal and financial affairs. You're hiring the lawyer to perform a service for you; shop around if the price or personality isn't right.

Second, you must be as comfortable as possible with any lawyer you hire. When making an appointment, ask to talk directly to the lawyer. If you can't, this may give you a hint as to how accessible the lawyer is.

If you do talk directly to the lawyer, ask some specific questions. Do you get clear, concise answers? If not, try someone else. If the lawyer says little except to suggest you turn over the problem—with a substantial fee—watch out. You're talking with someone who doesn't know the answer and won't admit it, or someone who pulls rank on the basis of professional standing. Don't be a passive client or hire a lawyer who wants you to be one. If the lawyer admits to not knowing an answer, that isn't necessarily bad. In most cases, the lawyer must do some research.

Also, pay attention to how the lawyer responds to the fact that you have considerable information. If you read this book, you know more about divorce and money than the average person. Does the lawyer seem comfortable with that? Does the lawyer give straightforward answers to your questions—or does the lawyer want to maintain an aura of mystery about the legal system? Pay attention to your own intuition. Many lawyers are threatened when the client knows too much—or, in some cases, anything.

Once you find a lawyer you like, make an hourlong appointment to discuss your situation fully. Your goal at the initial conference is to find out what the lawyer recommends and how much it will cost. Go home and think about the lawyer's suggestions. If they don't make complete sense or if you have other reservations, call someone else.

Finally, keep in mind that the lawyer works for you. Once you hire a lawyer, you have the absolute right to switch to another—or to fire the lawyer and handle the matter yourself—at any time, for any reason.

Online Legal Resources

A growing number of basic legal resources are available online. Nolo's legal resources at www.nolo.com and www.divorcenet.com include a vast amount of free legal information for consumers on a wide variety of legal topics.

In addition, a wide variety of secondary sources intended for both lawyers and the general public has been posted by law schools and firms. A good way to find these sources is to visit any of the following websites, each of which provides links to legal information by specific subject:

- www.divorcenet.com. This site provides divorce information for all 50 states and a lawyer directory as well.
- www.findlaw.com. This legal search engine is an excellent resource for do-it-yourself legal research.
- www.law.cornell.edu. This site is maintained by Cornell Law School's Legal Information Institute. You can find the text of some state court decisions. You can also search for material by topic.

Additional Resources

Below are names, addresses, and phone numbers of organizations that may be able to offer additional assistance.

Attorneys, Mediators, and Therapists

American Academy of Matrimonial Lawyers
209 W. Jackson Blvd., Suite 602
Chicago, IL 60606
312-263-6477
https://aaml.org

American Arbitration Association
1633 Broadway, 10th Floor
New York, NY 10019
800-778-7879
www.adr.org

American Association for Marriage and Family Therapy
112 S. Alfred Street
Alexandria, VA 22314-3061
703-838-9808
www.aamft.org

Association for Conflict Resolution
P.O. Box 5
Eagle, NE 68347-0005
614-262-2724
https://acrnet.org

Child Support

Office of Child Support Services
330 C Street, SW
Washington, DC 20201
703-506-2880
www.acf.hhs.gov/programs/css

Administration for Children and Families
U.S. Department of Health and Human Services
Child Support Enforcement
330 C Street, SW
Washington, DC 20201
202-401-9383
www.acf.hhs.gov

Custody

The Custody Project
www.thecustodyproject.org

National Parents Organization
www.sharedparenting.org

Domestic Violence

Futures Without Violence
100 Montgomery Street, The Presidio
San Francisco, CA 94129
415-678-5500
www.futureswithoutviolence.org

The National Domestic Violence Hotline
800-799-7233
www.thehotline.org

Appraisers

American Society of Appraisers (business appraisers)
2121 Cooperative Way, Suite 210
Herndon, VA 20171
703-478-2228
www.appraisers.org

Appraisal Institute (real estate appraisers)
200 W. Madison, Suite 1500
Chicago, IL 60606
888-756-4624
www.appraisalinstitute.org

Tax Assistance

Internal Revenue Service (IRS) (to obtain tax forms)
800-829-1040
www.irs.gov

National Association of Enrolled Agents (for a referral to an enrolled agent)
1730 Rhode Island Avenue, NW, Suite 400
Washington, DC 20036
202-822-6232
www.naea.org

Miscellaneous Financial Assistance

Institute for Divorce Financial Analysts
3622 Lyckan Parkway, Suite 3003
Durham, NC 27707
800-875-1760
www.institutedfa.com

Financial Planning Association (for a referral to a financial planner)
1290 Broadway, Suite 1625
Denver, CO 80203
800-322-4237
www.plannersearch.org

National Foundation for Credit Counseling (to find a consumer credit counseling office)
2033 K Street, NW, Suite 425
Washington, DC 20006
202-677-4300 or 800-388-2227
www.nfcc.org

Social Security Administration (to confirm work and benefits history)
800-772-1213
www.ssa.gov
(to get information pertaining to Social Security and women)
www.ssa.gov/women

Federal Trade Commission
202-326-2222
www.ftc.gov

Present Value Factors

This chart lets you calculate an estimate of the future value of an asset, such as a house. The figures in the first column represent the holding period, or number of years you would expect to retain the asset. The percentages across the top indicate the inflation rate. When you follow the two lines until they intersect, you have the future value factor. For instance, if you have a $200,000 house that you expect to hold for another seven years and if you assume a 4% inflation rate, the future value factor is 1.3159. Multiply that by $200,000, and you have an estimated future value of $263,180 for your house in seven years.

Present Value Factors							
Year	1%	2%	3%	4%	5%	6%	7%
1	0.9901	0.9804	0.9709	0.9615	0.9524	0.9434	0.9346
2	0.9803	0.9612	0.9426	0.9246	0.9070	0.8900	0.8734
3	0.9706	0.9423	0.9151	0.8890	0.8638	0.8396	0.8163
4	0.9610	0.9238	0.8885	0.8548	0.8227	0.7921	0.7629
5	0.9515	0.9057	0.8626	0.8219	0.7835	0.7473	0.7130
6	0.9420	0.8880	0.8375	0.7903	0.7462	0.7050	0.6663
7	0.9327	0.8706	0.8131	0.7599	0.7107	0.6651	0.6227
8	0.9235	0.8535	0.7894	0.7307	0.6768	0.6274	0.5820
9	0.9143	0.8368	0.7664	0.7026	0.6446	0.5919	0.5439
10	0.9053	0.8203	0.7441	0.6756	0.6139	0.5584	0.5083
11	0.8963	0.8043	0.7224	0.6496	0.5847	0.5268	0.4751
12	0.8874	0.7885	0.7014	0.6246	0.5568	0.4970	0.4440
13	0.8787	0.7730	0.6810	0.6006	0.5303	0.4688	0.4150
14	0.8700	0.7579	0.6611	0.5775	0.5051	0.4423	0.3878
15	0.8613	0.7430	0.6419	0.5553	0.4810	0.4173	0.3624
16	0.8528	0.7284	0.6232	0.5339	0.4581	0.3936	0.3387
17	0.8444	0.7142	0.6050	0.5134	0.4363	0.3714	0.3166
18	0.8360	0.7002	0.5874	0.4936	0.4155	0.3503	0.2959
19	0.8277	0.6864	0.5703	0.4746	0.3957	0.3305	0.2765
20	0.8195	0.6730	0.5537	0.4564	0.3769	0.3118	0.2584

Present Value Factors (continued)

Year	1%	2%	3%	4%	5%	6%	7%
21	0.8114	0.6598	0.5375	0.4388	0.3589	0.2942	0.2415
22	0.8034	0.6468	0.5219	0.4220	0.3418	0.2775	0.2257
23	0.7954	0.6342	0.5067	0.4057	0.3256	0.2618	0.2109
24	0.7876	0.6217	0.4919	0.3901	0.3101	0.2470	0.1971
25	0.7798	0.6095	0.4776	0.3751	0.2953	0.2330	0.1842
26	0.7720	0.5976	0.4637	0.3607	0.2812	0.2198	0.1722
27	0.7644	0.5859	0.4502	0.3468	0.2678	0.2074	0.1609
28	0.7568	0.5744	0.4371	0.3335	0.2551	0.1956	0.1504
29	0.7493	0.5631	0.4243	0.3207	0.2429	0.1846	0.1406
30	0.7419	0.5521	0.4120	0.3083	0.2314	0.1741	0.1314
31	0.7346	0.5412	0.4000	0.2965	0.2204	0.1643	0.1228
32	0.7273	0.5306	0.3883	0.2851	0.2099	0.1550	0.1147
33	0.7201	0.5202	0.3770	0.2741	0.1999	0.1462	0.1072
34	0.7130	0.5100	0.3660	0.2636	0.1904	0.1379	0.1002
35	0.7059	0.5000	0.3554	0.2534	0.1813	0.1301	0.0937
36	0.6989	0.4902	0.3450	0.2437	0.1727	0.1227	0.0875
37	0.6920	0.4806	0.3350	0.2343	0.1644	0.1158	0.0818
38	0.6852	0.4712	0.3252	0.2253	0.1566	0.1092	0.0765
39	0.6784	0.4619	0.3158	0.2166	0.1491	0.1031	0.0715
40	0.6717	0.4529	0.3066	0.2083	0.1420	0.0972	0.0668
41	0.6650	0.4440	0.2976	0.2003	0.1353	0.0917	0.0624
42	0.6584	0.4353	0.2890	0.1926	0.1288	0.0865	0.0583
43	0.6519	0.4268	0.2805	0.1852	0.1227	0.0816	0.0545
44	0.6454	0.4184	0.2724	0.1780	0.1169	0.0770	0.0509
45	0.6391	0.4102	0.2644	0.1712	0.1113	0.0727	0.0476
46	0.6327	0.4022	0.2567	0.1646	0.1060	0.0685	0.0445
47	0.6265	0.3943	0.2493	0.1583	0.1009	0.0647	0.0416
48	0.6203	0.3865	0.2420	0.1522	0.0961	0.0610	0.0389
49	0.6141	0.3790	0.2350	0.1463	0.0916	0.0575	0.0363
50	0.6080	0.3715	0.2281	0.1407	0.0872	0.0543	0.0339

Present Value Factors (continued)

Year	8%	9%	10%	11%	12%	13%	14%
1	0.9259	0.9174	0.9091	0.9009	0.8929	0.8850	0.8772
2	0.8573	0.8417	0.8264	0.8116	0.7972	0.7831	0.7695
3	0.7938	0.7722	0.7513	0.7312	0.7118	0.6931	0.6750
4	0.7350	0.7084	0.6830	0.6587	0.6355	0.6133	0.5921
5	0.6806	0.6499	0.6209	0.5935	0.5674	0.5428	0.5194
6	0.6302	0.5963	0.5645	0.5346	0.5066	0.4803	0.4556
7	0.5835	0.5470	0.5132	0.4817	0.4523	0.4251	0.3996
8	0.5403	0.5019	0.4665	0.4339	0.4039	0.3762	0.3506
9	0.5002	0.4604	0.4241	0.3909	0.3606	0.3329	0.3075
10	0.4632	0.4224	0.3855	0.3522	0.3220	0.2946	0.2697
11	0.4289	0.3875	0.3505	0.3173	0.2875	0.2607	0.2366
12	0.3971	0.3555	0.3186	0.2858	0.2567	0.2307	0.2076
13	0.3677	0.3262	0.2897	0.2575	0.2292	0.2042	0.1821
14	0.3405	0.2992	0.2633	0.2320	0.2046	0.1807	0.1597
15	0.3152	0.2745	0.2394	0.2090	0.1827	0.1599	0.1401
16	0.2919	0.2519	0.2176	0.1883	0.1631	0.1415	0.1229
17	0.2703	0.2311	0.1978	0.1696	0.1456	0.1252	0.1078
18	0.2502	0.2120	0.1799	0.1528	0.1300	0.1108	0.0946
19	0.2317	0.1945	0.1635	0.1377	0.1161	0.0981	0.0829
20	0.2145	0.1784	0.1486	0.1240	0.1037	0.0868	0.0728
21	0.1987	0.1637	0.1351	0.1117	0.0926	0.0768	0.0638
22	0.1839	0.1502	0.1228	0.1007	0.0826	0.0680	0.0560
23	0.1703	0.1378	0.1117	0.0907	0.0738	0.0601	0.0491
24	0.1577	0.1264	0.1015	0.0817	0.0659	0.0532	0.0431
25	0.1460	0.1160	0.0923	0.0736	0.0588	0.0471	0.0378

Present Value Factors (continued)

Year	8%	9%	10%	11%	12%	13%	14%
26	0.1352	0.1064	0.0839	0.0663	0.0525	0.0417	0.0331
27	0.1252	0.0976	0.0763	0.0597	0.0469	0.0369	0.0291
28	0.1159	0.0895	0.0693	0.0538	0.0419	0.0326	0.0255
29	0.1073	0.0822	0.0630	0.0485	0.0374	0.0289	0.0224
30	0.0994	0.0754	0.0573	0.0437	0.0334	0.0256	0.0196
31	0.0920	0.0691	0.0521	0.0394	0.0298	0.0226	0.0172
32	0.0852	0.0634	0.0474	0.0355	0.0266	0.0200	0.0151
33	0.0789	0.0582	0.0431	0.0319	0.0238	0.0177	0.0132
34	0.0730	0.0534	0.0391	0.0288	0.0212	0.0157	0.0116
35	0.0676	0.0490	0.0356	0.0259	0.0189	0.0139	0.0102
36	0.0626	0.0449	0.0323	0.0234	0.0169	0.0123	0.0089
37	0.0580	0.0412	0.0294	0.0210	0.0151	0.0109	0.0078
38	0.0537	0.0378	0.0267	0.0190	0.0135	0.0096	0.0069
39	0.0497	0.0347	0.0243	0.0171	0.0120	0.0085	0.0060
40	0.0460	0.0318	0.0221	0.0154	0.0107	0.0075	0.0053
41	0.0426	0.0292	0.0201	0.0139	0.0096	0.0067	0.0046
42	0.0395	0.0268	0.0183	0.0125	0.0086	0.0059	0.0041
43	0.0365	0.0246	0.0166	0.0112	0.0076	0.0052	0.0036
44	0.0338	0.0226	0.0151	0.0101	0.0068	0.0046	0.0031
45	0.0313	0.0207	0.0137	0.0091	0.0061	0.0041	0.0027
46	0.0290	0.0190	0.0125	0.0082	0.0054	0.0036	0.0024
47	0.0269	0.0174	0.0113	0.0074	0.0049	0.0032	0.0021
48	0.0249	0.0160	0.0103	0.0067	0.0043	0.0028	0.0019
49	0.0230	0.0147	0.0094	0.0060	0.0039	0.0025	0.0016
50	0.0213	0.0134	0.0085	0.0054	0.0035	0.0022	0.0014

Present Value Factors (continued)

Year	15%	16%	17%	18%	19%	20%
1	0.8696	0.8621	0.8547	0.8475	0.8403	0.8333
2	0.7561	0.7432	0.7305	0.7182	0.7062	0.6944
3	0.6575	0.6407	0.6244	0.6086	0.5934	0.5787
4	0.5718	0.5523	0.5337	0.5158	0.4987	0.4823
5	0.4972	0.4761	0.4561	0.4371	0.4190	0.4019
6	0.4323	0.4104	0.3898	0.3704	0.3521	0.3349
7	0.3759	0.3538	0.3332	0.3139	0.2959	0.2791
8	0.3269	0.3050	0.2848	0.2660	0.2487	0.2326
9	0.2843	0.2630	0.2434	0.2255	0.2090	0.1938
10	0.2472	0.2267	0.2080	0.1911	0.1756	0.1615
11	0.2149	0.1954	0.1778	0.1619	0.1476	0.1346
12	0.1869	0.1685	0.1520	0.1372	0.1240	0.1122
13	0.1625	0.1452	0.1299	0.1163	0.1042	0.0935
14	0.1413	0.1252	0.1110	0.0985	0.0876	0.0779
15	0.1229	0.1079	0.0949	0.0835	0.0736	0.0649
16	0.1069	0.0930	0.0811	0.0708	0.0618	
17	0.0929	0.0802	0.0693	0.0600	0.0520	
18	0.0808	0.0691	0.0592	0.0508	0.0437	
19	0.0703	0.0596	0.0506	0.0431	0.0367	
20	0.0611	0.0514	0.0433	0.0365	0.0308	
21	0.0531	0.0443	0.0370	0.0309	0.0259	
22	0.0462	0.0382	0.0316	0.0262	0.0218	
23	0.0402	0.0329	0.0270	0.0222	0.0183	
24	0.0349	0.0284	0.0231	0.0188	0.0154	
25	0.0304	0.0245	0.0197	0.0160	0.0129	

Present Value Factors (continued)

Year	15%	16%	17%	18%	19%
26	0.0264	0.0211	0.0169	0.0135	0.0109
27	0.0230	0.0182	0.0144	0.0115	0.0091
28	0.0200	0.0157	0.0123	0.0097	0.0077
29	0.0174	0.0135	0.0105	0.0082	0.0064
30	0.0151	0.0116	0.0090	0.0070	0.0054
31	0.0131	0.0100	0.0077	0.0059	0.0046
32	0.0114	0.0087	0.0066	0.0050	0.0038
33	0.0099	0.0075	0.0056	0.0042	0.0032
34	0.0086	0.0064	0.0048	0.0036	0.0027
35	00075	0.0055	0.0041	0.0030	0.0023
36	0.0065	0.0048	0.0035	0.0026	0.0019
37	0.0057	0.0041	0.0030	0.0022	0.0016
38	0.0049	0.0036	0.0026	0.0019	0.0013
39	0.0043	0.0031	0.0022	0.0016	0.0011
40	0.0037	0.0026	0.0019	0.0013	0.0010
41	0.0032	0.0023	0.0016	0.0011	0.0008
42	0.0028	0.0020	0.0014	0.0010	0.0007
43	0.0025	0.0017	0.0012	0.0008	0.0006
44	0.0021	0.0015	0.0010	0.0007	0.0005
45	0.0019	0.0013	0.0009	0.0006	0.0004
46	0.0016	0.0011	0.0007	0.0005	0.0003
47	0.0014	0.0009	0.0006	0.0004	0.0003
48	0.0012	0.0008	0.0005	0.0004	0.0002
49	0.0011	0.0007	0.0005	0.0003	0.0002
50	0.0009	0.0006	0.0004	0.0003	0.0002

Future Value Factors

This chart lets you calculate an estimate of the future value of an asset, such as a house. The figures in the first column represent the holding period, or number of years you would expect to retain the asset. The percentages across the top indicate the inflation rate. When you follow the two lines until they intersect, you have the future value factor. For instance, if you have a $200,000 house that you expect to hold for another seven years and if you assume a 4% inflation rate, the future value factor is 1.3159. Multiply that by $200,000, and you have an estimated future value of $263,180 for your house in seven years.

Future Value Factors							
Year	1%	2%	3%	4%	5%	6%	7%
1	1.0100	1.0200	1.0300	1.0400	1.0500	1.0600	1.0700
2	1.0201	1.0404	1.0609	1.0816	1.1025	1.1236	1.1449
3	1.0303	1.0612	1.0927	1.1249	1.1576	1.1910	1.2250
4	1.0406	1.0824	1.1255	1.1699	1.2155	1.2625	1.3108
5	1.0510	1.1041	1.1593	1.2167	1.2763	1.3382	1.4026
6	1.0615	1.1262	1.1941	1.2653	1.3401	1.4185	1.5007
7	1.0721	1.1487	1.2299	1.3159	1.4071	1.5036	1.6058
8	1.0829	1.1717	1.2668	1.3686	1.4775	1.5938	1.7182
9	1.0937	1.1951	1.3048	1.4233	1.5513	1.6895	1.8385
10	1.1046	1.2190	1.3439	1.4802	1.6289	1.7908	1.9672
11	1.1157	1.2434	1.3842	1.5395	1.7103	1.8983	2.1049
12	1.1268	1.2682	1.4258	1.6010	1.7959	2.0122	2.2522
13	1.1381	1.2936	1.4685	1.6651	1.8856	2.1329	2.4098
14	1.1495	1.3195	1.5126	1.7317	1.9799	2.2609	2.5785
15	1.1610	1.3459	1.5580	1.8009	2.0789	2.3966	2.7590
16	1.1726	1.3728	1.6047	1.8730	2.1829	2.5404	2.9522
17	1.1843	1.4002	1.6528	1.9479	2.2920	2.6928	3.1588
18	1.1961	1.4282	1.7024	2.0258	2.4066	2.8543	3.3799
19	1.2081	1.4568	1.7535	2.1068	2.5270	3.0256	3.6165
20	1.2202	1.4859	1.8061	2.1911	2.6533	3.2071	3.8697

Future Value Factors (continued)

Year	1%	2%	3%	4%	5%	6%	7%
21	1.2324	1.5157	1.8603	2.2788	2.7860	3.3996	4.1406
22	1.2447	1.5460	1.9161	2.3699	2.9253	3.6035	4.4304
23	1.2572	1.5769	1.9736	2.4647	3.0715	3.8197	4.7405
24	1.2697	1.6084	2.0328	2.5633	3.2251	4.0489	5.0724
25	1.2824	1.6406	2.0938	2.6658	3.3864	4.2919	5.4274
26	1.2953	1.6734	2.1566	2.7725	3.5557	4.5494	5.8074
27	1.3082	1.7069	2.2213	2.8834	3.7335	4.8223	6.2139
28	1.3213	1.7410	2.2879	2.9987	3.9201	5.1117	6.6488
29	1.3345	1.7758	2.3566	3.1187	4.1161	5.4184	7.1143
30	1.3478	1.8114	2.4273	3.2434	4.3219	5.7435	7.6123
31	1.3613	1.8476	2.5001	3.3731	4.5380	6.0881	8.1451
32	1.3749	1.8845	2.5751	3.5081	4.7649	6.4534	8.7153
33	1.3887	1.9222	2.6523	3.6484	5.0032	6.8406	9.3253
34	1.4026	1.9607	2.7319	3.7943	5.2533	7.2510	9.9781
35	1.4166	1.9999	2.8139	3.9461	5.5160	7.6861	10.6766
36	1.4308	2.0399	2.8983	4.1039	5.7918	8.1473	11.4239
37	1.4451	2.0807	2.9852	4.2681	6.0814	8.6361	12.2236
38	1.4595	2.1223	3.0748	4.4388	6.3855	9.1543	13.0793
39	1.4741	2.1647	3.1670	4.6164	6.7048	9.7035	13.9948
40	1.4889	2.2080	3.2620	4.8010	7.0400	10.2857	14.9745
41	1.5038	2.2522	3.3599	4.9931	7.3920	10.9029	16.0227
42	1.5188	2.2972	3.4607	5.1928	7.7616	11.5570	17.1443
43	1.5340	2.3432	3.5645	5.4005	8.1497	12.2505	18.3444
44	1.5493	2.3901	3.6715	5.6165	8.5572	12.9855	19.6285
45	1.5648	2.4379	3.7816	5.8412	8.9850	13.7646	21.0025
46	1.5805	2.4866	3.8950	6.0748	9.4343	14.5905	22.4726
47	1.5963	2.5363	4.0119	6.3178	9.9060	15.4659	24.0457
48	1.6122	2.5871	4.1323	6.5705	10.4013	16.3939	25.7289
49	1.6283	2.6388	4.2562	6.8333	10.9213	17.3775	27.5299
50	1.6446	2.6916	4.3839	7.1067	11.4674	18.4202	29.4570

Future Value Factors (continued)

Year	8%	9%	10%	11%	12%	13%	14%
1	1.0800	1.0900	1.1000	1.1100	1.1200	1.1300	1.1400
2	1.1664	1.1881	1.2100	1.2321	1.2544	1.2769	1.2996
3	1.2597	1.2950	1.3310	1.3676	1.4049	1.4429	1.4815
4	1.3605	1.4116	1.4641	1.5181	1.5735	1.6305	1.6890
5	1.4693	1.5386	1.6105	1.6851	1.7623	1.8424	1.9254
6	1.5869	1.6771	1.7716	1.8704	1.9738	2.0820	2.1950
7	1.7138	1.8280	1.9487	2.0762	2.2107	2.3526	2.5023
8	1.8509	1.9926	2.1436	2.3045	2.4760	2.6584	2.8526
9	1.9990	2.1719	2.3579	2.5580	2.7731	3.0040	3.2519
10	2.1589	2.3674	2.5937	2.8394	3.1058	3.3946	3.7072
11	2.3316	2.5804	2.8531	3.1518	3.4785	3.8359	4.2262
12	2.5182	2.8127	3.1384	3.4985	3.8960	4.3345	4.8179
13	2.7196	3.0658	3.4523	3.8833	4.3635	4.8980	5.4924
14	2.9372	3.3417	3.7975	4.3104	4.8871	5.5348	6.2613
15	3.1722	3.6425	4.1772	4.7846	5.4736	6.2543	7.1379
16	3.4259	3.9703	4.5950	5.3109	6.1304	7.0673	8.1372
17	3.7000	4.3276	5.0545	5.8951	6.8660	7.9861	9.2765
18	3.9960	4.7171	5.5599	6.5436	7.6900	9.0243	10.5752
19	4.3157	5.1417	6.1159	7.2633	8.6128	10.1974	12.0557
20	4.6610	5.6044	6.7275	8.0623	9.6463	11.5231	13.7435
21	5.0338	6.1088	7.4002	8.9492	10.8038	13.0211	15.6676
22	5.4365	6.6586	8.1403	9.9336	12.1003	14.7138	17.8610
23	5.8715	7.2579	8.9543	11.0263	13.5523	16.6266	20.3616
24	6.3412	7.9111	9.8497	12.2392	15.1786	18.7881	23.2122
25	6.8485	8.6231	10.8347	13.5855	17.0001	21.2305	26.4619
26	7.3964	9.3992	11.9182	15.0799	19.0401	23.9905	30.1666
27	7.9881	10.2451	13.1100	16.7386	21.3249	27.1093	34.3899
28	8.6271	11.1671	14.4210	18.5799	23.8839	30.6335	39.2045
29	9.3173	12.1722	15.8631	20.6237	26.7499	34.6158	44.6931
30	10.0627	13.2677	17.4494	22.8923	29.9599	39.1159	50.9502

Future Value Factors (continued)

Year	8%	9%	10%	11%	12%	13%	14%
31	10.8677	14.4618	19.1943	25.4104	33.5551	44.2010	58.0832
32	11.7371	15.7633	21.1138	28.2056	37.5817	49.9471	66.2148
33	12.6760	17.1820	23.2252	31.3082	42.0915	56.4402	75.4849
34	13.6901	18.7284	25.5477	34.7521	47.1425	63.7774	86.0528
35	14.7853	20.4140	28.1024	38.5749	52.7996	72.0685	98.1002
36	15.9682	22.2512	30.9127	42.8181	59.1356	81.4374	111.8342
37	17.2456	24.2538	34.0039	47.5281	66.2318	92.0243	127.4910
38	18.6253	26.4367	37.4043	52.7562	74.1797	103.9874	145.3397
39	20.1153	28.8160	41.1448	58.5593	83.0812	117.5058	165.6873
40	21.7245	31.4094	45.2593	65.0009	93.0510	132.7816	188.8835
41	23.4625	34.2363	49.7852	72.1510	104.2171	150.0432	215.3272
42	25.3395	37.3175	54.7637	80.0876	116.7231	169.5488	245.4730
43	27.3666	40.6761	60.2401	88.8972	130.7299	191.5901	279.8392
44	29.5560	44.3370	66.2641	98.6759	146.4175	216.4968	319.0167
45	31.9204	48.3273	72.8905	109.5302	163.9876	244.6414	363.6791
46	34.4741	52.6767	80.1795	121.5786	183.6661	276.4448	414.5941
47	37.2320	57.4176	88.1975	134.9522	205.7061	312.3826	472.6373
48	40.2106	62.5852	97.0172	149.7970	230.3908	352.9923	538.8065
49	43.4274	68.2179	106.7190	166.2746	258.0377	398.8813	614.2395
50	46.9016	74.3575	117.3909	184.5648	289.0022	450.7359	700.2330

Future Value Factors (continued)

Year	15%	16%	17%	18%	19%	20%
1	1.1500	1.1600	1.1700	1.1800	1.1900	1.2000
2	1.3225	1.3456	1.3689	1.3924	1.4161	1.4400
3	1.5209	1.5609	1.6016	1.6430	1.6852	1.7280
4	1.7490	1.8106	1.8739	1.9388	2.0053	2.0736
5	2.0114	2.1003	2.1924	2.2878	2.3864	2.4883
6	2.3131	2.4364	2.5652	2.6996	2.8398	2.9860
7	2.6600	2.8262	3.0012	3.1855	3.3793	3.5832
8	3.0590	3.2784	3.5115	3.7589	4.0214	4.2998
9	3.5179	3.8030	4.1084	4.4355	4.7854	5.1598
10	4.0456	4.4114	4.8068	5.2338	5.6947	6.1917
11	4.6524	5.1173	5.6240	6.1759	6.7767	7.4301
12	5.3503	5.9360	6.5801	7.2876	8.0642	8.9161
13	6.1528	6.8858	7.6987	8.5994	9.5964	10.6993
14	7.0757	7.9875	9.0075	10.1472	11.4198	12.8392
15	8.1371	9.2655	10.5387	11.9737	13.5895	15.4070
16	9.3576	10.7480	12.3303	14.1290	16.1715	
17	10.7613	12.4677	14.4265	16.6722	19.2441	
18	12.3755	14.4625	16.8790	19.6733	22.9005	
19	14.2318	16.7765	19.7484	23.2144	27.2516	
20	16.3665	19.4608	23.1056	27.3930	32.4294	
21	18.8215	22.5745	27.0336	32.3238	38.5910	
22	21.6447	26.1864	31.6293	38.1421	45.9233	
23	24.8915	30.3762	37.0062	45.0076	54.6487	
24	28.6252	35.2364	43.2973	53.1090	65.0320	
25	32.9190	40.8742	50.6578	62.6686	77.3881	
26	37.8568	47.4141	59.2697	73.9490	92.0918	
27	43.5353	55.0004	69.3455	87.2598	109.5893	
28	50.0656	63.8004	81.1342	102.9666	130.4112	
29	57.5755	74.0085	94.9271	121.5005	155.1893	
30	66.2118	85.8499	111.0647	143.3706	184.6753	

Future Value Factors (continued)

Year	15%	16%	17%	18%	19%
31	76.1435	99.5859	129.9456	169.1774	219.7636
32	87.5651	115.5196	152.0364	199.6293	261.5187
33	100.6998	134.0027	177.8826	235.5625	311.2073
34	115.8048	155.4432	208.1226	277.9638	370.3366
35	133.1755	180.3141	243.5035	327.9973	440.7006
36	153.1519	209.1643	284.8991	387.0368	524.4337
37	176.1246	242.6306	333.3319	456.7034	624.0761
38	202.5433	281.4515	389.9983	538.9100	742.6506
39	232.9248	326.4838	456.2980	635.9139	883.7542
40	267.8635	378.7212	533.8687	750.3783	1051.6675
41	308.0431	439.3165	624.6264	885.4464	1251.4843
42	354.2495	509.6072	730.8129	1044.8268	1489.2664
43	407.3870	591.1443	855.0511	1232.8956	1772.2270
44	468.4950	685.7274	1000.4098	1454.8168	2108.9501
45	538.7693	795.4438	1170.4794	1716.6839	2509.6506
46	619.5847	922.7148	1369.4609	2025.6870	2986.4842
47	712.5224	1070.3492	1602.2693	2390.3106	3553.9162
48	819.4007	1241.6051	1874.6550	2820.5665	4229.1603
49	942.3108	1440.2619	2193.3464	3328.2685	5032.7008
50	1083.6574	1670.7038	2566.2153	3927.3569	5988.9139

List of Professional Advisers

Attorney:

Name: _____

Address: _____

_____

Phone: _____

Email: _____

Financial Planner:

Name: _____

Address: _____

_____

Phone: _____

Email: _____

Accountant or Other Tax Professional:

Name: _____

Address: _____

_____

Phone: _____

Email: _____

Stockbroker/Money Manager:

Name: _____

Address: _____

_____

Phone: _____

Email: _____

Banker:

Name: _____

Address: _____

_____

Phone: _____

Email: _____

Mortgage Broker:

Name: _____

Address: _____

_____

Phone: _____

Email: _____

Retirement Planning Adviser:

Name: _____

Address: _____

_____

Phone: _____

Email: _____

Title Company Agent:

Name: _____

Address: _____

_____

Phone: _____

Email: _____

Real Estate Broker/Home:

Name: _____

Address: _____

_____

Phone: _____

Email: _____

Insurance Agent/Home:

Name: _____

Address: _____

_____

Phone: _____

Email: _____

Insurance Agent/Auto:

Name: _____

Address: _____

_____

Phone: _____

Email: _____

Insurance Agent/Life:

Name: _____

Address: _____

_____

Phone: _____

Email: _____

Other:

Name: _____

Address: _____

_____

Phone: _____

Email: _____

Other:

Name: _____

Address: _____

_____

Phone: _____

Email: _____

Other:

Name: _____

Address: _____

_____

Phone: _____

Email: _____

Other:

Name: _____

Address: _____

_____

Phone: _____

Email: _____

Index

NOLO   *Save 15%* off your next order

Register your Nolo purchase, and we'll send you a
coupon for 15% off your next Nolo.com order!

Nolo.com/customer-support/productregistration

On Nolo.com you'll also find:

Books & Software
Nolo publishes hundreds of great books and software programs for consumers and
business owners. Order a copy, or download an ebook version instantly, at Nolo.com.

Online Forms
You can quickly and easily make a will or living trust, form an LLC or corporation,
or make hundreds of other forms—online.

Free Legal Information
Thousands of articles answer common questions about everyday legal issues,
including wills, bankruptcy, small business formation, divorce, patents,
employment, and much more.

Plain-English Legal Dictionary
Stumped by jargon? Look it up in America's most up-to-date source for definitions
of legal terms, free at Nolo.com.

Lawyer Directory
Nolo's consumer-friendly lawyer directory provides in-depth profiles of lawyers all
over America. You'll find information you need to choose the right lawyer.

DIMO14